ON THE EDGE OF ANARCHY

STUDIES IN MORAL, POLITICAL,
AND LEGAL PHILOSOPHY

General Editor: Marshall Cohen

A list of titles in the series
appears at the back of the book

ON THE EDGE
OF ANARCHY

Locke, Consent, and the Limits of Society

A. John Simmons

PRINCETON UNIVERSITY PRESS
PRINCETON, NEW JERSEY

Library of Congress Cataloging-in-Publication Data
Simmons, A. John (Alan John), 1950–
On the edge of anarchy : Locke, consent, and the limits of society
/ A. John Simmons
p. cm. — (Studies in moral, political, and legal philosophy)
Includes bibliographical references and index.
ISBN 0-691-03303-X
ISBN 04483-X (pbk.)
1. Locke, John, 1632–1704—Contributions in political science.
2. Anarchism. I. Title. II. Series.
JC153.L87S57 1993
320.1'1—dc20   92-44658

This book has been composed in Linotron Palatino

Third printing, and first paperback printing, 1995

Printed in the United States of America
by Princeton Academic Press

3 5 7 9 10 8 6 4

CONTENTS

LIST OF ABBREVIATIONS   vii

ACKNOWLEDGMENTS   ix

INTRODUCTION   3

Part 1: Nonconsensual Relations   11

ONE. THE LOCKEAN STATE OF NATURE   13
1.1. Locke's State of Nature   13
1.2. The Moral, Social, and Historical Dimensions   23
1.3. The Point of State-of-Nature Stories   33

TWO. FORCE AND RIGHT   40
2.1. The State of War   40
2.2. How Rights Are Lost   46
2.3. Despotism: Slavery and Absolute Government   48

Part 2: Consent and Government   57

THREE. POLITICAL CONSENT   59
3.1. The Content of Lockean Consent   59
3.2. Consent, Contract, and Trust   68
3.3. The Appeal of Consent Theory   72

FOUR. THE VARIETIES OF CONSENT   80
4.1. Express and Tacit Consent   80
4.2. Majority Consent   90

CONTENTS

Part 3: The Limits of Society   99

FIVE. INALIENABLE RIGHTS   101

5.1. The Property of Inalienability   101
5.2. Locke on Inalienability   108
5.3. Locke's Commitments   119
5.4. Toleration   123
5.5. Inalienability and Absolutism   137

SIX. DISSOLUTION AND RESISTANCE   147

6.1. The Revolutionary Stance   147
6.2. The Right of Resistance   155
6.3. The Consequences of Dissolution   167
6.4. The Duty to Resist   178

Part 4: Consent and the Edge of Anarchy   193

SEVEN. THE CRITIQUE OF LOCKEAN CONSENT THEORY   197

7.1. Hume's Attack   197
7.2. The Meaning of Consent in Locke   202

EIGHT. CONSENT, OBLIGATION, AND ANARCHY   218

8.1. Consent and Voting   218
8.2. Consent and Residence   225
8.3. Duress, Hard Choices, and Free Choice   232
8.4. Lockean Anarchism   248

WORKS CITED   271

INDEX   285

ABBREVIATIONS

Two Treatises of Government—I or II, followed by paragraph number

An Essay Concerning Human Understanding—E, followed by book, chapter, and section number

Essays on the Law of Nature—ELN, followed by page number

A Letter Concerning Toleration—L, followed by page number

Two Tracts on Government—First Tract or Second Tract, followed by page number

An Essay Concerning Toleration—ECT, followed by page number

ACKNOWLEDGMENTS

Having come together from nearly ten years of work on problems in Lockean political philosophy, this book has benefited in a wide variety of ways from the assistance of others. The oldest parts of the book (in chapters 5 and 8) were read in paper form at many colleges and universities, and I must thank the audiences there for their help (despite my inability to remember their individual contributions). This older work was also supported by grants and fellowships from the University of Virginia, the University's Center for Advanced Studies, and the National Endowment for the Humanities. More recently, Julian Franklin and George Klosko generously made many helpful comments on the material in chapters 1 and 2. But a large part of this book (most of chapters 3, 4, 6, and 7) has not until now made it very far out into the world, having been read (and much improved) only by my friend and wife, Nancy Schauber (who also deserves credit for having convinced me to assemble the book in its current form), and by Jeremy Waldron, whose comments were essential in helping me present my ideas more clearly in a variety of places in the book. So however much I might be willing to try to get away with blaming the errors of my older work on the inattention of friends and colleagues, even I must acknowledge my sole responsibility for the vast majority of the mistakes that readers will encounter in this book.

Parts of this book contain material that has been previously published. Most of chapter 1 was published as "Locke's State of Nature," *Political Theory* (August 1989). Section 2.2 and most of the first three sections of chapter 5 appeared in "Inalienable Rights and Locke's *Treatises,*" *Philosophy & Public Affairs* (Summer 1983). Parts of sections 3.3 and 7.1, and most of sections 8.1, 8.2, and 8.3 were contained in "Consent, Free Choice, and Democratic Government," *Georgia Law Review* 18/4 (Summer 1984). I thank the publishers for their permission to reuse this material here. Finally, I wish to thank our friends and neighbors in St. Roman de Malegarde and Tulette (in the northern Vaucluse), and especially Peta and Yves, for the warmth and hospitality that made my writing so much easier.

ON THE EDGE OF ANARCHY

INTRODUCTION

This is a study in Lockean moral and political philosophy. I hope
that it will be read in conjunction with my earlier work in this area,
The Lockean Theory of Rights (Princeton University Press, 1992). But
the arguments of the present study in no way depend on those of
that earlier work, however much they might be illuminated by them.
As in *The Lockean Theory of Rights,* I try here to present, analyze, and
to a certain extent defend both John Locke's own theory in his *Two
Treatises of Government* (and elsewhere) and the best version of a
Lockean theory. Both books are concerned to explore, develop, and
criticize the Lockean conceptions of moral and political relationships, and together I hope they constitute a reasonably complete
discussion of that topic. But where *The Lockean Theory of Rights* concentrates specifically on Lockean moral theory (and even more particularly on the Lockean view of our basic moral rights and duties),
the present work is designed to examine the Lockean conception of
what I will call the "political relationship."

This way of stating my purpose (and of identifying the contrast
between my two works in Lockean theory) threatens from the start
to mislead. For Locke and Lockeans, of course, political philosophy
is a branch, a part, or an application of moral philosophy: "True
politics," Locke wrote, "I look on as a part of moral philosophy."[1]
Where *moral* philosophy is the general study of how *persons*[2] ought
to behave, and of the rights, duties, virtues, and moral knowledge
of persons that bear on how they ought to behave, political philosophy is the more specific study of how persons in their roles as members of political societies ought to behave, and of how they ought to
structure those societies to which they belong. Political philosophy,
then, will have to be concerned at its most basic level with the relationship among persons that defines political society and that
makes a person a member of such a society (i.e., with what Locke

---

[1] Letter to Lady Peterborough, in King, *Life*, 1:9.
[2] I use "persons" here to do the work of Locke's (less happy) technical term "men."
"Men" are, for Locke, rational, corporeal beings who are self-conscious and capable
of a reasonably high degree of self-control. They possess the modest capacities of
reasoning, understanding, and control typical of normal adult (and most adolescent)
human beings. See *Lockean Theory of Rights*, 82–84, 111–14, 201–3, 257–60.

3

calls "the original of society"), as well as with the consequent rights
("powers") possessed by members—both the "civil rights" of typical members and the "political power"[3] normally exercised by
those who govern the society. Locke identifies this "basic level" of
political philosophy as one of the two parts of "politics," "the one
containing the original of societies and the rise and extent of political
power, the other the governing of men in society."[4] On the latter
part of politics, Locke wrote relatively little and I will say nothing
of much significance here. On the former part, Locke wrote the
bulk of the *Treatises*, the *Letters Concerning Toleration*, and all that
established his preeminent place in the history of political philosophy. It is on this first part of "politics," as well, that I will focus in
this study.

"The political relationship" is that relationship among persons
that makes them members of the same political society. One's conception of this relationship will inevitably form the heart of one's
political philosophy. And Locke and Lockeans, of course, have a
distinctive view of the source of that relationship, the moral limits
on its possible extent, and the implications of the relationship for
appropriate forms of government. Locke also had a special terminology for referring to that relationship, on which we would do well
to be clear from the beginning. When "any number"[5] of persons
stand in the political relationship to one another, they are said by
Locke to constitute a "political society" (e.g., II, 89, 122; or "politic
society" [e.g., II, 102, 106]), "civil society" (e.g., II, 89, 95), "body
politic" (e.g., II, 95; or "polity" [e.g., II, 175]), or "commonwealth"
(e.g., II, 3, 89). Locke also frequently refers to them as a "people"
or a "community," and sometimes simply as a "society" (although
we must be careful here to distinguish such political associations
from the natural "community" or "society" of persons ["mankind"], by virtue of which persons are "distinct from all other creatures" [II, 128]). I take all of these terms in Locke's texts to pick out

---

[3] "Political power then I take to be a right of making laws . . . for the regulating
and preserving of property, and of employing the force of the community in the execution of such laws and in the defence of the commonwealth from foreign injury . . ." (II, 3). By "property" Locke here means the "lives, liberties, and estates"
of the society's members (II, 123).

[4] "Some Thoughts Concerning Reading and Study for a Gentleman," 400.

[5] See, e.g., II, 89: "wherever therefore *any number* of men are so united into one
society . . . , there and there only is a political or civil society"; or II, 95: "when *any
number* of men have so consented to make one community . . . they are thereby presently incorporated and make one body politic" (my emphases). But see my remarks
on the requisite number of members below in 1.1.

precisely the same relationship among persons;[6] and I will use these terms interchangeably in the discussions to follow. This might seem to some a mistake, especially given the special significance that a term like "commonwealth" had in the political discourse of the English civil war period. But Locke explicitly denies that his use of "commonwealth" is intended to convey anything more than "any independent community" or "a society of men" (II, 133). And this meaning, of course, is precisely what Locke intended for all of the other expressions listed above.

This, then, is what we may call groups of persons who stand to one another in "the political relationship." But what exactly is the substance of this relationship? While a thorough answer must await the chapters to follow, at least a sketch of an answer will be obvious to any careful reader of Locke's moral and political writings. Indeed, Locke's conception of the political relationship is probably the single most influential such conception in the history of political thought (as well as in the founding principles of existing political societies). The relationship that binds persons into one political society, according to Locke, is a particular kind of moral relationship among free persons, based in consent and consisting of a certain mutuality of rights and obligations. "Political" or "civil" are thus not for Locke (and Lockeans) purely descriptive, value-neutral terms. They are very much evaluative, morally loaded terms. The political relationship can arise only within groups of moral equals, all of whom enter the relationship from a state in which they are morally free to govern themselves and pursue their own (innocent) plans and activities.[7] "Political power" is the right possessed jointly by persons in this relationship, or by those trustees appointed by them, to make and execute binding laws for the society and to use the society's force to protect it from internal or external threats. The primary obligation

[6] See, for instance, II, 89, which appears to equate "political society," "civil society," and "commonwealth." II, 95 uses "civil society," "community," and "body politic" indiscriminately; and II, 101–6, 122, and 175 use "commonwealth" to mean "politic society," "political society," and "polity." II, 133 and 243 equate "commonwealth," "community," and "society," while II, 211 clearly identifies "society," "political society," "community," and "commonwealth." Numerous other similar indications of apparent synonymy among these expressions are present in Locke's writings.

[7] The political relationship can be entered only by those who either have never given up or have had restored their "natural freedom." It cannot be entered by those who either have already voluntarily surrendered this freedom (in joining and remaining a part of some other political society) or have lost (and not recovered) their freedom through wrongdoing. Those who do enjoy their natural freedom are all moral equals "in respect of jurisdiction or dominion over one another." They are all equally free of "the will and authority of any other man" (II, 54).

owed by each person to every other in a political society is to abide by those laws and to support whatever measures are "necessary to the ends for which they unite into society" (II, 99). Most important for Locke (and Lockeans), the political relationship is essentially voluntary and consensual. The mutual rights and obligations that are the substance of the relationship can arise only as a result of a consensual transaction, in which each member voluntarily surrenders certain rights and undertakes those obligations, on the understanding that the others do the same. "That which begins and actually constitutes any political society is nothing but the consent of any number of freemen . . . to unite and incorporate" (II, 99; see also, e.g., II, 95, 175).

Other sorts of apparently political relationships among persons are not, for Locke, true instances of political or civil society at all. To call a society "civil" or "political" is to say that it is morally legitimate; true politics, for Locke, is not just a matter of coherent structures of physical power. Where laws or other limits on their freedom are imposed on subjects without their consent (or the consent of their authorized representatives), where governors rule simply by force or where one social group oppresses another, there is no civil society (between the powerful and the powerless). Conquest, for instance, can never give genuinely political power over a people, no matter how just the cause that provoked it.[8] Absolute (unlimited) dominion within a group "is so far from being one kind of civil society, that it is as inconsistent with it as slavery is with property" (II,1 74; see also, e.g., II, 90). Governments that exercise power over their subjects that was not freely entrusted to them by those subjects, are simply "dissolved," no longer having any properly political power at all (II, 211–22, 232), regardless of how much physical control and power over their subjects they may continue to exercise. Indeed, since there are for Locke limits to what can be meaningfully (bindingly) consented to by a person, there are in his view necessary limits on political power (because that power can only be derived from consent). Those who use force beyond these limits leave the realm of the political relationship altogether, entering instead the realms of unlawful coercion and war.

We can extract from even this very brief summary of the core of Lockean philosophy three essential elements of a proper account of the political relationship:

[8] See, e.g., II, 175, 185, 196. This is, in fact, a major theme of the whole of chapter 16 of the *Second Treatise*.

(1) A position on the contrasting kinds of nonpolitical relationships that must precede, and may reemerge from, the
political relationship.

(2) A position on the kinds of voluntary, consensual acts or
practices that create the political relationship and civil
society.

(3) A position on (a) the source and extent of the moral limits
on the physical power that may be permissibly exercised
over persons by their political society or its governors, and
(b) the consequences of actions by political superiors that
transgress these limits.

The first three parts of this book deal, respectively, with these
three elements of the Lockean account of the political relationship.
Each of these parts aims to interpret, refine, develop, and criticize
Locke's position, with the ultimate intention of presenting the
strongest possible form of the Lockean position in each of the three
areas. Sometimes this process will involve excising or dramatically
revising elements commonly associated with the Lockean perspective (as in part 2's revision of the theory of tacit consent, or part 3's
rejection of the doctrine of inalienable rights). Sometimes the process will involve only clarification and development. But at all times
I aim to remain consistent with the spirit of Locke's political philosophy and to present the best possible defense of the resulting
account, so that at the close of part 3 we will have before us the
strongest conception of the political relationship that still deserves
to be called "Lockean." The fourth part of the book then turns to
the contemporary critique of the Lockean account, to possible avenues of escape for the Lockean, and to the threat of philosophical
anarchism that seems to lie in wait for a properly developed Lockean
political philosophy.

What I hope will emerge from this work are: a fuller understanding of Locke's political philosophy and some of its central concepts
(such as the state of nature, the state of war, consent, trust, dissolution, and the right of resistance); an indication of the directions in
which Lockean theory must be pushed if it is to represent a plausible
position in contemporary political philosophy; an assessment of the
best Lockean position; and an appreciation of the consequences of
a serious commitment to a Lockean political philosophy. Each of the
four parts of the book will be aimed at making a contribution to
achieving each of these objectives, although the emphasis early in
the book will be on the first two of these objectives, while later parts

will focus more on the last two. And each of these objectives seems to me quite clearly important, not only for reasons of historical accuracy and fairness, but for the advancement of political philosophy generally.

First, despite the healthy industry throughout this century in the production of articles, chapters, and books on Locke's political philosophy, much in that philosophy remains, in my view, badly misunderstood and hence unappreciated. Fundamental concepts in Locke's program are still discussed (and often dismissed) without paying careful attention either to the texts themselves or to the philosophical problems toward whose solution those concepts were introduced by Locke. Sometimes these misunderstandings seem willful. Some of them flow from unsympathetic caricatures of a great philosopher's work, as in George H. Sabine's exceedingly shallow analysis, which permits him to conclude that Locke's political philosophy is just "a series of compromises" between "really opposed philosophical positions," with "no logical structure";[9] or in John Plamenatz's anemic version of Locke, a Locke whose work is so "spoiled" by "ambiguities and false reasonings," "inconsistencies and confusions," and the "unconscious need to avoid unwelcome conclusions," that his political philosophy is on balance "superficial," showing "no novelty of method, largeness of design, or unusual penetration," and, indeed, making no "major contribution" at all to political or social theory.[10] More careful scholars have given us fairer accounts of Locke's political philosophy, showing more fully the foundations and the logical structure of that philosophy.[11] But this new care, surprisingly, has often also been accompanied by the dismissal of Locke's work as uninteresting "as a starting point for reflection about any issue of contemporary political theory."[12]

I will argue, by contrast, that Locke has much to say to the contemporary theorist, especially in his account of the state of nature, in his consent theory, and in his theory of resistance. When the basic concepts of Locke's political philosophy are clarified and analyzed, we can see the structure of a powerful and coherent voluntarist program in political philosophy, which must at least still be taken seriously by contemporary theorists. We can see this, of course, only if we surrender the predisposition to find in Locke's writings primarily code or dogma, only if we stop trying so hard to see all of

---

[9] *History of Political Theory,* 519, 537.
[10] *Man and Society,* 1:211–14.
[11] I have in mind here primarily Dunn, Tully, and Ashcraft.
[12] Dunn, *Political Thought,* x.

Locke's arguments as simply confused and desperate rationalizations in support of some (obvious or hidden) political agenda, only if we instead look carefully at his work as a body of sincerely philosophical theory. We will find systematic argument only where we look at texts with an eye to finding it. A serious philosopher's work surely deserves no less attention and regard than this. And none can deny that Locke merits the title "serious philosopher."[13]

When we are more careful and analytical with Locke's texts, of course, and when we treat them with greater philosophical sensitivity, we can see more clearly as well the kinds of changes in and developments of Locke's own theories that are required to allow Lockean theory to participate as a respectable player in contemporary political philosophy. I have argued elsewhere, for instance, that Locke's own theory of rights is based not only on theological, but also on secular foundational commitments; and this realization helps us to see that the best genuinely Lockean theory can be defended without appeal to either theological ethics or to any objectionably strong conception of the "naturalness" of rights.[14] So we can in fact begin our development of Lockean political philosophy with a perfectly secular account of individuals, their rights, and their powers to transfer or forfeit those rights. Similarly, we will see in the discussions below that the other most basic concepts of Lockean political philosophy can also be elaborated and combined in purely secular terms. These facts make clear that there is very real potential for a Lockean political philosophy whose theoretical commitments are no more suspect than those of any other political philosophy with realist or objectivist moral foundations.

My arguments in part 4 will suggest, though, that however carefully we fill out and articulate the best version of Lockean political philosophy, that philosophy will commit us to a quite different view of our actual, contemporary political lives, and to a quite different view as well of actual political life in Locke's own day, than anything Locke hoped for or expected. Our moral assessment of existing political communities and our account of the duties and rights of existing citizens will not be those that we might have guessed Locke would give. But in my judgment, the new Lockean view that will emerge at the end of this work is a better, clearer, more helpful view than Locke's own. The new Lockean analysis of the political rela-

---

[13] My defense of this approach to Locke's work is presented in the introduction to *Lockean Theory of Rights*. The approach is, I hope, vindicated in the remainder of that book and in this one.

[14] See *Lockean Theory of Rights*, chapters 1 and 2.

tionship and the new view of the relevance of Lockean theory to our understanding of actual polities, are both, I think, ones that force us to be more sensitive to the full range of moral considerations that bear on the basic decisions of political life that we must make here and now.

P A R T 1

NONCONSENSUAL RELATIONS

Throughout the *Two Treatises of Government* and his other major works, Locke strives to characterize and clarify the political by contrasting it with other familiar social or personal-interactive categories. Political *power* (right, authority), for instance, is contrasted with other types of rightful control that persons may exercise—most prominently, paternal (parental) and despotical power. Political *societies* are contrasted with other kinds of human societies, such as the "natural society" of "mankind," or voluntary, religious societies (churches). And what I have called the political *relationship* (which defines the bond among those who are members of the same political *society*) is also characterized in sharp contrast with other kinds of social relationships. In this case, the most important contrast drawn by Locke is with two kinds of nonconsensual relations among persons that may precede or reemerge from the political relationship. One such relationship—the state of nature (the subject of chapter 1)—may or may not involve coercive interactions between persons. The other relationship—the state of war (the subject of chapter 2)—is defined in terms of certain uses of unlawful coercion.

These are not, of course, the only kinds of nonconsensual relationships centrally discussed by Locke. He writes extensively as well, for instance, about the parent-child relationship. But the parent-child relationship is (rightly) taken by Locke to be a relationship between those who are not moral equals, all mature, rational humans being fully persons and their immature children being only potentially so. Because we accept the moral equality of persons, we have little trouble discerning today the manifold differences in content and justification between parental and political authority (at least largely, of course, thanks to Locke's efforts). As a result, the contrast between political and filial relationships, although undoubtedly absolutely central to Locke's polemical goals (e.g., his refutation of Filmer), is less interesting for our purposes than the

11

contrast Locke draws between political relationships and those non-consensual relationships that can hold between adult persons (who *are* moral equals). Thus, I will concentrate here on the ideas of the state of nature and the state of war, two such nonconsensual relationships. Our task in part 1 is to begin to better understand the Lockean conception of the political relationship by better understanding these two central nonconsensual relations among persons and their proper roles in Lockean political philosophy.

ONE

THE LOCKEAN STATE OF NATURE

1.1. Locke's State of Nature

The state of nature is in many ways the central concept at work in Locke's *Treatises*.[1] It is the concept with which Locke chooses to introduce the *Second Treatise* (II, 4). And it is only against and by means of the state of nature that he offers us accounts of political obligation and authority, the justification of civil government, the limits on political power, and the occasions for justified resistance. The state of nature defines for Locke the boundaries of the political. Understanding the state of nature is thus essential for understanding Locke's conception of the nature, content, and limits of the political relationship. But the state of nature is probably also the most misunderstood idea in Locke's political philosophy.[2] Locke has puzzled many generations of readers by appearing to offer inconsistent descriptions of the state of nature and by apparently allowing the concept to play too many roles in his theory. Is the state of nature a historical period that preceded governments? Or is it the state into which every person, even today, is born? Or is it simply an analytical device used by Locke to justify civil society, a convenient fiction with no actual historical instantiations?

Progress in understanding Locke's intentions has been made in recent literature, of course;[3] and it is, as a result, no longer fashionable to simply dismiss Locke's claims about the state of nature as bad history or bad psychology.[4] Nor is it as easy as it once was to accuse Locke of blatant inconsistency or deceptiveness in his de-

---

[1] There is only one mention of the state of nature in the *First Treatise* (I, 90), but Locke's arguments there are clearly consistent with the concept as it is articulated in the *Second Treatise*.

[2] Dunn, *Locke*, 46.

[3] Largely due to the work of Dunn (*Political Thought*, 97, 100–101, 106, 110–12) and Ashcraft ("Locke's State of Nature").

[4] For criticisms of this sort, see Aaron, *John Locke*, 273; Kendall, *Majority-Rule*, 75; Gough, *Political Philosophy*, 89.

scriptions of the social conditions persons would endure in the state of nature.[5] In spite of this progress, however, widespread obscurities and errors persist in discussions of Locke's state of nature, mistakes that often conceal the distinctive nature and virtues of the concept with which Locke chose to work. I will try in this chapter to remedy those mistakes. With the definition I present (in this section) in hand, many of the familiar worries about Locke's account are much easier to unravel. This definition will also enable us to locate both Locke's true confusions about the state of nature, which lie in rather different areas than is generally supposed, and the best way of understanding the value of Locke's concept of the state of nature to a Lockean program in political philosophy.

Locke begins chapter 2 of the *Second Treatise* by asking us to "consider what state all men are naturally in" (II, 4)—that is, the state of nature. The state of nature, of course, functions as the starting point in Locke's genetic account of the rise of civil societies. And the problems of life in that state serve to explain and justify the transition to political life. As a result, if we come to Locke fresh from a reading of Hobbes (as students often do), it is perhaps natural to suppose that Locke means by the state of nature roughly what Hobbes meant. For Hobbes (to simplify a bit), the state of nature can be defined as the state persons are (or would be) in living together without effective government over them. "Effective government" here means something like "government able to provide its citizens with adequate security against domestic and foreign assaults on their persons or property." To be sure, Hobbes fills out his picture of life in the state of nature in a way that is hard to confuse with Locke's picture.[6] But it is easy enough to believe that in their definitions of the state of nature, Hobbes and Locke simply agree.

Let me be more precise. We must distinguish in Hobbes the definition of the state of nature (as life without effective government) from the social and moral characterizations of that state and from claims about that state's historical instantiations. People can and do

[5] Variants of this attack can be found in Macpherson, "Introduction," xiv; Strauss, *Natural Right*, 224–26; Mabbott, *John Locke*, 143–46; Cox, *Locke on War and Peace*, 76–80; Jenkins, "Locke and Natural Rights," 152–53; Lessnoff, *Social Contract*, 60.

[6] Some, however, do argue for a "Hobbesian" Locke on this issue: see Strauss, *Natural Right*, 224–25; Cox, *Locke on War and Peace*, xx, 79, 93, 96, 99, 104, 165–67, 175, 182–83; Mabbott, *John Locke*, 145–46; Andrew, *Shylock's Rights*, 114; Pangle, *Republicanism*, 246; Kendall, "John Locke Revisited," 228. Cox argues that Locke actually used two quite different descriptions of the state of nature (*Locke on War and Peace*, 75–81), as does Macpherson (*Possessive Individualism*, 240–42, 245–46), while Goldwin holds Locke's view to be essentially Hobbesian but with some significant differences ("John Locke," 485).

actually live in the state of nature, on Hobbes' view of it, for people can live and have in fact lived together without effective government over them. When they do live in this condition, their lives will have certain social and moral properties. The social characterization of the state of nature in Hobbes is familiar (and quite different from what we find in Locke). Life in the state of nature is "solitary, poor, nasty, brutish, and short," a condition of war "of every man against every man," a war in which there is no industry, no culture, and no real society.[7] The moral condition of persons in the state of nature for Hobbes is less clear, although it seems fair to say that they have no moral rights or obligations at all in the ordinary sense—"the notions of right and wrong, justice and injustice, have there no place."[8] As for historical instantiations of the state of nature (i.e., actual occasions where persons lived together without effective government), Hobbes mentions savages in America, "civilized" persons during a civil war, and (at the international level) independent sovereigns.[9] Now Locke, of course, would accept little of this (although we must for him as well clearly distinguish his definition of the state of nature from his claims about its social, moral, and historical properties). Locke's social characterization of the state of nature seems considerably less bleak than Hobbes'; his moral characterization includes individuals with full-blown moral rights and obligations; and in Hobbes' list of historical instantiations of the state of nature, Locke would certainly make changes (primarily by adding to it). But for all of these disagreements, it is not difficult to suppose that Hobbes' and Locke's definitions of the state of nature are roughly the same.

This supposition is a common one among Locke scholars, who frequently claim that for Locke the state of nature is the condition of persons without (effective) government.[10] That view is, however,

[7] Hobbes, *Leviathan*, chapter 13, paragraphs 8–9.

[8] *Leviathan*, chapter 13, paragraph 13. Natural law binds only "in foro interno" in the state of war (*Leviathan*, chapter 13, paragraph 35); however we understand this claim, it does not refer to moral bonds of an "ordinary" sort. Similarly, the "rights" held by persons in this state are mere "liberties" (see 1.3). I refrain here from further comment on what I concede are difficult points in Hobbes scholarship.

[9] *Leviathan*, chapter 13, paragraphs 11–12.

[10] See Plamenatz, *Man and Society*, 1:220–21; Colman, *Moral Philosophy*, 177–78; Yolton, *Locke*, 57; Mabbott, *John Locke*, 142; Cox, "Introduction," xxi; Kendall, *Majority-Rule*, 64; Von Leyden, *Hobbes and Locke*, 99–100; Altham, "Reflections on the State of Nature," 134; Parry, *John Locke*, 57; Monson, "Locke's Political Theory," 192; Lemos, *Hobbes and Locke*, 88–89. To be fair, Colman characterizes the state of nature as the condition of persons "living together without *civil* society" (my emphasis), and "civil" (as we saw in the introduction) conveys for Locke some notion of legitimacy. Yolton may have something similar in mind. See also Vaughn, *John Locke*, 79. I argue below that this simple addition is also inadequate to give us a correct account.

mistaken in both obvious and more subtle fashions. In the most obvious case, persons can for Locke be living under effective, highly organized governments and still be in the state of nature—provided only that those governments are illegitimate with respect to them. Prominent instances mentioned by Locke are persons living under arbitrary, tyrannical governments (II, 17–20) and under foreign powers that have dissolved their society by conquest (II, 211). In both cases effective government and the state of nature are consistent.[11] At the very least, one wants to build into a definition of the state of nature that it is the condition of persons living together without *legitimate* government. Even this addition, however, will not suffice, for Locke mentions several classes of persons who can live under legitimate governments while remaining in the state of nature: visiting aliens (II, 9), minors under the age of consent (II, 15, 118), and those of defective reason (II, 60). What is clearly needed in any adequate definition of Locke's state of nature is some element that captures the distinctive moral component of that state. I will suggest such a definition momentarily.

But there is a second set of problems confronted in approaching the Lockean state of nature from a Hobbesian direction. For Hobbes, the state of nature is a condition persons are either in or out of (simpliciter).[12] And he virtually always writes of it as a condition that only *groups* of persons can be in or out of. Neither of these points squares well with Locke's concept of the state of nature (although Locke's own language is sometimes misleading). In the first place, Locke often writes of people being in the state of nature with respect to certain people and out of it with respect to others (at the same time). Thus, the princes of (legitimate *or* illegitimate) independent governments are in the state of nature with respect to each other (II, 14), although legitimate princes are (at the same time) out of that state with respect to fellow citizens of their commonwealths. And visiting citizens of an alien legitimate state are in the state of nature with respect to the state they visit (II, 9), but out of that state with respect to citizens of their own state. This suggests that the state of nature must for Locke be a *relational* concept, something not at all

---

[11] Contrary to, e.g., Lemos's claim that persons living under an absolute monarch are not in the state of nature, since they still have laws and judges (*Hobbes and Locke*, 116).

[12] It may seem that the sovereign in Hobbes is a counterexample to this claim, since it (or he) appears to be both in the state of nature (with other sovereigns) and out of it (with the citizens of its own commonwealth). This appearance dissolves when we remember that for Hobbes the sovereign *remains* in the state of nature, even with regard to the subjects who are out of it. See *Leviathan*, chapter 28, paragraph 2.

obviously true of Hobbes' parallel notion.[13] Second, while Hobbes virtually never writes of individuals being in the state of nature while those around them are not[14] (making his state of nature essentially a property of groups of persons), Locke's individuals are frequently in that position. Visiting aliens are, of course, in that position, and since every person for Locke is born into the state of nature (II, 15, 118, 191),[15] it is impossible to imagine a realistic society (no matter how legitimate) within which there are not many persons in that position.[16] Locke's state of nature is, then, both a more individualistic and a more relational concept than that of Hobbes. And the more closely we pattern our analysis of Locke's state of nature on Hobbesian notions, the more completely we will miss these essential features.

Now it may seem that in concentrating on the Hobbesian leanings of some scholars' accounts of Locke's state of nature, I have thus far managed to ignore Locke's most important claims about that state. Indeed, many take Locke to have given us a clear definition of the state of nature: "Want of a common judge with authority, puts all persons in the state of nature" (II, 19); "Men living together according to reason, without a common superior on earth, with authority to judge between them, is properly the state of nature" (II, 19).[17] Here (and elsewhere) Locke claims that wherever no one is entitled to settle controversies between two persons, wherever there

[13] Locke's clearest indication of the *relational* character of the state of nature comes in II, 145, where he uses the "in reference to" construction prominently (see also, e.g., II, 91 ["as much in the state of nature with all under his dominion as he is with the rest of mankind"] and II, 94 ["in the state of nature, in respect of him, whom they find to be so"]). As we will see (in 6.3), noting the relational character of Locke's state of nature is essential to a proper understanding of his theory of resistance. Since writing this chapter, I have found that Pangle also comments on the relational nature of Locke's concept (*Republicanism*, 247), while Kavka attributes a similar view to Hobbes (*Hobbesian Moral and Political Theory*, 88–89). I am not sure that I see the textual warrant for this interpretive claim in Hobbes' case, although Hobbes certainly could have held such a view without doing violence to his other positions.

[14] Even in those cases where the subject may legitimately resist the sovereign, it appears that this fact is no evidence that the subject is returned to the state of nature. See *Leviathan*, chapter 21, paragraphs 11–21.

[15] "A man is naturally free from subjection to any government, though he be born in a place under its jurisdiction" (II, 191).

[16] It appears that individuals within otherwise legitimate states may be returned to the state of nature by governmental violations of their rights. (I return to this issue in 6.3–6.4.) This is an additional instance of persons being in the state of nature while those around them are not. And, of course, were it not for Locke's odd account of tacit consent being given by mere residence (II, 119), many more people would be in this position (i.e., those who resided in but did not consent to membership in a legitimate civil society).

[17] See the parallel claims in II, 91.

is no authorized umpire to judge between them, those persons are in the state of nature. Those with no fair appeal to neutral arbiters may resolve their disagreements themselves, as the law of nature permits. The absence of an authorized common judge is taken by most of the scholars who are not influenced by Hobbesian notions to be (at least the essence of) Locke's definition of the state of nature.[18]

It is worth noting, first, that Locke's claims about the "common judge with authority" do not have the *form* of a definition; they have, rather, the form of a statement of a *sufficient condition* for being in the state of nature. Locke never, for instance, claims that it is only when there is no common judge that persons are in the state of nature (he never, that is, claims that this condition is a *necessary* one). For all we know (on the strength of these passages alone) there may be many quite different conditions also sufficient to put persons in the state of nature. A statement of a sufficient condition need not even approach a definition.

But lest this seem an idle, academic point, of no relevance to intelligent interpretation of Locke's text, I believe there is good reason not to want Locke to be offering his claims about the common judge as a definition of the state of nature. This is most easily seen if we remember Locke's claims about private contracts in the state of nature:

> For 'tis not every compact that puts an end to the state of nature between persons, but only this one of agreeing together mutually to enter into one community, and make one body politic; other promises and compacts, men may make one with another, and yet still be in the state of nature. . . . For truth and keeping of faith belongs to men as men, and not as members of society. (II, 14)

In other words, people may make promises and contracts with one another, transfer rights and undertake obligations, without leaving the state of nature. Only one particular and very special

---

[18] See, for instance, Laslett, "Introduction," 111; Goldwin, "Locke's State of Nature," 126–27, and "John Locke," 478–80; Aarsleff, "State of Nature," 100; Pangle, *Republicanism*, 246; Polin, "Justice," 272; Ashcraft, *Locke's Two Treatises*, 113; Farrell, "Coercion, Consent," 522–23; Medina, *Social Contract Theories*, 31; Anglim, "On Locke's State of Nature." Ashcraft comes closer to what I take to be the proper definition in his "legal statement of the state of nature," but still concentrates solely on establishing a judge ("Locke's State of Nature," 901). Strauss and Cox (along with others who *are* influenced by Hobbes) also use this definition (Strauss, *Natural Right*, 230; Cox, *Locke on War and Peace*, 73).

agreement takes persons out of the state of nature. Is that "special agreement" simply any agreement to set up a judge between persons? Is it simply any instance of one person transferring to another his natural right to judge for himself and punish violators of the law of nature (what Locke calls the "executive power of the law of nature")? It is hard to see how either of these claims could be plausibly maintained. For if it is possible for a large group of persons to surrender (in creating a civil society) the rights necessary to make a "common judge with authority," surely it is possible for a small number of people, *without* creating a civil society, to erect a common judge with equally legitimate authority. Why may not two persons in the state of nature authorize a third to settle conflicts between them (i.e., both surrender to the third their rights to judge for themselves)? I can see nothing in the nature of the rights or the transaction that would preclude this for Locke. Yet if two persons thus agreed to set up a common judge, surely this would be a purely private contract, after which they would still be in the state of nature. Simply erecting an authorized umpire would not be sufficient to constitute creation of a civil society. Among other things, this "common judge" would appear to lack the right to make law for those he judges between. The judge could, of course, interpret the law of nature for those who authorized him; for possessing the right to interpret the applicable body of law is part of what Locke means when he talks of being authorized to judge. But such a judge could not make civil law (which must be consistent with but will extend well *beyond* the requirements of natural law). In making a civil society, persons must give up not only their rights to interpret and execute natural law, but must as well create for their governors the right to make and enforce necessary civil laws whose content goes beyond that prescribed by the law of nature (see II, 128–30; and the discussion below in 3.1). Further, it seems, there would not be a sufficient number of people involved in a private agreement of the sort described to create a functioning society.[19] The one very special agreement that creates a civil society is considerably more complex, and involves the surrendering by citizens of far more rights, than any simple agreement merely to set up a common judge with authority.[20] Thus, while the absence of a common judge between per-

[19] Locke does, of course, say that "any number of men" may create a community or civil society (II, 89, 95). I do not find plausible the conclusion that three persons can make a civil society, but this point is not centrally important to my argument here.

[20] Creating a civil society involves, for instance, submitting one's possessions to the jurisdiction of society (II, 120).

sons is clearly a sufficient condition for those persons being in the state of nature, it does not appear to be a necessary condition. Common judges with authority may be present even in the state of nature.[21]

Exactly when an agreement is an agreement that creates a civil society, and when sufficiently many people are involved to create one, are questions to which Locke also provides (at least the frameworks for) answers. But he rightly concentrates his attention on one particular aspect of the agreement (the creation of an authorized judge) in his discussion of the state of nature, for it is this aspect of the agreement that solves the fundamental problems of life in the state of nature. It is still, however, only one aspect of the special agreement that creates a civil society. Without the rest of the agreement, persons remain in the state of nature. Thus, any acceptable definition of Locke's state of nature must make reference to (or otherwise capture the significance of) the full agreement that alone creates civil society and removes persons from their natural condition.

We might try to give an account of Locke's state of nature that refers to the full agreement as follows:

A person (A) is in the state of nature if and only if A has not voluntarily agreed to join some legitimate political community.

This definition (in the nontechnical sense of "definition"), while exceedingly simple, succeeds where the others we have considered

---

[21] A fact presupposed in Nozick's well-known discussion of these issues (*Anarchy,* chapters 2–6). See also Grant, *Liberalism,* 101–2. The state in which there is no common judge between any two people may be what Locke has in mind in referring to "the *perfect* state of nature" (II, 87; my emphasis); but this cannot be the *only* case of a state of nature. Notice that elsewhere Locke distinguishes "the ordinary state of nature" from the state of nature in which individuals find themselves when living under the (illegitimate) dominion of an absolute monarch (II, 91). (I reserve discussion of the hard case of people living under an effective but illegitimate ruler for chapter 6.) And, of course, the state of nature in which members of a civil society stand with respect to those outside it is quite different from the state of nature in which prepolitical persons stood with respect to one another (since members of a society have given their government the right to execute natural law both within and without their body). This much at least seems clear: Locke has in mind that many different specific conditions may qualify as "the state of nature." What all these states have in common is suggested below in the text. Locke may, of course, be using the expression "common judge" in a technical way, so that judges with authority in the state of nature simply do not count as "common judges" in the appropriate sense. But there is no announcement in the text that this is the case. And we could, I suppose, build enough into a phrase like "absence of an *effective,* legitimate common judge" to use it in a satisfactory definition of the state of nature. But I think the analysis I offer in the text is considerably more clear and direct.

failed in capturing the crucial element distinguishing the civil from the natural state—the voluntary agreement by an individual to perform according to the special terms of the contract that alone creates a civil society. This definition leaves open the precise content of the contract necessary to create a civil society. (Locke, of course, fills in much of that content for us, as we will see in subsequent chapters.) It also preserves the individualistic character of Locke's concept, since it allows that a single person may be in the state of nature (in virtue of not having agreed to join) while those around him are out of it.

But this definition is still flawed in two regards. First, it does nothing to capture the *relational* character of Locke's concept of the state of nature. And, second, this definition does not account for the cases of those who are *returned* to the state of nature from civil society. I propose, then, as an acceptable definition of Locke's state of nature the following:

A is in the state of nature with respect to B if and only if A has not voluntarily agreed to join (or is no longer a member of) a legitimate political community of which B is a member.

And then as a special case, falling under this account, we can say:

A is in the state of nature (simpliciter) if and only if A has not voluntarily agreed to join (or is no longer a member of) any legitimate political community.

Obviously, my definition has a great deal in common with those we considered earlier and rejected; but it squares with claims made by Locke for which they cannot account. Thus, while on my definition those not living under legitimate governments are, of course, in the state of nature, the definition accounts as well for Locke's claims that aliens, children, and madmen are in the state of nature even within legitimate political communities (their having either not agreed at all or not agreed voluntarily to join).[22] And while those who retain their executive rights and thus erect no judge over them are, of course, on this definition in the state of nature (the transfer of those rights being essential to any agreement to join a political

---

[22] It is, of course, an embarrassment for Locke that after saying visiting aliens have not joined the community (II, 9), he goes on to say that they have consented to the laws of their host countries in as full a sense as have most permanent residents (II, 119). For more discussion of the status of visiting aliens, see 4.1 below; and *Lockean Theory of Rights*, section 3.3.

community), the definition allows as well that private transfer of the executive rights leaves one in the state of nature.

The following picture, then, flows from this definition. Each person is born into the state of nature (simpliciter) (II, 191), and, barring a universal human community, each person stays in the state of nature with respect to at least some (and possibly all) others. Those incapable of consent (voluntary agreement) and those who choose never to consent remain in the state of nature (simpliciter). Those whose communities are dissolved (e.g., by foreign conquest) and those who are abused by otherwise legitimate governments are returned to the state of nature (simpliciter).[23] Persons who enter civil society (including princes) leave the state of nature with respect to fellow citizens, but remain in it with respect to all alien nations (II, 145, 183) and with respect to all noncitizens (i.e., those still in the state of nature [simpliciter]). All of these consequences of the definition I have offered seem to square precisely with Locke's claims about the state of nature.[24]

Perhaps the most important point to note about this definition is its strong moral flavor.[25] We have already distinguished between the definition of the state of nature, and the social, moral, and historical characterizations determined by it. Locke's definition clearly incorporates moral elements, making prominent use of distinctively moral notions (like legitimacy and voluntary agreement). No obvious social characterization flows from this definition, the state of nature being consistent for Locke with many different social circumstances. Hobbes' definition of the state of nature, by contrast, clearly incorporates elements of the social characterization; it was primarily the brute fact of absence of physical security that defined the state of nature for Hobbes, and an obvious social characterization (of life without security) follows immediately from his definition (given his account of human nature). It might be fair to say that, for Hobbes, the moral dimension of interpersonal life rests on and follows from

[23] Locke is careful to distinguish between dissolution of government and dissolution of society (II, 211). In the latter case, persons are returned to the state of nature (II, 211), while in the former it appears that the society regains those rights it entrusted to government, but no *individual* citizen returns to the state of nature (II, 243). I believe Locke means to say here that citizens remain out of the state of nature with respect to each other, but enter into it with respect to those (governors) who have abused their powers. The hardest case, of course, is that in which the government abuses only particular individuals, remaining legitimate with respect to the majority. See 6.3–6.4 for a detailed discussion of these questions.

[24] Accounts of the state of nature similar to that offered here can be found in Grant, *Liberalism*, 66; and Winfrey, "Charity versus Justice," 425.

[25] See Ashcraft, *Locke's Two Treatises,* 111ff.

the social dimension.[26] The sharp contrast between the social character of Hobbes' account of the state of nature and the moral character of Locke's illuminates, as we will see, some major obscurities in Locke's use of the state of nature.[27]

1.2. The Moral, Social, and Historical Dimensions

We have seen that Locke's state of nature is a concept with strong moral content. Because Locke's state of nature describes a possible (and frequently actual) relationship among people, Locke can give us more specific information about the substance of that relationship—for instance, about the moral and social characteristics (as well as historical examples) of its actual instantiations. There is, then, no inconsistency or confusion involved in Locke's using the state of nature sometimes as an analytical device (to explain and discuss the nature of the political relationship), sometimes to describe a historical condition of people, sometimes to describe a moral or social condition of possible or contemporary persons. All are perfectly proper applications of the concept.

Let us begin with the moral dimensions of the state of nature. Thus far our account of that content has been purely negative—that is, the state of nature is the state persons are in with respect to others when they have *not* consented to join with them (or have subsequently left) a legitimate commonwealth. Can we not give a full and positive moral characterization of Locke's state of nature? What is the moral condition of persons in the state of nature? What are their rights and duties? Locke often talks as if the moral condition

[26] I mean this only in the following senses: (a) natural law seems only to bind us to perform (*in foro externo*) when physical security (a "social fact") is guaranteed (*Leviathan*, chapter 15, paragraph 35); (b) consent (a moral notion) seems to follow from the mere presence of physical security (*Leviathan*, A Review and Conclusion, paragraph 7) and from the ability of others to take our lives when they please (other "social facts") (*Leviathan*, chapter 20, paragraphs 4–11).

[27] I have not yet mentioned the most interesting alternative account of what Locke means by the state of nature—the account offered by Dunn. For him Locke's state of nature is: "the condition in which God himself places all men in the world, prior to the lives which they live and the societies which are fashioned by the living of those lives. What it is designed to show is not what men are like but rather what rights and duties they have as the creatures of God" (*Locke*, 47; see the parallel claims in *Political Thought*, 97, 103). It is hard to argue with claims that capture so much of the true spirit of Locke's account, but Dunn's position seems to me not quite accurate. Persons can be in the state of nature long after they have changed the condition God set them in. As I argue below, there is no particular set of rights and duties possessed by all persons in the state of nature. Perhaps we can say that Dunn's claims give a fair characterization of that "original" state of nature to which each person is born, leaving aside later instantiations of that state (see 1.3 below).

of persons in the state of nature is reasonably simple to summarize: (1) Persons have all (and only) the duties defined by the law of nature, that law being eternal and immutable (e.g., II, 135), and there being in the state of nature no legitimate commonwealth that could impose on them any other duties. While the "particulars" of the law of nature are not discussed very carefully by Locke, the general form of these duties is clear—that is, they are duties to preserve oneself and others (by, for instance, not harming persons in their lives, liberty, health, limb, or goods [II, 6]).[28] (2) Persons enjoy in the state of nature their full complement of natural rights (which correlate with the natural duties of others to respect those rights). Each person is "born to" this set of rights, and "receives" them fully on reaching maturity (II, 55, 59). Natural rights are a "grant or gift from God" (I, 116), which persons possess intact until (if ever) they consent to enter a legitimate civil society, surrendering some of these rights in the process. While Locke is again sketchy on the particular rights we possess, they include rights to freely pursue harmless activities, to do what is necessary to preserve oneself and others, and to "execute" the law of nature (II, 4, 129). This is the account of persons' moral condition in the state of nature that can be drawn most easily from Locke's texts.

But it simply cannot be the whole account (nor do I think Locke intends it to be). This account is adequate as an account of (what we might call) the "original" state of nature in which newly mature individuals find themselves.[29] But if my claims about Locke's state of nature have thus far been even reasonably accurate, a full moral characterization of the state of nature would seem to be impossible. For, in the first place, we must specify at least two sorts of moral conditions for persons in the state of nature: the conditions for mature, rational individuals, and the conditions for children and incompetents. Where mature persons in the state of nature may possess the "full complement" of rights and duties, those who are not fully rational (and are thereby also in the state of nature) clearly do not. Because a law only binds those to whom it is promulgated, and because the law of nature is promulgated by reason, those deficient in reason are not properly under the law of nature at all (II, 57–60). Presumably, this means that children and incompetents lack

[28] For a fuller discussion of the content of the law of nature, as articulated by Locke, see my *Lockean Theory of Rights*, section 1.5.

[29] Even the "original" state of nature may, to be completely precise, involve different rights and duties for different persons, since newly mature persons will often have, for example, different property rights as a result of differential inheritances.

at least some of the duties and rights defined by the law of nature.[30] Further, of course, those in prepolitical or nonpolitical states of nature will have different sets of rights and duties than those who are merely in different civil societies. For while these latter persons are *also* in the state of nature with respect to one another, they will have surrendered to their societies or governments certain rights (such as the natural executive right) that are typically possessed by prepolitical or nonpolitical persons.

But even leaving aside children, incompetents, and legitimate or illegitimate states, it is easy to see that the moral characterization of the state of nature summarized above cannot be adequate. We need only remember our earlier observation about private contracts being consistent with Locke's state of nature. Since the point of contracts is precisely to alter the existing structure of rights and duties, mature persons in the state of nature are perfectly capable of changing the rights and duties that were their "original" grant from God. Where I was originally free to pursue any harmless activity, I may by promise or contract transfer a portion of this right to another and undertake a duty to respect that right (as when I promise to help you on Friday, thereby giving you the right I initially possessed to determine how I will spend Friday). The one to whom I make my promise has greater right and less duty toward me than before the promise. My point is not that the law of nature somehow ceases to bind; there is a clear sense in which it is eternal, as Locke claims. The point is rather that the specific rights and duties granted originally to each under natural law may be altered. Consent, as it were, carves the boundaries of natural law. And any rights that can be transferred in the trust that creates civil government can in principle be transferred in private transactions within the state of nature. As we have seen, this includes our natural executive rights. The only rights that could not be transferred would be those that are in principle inalienable (see Chapter 5).

If this is correct, there is no specific moral characterization of the state of nature that can be given even for mature adults. No adults in the state of nature will necessarily possess any particular set of rights or duties. Which rights and duties they possess will follow from their specific moral histories (the nature of promises, contracts, and other morally relevant activities).[31] The best we can do is this: since being in the state of nature with respect to another consists in

[30] On the rights and duties of children and incompetents, see *Lockean Theory of Rights*, chapter 4.
[31] Dunn, *Political Thought*, 112.

25

not having entered into with another (or having been released from) one special sort of transaction (that one which alone creates a legitimate civil society between them), each person in the state of nature with respect to another lacks the one distinctive sort of moral obligation (toward that other) which that transaction creates—what we normally refer to as "political obligation."[32] All persons in the state of nature (simpliciter), then, have no political obligations; and all persons in the state of nature with respect to each other lack *mutual* political obligations. That moral characterization of Locke's state of nature, however thin and negative, is, I think, the best we can offer (although it will, of course, become a more substantial characterization once we have seen, in chapter 3, just what a legitimate civil society is for Locke, and just what sort of transaction creates one).

What, then, of the *social* characterization of Locke's state of nature? By contrast with Hobbes' thoroughly bleak characterization (to which any form of effective government at all would be preferable), the Lockean state of nature receives mixed reviews. It is a state of limited safety and considerable uncertainty, a state of significant but not desperate "inconveniences," a state to which only certain limited forms of political society will be preferable. The state of nature is one of "uncertain peace," in which people are able to follow the law of nature but do not always do so,[33] a state caused by the "tension between man's natural sociableness and his equally natural desire for personal happiness."[34] Indeed, even if there were not this natural tension in human nature, it would be surprising if Locke's social characterization of the state of nature were not "mixed." For in both *Treatises* there are ample suggestions that the state of nature might take many different forms.[35] At the lower end of the spec-

---

[32] See Cohen's claim that natural freedom in Locke is the absence of political obligations ("Structure, Choice, and Legitimacy," 313). I explain the concept of political obligation in *Moral Principles and Political Obligation*, chapters 1 and 2. I return to this subject below in chapters 3, 4, 7, and 8.

[33] Ashcraft, "Locke's State of Nature," 902–3. Although "according to the law of nature all men alike are friends of one another and are bound together by common interests" (ELN, 163), many clearly have some trouble obeying the law (out of ignorance, neglect, weakness, and bias—ELN, 115, 129, 133–35, 141, 165, 191). The "*greater* part" of persons are "no *strict* observers of equity and justice," making our enjoyment of our freedoms in the state of nature "very uncertain" (II, 123; my emphases). The law of nature is "plain" to each person. Laziness, bias, passion, and partiality are "apt" to produce immoral conduct with some regularity (II, 124–25, 136), but *not* with the frequency of a Hobbesian war of all against all.

[34] Colman, *Moral Philosophy*, 185. A similar version of this tension is described in Parry, *John Locke*, 61. On the Thomist view of our natural sociability, see Skinner, *Foundations of Modern Political Thought*, 2:157–58.

[35] Particularly, in the *Second Treatise*, chapters 5 and 8. On the "stages" of the state

trum, the state of nature could be a reasonably primitive state, with no ownership of land and few movable possessions. For the inconveniences of this state of nature, where there is little to covet, Locke allows that monarchical government would be appropriate (II, 107). At the upper end of the spectrum, the state of nature could be quite civilized, with property in land, money, commerce, cities, and the like (all things that would be impossible in Hobbes' state of nature, and things which, in Locke's view, both call for greater safeguards in government than a simple monarchy could supply [II, 111] and are unlikely to persist for long without the emergence of civil society). It would be surprising if all points on this spectrum involved the same kinds of social problems and benefits, and Locke never suggests that they do. What he does suggest is that the state of nature will always have one specific kind of social problem, and it is on this problem that he concentrates his attention. In every state of nature there will be the problem that persons are judges in their own cases. Where there is no common judge with authority, persons may be partial or vengeful in exercising their natural executive rights, possibly leading to feuds, conflicts, and war (II, 13). This kind of social problem plagues all forms of the state of nature, and the insecurity it causes is the primary reason for seeking the protection of a (properly limited) civil government (II, 13, 21).[36]

Just how bad will this problem be? On his answer to that question, of course, Locke has taken something of a beating. He seems to describe the state of nature first as "a state of peace, good will, mutual assistance, and preservation" (II, 19) and then as a state we should be very eager to escape (II, 21). The first description leaves us wondering why a civil society would seem a desirable alternative to the state of nature at all; the second leaves Locke looking like Hobbes after all. And the inconsistency leaves Locke looking confused. The range of explanations for these passages, sympathetic and unsympathetic, is familiar to any student of the literature on Locke's political philosophy: Locke's real position is like Hobbes',[37]

---

of nature, see Ashcraft, "Locke's State of Nature," 910–12, *Revolutionary Politics*, 218–21, and *Locke's Two Treatises*, 144–47; Pateman, *Political Obligation*, 66–67; Pangle, *Republicanism*, 245–47; Macpherson, *Possessive Individualism*, 211; Replogle, *Recovering the Social Contract*, 201–3; Anglim, "On Locke's State of Nature"; Den Hartogh, "Made by Contrivance," 201–2.

[36] Tully takes these social problems to be caused (in large measure, at least) by the invention of money (*Discourse*, 150–51). I consider his views on this question (and argue against them) in *Lockean Theory of Rights*, 304–5.

[37] Strauss, *Natural Right*, 224–32. Or even *worse* than Hobbes (Macpherson, "Natural Rights," 234).

a position to which he was converted as he wrote;[38] Locke is deliberately inconsistent in order to conceal gaps in his argument;[39] he has different views of the state of nature before and after the invention of money;[40]this last hypothesis is mistaken, and Locke was just inconsistent;[41] Locke is not inconsistent at all and there is no confusion.[42]

What is puzzling about the various charges of confusion and indecision, is that they charge Locke with a particularly silly and shallow sort of confusion. This is not a deep, theoretical problem on which even a very intelligent person might be expected to become muddled. Indeed, the charges often amount to a claim that Locke was inconsistent or changed his views over the course of three or four paragraphs of text.[43] Only the strong antecedent desire to defend a particular interpretation of the text would make such a reading attractive. In fact, the apparent inconsistencies are strikingly easy to explain. Locke never really characterizes the state of nature as "a state of peace, goodwill, mutual assistance, and preservation," any more than he describes it as a state of "enmity, malice, violence, and mutual destruction" (II, 19). Both descriptions are of *possible* states of nature, but neither is of *the* state of nature. The contrasting descriptions in II, 19 are quite plainly intended as descriptions of the best and the worst that the state of nature can be. Where persons almost always abide by the laws of nature, the state of nature will be one of peace, goodwill, and the like; where persons disregard the law, the state of nature will be a state of enmity, malice, and so on.[44] But since people will almost always behave in a way that falls between these extremes, the social characterization of the state of nature that dominates the *Treatises* is also a mixed account, of the sort with which we began. As Locke puts it, our social condition is one of "mediocrity."[45] No amount of struggling will make other pas-

---

[38] Cox, *Locke on War and Peace*, 74–79; Mabbott, *John Locke*, 143–46.

[39] Jenkins, "Locke and Natural Rights," 152–53.

[40] Snyder, "Locke on Natural Law," 745–48.

[41] Macpherson, *Possessive Individualism*, 240–46; Best, "Innocent," 168.

[42] Ashcraft, "Locke's State of Nature," 901-7; Colman, *Moral Philosophy*, 180–85; Aarsleff, "State of Nature," 99.

[43] Cox uses this fact to support the quite different conclusion that Locke is deliberately (if deceptively) trying to describe two completely different states of nature (*Locke on War and Peace*, 7, 75–81). The arguments in the text below are, I think, more than adequate to discredit that reading of the text.

[44] Den Hartogh, "Made by Contrivance," 199–200. The state of war, while not a necessary feature of the state of nature, is consistent with it. See Parry, *John Locke*, 60; Colman, *Moral Philosophy*, 183; Medina, *Social Contract Theories*, 30–31; and 2.1 below.

[45] Journal entry dated March 20, 1678, cited in Ashcraft, "Locke's State of Nature," 907.

sages in Locke yield anything but a "mixed" social characterization.[46]

Whatever stand we choose to take on that question, however, it is worth noticing that *any* social characterization of the state of nature given by Locke would represent a confusion on his part. The problem is not that the state of nature might be either very primitive or reasonably civilized, so that no one description would apply uniformly. For, as we have seen, Locke tried to isolate that "inconvenience" that would plague *any* state of nature—namely, the want of a common judge with authority. But what Locke seems not to keep carefully in mind in his descriptions is that his state of nature is not just a state without government (as Hobbes' was). It is rather a state of not being a member of the same legitimate commonwealth as another. It follows from this, of course, that the want of a common judge characteristic of the state of nature will not create anything like the same problems for various state of nature situations. Prepolitical persons, of course, and persons whose society has collapsed, will suffer the kinds of insecurity and inconvenience Locke describes in the *Second Treatise*. But persons living under a repressive and tyrannical government will face a quite different set of problems. They are equally in the state of nature, and equally lack a common judge with authority; but they *do* have a common judge *without* authority. Illegitimate governments may nonetheless be highly structured with complex legal systems. The social problems of life in such a state will be very different from those of that state of nature in which all persons are judges in their own case (and in which the outbreak of war between private individuals is the primary worry). Others living in the state of nature (without a common judge with authority) may face no serious problems at all. Children or aliens living in a commonwealth that is legitimate with respect to most of its citizens will presumably be living in a moderate, peaceful society. While they have no judge over them (with authority to

---

[46] Even the "worst" of Locke's other descriptions (e.g., II, 123) in no way contradict his claims that the state of nature is preferable to many possible forms of political life (e.g., II, 93), and do not even approach the descriptions offered by Hobbes. These grim descriptions (designed to stress the dangers of the state of nature) are counterbalanced by brighter ones (designed to stress the benefits). Even this mixed social characterization, however, is sufficient to make entry into civil society rationally preferable, so that persons will seldom stay long in the state of nature when a limited government is an alternative (II, 101, 122). I take my position on this point to be consistent with those of Ashcraft ("Locke's State of Nature") and Colman (*Moral Philosophy*, 180–84), who offer further support for the claims I make here. As Ashcraft elsewhere puts it, Locke's view in both the *Essay* and the *Treatises* is that persons are fallible, not wicked (*Locke's Two Treatises*, 236–38).

settle disputes between them and citizens of the commonwealth), they will probably be treated well, leading lives burdened with few of the inconveniences Locke describes. Life in *this* state of nature may be quite acceptable. The point here is only that Locke's concept of the state of nature is compatible with an extremely wide range of possible social circumstances.[47]

For Hobbes, the definition of the state of nature is social in character. It is thus compatible with only a very limited range of social characterizations. For Locke, however, the state of nature is a human moral (and relational) condition. Locke's concept of the state of nature, unlike Hobbes', does nothing to limit the possible social descriptions of persons in that condition. When Locke attempts a social characterization of the state of nature, in response to the social characterizations offered by others, he succumbs to a confusion, for he is entitled to no particular social characterization. The state of nature is not necessarily characterized by the inconvenience of having no common judge. There is only the inconvenience of having no *legitimate* common judge, which may or may not be a *social* problem (and where it is a social problem, it will not always be of the same sort). The best Locke can do is to describe the social position of persons in one kind of state of nature. We can, I suppose, take Locke to be intending to do just that in the *Second Treatise*. But it surely seems more likely that Locke is simply confused on this point, either by the genetic account he offers of the formation of political society (which concentrates his attention on the social condition of pre-political and nonpolitical states of nature), or by the fact that earlier theorists who employed a concept of the state of nature had offered social characterizations of it (which they, unlike Locke, were entitled to do).

I turn now to Locke's historical arguments and his claims about historical instantiations of the state of nature. Like Hobbes, Locke offers us observations about times and places when actual groups of persons have been in the state of nature. Unlike Hobbes, however, Locke spends rather a long time with historical claims. His historical worries about the state of nature begin as early as II, 14, and a large part of chapter 8 (especially II, 100–115) is devoted to them. In light of the moral character of his state of nature, what (if anything) can these arguments be supposed to add to the support of Locke's position? Locke concerns himself with finding historical

[47] This may be part of what Dunn is driving at when he writes that the state of nature has no "empirical content" (*Political Thought*, 103, 110). See also Ashcraft, *Revolutionary Politics*, 581.

examples of groups of people in the state of nature who voluntarily band together to form commonwealths. But why does he bother? What does it matter to his project whether or not he can present such examples?[48] Presumably, all he needs to show to support his claims about the state of nature is that everyone (including those persons born in political society) is in the state of nature originally. He need not show that everyone was in that state at the same time, or that everyone in each community was in that state at some time, or even that the *origin* of *any* political community was legitimate (i.e., the voluntary consent of all involved).[49] On the face of things, at least, even if Locke were able to show none of these things, his moral concept of the state of nature would in no way be suspect. He notes himself that "at best an argument from what has been, to what should of right be, has no great force" (II, 103), and his most central arguments in these passages (e.g., II, 113) are logical, not histori-cal.[50] So what is Locke up to with his historical arguments?

Undoubtedly, one answer is that Locke wishes to meet Filmer (whose arguments are scriptural-historical) on his own ground.[51] He wants to respond to Filmer's claims that patriarchal monarchy is the natural (and hence legitimate) form of government,[52] claims to which Locke in fact makes several concessions. Locke tries to show, in response to Filmer's explicit challenge to do so (*Patriarcha*, II, 5–7), that it is just as natural to form other kinds of governments (given other kinds of social conditions), that there is historical evidence of persons having done just that, and that even the establishment of a monarchy is evidence that individuals were naturally free to es-

---

[48] Worries about this portion of Locke's argument have often led to quick claims of a basic confusion on his part. See, e.g., Cook, "Introduction," xv-xvi; and Kendall, *Majority-Rule*, 75.

[49] That the historical origin of government is irrelevant to its legitimacy, on Locke's principles, seems clear. If government's origin is, say, conquest, subsequent (free) consent to the conqueror can make the government legitimate (e.g., II, 192). If its origin is consent, subsequent tyranny or usurpation can make it illegitimate.

[50] Locke seems extremely sensitive to the dubious value of historical argument to his project. Not only does he offer the reminder in the midst of his historical argu-ments in the *Second Treatise* (II, 103; see also II, 180), but the *First Treatise* is full of such warnings (e.g., I, 56–59, 106, 129). This care makes his use of such arguments even more curious. Thomas seems to believe, oddly, that Locke is really intending in these passages to reinforce his rejection of all appeals to history or tradition (*There to Here*, 118).

[51] Dunn, *Political Thought*, 101, and *Locke*, 50; Herzog, *Without Foundations*, 74–75. Most directly, of course, Locke wishes to counter Filmer's argument that there is no historical evidence of the election of kings or, more generally, of government by con-sent (*Patriarcha*, II, 6–7).

[52] *Patriarcha*, II, 9–14. Here Filmer claims that the *naturalness* of monarchy (among other things) shows that it is the form of government that God intended for people.

tablish a government. Now this would all be well and good if Locke were (oddly) presenting his case as a detached criticism of another author whose positions bore no logical relation to his own. But the arguments of chapter 8 are not presented in this way. They are presented as if they lend support to Locke's own position; and, in particular, they are presented as if they are evidence for the conclusion that persons are *naturally free* (i.e., born into the state of nature with the right to determine the course their political [and nonpolitical] lives will take). Now since being "naturally free" in Locke does not mean being *physically free* to create, join, or remain outside a commonwealth, but rather means having the *right* to do so (e.g., II, 22, 54),[53] it is hard to see how historical evidence could in any way bear on his conclusion. Is Locke, then, hopelessly confused in these passages?

The more reasonable answer, I think, is that Locke is both rather unclear in his wording and a bit carried away by his arguments. What I believe Locke is really driving at is that history shows that we all *regard* ourselves as naturally free, act as if we are, and have always done so (this belief, then, is not, for instance, simply a product of recent social conditioning or a particular ideological stance). This is in fact the way he puts some of the conclusions he draws from his historical arguments: "'Tis plain mankind never owned nor considered any such natural subjection" (II, 114); there is little room for doubt "what has been the opinion, or practice of mankind, about the first erecting of governments" (II, 104). And they are conclusions one could be entitled to reach from historical inquiry.

Now, of course, these conclusions prove nothing that is logically related to Locke's main position on the state of nature. Even if we did believe ourselves born free of subjection to any government, a fact Filmer and others (e.g., Hume) have denied, this would in no way prove that we are all naturally free. But Locke can, perhaps, be excused for excessive enthusiasm in his conviction that the opinion of humankind through the ages shows us "where the right is" (II, 104). Insofar as we believe persons to be on the whole rational beings, it would be surprising if the consensus of persons throughout history did not point us in at least the general direction of the truth. And this is particularly the case where *moral* truth is concerned, and where one believes (as Locke at least sometimes seemed to [see, e.g., II, 12]) that basic moral distinctions are perceived by reason with relative ease. So Locke's historical arguments are at

---

[53] On "natural freedom" in Locke, see *Lockean Theory of Rights*, 85–87.

32

least relevant to the support of his position on the state of nature. They help to show "how *probable* it is, that people . . . were naturally free" (II, 112; my emphasis). This is a respectable, if not decisive, role for history to play in Locke's arguments.

1.3. The Point of State-of-Nature Stories

With this understanding of Locke's definition of the state of nature (and of the force of his various claims about that state), the point of using a concept like the state of nature appears more clearly. Its role in Locke's political philosophy can be seen to share some features of its role in Hobbes, for instance, but to depart from Hobbes in other regards. Both Hobbes and Locke, at the most obvious level, use the idea of the state of nature to offer a vivid portrayal of the stakes in the choice between government and anarchy (in Locke's sense of that word—i.e., having "no form of government at all" [II, 198]). For Locke, of course, the only intelligible choice is between some limited form of government and anarchy, the absolute government favored by Hobbes appearing to him clearly worse than the worst consequences of anarchy (perhaps a dubious assumption by Locke—see 2.3 below). In any event, anarchy loses out for both Hobbes and Locke. And both use the idea of the state of nature to formulate general conditions for governmental legitimacy, the rule being (roughly) that a government can be legitimate only if it fosters conditions rationally preferable to those in the state of nature. For Hobbes, a government has authority and ought to be obeyed if it passes this test;[54] for Locke, a government is capable of having authority if it passes (only citizens' consent gives authority, but arbitrary governments that fail the test are ones to which binding consent cannot even be given [II, 23; and 2.3 and 7.2 below]). We can see now, of course, that in none of this can Locke be taken to be comparing limited government with *the* state of nature, since not all instances of the state of nature are anarchical (i.e., one can live within the jurisdiction of some government and still be in the state of nature [II, 191]). The contrast Locke draws bears not so much on the choice each must make between joining an already existing commonwealth or not doing so, but rather on the choice between having

---

[54] Hobbes, *Leviathan*, chapter 21, paragraph 21. Consent is also necessary for authority in Hobbes, of course, although it can be acquired simply by sufficient exercise of force. For an argument that Hobbes really relies here on hypothetical contractarian ideas, see Kavka, *Hobbesian Moral and Political Theory*, chapters 5 and 10.

governments at all or not having them (and, in this sense, the point is reasonably close to Hobbes').

It is often said as well that the point of Locke's use of the state of nature is to elucidate human nature through his account of how life would be (is) in that state.[55] This is certainly part of Hobbes' aim in utilizing his socially defined state of nature. And while to a certain extent this is clearly true of Locke as well, it cannot (or, at least, should not) be Locke's primary intention. For Locke's state of nature, as we have seen, simply has no determinate social characterization. There is no one picture that can be offered of what the state of nature is like, and so no simple conclusion that can be derived from that picture about the character of human nature. A moral we can draw from this, and one to which Hobbes would have done well to attend, is that human nature is revealed as much in our responses to social and political settings as it is in our responses to asocial chaos and insecurity. But in Locke the primary point of the state of nature is not to reveal human nature in any of its particular guises. It is rather to describe a certain *moral* human condition. It is tempting to say that the moral condition in question is the condition into which God placed persons (or the condition into which mature persons rise, when they receive their moral birthright), or that the relevant condition is the moral condition of persons prior to its modification by their complex social and political interactions. And there is no denying that Locke sometimes speaks in these ways. But, as we have seen, none of these ideas can be quite right, for Locke's state of nature has no precise moral characterization either. The moral condition that the state of nature describes is simply the moral relationship of *noncitizens*—the condition of not being a member of the same legitimate civil society as another. And it is hardly surprising that this should be the point of a central concept in a book whose primary focus is the nature and importance of legitimate government.

State-of-nature stories "also will serve explanatory purposes" (as Robert Nozick argues). They supply us with a "fundamental potential explanation" of the whole political realm; they "pack explanatory punch and illumination. . . . We learn much by seeing how the state could have arisen, even if it didn't arise that way."[56] It is easy

---

[55] See, for instance, Cook, "Introduction," xv-xvi; Aarsleff, "State of Nature," 100; Seliger, *Liberal Politics*, 83, 90, 93–94, 99–100; Medina, *Social Contract Theories*, 29.

[56] Nozick, *Anarchy*, 6–8, 8–9. Nozick does, of course, identify as well the point that was important to both Hobbes and Locke: "If one could show that the state would be superior even to [the] most favored situation of anarchy, the best that realistically

to misunderstand Nozick's remarks (given his refusal to say exactly *what* we learn about the state from state-of-nature stories). It might seem, for instance, that Nozick is trying to argue that particular states are legitimate if they could have arisen from a state of nature by legitimate means (regardless of how they *actually* arose). This, however, would seem to conflict dramatically with his more general insistence that the legitimacy of a state of affairs depends importantly on how it came about, on the *actual* history of the situation.[57]

Nozick's remarks about the "explanatory" uses of state-of-nature stories, however, are not intended to address questions of justification (rather than those of "explanatory political theory," as Nozick himself asserts). Nozick seems to me correct in his claim that we can learn much about the political realm by beginning in nonpolitical terms "with fundamental general descriptions of morally permissible and impermissible actions, and of deeply based reasons why some persons in any society would violate these moral constraints, and [going] on to describe how a state would arise from that state of nature."[58] We learn about the (or one) point of political institutions, about rational limits on their nature and extent, about the source of the rights they exercise, about the enduring problems with which they must be designed to cope, about the moral condition of persons in political society,[59] and so on. Locke's state-of-nature story, like Nozick's, shows us precisely these kinds of things (and, being a more accurate story in my view, shows them more accurately).

---

can be hoped for, or would arise by a process involving no morally impermissible steps, or would be an improvement if it arose, this would provide a rationale for the state's existence; it would justify the state" (p. 5). Presumably, Nozick means (as did Locke) that this would provide a general justification for having states at all, not that it would justify (in the sense of "legitimize") any *particular* states. Whether Nozick also means (as Locke did) that such a justification is a necessary (but not sufficient) condition for the legitimacy of any particular state, is not as clear. It seems likely, however, that he does *not* mean this, since it seems that any government to which its citizens have freely consented will be legitimate for Nozick, even if that government is *not* an improvement over the state of nature.

[57] Ibid., e.g., 151–52. Seeing this conflict, Brown rejects Nozick's state of nature as "irrelevant" (*Modern Political Philosophy*, 98–99).

[58] *Anarchy*, 7.

[59] Nozick assumes that "no new rights 'emerge' at the group level" (ibid., 90), so that the rights of citizens and governors must simply be the sum of the rights possessed by those persons in the state of nature. Locke's position on this point is less clear. For despite his overt insistence on consent as the source of "new rights at the group level," he may well accept arguments using an analogue of the principle of fairness, by which new rights *do* emerge at the group level (i.e., rights to cooperation held against those who accept the benefits of our joint sacrifices). See 8.4 below; and Den Hartogh, "Express Consent," 108.

At a more general level, we must make one final observation about the point of state-of-nature stories. Now I will be concerned no longer with their point within political philosophies like those of Hobbes, Locke, and Nozick, but rather with where the use of these stories *places* such political philosophies on the map of possible views. Any political philosophy that utilizes the idea of a state of nature is fundamentally opposed to what we may call "political naturalism." Although it comes in many forms and degrees of dilution, political naturalism in its strongest form is the view that the natural condition of humans is a *political* condition; that persons are naturally subject to political authority; that we cannot understand persons, morality, or social interaction except in terms that already presuppose political organization of some sort. Contemporary political naturalists most often take their inspiration from Aristotle or Hegel. Those naturalists with whom Locke was most concerned, of course, were the rather less interesting defenders of the divine right of kings, theorists like Filmer (whose patriarchalist theory of authority, remember, maintained that every person since Adam has been naturally subject to the paternal/political authority inherited from that first man).

State-of-nature theory, by contrast, is individualistic in the following sense: persons and much of their social interaction (and, most often, their morality) may be understood in purely *apolitical* terms. The political realm must be seen as a contingent, nonessential aspect of human life, despite its being typically achieved in human groups (much as having two arms is a nonessential but typical feature of human beings). State-of-nature theory is also usually voluntaristic with regard to questions of political membership and obligation.[60] Political voluntarism (about which much more will be said in subsequent chapters) is the view that political relationships among persons are morally legitimate only when they are the product of voluntary, willing, morally significant acts by all parties. State-of-nature theory need not be voluntaristic in this sense; for contingent nonvoluntary relationships (like the receipt of benefits by some from others) between persons, or between individuals and governments or societies, might be taken to establish political ties. But in its strongest, Lockean form, state-of-nature theory is individualistic (antinaturalist) and voluntaristic.

The Lockean assertion that each person is born free in the state

<hr>

[60] See Lessnoff's related discussion of social contract theory, its opposition to "naturalistic" and "supernaturalistic" theories of political authority, and its commitments to individualism and voluntarism (in *Social Contract*, 6–9).

of nature is one way of asserting (correctly, in my view) that we are not born into political communities, however clearly we may be born within their territories (II, 191). We are not naturally citizens; we must do something to become citizens. The course our lives take should be determined as fully as possible by our own voluntary choices, and birth within the territory of a state is not the product of any choice we make. This is to stress the artificiality of government (however natural it may be for us to create it), and to stress that its moral rights against us (and duties toward us) can only be the sum of what it receives from us (or what is otherwise independently generated by us) in the process that creates it. If we are not naturally citizens, we must be naturally something else; and the state of nature is a way of talking about that "something else," a "something else" we sometimes remain (by disability or by choice) and which we always remain in part.

From this Lockean perspective, the fundamental defect of political naturalism is its reliance on what we might call "the communitarian fallacy." This is the fallacy of inferring the truth of political naturalism from certain kinds of simple, true premises about people and societies—for instance, that we all grow up and are socialized in political communities, or that it is perfectly natural (expected) for people to create new political societies where old ones break down or where none otherwise exist. But these kinds of simple facts are plainly inadequate to establish the truth of political naturalism. For political naturalism must make the far stronger claim that persons are *necessarily* political, hence *essentially* related to political societies or subject to political authority. Only in (certain sorts of) political societies, naturalists claim, can there be fully developed, autonomous persons, with moral rights and duties and the capacity to make informed choices. These stronger claims, however, have never been adequately defended, nor do they seem at all initially compelling.[61] Persons may fully develop within isolated families and nonpolitical societies, even if they typically do not. If they may, however, Lockean state-of-nature theory has much of what it needs to defeat the challenge of naturalism. If persons are not *essentially* political, then their political relationships are properly viewed as contingent, perhaps resting on the contingent performances that create artificial political constructions. To claim that my mere birth and socialization under a government are sufficient to legitimate its au-

---

[61] See my *Lockean Theory of Rights*, 109–16; and Green, *Authority of the State*, chapter 7.

thority over me, is no more plausible than to claim that a child owes lifelong obligations to the first adult who merely finds it (or gives birth to it), regardless of the nature of their subsequent relationship. To claim either is to let morality be determined by a spin of the wheel of fortune. The assertion that our natural moral condition is *non-political*, by contrast, is a refusal to accept mere accidents of birth as the source of substantial moral differences among persons. It is from this compelling foundation that Lockean political voluntarism begins and develops.

Hobbes, Locke, and Nozick are all equally participants in the voluntarist program in political philosophy, of course, and much of the point of "state-of-nature talk" in their work can only be appreciated in light of this fact.[62] But it is worth noticing, finally, that the state of nature defined by Locke (and Nozick) functions much more naturally within this program than does the parallel notion in Hobbes. This can be seen by attending to their respective moral characterizations of the state of nature. In Locke, persons in the state of nature have full-blown claim rights, rights that correlate with the duties of others to refrain from interfering with their exercise. While only knowing a person's history in Locke's state of nature will tell us *which* rights he has, whatever rights he has will have this character. In Hobbes, by contrast, persons in the state of nature have not full-blown rights, but mere moral liberties (the moral analogue of what Hohfeld called "liberty rights"). Each person has the "right of nature," which is a "right to everything, even to one another's body."[63] Competitive rights of this sort (where each person has a right to everything) can only be understood as the moral liberty each person has in the absence of obligation (i.e., "person A is at liberty to do act X" means only "A has no obligation not to do X"). What these "rights" lack, which leaves them short of "full-blown" rights, is the duty others have to refrain from interfering with the right's exercise.

But the Hobbesian picture of persons in the state of nature, armed only with their "rights of nature," severely undercuts the voluntarist conception of authorizing a government (or a community) by transfer of right. Our normal idea of authorization is that it is a way of

---

[62] The voluntarist character of all their theories is diminished by certain aspects of their positions—Hobbes' by his belief that coerced consent is binding; Nozick's by his use of a compensation principle to absorb nonconsenters into the state; Locke's by his view that (tacit) consent can be given passively (by mere residence, for instance). See my discussion of these matters in chapter 8 below and in "Voluntarism and Political Associations," 19–21.

[63] *Leviathan*, chapter 14, paragraphs 1–5.

improving the moral position of others, giving them an authority they lack. When I authorize your actions I make things previously forbidden permissible for you. In Hobbes, however, authorization of the sovereign cannot fit this model. The sovereign (as a person or group that also began in the state of nature) *already* had a right to everything. Everything was permissible for him before the "authorization," so there is no way that the contract with his subjects can improve his moral position. There is no sense in which, for instance, if I had not authorized him he could not have legitimately controlled me (if he had the physical power to do so).[64] Thus, Hobbes can make no real sense of the voluntarist idea of authority or of the view that a government's rights can only be those that its citizens transfer to it.

In this regard, Locke's state of nature fares much better. Because it is populated by persons with full-blown moral rights, Locke's state of nature can fit with the voluntarist conceptions of authorization and transfer of rights to produce a coherent voluntarist account of the nature of the citizen-state relationship. Its role in this account explains much of the point of Locke's concept of the state of nature. And insofar as one finds this voluntarist program compelling (as I do), one has good reason to take seriously Locke's state of nature as a central concept in political philosophy.

The political (civil) relationship, then, can be defined by the Lockean in terms of free departures from the natural moral condition of humankind (as we will see in more detail in part 2). But there are, of course, also certain "unnatural" nonconsensual relationships in which persons can find themselves that not only have great moral significance, but are also extremely important in understanding the limits of civil society. Chief among these are those relationships arising from the unlawful (i.e., morally wrongful) use of force, to which I turn in chapter 2.

[64] The only moral effect of authorizing the sovereign in Hobbes is to convert his liberty right to everything into a *protected* liberty right (or *claim* right) to everything (i.e., the subjects undertake the obligation to allow the sovereign exercise of his right [*Leviathan*, chapter 28, paragraph 2]). Nothing new becomes morally permissible for the sovereign as a result of the contract that gives him his new "authority." This problem in Hobbes is much discussed in the secondary literature and may well be a function of Hobbes' unsuccessful attempt to merge his earlier views with a later "authorization" model.

T W O

FORCE AND RIGHT

2.1. The State of War

Locke never presents his general views about the morality of violence in any clear, systematic fashion; and we will not be able to see the whole of his position until we return to this question in chapter 6. But Locke does discuss prominently the nature and consequences of one sort of appeal to violence: that which initiates a state of war between persons. The constant danger of the state of nature degenerating into a state of war (and the uncertainty of enjoyment of property that this causes) is the chief reason Locke mentions for preferring a limited government (civil society) to the state of nature. The possibility of war is thus an important element in Locke's state-of-nature story. But Locke's definition of the state of war and his account of its moral consequences were also very important to his practical political aims—that is, the exclusion of, and later resistance to, a Catholic king on the English throne. The initially precise definition of the state of war that Locke offers in the *Second Treatise* immediately ranges quite far afield, almost certainly for the purpose of more obviously displaying James II's relation to the English people as a state of war. Here, however, I will concern myself only with the plausibility of Locke's theoretical position.

Locke's first account of the state of war is: that state in which one person has declared "by word or action . . . a sedate settled design, upon another man's life" (II, 16). Premeditated, cold-blooded killing (or any indication of the intention to do so) initiates a state of war between the aggressor and the (would-be) victim. "Hasty" or "passionate" killings (or attempts) are specifically excluded by Locke, meaning (I assume) that less severe punishments, and perhaps even less violent means of resistance, are appropriate in these cases (as both common moral intuitions and the law typically allow). Passionate killers are both less blameworthy for their acts and more

40

likely to soon regain their commitment to "reason" than are cold-blooded killers.

Almost before his first definition of the state of war is explained, however, Locke extends the account: anyone "who attempts to get another man into his absolute power, does thereby put himself into a state of war with him; it being to be understood as a declaration of a design upon his life" (II, 17). Since my freedom, Locke argues, is "the fence" to my preservation, one who would take away my freedom "must necessarily be supposed to have a design" on my life as well. A thief who uses force to get me in his power, for instance, has "put himself into a state of war with me" (II, 18). Now this argument is clearly quite a bad one as it stands. The attempt to get another in one's power indicates precisely an intention not to kill, but rather only to control or use another in some way. The man who robs me at swordpoint clearly has designs only on my money; if he had designs on my life as well, he would run me through first, and then take the money from my more cooperative corpse. Trying to enslave others, likewise, shows a design only on their freedom, not on their lives (since slaves are valueless without their lives); indeed, enslaving some people might improve their chances of survival.[1]

Now I am obviously not trying to deny that attempting to get another in one's power is wrong.[2] Physical control over others does give you the power to kill them if you please (even if it in no way indicates any intention to kill), and no one ought to be subjected in this way to another's whims. Locke has more than enough theoretical machinery to show this is wrong. It "tends to" the destruction of others, by making them vulnerable to such whims (thus violating the law of nature [II, 6–7]) and it uses others in the strongest possible sense (which we are forbidden to do [II, 6]).[3] But attempting to get another into your power is *not*, on Locke's initial definition, a way

[1] Locke's argument will not even work as an instance of what is sometimes called in the law "constructive intention"—where one is counted as having an intention simply by virtue of performing an act that is normally accompanied by that intention.

[2] Although we must qualify our claims more carefully than Locke does, to exclude lawful police or jailers (or military officers, for that matter, who, according to Locke, may legitimately wield absolute power [II, 139]). Presumably, they may be assumed to lack the intentions to kill those they control, where unlawful aggressors may not. If this would be Locke's rationale for excluding them, the test for the state of war is perhaps not the intentions others may be assumed to have but rather those we have no good grounds for ruling out (so that a reliably nonviolent person who gets me in his control has not initiated a state of war either?).

[3] On Locke's use of both rule-consequentialist and Kantian styles of moral argument, see *Lockean Theory of Rights*, chapter 1.

of initiating a state of war (however much Locke may want to use the strongest possible language in condemning absolute rule—the inevitable consequence of popery, in his view). Locke must change either his definition, or his conclusion about absolute power.

Nor is this the end of Locke's ever-widening account of the state of war. Eventually, the state of war becomes that state begun by any wrongful use of force (II, 155, 181, 227, 232), including any occasion on which a king "dethrones himself" by a breach of trust (II, 239) (see 6.2 below for a detailed discussion of these claims). Apparently, such uses of force without authority are alleged by Locke to create a state of war regardless of whether they involve any intention to kill or to get another under one's absolute power. Perhaps Locke believes that the only possible point of wrongful uses of force is to try to gain control of another, but charity would seem to require us to look for a better reading of the text. For Locke surely does not want to say that when my calm, premeditated response to your insult is to punch you in the nose, I have created a state of war by declaring an intention to kill you or make you my slave. This kind of wrongful use of force should clearly be treated more like lesser, nonviolent crimes than like murder. The best we can do for Locke on this subject, I think, would involve: (1) reading "use of force without right" to really mean "use of force without right for the purpose of gaining absolute power over another"; and (2) expanding Locke's initial definition of the state of war to cover both cases of intent to kill and cases of intent to deprive others of their freedom. Killers and enslavers (and those who attempt to be either) would then count as makers of war. Lesser users of wrongful force would not.[4] This position seems to me both reasonably plausible and at least broadly consistent with the spirit of Locke's claims about the state of war; and it will allow Locke to use the concept of the state of war in the ways his arguments (and practical purposes) require.

How does this Lockean state of war relate to the state of nature (which "some men have confounded" [II, 19][5])? Like the state of nature, the state of war must be a relational concept. A's wrongful aggression against B puts A and B in a state of war with respect to

[4] Both kinds of users of unlawful force might be "resistible" under our general rights of self-defense. But considerations of proportionality would dictate both different allowable defensive responses and different permissible punishments.

[5] Hobbes, of course, was often taken to have "confounded" the two, although he seems innocent of the charge. Hobbes did not conflate the state of nature and the state of war; he claimed only that they necessarily coexist. Hobbes' definition of war as the mere willingness and preparedness to fight, however, is inadequate, and on that point Locke seems correct.

each other. But B is not thereby in a state of war with respect to his peaceful neighbor, C, or any other person but B.[6] The state of war is certainly not *coextensive* with the state of nature, however, even if it is *consistent* with it (see 1.2 above). Any time two people are in the state of war with one another, they must be in the state of nature with respect to one another. For the state of war excludes the possibility of civil society (II, 90); and the absence of civil society between persons (as we saw in 1.1) defines the state of nature.[7] But the state of nature (as we have seen) need not be a state of war. The state of war between persons, then, implies that they are in the state of nature with respect to each other, but not vice versa.

The moral consequences of the state of war are clear and dramatic in Locke. The aggressor who initiates a state of war with another (hereafter, the "warmaker") forfeits all of his rights, including the rights not to be killed (arbitrarily) or enslaved. He is "stripped of all property [i.e., rights]" (II, 173; see also II, 85, 172). Not only, then, can the warmaker not gain rights over others by his employment of force, he is himself deprived of those rights he formerly possessed. The reason, Locke claims, is that the warmaker has rejected the law of reason and is no longer under it (and so no longer enjoys the protection it affords to those under it) (II, 16). By choosing the rule "of force and violence" (II, 16) instead, the warmaker undoes his own personhood, making himself like a beast of prey, a "dangerous and noxious creature," who may be destroyed, enslaved, or otherwise used at will (II, 16, 172, 181).[8] The state of war, once it is begun

[6] Whether A, by quitting reason and making war on B, also enters into a state of war with C (and the rest of humankind), against whom he has *not* aggressed, is unclear from the text. While A has made clear no intention of abusing anyone but B (which militates against this possibility), he has made himself a dangerous beast that anyone may justly destroy (which argues for a more general state of war). Textual evidence, I think, favors the former line, for Locke speaks of a state of war against "some men, or party of men," and only "the sufferers" seem to be at war with the aggressor (II, 20).

[7] II, 19 should *not* be read as saying (nor does it really entail) that the state of nature and the state of war are not compossible; II, 19 must mean only that the defining characteristics of these two states are very different (*not* that both sets of defining characteristics may not be simultaneously realized). Dunn is thus mistaken, I think, when he claims that "it is logically impossible for the state of nature to be a state of war" (*Political Thought*, 181n; see also Lemos, *Hobbes and Locke*, 87). See 6.3 below for further discussion of this point and of those scholars' views that agree with the reading defended here.

[8] Indeed, Locke suggests that by quitting reason persons can sink "*below* the level of beasts" (I, 58; my emphasis). This analogy with beasts of prey, of course, is far from perfect. Wild animals are more like hot-blooded, passionate killers than they are like the sedate, premeditative warmakers Locke elsewhere discusses. Anthropocentrism aside, one would expect beasts of prey to be treated more like perma-

43

by the warmaker, ends differently in civil society and in the state of nature. In civil society, the state of war ends with the end of the use of force. We are entitled to resist a warmaker with force until he desists; and then we must allow the law to resolve matters (the state of war consists in "the enmity of the parties, where they have no superior to appeal to" [I, 131]). In the state of nature, where there is no common judge to appeal to, the state of war, once begun, continues until either the warmaker is destroyed[9] or he offers peace to his victim (with reparation for injuries and security for the future) (II, 20).[10]

Locke sometimes writes as if *any* deliberate breach of the law of nature counts as "quitting reason," but this is clearly not his considered view. Only the making of war counts as abandoning reason (and personhood). "Lesser breaches" of the law involve lesser (not total) forfeitures of right, justifying punishments less severe than death or enslavement (II, 12; see 2.2 below). But it is worth asking in passing just *why* lesser breaches do not also count as quitting reason. If the laws of nature are all equally "laws of reason," why is breaching one of them (that forbidding murder) any more a way of abandoning reason than breaching another one (say, that forbidding theft)? A chronic thief (whose weak stomach is all that keeps him from violence) may have abandoned reason more fully than one whose only offenses are the very occasional, cold-blooded murders of those who insult him (or so it seems). Perhaps Locke's view is

nently deranged and homicidal mental patients than like killers who coolly choose a life of violence (and presumably the former are to be confined and cared for, not used or destroyed). Locke does not really want to claim that mere dangerousness (even permanent dangerousness) justifies arbitrary rule. It is because animals are also given to us for our use (by God) that ("passionate") dangerousness justifies their free destruction. The comparison of evil persons to "noxious beasts" most directly follows Grotius, who compares them to "foxes and harmful serpents" (*De Jure Praedae Commentarius*, 90); but the same kind of point is made in Aquinas (*Summa Theologica*, II, Q64, A2).

As a result of this view of warmakers, of course, Locke's view of war falls into the most extreme class of just war theories, according to which the justice of one's cause can justify *any* conduct, no matter how harsh, toward enemy combatants or leaders (and according to which unjust warmakers have no rights to carry on the conduct of war at all). There is no logically separate issue of *jus in bello*; *jus ad bellum* determines all. Walzer claims that a similar view is the best rendering of General Sherman's remark that "war is hell" (*Just and Unjust Wars*, 32–33).

[9] Note that the state of war does not end with, say, the enslavement of the warmaker, since such subjection is a continuation of the state of war between them (II, 24).

[10] Here Locke writes as if the victim is obliged to accept reasonable peace terms, once they are offered. This seems inconsistent with the idea that war gives the victim arbitrary power over the warmaker (II, 85), and that only a (nonobligatory) decision to contract with the warmaker ends the state of war (II, 24).

that some offenses are simply more directly contrary to reason than others. Killing, for instance, seems to conflict more directly with the fundamental law of preservation than does theft, even if both are in some measure contrary to reason. And remembering that Locke's reasoning seems often to be rule-consequentialist in nature, it is certainly true that as a rule thieves are less likely than murderers to have left morality completely behind.

This is also the place, I think, to remember that we have not yet seen very clearly just what the rationale for the moral standing of warmakers is. For Locke at various times identifies three different sources of that standing. Warmakers: (1) are not under the law of nature (and hence are rightless); (2) are dangerous to humankind (like beasts of prey); and (3) have deliberately quit or abandoned reason. But (1) cannot account for the whole of the warmaker's moral position, since other beings (infants, madmen, idiots, animals) are apparently not under the law either, but require quite different treatment than warmakers. Neither does (2) seem to do the entire job. For in the first place, madmen may be equally dangerous to humankind. And in the second place, warmakers are not really reduced to the same status as beasts of prey. They cannot be hunted or punished for sport,[11] nor can they be kept for food or skinned for clothing. Most important, they can be forgiven and contracted with, taken back into the community of persons.[12] This leaves (3), which is the real key to the warmaker's moral standing. Only the warmaker deliberately quits reason as the rule for his life. Animals and madmen are incapable of making this choice. It is this free choice to take advantage of the peaceful pursuits of others, in the most dramatic of fashions, which strips warmakers of their rights and reduces them to their degraded moral standing.[13] Such choices to take ad-

[11] Those who forfeit rights make themselves vulnerable to the responses or punishments of others only when these are undertaken for the right kind of reason. Not just any kind of response to a warmaker counts as self-defense or punishment (the primary reasons for which we may harm others, along with defense of others or property). See Lockean Theory of Rights, section 3.5.

[12] Dunn, Political Thought, 107–10.

[13] Their freedom to make this choice seems essential to Locke's arguments, since once the warmaker quits reason, he is no longer under the law of nature. As such, he is not free any longer (II, 57). Freedom being necessary for morality and for the praiseworthiness or blameworthiness of actions (E, 1. 2. 14), it seems we cannot blame the warmaker for the crimes he commits after quitting reason. But we *can* blame him for the free choice he made to quit reason (much as we often blame the drunken criminal for his actions at least largely because of his choice to put himself in a condition in which he would have no self-control). On the necessity of freedom and self-mastery for morality (praise, blame) in Locke, see, e.g., Polin, "John Locke's Conception of Freedom"; and Arnhart, Political Questions, 221.

vantage are the source of all forfeiture, but the warmaker carries this process to its logical extreme.

2.2. How Rights Are Lost

Forfeiture, of course, is not the only way in which we can lose rights that we have. Joel Feinberg has pointed to three different ways in which rights can be lost: they can be (a) voluntarily given away or exchanged; (b) lost involuntarily through negligence or wrongdoing; or (c) taken away by some other party.[14] Locke, similarly although less clearly, identified these three kinds of right-loss in the *Treatises*. The distinction between (a) and (b) plays a major role in the *Second Treatise*, for political power and despotical power can be distinguished by pointing to (a) and (b), respectively, as the means by which the individuals subject to these powers have lost the relevant rights (as in II, 171–73). This distinction is probably most clearly stated, however, in the *First Treatise*: "a father cannot alien the power he has over his child; he may perhaps to some degrees forfeit it, but cannot transfer it: and if any other man acquire it, 'tis not by the father's grant, but by some act of his own" (I, 100). Here Locke (following Grotius) observes the difference between *alienation* (voluntary transfer or loss) and *forfeiture* (involuntary loss through wrongdoing).[15] The third way in which a right may be lost is not discussed as directly by Locke, but he clearly assumes a position on this subject throughout the *Treatises*. Indeed, his position is the occasion for one of his infrequent agreements with Filmer: "in grants and gifts that have their original from God or nature [i.e., natural rights], no inferior power of man can limit; or make any law of prescription against them" (I, 116; see also I, 6, 63). The "law of prescription" to which Locke and Filmer refer is a law annulling or

---

[14] Feinberg, "Voluntary Euthanasia," 110–14. See also Vlastos, "Justice and Equality," 38–39.

[15] I would not like to exaggerate the sharpness of this distinction as I have drawn it here. There is, of course, a technical sense in which any forfeited right can at the same time count as alienated, according to these simple definitions of the terms, since by committing a crime that forfeits rights with the intention of losing those rights, one can accomplish both a forfeiture and a voluntary loss of right. Defining alienation as a deliberate, willing loss of rights (as in McConnell, "Nature and Basis of Inalienable Rights," 28) will not, of course, solve this problem. More precise definitions can, I think, eliminate the overlap by specifying the *transactional* nature of alienation, but they will serve no real purpose here. It is necessary only that we acknowledge that wrongdoing even with knowledge of the moral or legal consequences cannot be counted in any interesting sense as the same kind of source of right-loss as alienation (contra Nino, "Consensual Theory of Punishment").

taking away a right, prescription being any way (although typically legal) of limiting or restricting another's right without that person's participation.[16] Let us, then, call our third way of losing a right (method [c] above) *prescription*.[17]

These distinctions are extremely important in avoiding both confusions about properties of rights such as "inalienability" or "imprescriptibility" (as we will see in chapter 5), and confusions about the force of some of Locke's central arguments.[18] For this reason, a bit more elaboration on the distinctions would not, I think, be out of order. First, a right need not be permanently lost for it to be genuinely alienated, forfeited, or prescribed (although this seems clearest in cases where the right changes hands). There is no oddity in the idea of a right being, for a specified period of time only, alienated (as in a contract granting temporary property rights), forfeited (a criminal might forfeit freedom of action for a period of years), or prescribed (the state might withdraw certain rights in times of civil crisis). These kinds of cases would count as genuine losses of right, for our purposes, because control over the exercise of the right changes hands. Rights that we merely decline to exercise in some particular case, on the other hand, are not lost, for we retain control over all future exercises of those rights. I may decline to exercise my property rights by allowing the neighborhood children to play baseball in my yard; but I retain the rights, for I may elect to withdraw my permission after I discover the inevitable broken windows and trampled shrubbery. A right is genuinely alienated (forfeited, prescribed), then, only if control over the exercise of the right is, permanently or temporarily, lost to another (or lost altogether).

In addition, of course, each of these ways of losing a right will affect the resulting distribution of rights and obligations differently, depending on whether the right is simply lost or, instead, changes

[16] The legal doctrines of (positive and negative) prescription (and the corresponding moral questions at issue in Locke) have to do with the loss or limitation of rights (or obligations) and the acquisition of rights as a result (respectively) of passage of long times without use (or enforcement) or longstanding use. The more general use of "prescription," however, referred simply to limiting or annulling another's right, regardless of whether that right had been long unused. For a brief discussion of the concept of prescription in property law, see Reeve, *Property*, 165.

[17] Locke is not always perfectly clear on the distinction between alienation and prescription. In I, 116, for instance, he seems to confuse the question of "whether the eldest son has a power to part with" a right (i.e., whether the right is *alienable*) with the question of that right's prescriptibility.

[18] As when Macpherson argues that Locke's right of self-defense "is not entirely inalienable" by showing (a non sequitur) that it "can be forfeited" by an act that deserves death ("Natural Rights," 230).

hands. Thus, Hobbes observes that "right is laid aside either by simply renouncing it or by transferring it to another."[19] When I alienate a right by transferring it (as when I promise, contract, trade, or give a gift), I not only remove obligations that others had toward me (to respect the right), but I undertake new obligations to those to whom the right transfers. If, on the other hand, the alienation was a renouncement, only the first of these changes occurs; I undertake no new obligations, but simply render some actions nonobligatory for others. And an analogous distinction can be drawn for each of the nonvoluntary kinds of right-loss. A forfeited right might be simply forfeited (as when a convicted felon forfeits the right to vote), or it might be forfeited to some other person, such as the one wronged. Locke in fact seems to employ both of these notions of forfeiture in his arguments.[20] Finally, in the case of prescription, in order to distinguish usefully between rights that can be forfeited to someone and rights that can be prescribed, we must say that a prescriptible right is one that can be annulled or withdrawn even in the absence of negligence or wrongdoing. The party empowered to annul might be, among others, the state. And in any case, we can again distinguish between annulment, where the right is simply lost, and cases of expropriation or redistribution, where the right transfers to the empowered party or to some third party.

Locke seldom refers to prescription in his work, since (as I will claim in chapter 5) none of our natural rights (Locke's primary concern in the *Treatises*) is prescriptible. The distinction between alienation and forfeiture, however, is at the center of Locke's arguments against slavery and absolute government, to which I now turn. While we will return to these arguments in chapters 5 and 6, we have now examined the basic elements of the arguments—the state of nature, the state of war, and the loss of rights through alienation or forfeiture—and can lay out their basic structures and difficulties.

2.3. Despotism: Slavery and Absolute Government

Locke begins the *First Treatise* with these words: "Slavery is so vile and miserable an estate of man, and so directly opposite to the generous temper and courage of our nation; that 'tis hardly to be conceived, that an Englishman, much less a gentleman, should plead for it" (I, 1). Filmer (the gentleman whose pleading is hardly to be

[19] *Leviathan*, chapter 14, paragraph 7.
[20] See *Lockean Theory of Rights*, section 3.5.

conceived), of course, was concerned to defend not so much the institution of (personal) slavery as that of absolute government, or "political slavery" (Filmer is "the great champion of absolute power" [I, 2]). So Locke illustrates in the first words of the *Treatises* an important fact about the arguments he will attempt to counter: the case for (or against) the possibility of legitimate slavery and the case for (or against) political absolutism tended to go hand in hand in the natural law tradition. The moral possibility of personal slavery was taken by many of the prominent defenders of absolutism (for instance, Suarez, Pufendorf, and [at times] Grotius) to be what established the moral possibility of absolute government. Locke, in opposing these arguments, will similarly argue that the moral *impossibility* of slavery's origination in certain sources establishes the moral impossibility of political absolutism.

I will not here discuss the question of Locke's attitude toward the actual institution of slavery of his day. He was, of course, financially involved in the African slave trade and did nothing to oppose the practice in his practical political activities under Shaftesbury. Whether he genuinely believed that African blacks were justly enslaved or was simply pursuing the time-honored practice of "immoral evasion"[21] is a question that has been amply addressed elsewhere.[22] Here I will deal only with Locke's philosophical commitments (which, conjoined with any even remotely plausible factual and moral premises about African blacks, clearly entail that the slave trade of Locke's day was grossly immoral).

Locke never offers a factual definition of slavery (in value-neutral terms). He is concerned only with the moral condition of slavery, which is the condition of being rightless and under the despotical power of another (II, 85). Despotical power,[23] Locke tells us, is "an

[21] Dunn, *Political Thought*, 175n. One might speculate that Locke's personal views rested on his taking African blacks to be less than human; but in his writings he seems to allow that other races share in the natural equality of humankind (see Wood, *Politics of Locke's Philosophy*, 132–34). Locke did, however, try to characterize African blacks as captives taken in a just war; Seliger suggests that Locke might have (quite implausibly) taken them to be unjustly resisting the use of waste (common) lands by Europeans ("Locke, Liberalism, and Nationalism," 28).

[22] On Locke's personal involvement with slavery, his personal beliefs, and the bearing of his philosophical position on the actual slave trade, see, e.g., Farr, " 'So Vile and Miserable an Estate' "; Loewenberg, "John Locke and the Antebellum Defense of Slavery"; Polin, *La Politique Morale de John Locke*, 277–81; Parry, *John Locke*, 70; Seliger, *Liberal Politics*, 114–24.

[23] Which Locke contrasts with paternal (or parental) and political power (*Second Treatise*, chapter 15), returning to a traditional distinction that he felt had been lately ignored (particularly by Filmer, but also, one might suppose, by Hobbes and many others).

absolute, arbitrary power one man has over another, to take away, his life, whenever he pleases" (II, 172) (and also a power, it is understood, to do any lesser harm to another at will). Locke's argument against slavery (despotical power) consists in denying three possible sources as legitimate grounds of despotical power (although, as we have seen, he does *allow* one ground for the legitimate enslavement of another). We can read chapters 3, 4 and 6 of the *Second Treatise* as being aimed at blocking these three potential arguments for justified slavery:

(1) Despotical power cannot be acquired by aggression or unlawful conquest. As we have seen, the aggressive use of force creates a state of war, which, far from yielding new rights of dominion for the aggressor, in fact forfeits those rights he has.

(2) Despotical power cannot be acquired by compact (alienation of rights): "Man, not having the power of his own life, cannot, by compact, or his own consent, enslave himself to anyone" (II, 23; see also II, 135, 172). We ourselves lack the rights that would have to be transferred to others to give them despotical power over us.[24]

(3) Despotical power cannot come from nature (II, 172–73). Persons are naturally free and equal (II, 4), so none could have natural dominion over others. And parental power is limited by the point of parents' having power over their children—namely, the good of the children (II, 64–65, 74). It cannot possibly be despotical (contrary to Filmer's view).

Nature can give only (limited) parental power. Compact can give only (limited) power of other sorts (e.g., political or "economical"[25]). Force can give no power at all. Each of these arguments, of course, takes on a powerful tradition of thought about the justification of slavery. For Locke there is only one source of legitimate slavery: "the perfect condition of slavery . . . is nothing else, but the state of war

---

[24] It is worth noting here that any weakening of Locke's apparently absolute ban on suicide may result in a corresponding weakening of the claim that we lack the power (rights) necessary to give another despotical power over us. See *Lockean Theory of Rights*, section 1.5.

[25] The extreme case of this (limited) economical power is apparently what Locke calls "drudgery" (II, 24)—a state of rightful servitude that does not involve a master's right to kill or maim at will. Why Locke (apparently) thinks selling oneself into drudgery is legitimate (based only on the fact that the Jews [and others] actually did this) is unclear (given that people have also actually sold themselves and others into slavery). I return to these issues in chapter 5.

continued, between a lawful conqueror, and a captive" (II, 24). Only captives taken in a just (defensive) war can legitimately be held as slaves (II, 85, 172), for they have forfeited all of their rights, making unlimited (despotical) power over them possible.[26] Despotical power can end, in the same way that the state of war ends (since slavery is only the state of war continued)—with the death of the slave or an agreement between lord and slave to live in peace (and hence to limit the lord's previously unlimited rights over the slave) (II, 20, 24, 172).[27]

Locke's case against political absolutism (for Locke a kind of "mass slavery") has the same basic structure as his case against slavery, with one salient exception: there is no possible source of legitimate absolute rule over a political society (analogous to the case of despotical power over a captive taken in a just war). And his equation of both the attempt to enslave and the attempt to wield absolute political power with all other simple cases of initiating a state of war, yields a position with great rhetorical impact. The king who tries to establish an absolute dominion turns out not to be interestingly different from the moral viewpoint than a thief (II, 17–18), "petty villain" or pirate (II, 176), unscrupulous "petty officer" or constable (II, 202), or unlawful slaver (II, 22–23). A king like James would have no special status that justified the aggressive invasion of his subjects' rights.[28]

[26] Despotical power is thus the limiting case of our natural executive right, the right to punish those who break the natural law. For if the executive power is given by others' forfeitures, despotical power is similarly given by the total forfeiture of rights. It is rather hard to see, of course, how we can forfeit rights that we cannot alienate, when the reason given for our inability to alienate them is that we do not possess them (II, 23). Locke's position seems at first appearance to be that we can forfeit rights we do not have! I try to make a bit more sense of Locke's position in chapter 5.

[27] Exactly how one can make a compact with a slave, who has no rights and is not under the law of nature, is unclear. It would appear to be about as easy as making a compact with a lion, an infant, or a madman. One can, of course, unilaterally assume certain obligations toward one's slave, but that does not amount to a compact. Only after the slave regains his rights would he seem to be a possible participant in the agreement that gives him his rights (a problem of Rousseauian proportions). This suggests (what is noted in 2.1 above) that slaves may not really be reduced so low as animals in their moral standing. But what rights (or other moral traits) they retain is not clear from the text. Neither is it clear why, if a slave reaffirms his commitment to the law of reason, leaving the rule of force behind, this by itself should not be enough to bring him once more under the law of nature and alter his moral standing. These are just a few of the many puzzles about Locke's theory of slavery that I do not here make any attempt to solve.

[28] On the importance of this "moral equivalence" argument to Locke, the radical Whigs generally, and the Rye House plotters in particular, see Ashcraft, *Revolutionary Politics*, especially 397–401.

But if Locke's condemnation of absolutism is rhetorically powerful, it is also muddied by a particularly gross equivocation on the term "absolute power." Locke uses it to mean both despotical power (a moral right to absolute, arbitrary rule) and mere physical control over another (which gives one the physical power to take the other's life at will). In II, 23, for instance, where Locke says we cannot voluntarily put ourselves under another's "absolute power," he is clearly using "absolute power" in the first, moral sense (since we obviously can put ourselves in another's physical control). But in II, 17, where Locke says that an attempt to get another in one's "absolute power" initiates a state of war, he must be using "absolute power" in the second, physical sense. For the attempt to get another in one's moral "absolute power" can look like a rather silly, innocuous attempt to do the morally impossible (as when I politely ask you to give yourself to me as a slave).[29] It need not involve any use of force at all, although it must (on Locke's view) involve a confusion. Perhaps Locke only means that the (confused) attempt to gain moral absolute power by subjecting others to physical absolute control initiates a state of war. But if this is his meaning, he expresses it very poorly, both here and elsewhere in the text. I will use the term "absolute power" only to mean moral (despotical) power, as I believe Locke meant to (or should have).

In spite of these ambiguities, however, the structure of Locke's argument against political absolutism seems clear. The core of the argument, of course, is the same three-part rejection of possible grounds of absolute power that we saw in his argument against (personal) slavery. A king cannot get absolute power by aggressive conquest or usurpation (contra, e.g., Filmer [*Patriarcha*, I, 6] and the popular reputation of Hobbes), by compact (contra, e.g., Suarez, Pufendorf, and the *real* Hobbes), or by extension of some natural power (contra Filmer's derivation from the paternal power of Adam and the patriarchs [*Patriarcha*, I, 3–10]).

But Locke also adds to the case against slavery to produce a total rejection of legitimate political absolute power. In the first place, he specifies limits on the rights of even just conquerors. They cannot, by their legitimate enslavement of warmakers, come to have absolute power over the wives, children (etc.), property, or land of the warmakers (II, 177–84). Thus, one cannot derive absolute political power by, as it were, mass forfeiture (a fourth possible source). Here

---

[29] Indeed, even the actual possession of moral absolute power (i.e., despotical power) need not involve physical control over others, as when the lawful conqueror loses control of his lawful slaves.

the disanalogy between personal slavery and absolute political power makes it possible for Locke to utterly deny the legitimacy of the latter (while affirming the legitimacy of the former in special cases). Locke expresses this utter denial at times by saying that absolute power is inconsistent with civil society: "absolute government, which by some men is counted the only government in the world, is indeed inconsistent with civil society, and so can be no form of government at all" (II, 90; see also II, 137, 175). What makes a society a civil society (i.e., a legitimate political community) is precluded by absolute dominion of one (or some) over others.[30]

There is, however, another component of Locke's case against absolute political power that I have not yet mentioned. It is not only morally impossible to subject oneself to the absolute power of another. It would be an irrational choice for a person to make. No sensible person would prefer absolute subjection to the state of nature (here meaning "anarchy"), any more than one would flee the "mischiefs" of "polecats or foxes" while thinking "it safety, to be devoured by lions" (II, 93). Locke's reasoning runs as follows: in the state of nature, no matter how bad things get, we are at least at liberty to arm ourselves and use our wits in self-defense; and we face as foes only single persons or small groups. In a legitimate absolute monarchy, however, we would have disarmed ourselves and laid aside our rights to resist; and the monarch, with his command of police and armies, would be elevated to the status of an irresistible foe. It is far worse to be "exposed to the arbitrary power of one man, who has the command of 100,000" than to be "exposed to the arbitrary power of 100,000 single men" (II, 137).

As stated, at least, this argument is not very convincing. As Gregory Kavka has observed,[31] the likelihood of being attacked is probably considerably higher in a state of nature with one hundred thousand bad persons than in an absolute monarchy with one, extremely powerful bad person. This may make it more sensible to opt

---

[30] This looks as if it makes "legitimate absolute government" an internally contradictory notion. Now an opponent could reasonably reply to Locke here that Locke's definition of civil society is only one possible definition. He should not be allowed to win the day by stipulation. But, of course, Locke's arguments against the four possible sources of absolute power are not stipulative. They show (if successful) that nothing even interestingly resembling a state can be rightfully ruled by one with absolute dominion. For there is no remaining source of such power (over an enduring political body) not disposed of by Locke. One need not, then, treat Locke's argument against absolutism as an argument by stipulative definition (or as one using the "definitional stop").

[31] *Hobbesian Moral and Political Theory,* 227. See also Hampton, *Hobbes and the Social Contract,* 192–95.

for a small chance of attack by an overwhelming force than to opt for a large chance of attack by weaker (but still threatening) persons. Whether it is irrational to choose an absolute monarchy seems to turn, contrary to Locke's suggestion, on just how bad your state of nature is (or would be) and just how bad the particular monarchy (and monarch) you could choose is (or would be).

But quite apart from these concerns, it is appropriate to wonder just what point Locke is trying to make here. Is he simply arguing that even if you could empower an absolute monarch (which, of course, you cannot, no matter how badly you might want to), it would be irrational to do so? Or is the irrationality of the choice what is supposed to make it impossible to empower the monarch? Locke may have in mind here (as I suggested in 1.3) that a government that is not even rationally preferable to the worst kind of state of nature is not one that can even be a candidate for legitimacy.[32] But I reserve my final comments on this argument until 5.5, where I will also offer a final evaluation of Locke's (and the Lockean) case against slavery and absolutism.

I conclude this chapter with a last exegetical point about Locke's arguments against absolutism. We have thus far discussed Locke's claims as if it were perfectly clear what Locke means by terms like "absolute" and "arbitrary." He seems to use these terms interchangeably (e.g., II, 222), sometimes talking about power as "absolute," sometimes as "arbitrary," and sometimes as "absolute, arbitrary." Always the sense conveyed is "unlimited" (I, 9, 68–70)—that is, one with absolute or arbitrary power over a "person" has no (moral) limits on what he may do to that person. Anything goes. But this impression may be misleading. For Locke, in at least one passage (II, 139), clearly tries to distinguish *between* absolute and arbitrary powers: "even absolute power, where it is necessary, is

[32] We should be careful not to leap from this reading to a more general, hypothetical-contractarian reading of Locke's standards for governmental legitimacy. Pitkin, for instance, has read Locke as "really" holding that personal consent is irrelevant to legitimacy of government and citizens' obligations. All that is relevant is whether "the government is such that you *ought* to consent to it," whether it is one that rational persons in a hypothetical state of nature would have opted for ("Obligation and Consent-II," 39). But this "Rawlsian" reading of Locke on legitimacy must surely be rejected in the face of the textual evidence (as I will argue in 7.2). Personal consent, I think, is the sole ground of governmental legitimacy and political obligation in Locke, although consent is not always sufficient to obligate one or to legitimate government. The rational preferability of a government to the worst state of nature may be intended to limit our binding consent, by establishing minimal conditions for legitimacy. But without our consent, this rational preferability cannot by itself establish the legitimacy of a government.

not arbitrary by being absolute, but is still limited by that reason, and confined to those ends, which required it in some cases to be absolute." Locke's example to clarify his distinction is that of military discipline. For the good of the army (and, ultimately, of the commonwealth), superior officers command the absolute obedience of those below them in rank, and may punish them with death for disobeying "the most dangerous or unreasonable" orders. But these same officers may not take the property of their subordinates, since that right is not necessary to preserving the army (and the commonwealth).

Unfortunately, this example does not uniquely determine the distinction Locke has in mind. The natural readings of this example are two: (1) Absolute power is only to be used for a particular purpose; arbitrary power is not *for* anything. (2) Absolute power is the power to do anything at all, but only within a particular sphere of action (defined by the "purpose" of the power); arbitrary power is the power to do anything at all, with no limit on "spheres" (so that arbitrary simply means "absolute in *all* spheres of action"). Of these, (2) seems preferable, since Locke allows that officers have a right to obedience even when they command "unreasonable" things, not directly related to the purpose that the absolute power serves (as long as they are "military" things). Commands that do not advance the good of the army are still to be obeyed. (2), however, has its own problems, since Locke elsewhere mentions arbitrary powers that are limited to a particular sphere of action. Indeed, Locke seems to define "prerogative" (which, of course, he allows) as "an arbitrary power in some things left in the prince's hand to do good, not harm to the people" (II, 210). A third possibility, however, is suggested slightly earlier: (3) Absolute power operates by standing, promulgated rules; arbitrary power is exercised "at pleasure" (II, 137) and by "extemporary decrees" (II, 136).[33] But, of course, the commands of the military officer, who has only absolute power, are often "extemporary decrees," dictated not by rules but by situations.

My own preference (which I unblushingly concede to be a bit arbitrary) is for version (2) of the distinction; but I can see no version of it that squares well with the whole of the *Treatises*. For that reason, I have treated "absolute" and "arbitrary" as synonymous throughout this chapter, as Locke seems mostly to do in the *Treatises*. The safest position, however, is to maintain that while Locke did not clearly reject either "arbitrary" or "absolute" power in government, he certainly rejected "absolute, arbitrary" power.

[33] Grant seems to favor this reading of "arbitrary" in Locke (*Liberalism*, 72–73).

PART 2

CONSENT AND GOVERNMENT

Part 1 has explored the contrasts drawn by Locke between the political relationship and two important nonconsensual relations—the state of nature and the state of war. Many of Locke's arguments on those subjects, we have seen, can play useful roles in any voluntarist political philosophy. Those arguments are employed to show that membership in civil society cannot be a product of force (or prescription of rights), of birth (either because of family status or geographical location), or of moral wrongdoing (and forfeiture of rights). Only free consent can remove persons from their natural condition.

In part 2, I turn to a more careful description of the Lockean ideal of government by consent, in an effort to understand the nature and content of the special transaction that moves persons from their natural moral condition to their political condition. We must understand first the precise content of that transaction (the subject of chapter 3), in order to see what rights members of political societies should be understood to have surrendered and retained, what obligations they have assumed, and what powers can legitimately be wielded over them. More generally, we must begin to examine the relation of a political society to its government. Further, of course, we know that whether or not political societies were ever created ex nihilo by the mutual consent of persons, existing political societies face a constantly renewed supply of new residents and potential members. If only consent can establish the political relationship among persons and give some political power over others, how can existing societies claim to act legitimately when they attempt to impose existing law on new generations of residents? Locke's answer to this question lies in his account of the variety of ways in which political consent may be given (the subject of chapter 4).

At the conclusion of part 2 it will still remain to discuss more completely the limits on and details of the consensual transaction that for Lockeans grounds the political relationship. That task will be one of the jobs of parts 3 and 4 of this study. In part 2, however, I propose only to deal in reasonably broad strokes with the basic Lockean model of the legitimate political relationship.

THREE

POLITICAL CONSENT

3.1. The Content of Lockean Consent

Artificial political bodies (civil societies) and governments cannot for Locke (or Lockeans) possess rights naturally; only persons have that capacity. The question then arises: how may political communities and governments obtain rights from (and over) free persons who possess them in their natural condition? Locke's famous answer defines the essence of the political relationship for the voluntarist.[1] It identifies only one possible process by which such political rights ("power") can be secured. Only fully voluntary alienation by the rightholder—consent (contract, trust)—can give another person or body political power over the rightholder:[2] "Men being . . . by nature, all free, equal and independent, no one can be put out of this estate, and subjected to the political power of another, without his own consent" (II, 95). "No government can have a right to obedience from a people who have not freely consented to it" (II, 192).

These claims are intended to mean, I believe, that for Locke only consent can ground a person's political obligations (the logical cor-

[1] This voluntarism, of course, was not much in evidence in Locke's early works (such as the *Two Tracts* and the *Essays on the Law of Nature*), where the lawmaker's rights are, for instance, said to be "borrowed from God" (e.g., ELN, 187) and our obligations to obey are derived simply from God's command that we obey magistrates (e.g., First Tract, 159; Second Tract, 226). Locke's voluntarism apparently emerged only with the maturity of his thought (perhaps as a result of his practical political experience and more active political plans). The claim that Locke's doctrine was essentially the same in his early and later works (as advanced by, e.g., Macpherson in *Possessive Individualism*, 258–61) is mistaken in its identification of both the rights that individuals surrender and how governments obtain them (as I argue below). On the development of Locke's voluntarism, see Riley, *Will and Political Legitimacy*, especially 69–71.

[2] Neither forfeiture nor prescription can yield political power. Other kinds of power, such as paternal or despotical power, arise from other sources. Locke occasionally overstates his position by claiming that consent is necessary for subjection "to any earthly power" (e.g., II, 119). But his considered position is clearly only that consent is the sole possible source of *political* power.

relates of political power),[3] and that only consent can remove a person from the state of nature (see II, 15; and 1.2 above). And Locke's wording, here and elsewhere, makes it clear that by "consent" he means the actual, personal consent of each individual (as I argue at length in 7.2). It is consent alone that makes civil society (i.e., legitimate political society), along with the political rights and obligations such a society necessarily involves.

By political power, remember, Locke means the right of making law for the society and of using that society's force to execute the law and protect the society (but all only for that society's own good) (II, 3). This includes the right to have morally acceptable, lawful commands obeyed by the society's members (political power is the right "to command and be obeyed" [I, 120]). The logically correlative obligation of each member of the society, the member's "political obligation," is (a) to obey valid laws (which for Locke means obedience only to those civil laws whose demands do not contradict those of natural law) and (b) to support the society in those other ways necessary to its continued effective (just) functioning (which will typically include paying necessary taxes, contributing one's physical "force" to assist in domestic law enforcement or national defense, etc.).[4]

[3] Snare prefers to say that there are "two consents" involved here: one (like a promise) that creates the citizen's obligation and another that transfers rights to the political body ("Consent and Conventional Acts," 36). Since I take the point of consent normally to be both to transfer rights and to undertake obligations, I see no advantage in this analysis. Others, as we will see, have denied that consent in Locke is thus tied to either political obligation (e.g., Dunn) or governmental or political rights (e.g., Gough).

[4] Each member "engages his natural force . . . to assist the executive power of the society, as the law thereof shall require" (II, 130), this being taken by Locke to include assistance in federative matters, where "the force of the public" is employed in making war (II, 145–48). Similarly, each must be understood to have agreed to pay "his proportion" of the necessary expenses involved in maintaining a government and extending to all members the protection it provides (II, 140). I return to discussion of the specific content of political obligation in chapters 7 and 8.

Kilcullen has argued that political obligation cannot be understood in this way as (in large part) a moral obligation to obey the law, because, he claims, to feel morally obliged not to (e.g.) commit murder "is not to acknowledge any political obligation in the proper sense" ("Locke on Political Obligation," 324). This argument, however, does not take seriously the word "obey" (as it is used in my account). To genuinely *obey* the law (rather than to simply *do* the same act that happens to be required by law) is to do what law requires because it requires it. A moral obligation to obey the law (part of one's political obligations), where the law's only requirements (say) are to do A and B, is not identical to a moral obligation specifically to do A and B (which obligation would continue even if the legal requirements to do A and B were changed). There is, then, no problem in this characterization of political obligation, which is quite distinct from our obligations to perform acts described independent

Consent can take persons out of the state of nature into civil society in one of two ways: they can join together with other persons who are also in the state of nature (simpliciter) to make "one people," a new body politic; or they can "incorporate with any government already made" (II, 89) (i.e., join with others who are still in the state of nature with respect to them, but not with respect to one another). While the process will clearly differ in the two cases, the moral content of the consensual transactions is, Locke claims, largely the same.[5] Whether joining or creating a commonwealth, the same rights are surrendered by the individual to the body (and the same obligations to it are correlatively undertaken). These acts constitute the "one very special agreement" (referred to in 1.1 above) that alone begins the political relationship among persons and creates civil society.[6]

In the most general terms, each person's consent must surrender to political society "all the power necessary to the ends for which they unite into society" (II, 99), that is, "as much of his natural liberty in providing for himself, as the good, prosperity, and safety of the society shall require" (II, 130). Each surrenders these rights and undertakes an obligation to respect the exercise of these rights by their new holders. More specifically, Locke suggests that each person gives up two different kinds of rights on entering civil society.

---

of their legal standing.

Kilcullen also argues (contrary to my claims here) that political power in Locke does not derive from consent (although what he calls "political authority" does), and that political obligation and political power are as a result not logical correlates (pp. 323–26). I reply to these arguments in note 13 below.

[5] This claim requires qualification, given Locke's view that the obligations of tacit consenters, while otherwise identical in extent, have a different force or duration than those of express consenters (see 4.1 below). What is certainly true is that the moral content of the consensual transactions is the same for those who either expressly create a society or expressly join an already existing society.

[6] Exactly how literally we are to take Locke's talk of "incorporation" and of creating a new "body" is unclear to me. A "body politic" or "people" is spoken of by Locke as something that can act, will, judge, have interests, and possess rights. Civil society thus seems to be for him at least a reasonably strong sort of civil partnership (as in the Roman *societas*). But it is unclear whether civil societies are conceived of by Locke in a nonreductionist or holistic way—i.e., as independent corporate agents, with rights and duties that are not reducible to or analyzable in terms of the rights and duties of their constituent members. Social groups are, on this nonreductionist view, more than collections of individuals standing in complex relations to one another. Locke's language sometimes suggests such a nonreductionist view of societies. But the overall tone of Locke's work and the rigorously individualistic character of his account of society's formation (according to the reading for which I argue in the text) both argue for a reductionist reading of Locke's corporate language. I return to this question again in chapter 6.

The natural executive right each "wholly gives up" (II, 130),[7] transferring this right to one "common judge" over all the members (who also judges in "federative" matters between members and nonmembers). This right, then, when ultimately exercised by government, becomes its executive and federative powers (II, 144–48)—that is, its right to interpret the law and direct the community's use of force. Second, each relinquishes a portion of the right of self-government—that right made up from the "liberty of innocent delights" and the right "to do whatsoever he thinks fit for the preservation of himself and others within the permission of the law of nature" (II, 128). The right of innocent delights is retained, while the rest is given up only as "far forth as the preservation of himself and the rest of society shall require" (II, 129).[8] This right, in the hands of government, becomes a significant part of its legislative power (II, 143),[9] while the well-known limits on legislative power specified by Locke (in II, 135–42) are determined in part by the natural rights that individuals retain even within civil society.[10]

The simple distinction Locke draws between two kinds of rights that must be surrendered on entrance to civil society is, I think, both extremely important and, quite simply, the correct position to take

---

[7] Although we should note that Locke appears to claim elsewhere that individuals always *retain* their right to take reparation for damages done them by offenders against the law of nature (II, 11).

[8] Among those who argue (correctly, in my view) that some natural rights are retained by individuals after consenting to enter civil society are Plamenatz, *Man and Society,* 1:217; Goldwin, "John Locke," 496; Aaron, *John Locke,* 279; Brandt, *Ethical Theory,* 443; Hacker, *Political Theory,* 266; Barker, "Introduction," xx; DeBeer, "Locke and English Liberalism," 41. It may be worth remembering that the Ninth Amendment to the American Constitution refers explicitly to the rights "retained by the people."

[9] Note that legislative power is defined by Locke as "a right to direct how the force of the commonwealth shall be employed for preserving the community and the members of it" (II, 143). This is clearly just the political version of the first power specified in II, 126 (i.e., it is clearly the collection of all the members' "first powers").

[10] These limits are that legislative power (a) cannot be arbitrary (II, 135); (b) must operate by means of promulgated laws and known, authorized judges (II, 136–37); (c) cannot be used to take property without the owner's consent (II, 138); and (d) cannot be transferred by government to other hands (II, 141). (Locke's final list of these limits in II, 142 is slightly different from, but consistent with, the limits emphasized in the preceding text, as summarized above.) As we will see in chapter 5, these limits are set in part by the limits of each person's rights over *self* (as specified by the law of nature). But the legislative power must also be limited by the rights that each person retains in society (e.g., retained property rights, which are the justification for limit [c]). Note that Locke says the "bounds" of the legislative power are set both by the law of nature and by the content of the trust (II, 142)—and the content of the trust is itself limited by the rights individuals retain, since all of the rights that they surrender are eventually put in the hands of government.

in a voluntarist account of the political relationship.[11] If the government's right to make and enforce law were only its subjects' natural executive rights (suitably transferred to government), the government could only legitimately make and enforce civil laws whose requirements coincided with those of natural law (as we saw in 2.1). For the natural right to punish, as exercised by independent individuals in the state of nature, is only a right to punish transgressors of *natural* law (II, 7). But while many of the acts a political society will wish to legally proscribe will, of course, also violate natural law (e.g., murder, violence, theft), many others quite clearly will not. Regulatory statutes of all sorts, many tax laws, many "morals" laws, laws designed to control the society's economy, and so on, all prohibit (or require) acts that are not prohibited (or required) by any plausible description of natural law. Governments, then, can only legitimately prohibit activities in such areas if they secure from their subjects additional rights to make laws in areas of morally "indifferent" conduct (those areas where each can in the state of nature do "whatsoever he thinks fit"), conduct *not* specifically required or prohibited by natural law. I take this insight, and the required solution to the problem, to be the point of Locke's arguments in II, 128–30.[12]

Laws concerning "indifferent" conduct must still, of course, be *consistent* with natural law in order to be legitimate: "the rules that they make for other men's actions must . . . be conformable to the Law of Nature" (II, 135). But the natural executive right possessed outside of civil society does not include the right to make laws for others and punish them for violations where the conduct in question is morally indifferent. I may not, in the state of nature, make it a law that your tribe can only gather acorns east of the river and south of the large rock, and then punish you for violations; for there is no natural law restriction on the area in which your tribe may gather. But a lawful government might be entitled to make such a law, in

---

[11] See my more complete defense of these claims in *Lockean Theory of Rights*, section 3.6.

[12] Locke's sensitivity to the problem is evident even in his early *Two Tracts*, where he distinguishes between the magistrate's power to require morally obligatory conduct and his power in the area of indifferent conduct. Locke claims there that if the magistrate is not left free to legislate concerning indifferent conduct, then he could only require again that which is already required by natural law, in which sphere "the power of the magistrate seems to be no greater than that of any private citizen" (Second Tract, 228). Locke solves the problem in the *Second Treatise* by distinguishing two kinds of rights that subjects might transfer to their political superiors.

order, say, to better coordinate gathering activities.[13] It is only by surrendering a portion of the right of self-government that the citizen can legitimate such civil laws, laws that prohibit (or require) actions that are naturally indifferent, thus making it permissible that "the laws of the society in many things confine the liberty he had by the Law of Nature" (II, 129).

The political power of government, then, is the sum of those rights government ultimately receives from all of the individuals who consent to be members of the society it governs.[14] Political power's "domestic" component essentially consists of the rights to make laws limiting members' liberty for the public good and to enforce those laws with punishment.[15] Locke sometimes identifies this power in other terms: the "power of the magistrate" (II, 65), the "authority to command" (I, 81), the "right to obedience" (I, 81; II, 151), and the "power or right of government" (I, 120); and he even occasionally uses the language of "sovereignty" to characterize it.[16]

---

[13] Kilcullen's claim that political power in Locke (i.e., the government's right to make and enforce law) does not require consent (and so is not correlative with the political obligations of subjects) turns crucially on his failure to note that this power requires more than simply the natural executive right (actually, Kilcullen notes this possibility, but dismisses it as making "no difference" to his argument ["Locke on Political Obligation," 324n]). Only consent can give the government the important power to legislate indifferent things. But further, even if this were *not* a problem, even that aspect of political power that simply amounts to interpreting and enforcing natural law is not by any means identical to the natural right to punish possessed by individuals in the state of nature. For political power is an exclusive right to punish, exercised without domestic competition and on behalf of an entire people. ("For all force [as has often been said] belongs only to the magistrate, nor ought any private persons at any time to use force unless it be in self-defense against unjust violence" [L, 132].) Individuals in the state of nature do not have any right to such a monopoly on force. Acquiring the monopoly that constitutes political power again requires the consent of subjects, even if punishing a moral wrongdoer without possessing that monopoly would have been lawful independent of such consent.

[14] See Pitkin, "Obligation and Consent—I," 994–95. Gough, oddly, seems to deny this (*Political Philosophy*, 54–55); Hacker, even more oddly, argues that governments in Locke cannot have rights at all, but only "powers" (in the sense of "abilities") (*Political Theory*, 266–67). See also Den Hartogh, "Express Consent," 666. But Locke clearly affirms the view I have attributed to him in the text, both in II, 88 ("and herein we have the original of the legislative and executive power of civil society") and in II, 171 (see below).

[15] Locke likes to emphasize specifically the right to impose capital punishment in discussing political power, although this is clearly only one kind of punishment that a legitimate government might employ (see, e.g., II, 3, 65). It is tempting to read Locke as trying to identify with this emphasis one particularly central or essential component of political power. But while this may well be Locke's view, it is hard to see why governments that decline to use the death penalty should be taken to be exercising an interestingly impoverished form of political power.

[16] As in I, 129–32, where the "marks of sovereignty" he identifies include aspects of political power, as that power is subsequently defined. Locke, however, generally

But in whatever terms, political power is simply "that power which every man, having in the state of nature, has given up into the hands of the society, and therein to governours" (II, 171).

The account here offered of the moral content of Lockean political consent is not uncontroversial. Many have argued, for instance, that Locke's citizens must be understood to have surrendered all of their natural rights in creating or joining civil society, retaining none.[17] And while the passages cited above seem reasonably clear in implying the contrary, there is no denying that other passages in the *Second Treatise* could be marshalled to support such a reading—for instance, where Locke writes that "men give up all their natural power to the society which they enter into" (II, 136; see also II, 131). The choice, then, is between a reading of Locke on which individuals retain certain natural rights (i.e., those whose surrender is not needed for peaceful society)—rights held against the community, not just its government—and one on which all rights are given up to the community, to be redistributed to individuals by the community (depending on its needs) in the form of civil or institutional rights (a la Rousseau).[18] On the latter view, only the community (not individual citizens) can have rights against the government, and individual citizens have only those rights the community grants them (i.e., they have no secure, permanent rights even against the community, having surrendered all to the community's judgment).

Locke's *Treatises* are probably as unclear on this crucial point as on any other. Which reading we choose will vitally affect our view

---

avoids directly utilizing the idea of sovereignty in the central aspects of his positive presentation in the *Treatises*. See Grant, *Liberalism*, 76–79. This essay contains no extended discussion of sovereignty or of how traditional conceptions of sovereignty relate to Locke's position, in part because I can add little to Franklin's careful study of these matters (*John Locke and the Theory of Sovereignty*). In chapter 6, I do comment briefly on the significance of Locke's theory of resistance for classical conceptions of sovereignty.

[17] Kendall, *Majority-Rule*, e.g., 62, 103–4, 112–13, and "John Locke Revisited," 221; Strauss, *Natural Right*, 231–32; Cox, *Locke on War and Peace*, 115–23, 148; Macpherson, *Possessive Individualism*, 256–61; Waldron, "Enough and as Good," 327 (although Waldron's position on this point is unclear; see note 21 below). Parry makes the puzzling claim that Locke's contractors "surrendered their right to enforce the law of nature and no other rights" (*John Locke*, 98); his view seems to have been anticipated in Grady, "Obligation, Consent," 282, 284; and followed in Den Hartogh, "Express Consent," 660, 667; and Lessnoff, *Social Contract*, 61–62.

[18] There is a third choice, closely related to the first: that the contract amounts to a kind of "limited blank check," an agreement to give up the rights required by society (but *only* those) when they are needed (as opposed to determining in advance which rights are needed). On this reading, like the first, citizens retain those rights that are not needed by society, but, unlike the first, surrender rights in stages as the needs of society become apparent.

of the entire tenor of Locke's project, our view, for instance, of whether we take Locke's methodological individualism to have led him to any serious form of political individualism. Locke's lack of clarity in the *Treatises* is complicated by the fact that his early views of these matters, in the *Two Tracts on Government*, quite clearly *do* favor one reading over the other. They favor the second reading outlined above, the reading of the *Treatises* that I have opposed.[19] In the First Tract, for instance, Locke writes that it is "the unalterable condition of society and government that every particular man must unavoidably part with this right to his [entire] liberty and entrust the magistrate with as full a power over all his actions as he himself hath" (p. 125); and in the Second Tract: "every individual surrenders the whole of this natural liberty of his, however great it may be, to a legislator" (p. 231).

Nonetheless, I will argue for the first reading, on which persons retain a portion of their natural rights (and here, I think, the influence of the Levellers on Whig, and consequently on Locke's, thought is apparent). Locke's views on the political transfer of rights, I will suggest (in chapters 5 and 6), changed with his views on the right to toleration and the right of resistance. We cannot, I think, make sense of his claims in either area in his later works, without embracing the first reading. And it is easy to see how it was Locke's argumentative needs in the *Two Tracts* that there required him to defend the view that individuals must surrender all of their rights (a view he was later to abandon). For Locke there wants both to deny to citizens a right of resistance and to defend the magistrate's right to legislate indifferent religious matters (i.e., matters of worship neither required nor forbidden by God's law). The first ambition is obviously aided by denying any retained liberty to subjects. And the second ambition is advanced by Locke by arguing that a magistrate may lawfully command whatever a subject may rightfully do (First Tract, 125–26; Second Tract, 231), a claim that follows trivially from the position that subjects transfer all of their rights to the magistrate. But once Locke surrenders these ambitions, as he clearly does by the time of the *Two Treatises* and *A Letter Concerning Toleration*, there is no further need for that view of the political transfer of rights. Locke's views changed, both on what rights *must* be transferred to government, and on what rights *can* be transferred.[20]

[19] This, of course, is part of Macpherson's reason for favoring the second reading. See note 1 above.

[20] This change was related to Locke's change of view on the best strategy for managing religion in civil society. Whether civil peace and prosperity (the proper ends

I have argued elsewhere, for instance, that Lockean citizens in civil society must be supposed to retain significant portions of their natural rights in land and all of their rights in other material property.[21] Similarly, the right of innocent delights is clearly excluded by Locke (in II, 128–30) from the consensual transfer that creates political power. (And who, in any event, could imagine Locke denying that a citizen has a clear right to smoke a pipe or whistle a favorite tune?) And the language of II, 129 is obviously intended to convey as well that the rest of our right of self-government (what Locke calls "the first power") is surrendered only in part, to the extent necessary for society's preservation.

This is not, of course, to argue that Locke's (mature) position on the political transfer of rights is without difficulties for him. Locke argues, for instance, that each citizen surrenders (in part) the right "of doing whatsoever he thought fit for the preservation of himself and the rest of mankind" on entrance into civil society. But if the law of nature, which commands the preservation of humankind, is "an eternal rule to all men" (II, 135), then each person always has a duty to preserve self and others, in or out of civil society.[22] And if each has that duty, each also has the right to preserve self and others (i.e., the right to do one's duty). How, then, can Locke claim that even a part of this right has been given up by citizens (a question to which we will return in chapter 5)? One simple answer available to Locke is claiming that the "part" of this right that is surrendered is only the privilege of acting *first* in attempting to preserve self and others. The community obtains from each the right to act first in preserving its citizens and promoting their good (analogous to the "right of first try" that parents possess in rearing their children[23]), by obtaining from each the right to act before that individual. This precludes the anarchic results that might seem to result from citizens following their own judgments while legislators and judges try

---

of civil government) are best served by imposing religion or by tolerating it will partially determine which rights must be transferred from citizens to government. And on this question of strategy, Locke's views clearly changed. See Kraynak, "John Locke," 53–55.

[21] What is surrendered is only those rights over property necessary for societal or governmental jurisdiction (II, 120–22); and jurisdiction over property is not identical to community or governmental possession of all rights in the property at issue. See *Lockean Theory of Rights,* sections 4.4 and 6.1; and Waldron, *Private Property,* 137.

[22] This claim is independently plausible from an intuitive Lockean perspective. For it seems clear that Locke would want to contend that even citizens in a legitimate commonwealth have duties to refrain from suicide, keep their promises, or save a starving man—whether or not these acts are commanded by the state as legal duties.

[23] See *Lockean Theory of Rights,* 178–84.

to follow theirs. Where the community is unable or unwilling to preserve its citizens, however, individuals retain the right (and duty) to "act second" themselves, even to the point of actively resisting a government that fails to observe natural law.[24]

3.2. Consent, Contract, and Trust

With this understanding in hand of the moral content of the transfer of right that creates political society, we can look more closely at the process of transfer (which is more complicated than I have thus far indicated). A complete political society, Locke suggests, is created in two logically separable stages (which may or may not be separated by an interesting temporal gap). The society itself is created by a contract among all those who wish to be part of it. The society's government is formed by society's granting a separate trust, which conveys to government the political power which was previously invested in the society by its members.[25] Political power is given first "into the hands of the society, and therein to the governors whom the society has set over itself, with this express or tacit trust: that it shall be employed for their good and the preservation of their property" ([II, 171]; see also II, 243). While the creation of the "Legislative" (the "soul" of the commonwealth) is "the first and fundamental act of society" (II, 212), the body politic is created "by barely agreeing to unite into one political society" (II, 99).[26] Consent to membership in the body politic must be unanimous ("by the consent of every individual" [II, 96]), for only a person's *own* consent

[24] Interestingly, the only place where Locke explicitly approaches this style of reasoning seems to be in connection with the *executive* right, which Locke says is "wholly" given up in civil society. Locke argues that I have a right to preserve myself (by, e.g., killing a thief) even in civil society, if the law "cannot interpose to secure my life from present force" (II, 19).

[25] See, e.g., Parry, *John Locke*, 99; Pateman, *Political Obligation*, 69–79; Mabbott, *John Locke*, 151; Pitkin, "Obligation and Consent—I," 994. Sabine claims that Locke did not explicitly employ a "two-stage contract," since he had no real interest in formal clarity (*History of Political Theory*, 532–33). This assertion seems mistaken, at least if one counts the trust as analogous to the second stage in earlier contractarian accounts.

[26] Thus, political society logically precedes government for Locke. Grant argues that Locke can be understood to be using two senses of the term "government" in his work. In the technical sense, government is that which is created by the trust from society. But the society itself, at its creation, is also a kind of government: "then the form of government is a perfect [majority rule] democracy" (II, 132). Locke does sometimes use "community" and "government" interchangeably (e.g., II, 95), and the society and the government it entrusts do hold the same political power (although on different terms). So Grant's suggestion seems reasonable. See *Liberalism*, 103–6; and Tarcov, "Best Fence," 205.

can remove that individual from the state of nature. But this consent *entails*, Locke believes, consent to rule by the majority of the members in all subsequent matters (including, of course, the creation of government) (II, 95–99; I return to this matter in 4.2).

After the first creation of the commonwealth (or after an initially *illegitimate* society has been rendered legitimate), individuals may join it by consenting to those same terms of incorporation to which the original members agreed (II, 89) (or should have agreed), including majority rule and the authority of any legitimate government the previous members may have installed.[27] The new member's rights are simply "added to" the political power of the society (and from there entrusted to government).

All of this is accomplished only by consent. Locke's most famous discussion of consent, of course, concerns the consent given by those who join (or otherwise enjoy the dominions of) already existing commonwealths. But I will take the term "consent" to be for Locke a blanket term covering all instances of deliberate, voluntary alienation of rights (and undertakings of obligation)—including not only what we might narrowly call consenting, but also promising, contracting, entrusting, and so on.[28] This is not just Locke's account of consent, but a quite plausible account in its own right. While we can obviously distinguish in certain ways such acts as consenting, promising, contracting, and entrusting, there is also a perfectly natural sense of "consent" on which promising, contracting, and entrusting are simply *kinds* of consenting.[29] We can describe as acts of consent any acts that deliberately and suitably communicate to others the agent's intention to undertake obligations toward and/or convey rights (or permissions) to those others. One can, on this account, consent insincerely (by deliberately communicating to others an intention one in fact lacks). And acts of consent can, of course, fail to alter the existing distribution of obligations and rights, for consent is not sufficient to ground obligations and convey rights.[30] But consent can be defined in terms of the agent's deliberate and

[27] The differences between express and tacit consent, with regard to membership in the commonwealth, are discussed below in 4.1. On the content of a "joiner's" consent, see Grant, *Liberalism*, 119–21.

[28] See Pateman, *Political Obligation*, 71. Note that consent is given in Locke not only to society, but also to government (e.g., II, 121).

[29] Raz, *Morality of Freedom*, 82–83; Green, *Authority of the State*, 167. This seems to me more plausible than the view that consent is really a kind of promise, as claimed in Weale, "Consent," 68–69; and Den Hartogh, "Made by Contrivance," 214.

[30] We can consent to (virtually) anything; but we can only convey to others rights over a very limited class of acts or objects (Weale, "Consent," 66–67; Raz, *Morality of Freedom*, 84).

effective communication of an intention to bring about this kind of change.[31]

Regardless of how broadly we understand the term "consent" (or Locke's use of it), however, Locke clearly intends as well to point to (and rely upon) substantive and important differences among the various kinds of voluntary alienations.[32] In particular, the distinction just discussed between the *contract* that creates society and the *trust* that creates its government is meant by Locke to bear considerable weight. It is certainly important to Locke both that invoking the concept of a trust makes this political relationship mirror certain aspects of his view of our relation to God and that doing so constitutes a significant departure from medieval assertions of a contract between people and ruler.[33] Locke's employment of the idea of a trust is especially important in its consequences for his theory of resistance, as one of his clearest discussions of the idea reveals:

> The Legislative being only a fiduciary power to act for certain ends, there remains still in the People a supreme power to remove or alter the Legislative, when they find the Legislative act

[31] Raz prefers to analyze consent in terms of the agent's beliefs rather than intentions (*Morality of Freedom*, 81–83). But as Green argues (and as we will see in 8.4), while we might sometimes call an act one of "consent" even where the intention to bind oneself was lacking, the principle in such cases under which we argue for holding a person liable for that "consent" is very different than that to which we appeal in cases of intentional undertakings of obligation. Where intention is absent, we appeal rather to a principle of "estoppel" (to protect the interests of those who relied on the "consent") (*Authority of the State*, 163–64).

It is important to see that the intention relevant to a proper analysis of consent is the intention to alter the existing distribution of obligations and rights, and not the intention to "induce reliance" in another (as is claimed in Weale, "Consent," 68–69, and rejected in Raz, *Morality of Freedom*, 96). While consenting to something may (or may not) induce others to rely on one, one's obligation to abide by one's consent is not explained by this reliance. Another's reliance is not necessary for me to have a consensual obligation. Nor is even quite deliberate, voluntary creation in another of reasonable expectations sufficient to generate an obligation not to frustrate those expectations (if, for instance, conventional or otherwise appropriate means of creating expectations were not employed; see my "Reasonable Expectations").

[32] Schochet emphasizes the importance of the distinction between *contract* and *consent* for Locke, although Locke clearly (in my view) uses "consent" to cover cases of "contract" in many places in the *Treatises* (e.g., II, 95–98, 112, 122, 171, etc.). See Schochet, "Family," 94, and *Patriarchalism*, 262–63. See also Snare's more general discussion of the different kinds of consent acts in Locke, in "Consent and Conventional Acts."

[33] See *Lockean Theory of Rights*, 53–54, 77–78, 97–99, 260-64. On the history of the use of "trust" in political theory, see Gough, *Political Philosophy*, chapter 7. On Locke's use of the concept in his theory of resistance (noted below), see ibid., 161. Hampton has argued that Locke is not really using the idea of a trust in his theory at all (*Hobbes and the Social Contract Tradition*, 248n). My arguments here and in chapter 6 are, I think, good grounds for believing her claim to be false.

contrary to the trust reposed in them. For all power given with trust for the attaining an end, being limited by that end, whenever that end is manifestly neglected or opposed, the trust must necessarily be forfeited and the power devolve into the hands of those who gave it. (II, 149)

This passage isolates a number of important features of Locke's understanding of trusts, which make the idea particularly suitable for effectively conveying a particular conception of the moral relation between a people and their government:[34]

(1) Unlike a contract, which binds parties to specific performances, a trust sets an end to be pursued (and grants rights only for the purpose of pursuing that end).

(2) The end establishes a responsibility on the part of the trustee (in this case, "to preserve the members of that society in their lives, liberties, and possessions" [II, 171]). A contractually alienated right, by contrast, typically carries no specific limitations on the new rightholder's use of it.

(3) Pursuit of an end requires discretion (think here of Kant's characterization of imperfect duties). Thus, a trustee must be allowed prerogative in the employment of entrusted rights for pursuing the end (II, 159–68).

(4) Because it is a trust, and not a contract, no consideration need be given for it to bind. The trustee need not personally benefit in order to be bound to pursue the assigned end.[35]

(5) Because a trust conveys more of a privilege than a claim (unlike a contract), and so is only a conditional alienation, the settlor may withdraw the trust without injury to the trustee. Trusts are revokable in a way that executed con-

[34] Specifically, the people in Locke occupy two of the three standard roles in fiduciary relations—they are both settlor (trustor) and beneficiary, with their government as trustee. See Barker, "Introduction," xxiii–xxiv. Von Leyden's account of Locke on trusts emphasizes (4), (5), and (6) below (*Hobbes and Locke*, 128–32). Dunn's account, by contrast, concentrates on (1), (2), and (3) below (*Political Thought*, 162, and "The Concept of 'Trust,'" 296–97). Both aspects of the fiduciary relationship Locke has in mind need emphasis. Lessnoff argues that trusts should actually be thought of as special kinds of contracts, involving promises by both settlor and trustee, with at least one promise (presumably the settlor's) being conditional on proper performance by the other party (*Social Contract*, 4–6). As the analysis below suggests, this does not capture the full measure of the differences between contracts and trusts (at least as these notions are used by Locke).

[35] Gough, *Political Philosophy*, 139.

tracts are not, so that entrusted rights are not irrecoverably lost.[36]

(6) The settlor is the judge of when and whether the trustee has acted contrary to the trust, thus forfeiting the entrusted rights.[37]

Legitimate governments, then, hold their political power only for the purpose of advancing the good of the people who created them (or subsequently consented to their authority), never for advancing their own good. They may act outside of the law (and otherwise use discretion) in order to more effectively serve this purpose. But when the people judge them to have failed in their task, their power is forfeit and resistance to them becomes legitimate. It is this arrangement to which each member of the commonwealth is committed by political consent, and this limit on the power of governors over the governed that consent establishes.

3.3. The Appeal of Consent Theory

Political power, Locke tells us, "has its original *only* from compact and agreement, and the mutual consent of those who make up the community" (II, 171; my emphasis). Let us draw from this claim (and from those examined above) the essential premise of Lockean consent theory: that free consent by citizens is not only (normally) sufficient, but *necessary* for legitimate political authority and political obligation (see 7.1). That this consent theory has great appeal, far beyond the structure of Locke's work or the character of Locke's time, is undeniable. Americans learn at their mothers' knees that governments derive "their just powers from the consent of the governed," and it is a view that is widely (and uncritically) accepted today by most citizens of modern democracies (among others). What accounts for the attractiveness of the doctrine that only consent can make a government legitimate?[38]

Some of what made the doctrine attractive to Locke would un-

---

[36] See Cranston, "Government by Consent," 74; Tuck, *Natural Rights Theories*, 146–47; Gough, *Political Philosophy*, 122n; Barker, "Introduction," xxiii–xxiv.

[37] "Who shall be the judge whether his trustee or deputy acts well, and according to the trust reposed in him, but he who deputes him, and must, by having deputed him have still a power to discard him when he fails in his trust?" (II, 240). Whether the people wrong their trustee (government) by removing it when they mistakenly judge it to have breached its trust is a question to which I return in 6.4.

[38] See my earlier discussion of this question in *Moral Principles and Political Obligations*, chapter 3.

doubtedly not interest us today. But at least a large part of what appealed to Locke about consent theory, I contend, is precisely what continues to appeal to us today. In the first place, for instance, consent (voluntary alienation) is a convincing source of our political ties for both Locke and ourselves, because, more than any other, consent is a clear and uncontroversial ground of special obligation and right-transfer.[39] For Locke, consent (promise, contract) binds even God, its moral force is so clear and indisputable (I,6; II, 195); indeed, Locke wonders if there can "be anything more ridiculous" than to make a pledge and then break it (II, 194). It is consent that makes society possible on Locke's view.[40] And we share with Locke, I am suggesting, this intuitive conviction: "that men should keep their compacts is certainly a great and undeniable rule in morality" (E, 1.2.5).

Other sources of the appeal of consent theory are also common to Locke and many of us today. For Locke, the emphasis on consent is an emphatic denial of the legitimacy of force and conquest as a source of political authority.[41] Free consent (as the only legitimate source of such authority), of course, is the ground most clearly opposed to force. I assume that on our agreement with Locke in this matter, no argument is necessary. Nor is it necessary to dwell long on our agreement with Locke on the right of a people to resist a government that oppresses them or acts consistently contrary to their expressed aims and commitments. Consent theory is specially connected to this view of the right of resistance.[42] While other theories may also, of course, affirm the right to resist illegitimate government, on other theories a government that acts contrary to its people's will may still have moral standing for unrelated reasons (its institution by God, the historical contract in which it originated, the benefits it still provides, etc.). According to Lockean consent theory, a government that steadily and deliberately fails to act within the terms of its trust has no moral standing at all (as a government), and so may be resisted without fear of moral impropriety.[43]

[39] Ibid., especially 69–70.

[40] See *Lockean Theory of Rights*, 65; Dunn, "Concept of 'Trust,'" 287–88, and *Locke*, 52. The importance of promise-keeping to society's maintenance in Locke can be plainly seen in the limits on toleration that he stresses: papists are not to be tolerated (in part) because the pope can release them from oaths and promises to their rulers (ECT, 188); atheists are not to be tolerated because "promises, covenants, and oaths . . . can have no hold upon" them (L, 156).

[41] See 2.3 above. This point is made forcefully in Dunn, *Political Thought*, 144–45, and "Consent," 47.

[42] See Shapiro, *Evolution of Rights*, 288.

[43] This, it seems to me, is the "logical connection" between Locke's consent theory

But all of this still ignores the deepest and most important continuity between Locke's reasons for embracing consent theory and our own. Because many of us agree with Locke about the importance of the individual's right of self-government or autonomy, we are with Locke drawn to the conclusion that consent is the only ground of political obligation and authority that is consistent with the natural moral freedom to which we are committed. The Lockean person's natural condition, remember, is one of perfect freedom (from the political authority of others). Persons are not born subjects, just because they happen to be born within the territories of states (II, 118).[44] It follows from this, of course, that attempts by others to govern us will require some special justification—a justification consistent with and respectful of our natural freedom. But what kind of justification could this be? If another's being wiser or more able were sufficient justification for his governing and controlling us, we would have to concede that we had, after all, no natural claim to choose for ourselves how our lives will go.[45] Only the view that the free choices of those subject to political authority are necessary to legitimate it seems consistent with the natural right of self-government.[46] Consent is an act only a free person can perform; it is a use, not a breach, of one's freedom. Because consent is an *intentional*, deliberate act, which requires knowledge and awareness of circumstances, one's freedom cannot be undermined by allegedly consensual obligations (or alienation of rights) that are accomplished unwittingly or under duress.[47] Indeed, it is virtually analytic for Locke that the political transfer of rights can only be achieved by consent. For a person's rights are personal property (e.g., II, 87), and property cannot be taken without its owner's consent (II, 138).[48]

No government can allow complete liberty (this *is* analytic: E, 4.3.18). But the method of consent comes as close to this ideal as possible. Consent invests governmental acts with the moral signif-

---

and his theory of resistance. Plamenatz denies that any such connection exists (*Man and Society*, 1:231–32). We will see in chapter 6, however, that this Lockean position, as I have just expressed it, needs to be in certain ways qualified (e.g., to take account of the necessity of the people's judgment that government is in breach of its trust).

[44] See 1.3 above; and Dunn, *Political Thought*, 136–38.

[45] See the discussion of these points in Beran, "What Is the Basis of Political Authority?" 490–93, and *Consent Theory*, 34–36.

[46] See Pateman, "Women and Consent," 150–51; Richards, *Toleration and the Constitution*, 101; Lemos, *Hobbes and Locke*, 81.

[47] *Moral Principles and Political Obligations*, 69–70.

[48] This claim requires careful statement. Rights can be forfeited to others without the consent of their original holder, but not "taken from" the rightholder. And only wrongdoing can accomplish a forfeiture (see 2.2).

icance of the free choices of individuals. It has been argued, by contrast, that Locke was mistaken in thinking that his acceptance of our natural freedom committed him to consent theory. For once governments are established that protect *others'* freedom, we have a duty to accept the authority of these governments, whether we have agreed to be subject to them or not.[49] This claim, however, betrays a misunderstanding of the substance of Locke's (and the Lockean) doctrine of natural freedom. Others act wrongly if they act in ways that limit our natural freedom to dispose of our rights as God's law and our own wills dictate. Others cannot acquire authority over us by wrongly making it difficult or impossible to reject that authority without disadvantaging them. Indeed, others may only permissibly form a society among themselves (without me) provided that their doing so does not harm me in my freedom: "This [joining to form a commonwealth] any number of men may do, *because it injures not the freedom of the rest*; they are left as they were in the liberty of the state of nature" (II, 95; my emphasis). No one, then, whether born in the territories of an established state or not, is either born obligated to obey any political authority, or born with an obligation to consent to any particular political society's authority.[50] These are fundamental tenets of Lockean consent theory. They are a significant source of its enduring appeal, in my view, largely because they are correct.

However appealing we might find it, though, we should not try to pretend that Lockean consent theory offers the only account of political obligation and authority that has any real potential. Opposing views with many serious and thoughtful adherents are ranged in a wide variety of theoretical distances from Lockean voluntarism. We saw in 1.3, for instance, that Lockean individualism and voluntarism are opposed most dramatically by various naturalist and communitarian theories, according to which the obligation to obey one's political superiors follows simply (or even trivially) from one's identity as a person or as a member of a certain kind of community. Less dramatically, of course, Lockean theory is opposed by more individualistic virtue theories, which maintain that political

---

[49] Plamenatz, *Man and Society*, 1:224.

[50] See my discussion of this point in *Lockean Theory of Rights*, 66–67; and Lessnoff, *Social Contract*, 62, 98. Even if Locke's view is (as I believe it is not) that each person has an obligation to consent to and enter civil society (a familiar enough Puritan view), this still does not amount to an obligation to enter any particular political society (e.g., the one I happen to have been reared in): each reaches maturity as "a freeman, at liberty what government he will put himself under" (II, 118). This, of course, is the crucial point for the force of consent theory.

obedience, allegiance, or civility are important aspects of moral virtue.[51] Less dramatically still, Lockean consent theory can be contrasted with straightforwardly individualistic theories that simply identify different (or additional) grounds of political obligation than consent. Thus, "benefit/reciprocation theories" take political obedience (etc.) to be morally required reciprocation for benefits received or accepted from the workings of one's legal and political institutions. Such theories might appeal either to a principle of gratitude or to one of fairness to justify their claims. "Quality of government theories," while also typically individualistic in character, reject the idea that political obligations must flow from specific transactions between citizens and states, basing those obligations instead on the independent moral importance of supporting just, useful, or worthy (etc.) laws or governments. I class both utilitarian and hypothetical contractarian theories of political obligation as quality-of-government theories.

We will return to some of Lockean consent theory's individualist competitors in 7.2 and 8.4. But the contrast on which I want to concentrate for a moment here is in a way the least dramatic of all, and hence a matter of rather subtler theoretical distinctions. Many (especially recent) political philosophers have, like Locke, employed in their theories of obligation or authority the ideas of consent or contract; but they have at the same time rejected the Lockean consent theory outlined above. Their theories thus constitute the most immediate challenge to Lockean consent theory. For they threaten to capture what is appealing about Lockean theory while dispensing with central aspects of that theory.

All of the theories I have in mind here, while utilizing some notion of consent, reject the central Lockean claim that an actual act of consent is necessary for each person's political obligations or duties. Hypothetical contractarians maintain, for instance, that our political obligations (duties) are to support those institutions that *would be* agreed upon by hypothetical persons of some description (typically, rational, self-interested, and in some ways ignorant) in an original position of equality and nonsubjection.[52] The actual consent of specific persons (or the absence of such consent) is irrelevant (or at least secondary) to a determination of their political duties. Yet, it is

---

[51] Hume, *Treatise*, 3.2.7–10; Green, *Authority of the State*, chapter 9.

[52] Lessnoff (*Social Contract*, 91) distinguishes hypothetical contract theories (which appeal to what people could or would have chosen) from ideal contract theories (which appeal to what they ought to have chosen). Where the choosers are idealized (as in the theories I am discussing here), however, the distinction tends to dissolve.

claimed, this view captures much of the force and appeal of classical Lockean consent theory:

> No society can, of course, be a scheme of cooperation which men enter voluntarily in a literal sense. . . . Yet a society satisfying [hypothetical contractarian demands] comes as close as a society can to being a voluntary scheme, for it meets the principles that free and equal persons would assent to under circumstances that are fair. In this sense its members are autonomous and the obligations they recognize self-imposed.[53]

Radical participation theorists also reject the idea that specific acts of consent are necessary (or sufficient) for each person's obligations, although they stress as the alternative not some hypothetical version of consent. Rather, their emphasis is placed on "the theory and practice of participatory or self-managing democracy":[54] only serious, ongoing participation in the practices of such a democracy counts as giving true consent (and hence creating and maintaining political obligations). Others agree that political consent is better thought of as "ongoing and diffuse" than as a specific act,[55] and they insist as well on a less individualistic conception of consent than is utilized in classical consent theory. But now we are asked to think of the "consent of the governed" not in terms of acts or ongoing performances by citizens, but instead in terms of the responsiveness of the state to its people (conceived of as a single corporate agent). States that are responsive and unoppressive toward those who reside in their territories are legitimate and are owed obligations of obedience; they enjoy the consent of the governed.[56]

I cannot here respond to these "revisionist consent theories" with the care they clearly merit. But my advocacy of the Lockean perspective requires at least a brief reply, as well as a defense of my view that only the Lockean version of consent theory preserves the intuitive appeal of consent theory summarized above. To radical participation theory the Lockean can respond primarily by insisting on additions. For the Lockean need not insist that only discrete acts (however we might try to explain such a concept) can properly be counted as acts of consent. Ongoing (voluntary, informed, serious)

---

[53] Rawls, *Theory of Justice*, 13. Indeed, Locke himself has been read as a defender of hypothetical contractarianism, although I postpone until 7.2 my full defense of reading Locke as an actual-consent theorist.

[54] Pateman, *Problem of Political Obligation*, 1.

[55] Herzog, *Happy Slaves*, 193, 196.

[56] Ibid., 202–15.

political participation can be counted by the Lockean as giving consent of the appropriate sort, just as Locke himself (although not very convincingly) was willing to count the ongoing process of continued, voluntary residence as giving consent. The Lockean must insist, however, against much participation theory, that discrete acts of consent *can* ground political obligations, provided these acts are genuinely voluntary and adequately informed. And the Lockean will have good reasons for this insistence: for many of the same values (and, from the Lockean point of view, the most important ones) that are promoted by schemes of active, democratic political participation are also promoted by allowing individuals free choice in where their political allegiance will lie, and by permitting persons to commit themselves to their choices by discrete acts of consent. Our practices of promising and contracting have quite apparent justifications. And provided only that the range of possible commitments is appropriately limited (as it will be in any Lockean theory), there is no reason to suppose that political versions of promises and contracts are morally suspect.

As for hypothetical contractarianism and "consent-as-responsiveness theories," the most obvious objection to them (as developments of consent theory) is that both actually constitute clear retreats from genuine consent theory to what I earlier called "quality-of-government theories." Both are only superficially forms of consent theory at all. For both really base our duties or obligations not on anyone's actual choices, but on whether our governments (states, laws) are sufficiently just, good, useful, or responsive to secure the hypothetical support of ideal choosers. And the choices of such ideal parties are, of course, necessarily guided solely by the actual merits of the governments (institutions, schemes) in question; they can only choose that which is in fact best for them. But then it seems only honest to acknowledge that the "contract" in hypothetical contractarianism is simply a device that permits us to analyze in a certain way quality of government, rather than the actual ground of political duty. And once consent is abandoned as the ground, we have also abandoned much of what is most compelling about classical consent theory—namely, the clear, uncontroversial ground of obligation on which it relies, and the high value of self-government with which it remains consistent. Theories that simply base political duties in governmental justice or responsiveness (etc.) plainly lose the latter source of consent theory's appeal (for individual choice or rejection of allegiance becomes unimportant to obligation); and they arguably lose the former as well.[57] It simply will not do to respond that the Lockean consent theorist's demand for actual consent (in the interest of individual autonomy) is silly, given that no actual societies permit (or can permit) their residents full autonomy.[58]For it may well be, as Lockeans insist, that societies that refuse to permit or fail to facilitate free choice of political allegiance are simply illegitimate, however many such societies might actually exist. It is that possibility to which we will return in earnest in part 4.

[57] It is not unreasonable (or even unusual) to ask why we should take ourselves to have a duty to support arrangements that merely would be chosen by ideal choosers (Kavka, *Hobbesian Moral and Political Theory*, 399). The counterfactual claim at issue, remember, is not that the choice is one that *I* would have made (as when the doctor tries to justify treating my unconscious body [without my actual consent] by appealing to what I would consent to were I able). It is rather that the choice is one that ideal persons in special circumstances would have made. And if the theory tries to make the choosers *less* ideal (so they are more like me, and their choices more like the ones I would make), the theory loses whatever advantages it gained by associating justification and legitimation with the "best" (soundest, most rational) choices. In any event, however, it is certainly possible for the Lockean consent theorist to argue that one's free *acts* have a very different moral significance than even extremely reliable counterfactual claims that could be made about how one *would* act.

[58] Herzog takes the classical consent theorist's demand for individual autonomy to be an impossible demand that each person "have his way" even in society (*Happy Slaves*, 201–2). But this is not, of course, a fair rendering of that demand. The Lockean demand is only a demand either to be left alone (to one's natural freedom) or to be allowed to freely choose the political society within which one will surrender the right to "have his way." And, in any event, the right to "have one's way" is at its fullest (for the Lockean) only a right to act in ways consistent with one's own duties and the rights of others. The Lockean demand for individual autonomy is only a demand for that which is consistent with all others possessing the same.

FOUR

THE VARIETIES OF CONSENT

4.1. Express and Tacit Consent

There is, Locke tells us, "a common distinction of an express and a tacit consent, which will concern our present case" (II, 119). Locke is less clear on the substance of this distinction, however, than he is on the political applications and consequences of tacit consent:

> I say that every man that hath any possession or enjoyment of any part of the dominions of any government, doth thereby give his tacit consent, and is as far forth obliged to obedience to the laws of that government, during such enjoyment, as anyone under it; whether this his possession be of land to him and his heirs forever, or a lodging only for a week; or whether it be barely travelling freely on the highway; and in effect, it reaches as far as the very being of anyone within the territories of that government. (II, 119)

Locke's remarks here may seem to suggest that those who join together to create a new political society (from out of the state of nature [simpliciter]) must be express consenters, since one can hardly "enjoy the dominions of a government" until those dominions exist. Elsewhere, however, Locke plainly refers to political societies that begin in the purely tacit consent that is given to a continuation of the natural preeminence of fathers or especially able persons.[1] Thus, enjoying the dominions of an established govern-

---

[1] Locke writes of the father of the family who becomes its prince (and, as a result, wields political, not merely paternal power), suggesting that the process that converts the family into a political society is the giving by the children of "a tacit, and scarce avoidable consent" to their father's rule (II, 75). Similarly, "some one good and excellent man" may be changed from able leader to legitimate ruler (thus creating a new civil society) "by a tacit consent" of other persons to his rule (II, 94). In both cases tacit consent is sufficient to create a new polity, but in neither case is that consent a matter of enjoying the dominions of an established government (since no society exists when the consent is given). In both cases, I will claim, the tacit consent

80

ment would seem not to be the only way in which tacit consent may be given to the political authority of others (see below). This much at least is perfectly clear, however: those who join an already existing political society, and all of the subsequent generations (beyond the first) of a society's residents, can begin the political relationship and become subject to society's laws by giving either express or tacit consent. And it is after all with these people, more than with those who make new political societies out of the state of nature, that we are chiefly acquainted in our actual political lives.

Locke's distinction between express and tacit consent is intended by him not only to distinguish various forms in which consent may be given, but also to specify the force or duration of the resulting consensual obligation. The tacit consenter's obligation to obey, according to Locke, "begins and ends with the enjoyment" (II, 121), so that he is free to "quit" his "possession or enjoyment" and go elsewhere, without encumbering bonds. Not so for the express consenter, who has "given his consent to be of [the] commonwealth"; an express consenter is "perpetually and indispensably obliged to be and remain unalterably a subject to it, and never again be in the liberty of the state of nature," his obligations ending only if he is cast out of society or its government dissolves (II, 121). Nothing but express consent can make persons "subjects or members" of the commonwealth (II, 122), Locke seems to say.

So we appear to have two classes of possible consenters, two ways in which a person can enter with others into some form of the political relationship. One can consent to (permanent) membership in the society directly and explicitly (expressly); or one can give one's consent indirectly (tacitly), to a more conditional membership, through the performance of other kinds of acts that nonetheless have much of the same significance and binding force of explicit acts of consent.

The problems raised by Locke's claims in these passages are many and familiar. Locke seems at times to be trying to distinguish those who expressly join themselves to the society from those who merely "submit" to the government's laws for a (perhaps indefinite) time. But given the apparent paucity of express consenters (both in Locke's day and our own), this distinction would seem unhelpfully

---

consists in the performance of not explicitly consensual acts that nonetheless constitute the making of a morally significant choice in a clear choice situation. Tacit consent in the case of one who enjoys the dominions of some established government similarly consists of different, but still not explicitly consensual acts that constitute choice.

to lump together most landholders, native-born residents, resident aliens, tourists, and the like, as mere "submitters," leaving almost no real members.[2] On the other hand, Locke sometimes seems to want to distinguish not two classes but three: "foreigners" living under the government, "denisons," and full "subjects or members" (II, 122).[3] But it is hard to distinguish three classes of residents with Locke's twofold distinction between express (permanently obliged) and tacit (temporarily obliged) consenters. And, of course, we would like to see foreigners distinguished from subjects not by the form (tacit or express) of their consents, or by the duration of their obligations, but by the content of their consent (i.e., what they consent to) and the substance of their rights and obligations. For instance, subjects, but not foreigners, might have rights of political participation and obligations to help defend the society in times of war or other crisis. Matters are not helped by Locke's rather casual use of the terms "member" and "subject," although he seems mostly to want to reserve both terms to describe express consenters (who become members of society and subjects of its government [II, 119]), while allowing that tacit consenters may be "subject to" the laws, perhaps without being "subjects" (members) of the commonwealth.[4] Nor is Locke's distinction supported by any obvious reasons why he would want to deny express consenters the right to free emigration, which is so happily granted to tacit consenters.[5]

[2] Waldman, "Note on John Locke's Theory of Consent," 46–47.

[3] Dunn mentions "Members, Subjects, and those 'subject to the laws'" as three possible classes Locke might have had in mind ("Consent," 41). I suggest below that this is probably not Locke's intended use of "subject."

[4] "Member" is used to mean "perpetual subject" in II, 122, which suggests a distinction between "members" and (nonperpetual) "subjects." It is, I think, the prevailing view among Locke scholars that Locke thus intends to distinguish "members" from "subjects." But the text does not seem to support this view. In the very same paragraph (II, 122), Locke uses "subjects or members" as if the terms are interchangeable, as he does also in II, 121 ("a subject to it" and "a member of it" seem to be equated); II, 120 (one who "incorporates" is described as a "subject"); II, 119 (express consent makes one "a perfect member of that society, a subject of that government"); II, 117 (where "becoming a member" puts one as much under government "as any other subject"); II, 116 (the father who is bound to a "perpetual subjection" is described only as "a subject" of the commonwealth). The problem with this reading is not just that it leaves no term to describe tacit consenters (who are most often described as "submitting" to government). Locke also says that persons remain in the state of nature "til by their own consents they make themselves *members* of some politic society" (II, 15; my emphasis). This remark, given the present reading, raises the disturbing (but intriguing) possibility that tacit consenters (who may not be members) are still in the state of nature with respect to members—something Locke actually claims about visiting aliens in II, 9. I try to resolve these difficulties below.

[5] This is not, of course, to say that no reasons can be imagined. Locke was, of

The answers to these puzzles would be clearer if we had a more obvious answer to the question of who counted in Locke as *express* consenters, the "perfect members" of society. Locke says nothing explicit on the subject,[6] but he elsewhere counts as "express" any consent that is "stated" (ELN, 161), and he here contrasts express consent with consent given without any "expression of it" (II, 119), assimilating it to "actual agreement," "express declaration," and "positive engagement" (II, 121–22). Tacit consent, by contrast, seems to be for Locke consent given without words or explicit signs ("expressions"), given rather by other behavior that constitutes the making of a morally significant choice in a clear, noncoercive choice situation.[7] The choice in question (in political cases of tacit consent) could be the choice to participate in a society's scheme of benefits and burdens, indicated by the (not explicitly consensual) willing enjoyment of its government's dominions (as in II, 119); or it could be the choice to elevate a nonpolitical leader to the status of a political ruler (as in II, 74–76 and II, 94), a choice indicated by freely opting to treat that person as the leader of a society. Regardless of whether

---

course, much taken with the solemnity and weight of express oaths and promises, and so might easily have supposed that this made express (but not tacit) consent permanently binding. And, of course, a commonwealth cannot have its members running off every time there is a war to be fought or a burden to be borne (although this seems as true of its tacit-consenting residents as of its express-consenting members). Seliger finds Locke's remarks on the right of emigration "ill-considered" and "irreconcilable . . . with the details and main line of his argumentation" (*Liberal Politics*, 279–80). It is fairer to say that "Locke gives no reason for this position . . . and it seems not to have any function in the structure of the theory" (Dunn, "Consent," 42).

[6] Which Dunn calls a "damaging lacuna in Locke's theory" ("Consent," 40, *Locke*, 50–51, and *Political Thought*, 134). See also Parry, *John Locke*, 104; and Hampsher-Monk, "Tacit Concept of Consent," 136, 138.

[7] I have argued elsewhere that calling consent "tacit" only refers to its distinct mode of expression—in this case, silence or inactivity in response to a clear (i.e., apparent and noncoercive) choice situation (see *Moral Principles and Political Obligations*, especially 79–84). While Locke believed (mistakenly, in my view) that tacit consent binds less completely than express consent, his view of tacit consent is in other respects very much like the one detailed in *Moral Principles and Political Obligations* (as I argue further in 7.2 below). For other similar accounts of tacit consent, see, e.g., Beran, *Consent Theory*, 8; Bennett, "Note on Locke's Theory," 227–29; Feinberg, *Harm to Self*, 183–84; Den Hartogh, "Express Consent," 106.

Some of Locke's own examples and accounts of tacit consent are unhelpful or confused. For instance, the "tacit consent" supposedly given to the use of money (II, 50) cannot really be counted as binding consent at all, but only as what Locke elsewhere calls "natural [i.e., nonbinding] consent" (see the discussion in 7.2). The same is true of the "tacit consents" mentioned in the *Essay* (e.g., E, 1.3.22; 2.28.10; 3.2.8), which clearly concern only conformity in social practice and opinion (ELN, 165). Similarly, Locke's definition of a "tacit contract" as one "prompted by the common interests and convenience of men" (ELN, 161) is unhelpful, since it identifies a characteristic of tacit consent that does not distinguish it from express consent.

we agree with Locke that such behavior actually does constitute the making of a morally significant political choice, it seems fair to infer that Locke wants to count as tacit political consent all acts that inexplicitly constitute the free assumption of the burdens of membership in a political society.

It seems reasonable to conclude as well, then, that when Locke speaks of express consent, he has in mind primarily explicit verbal or written agreements to become a member of society and a subject of its government (and also, no doubt, direct but verbally "imprecise" or nonverbal expressions of such agreement—such as shouting "aye" or raising one's hand in appropriate contexts).[8] In actual practice, express consent could take the form of "oaths of allegiance and fealty" (II, 151) "or other public owning of, or submission to the government of their countries" (II, 62).[9] It is hard, of course, to see how Locke could have thought that a society would have many real members, if membership were contingent on having taken such an explicit oath. Few existing societies (that would today be taken by most people to be legitimate) have in their populations many oath-takers of this sort. And although there was a long history of imposed loyalty oaths in sixteenth- and seventeenth-century England, these oaths were taken primarily with reference to specific religious or political tenets, or to forswear allegiance to some foreign power or domestic competitor. They were not oaths of membership; refusal to consent was not taken to leave one in (or to return one to) the state of nature (but rather, if anything, only to leave one vulnerable to civil punishment as a citizen).[10] Locke might, of course, have imagined or hoped for rather dramatic changes in political behavior and conventions.[11] Yet quite independent of any changes he

[8] Waldman, "Note on Locke's Concept of Consent," 45–46; Russell, "Locke on Express and Tacit Consent," 292, 295. Riley certainly overstates the point, however, when he claims that express consent "is no problem for Locke" (*Will and Political Legitimacy,* 96).

[9] Dunn, "Consent," 41; Russell, "Locke on Express and Tacit Consent," 295; Farr and Roberts, "John Locke on the Glorious Revolution," 391; Den Hartogh, "Express Consent," 106.

[10] On the importance of oaths of allegiance in Locke's day, see Herzog, *Happy Slaves,* 186–92; MacCormick, "Law, Obligation and Consent," 400–401; Cranston, *John Locke,* 320; Ashcraft, *Locke's Two Treatises,* 169, and *Revolutionary Politics,* 594.

[11] Farr and Roberts argue, for instance, that Locke (like various radicals in 1689) wanted to require express consent (loyalty oaths) of all citizens, in order to establish a "firm" bond to the new government ("John Locke on the Glorious Revolution," 390–93, 398; see also Den Hartogh, "Express Consent," 109–14). Their argument is based on Locke's manuscript (called by Laslett) "A Call to the Nation for Unity," which they date in April 1690. To be fair, however, this manuscript never uses the term "consent" at all. And a requirement of express consent in *one* country (Locke's

might have envisioned, Locke seems to believe that all legitimate commonwealths will have "a multitude" of such consenters, who "separately" make themselves "members" (II, 117).

There is, I think, no way of reading Locke here that makes sense of his arguments without also charging him with (at least) imprecision and incompleteness in his presentation. Given that necessity, however, I believe the best way to read Locke's remarks on express and tacit consent (in II, 119–22) is as follows:

Locke wishes first and foremost to distinguish those who have a serious stake in the commonwealth's preservation and well-being from those who do not. This "stake" can be indicated in a variety of ways: taking a solemn oath of allegiance (or otherwise giving express consent—i.e., making a direct and morally serious commitment), owning and residing on land in its territories, being born and reared (and rearing one's own family) in the commonwealth. Others, who merely travel through or reside temporarily within the commonwealth—those who are not somehow committed to the community—lack this stake. All are obliged to obedience by virtue of their oaths or enjoyment of the commonwealth's domains. And all but those who take solemn oaths of perpetual subjection are free to emigrate. But only those who have a stake in the community are to be considered its members or subjects. This class will include oath-takers (native-born or naturalized), landowning residents, and the native-born (be they propertied or propertyless). Those who are merely "passing through" are bound to obey the same laws for preserving public order, as much as are society's members. But they lack political obligations and rights in the fullest sense, the true mark of citizens or members. In an important sense, they remain in the state of nature with respect to the members of the society (as Locke claims in II, 9); for while they are obliged to obey the law while in the commonwealth, they lack the more general obligation to support it in all the ways "necessary to the ends for which" its members are united (they are not, for instance, obliged to pay routine taxes to maintain its government or to aid in its defense, nor are they required to use their power to help enforce the law, where this is needed). And while foreigners will enjoy the law's protection, they will enjoy it not as a right (as subjects do), but as "a local protection

England) would hardly solve for Locke any of the general theoretical problems concerning governmental legitimacy with which we are concerned here. Further, of course, requiring loyalty oaths of all residents runs into very serious problems with a voluntariness condition on binding consent (discussed in 8.3 below). See Herzog, *Happy Slaves*, 192.

and homage" appropriate to those with whom we are at peace (II, 122)—just as an outsider who temporarily lives with a family cannot claim a family member's rights. Subjects, by contrast, have left the state of nature with respect to one another and have entered the political relationship—which they cannot do "til by their own consents they make themselves *members*" of the community (II, 15; my emphasis).

If these are, in fact, Locke's intentions, they are admittedly ill-served by some of what he says and much of how he says it (in II, 119–22)—including, most important, in his very central presentation of the express-tacit distinction. For on my reading, both members (subjects) and nonmembers can be tacit consenters; so the express-tacit distinction will not usefully divide them. Locke's central presentation of the distinction is no doubt meant to emphasize the joint grounds for demanding obedience from all within the state's territories, and to distinguish the perpetually from the non-perpetually obliged.[12] But it also confusingly suggests that landowners have the same standing as visiting aliens. Locke never says this, of course. Indeed, while he calls those who inherit land tacit consenters in II, 120–21, he quite clearly calls them members in II, 116–17.[13] Only in II, 122 does Locke actually seem to be committed to the view that resident landowners (who are only tacit consenters) cannot be members; and even in that passage he is clearly concerned to distinguish foreigners from members (not tacit-consenting landowners from members).

Suppose for a moment that I am right in claiming that the intended force of Locke's remarks on tacit and express consent is (at least in part) to distinguish those who do from those who do not have a stake in the community. This is a distinction that must, of course, be made in any respectable voluntarist political philosophy, and it is to Locke's credit that he at least attempts to do so. But a defensible Lockean theory must draw the distinction rather differently than Locke does, for the reasons enumerated above. We can allow, first, that there is a perfectly legitimate point to be made in

[12] See Ashcraft's argument that Locke is in these sections concerned with the question "Who is free to *leave* the state?" (*Locke's Two Treatises*, 179–82).

[13] The membership of tacit-consenting landowners is important to Locke's case. For Locke wishes to give not only a moral but a territorial account of the state (see Lessnoff, *Social Contract*, 65)—according to which a civil society's territory is that land that was subjected to its jurisdiction by its members (in joining the society), along with common ground surrounded by that land or otherwise conceded to the society by other societies (or so Locke's remarks in II, 45 seem to suggest). If tacit consenters who inherit land are not members, this account will be severely strained.

appealing to the difference between express and tacit consent. Consent can either be given by explicit or direct verbal, written, or behavioral performances, in which case the content of the act of consent (what is consented to) will be for the most part perfectly transparent; or consent can be given by certain other actions, which can constitute consent by virtue of being free, deliberate responses to clear choice situations.[14] And in these latter cases, the content of the consent will have to be inferred from the context and understandings that surround the performance of the act. Obligations can arise from either sort of consent, including obligations to obey the law, support the government, serve in the military, and so on.

But, contrary to Locke's apparent suggestion, *both* members *and* nonmembers of a civil society may consent to appropriate restrictions *either* tacitly *or* expressly. A visiting alien may expressly consent to obey the law as she enters the society's territories, or she may tacitly consent to that same restriction (under normal conditions) simply by freely and deliberately (knowingly) crossing the border, where doing so has the clear and defensible conventional significance of agreeing to obey. Similarly, one may become a member of that civil society either by taking an explicit oath or by freely and deliberately performing other acts (if any) that have the clear and defensible conventional significance of undertaking membership. The difference between the visiting foreigner and the member lies not in the *forms* of their consensual acts, but in the *contents* of those acts. Visiting aliens consent only to obedience to the law of the land (and to liability to appropriate penalties for violations) during such period as they enjoy the territories of the society. Members are made of only those who consent to significantly more than this (including, for instance, helping in the defense of the society, supporting it in ways that go beyond mere obedience to law, perhaps paying taxes, and, in general, doing whatever is necessary to make an effective, just society possible). Tacitly consenting members are those who perform acts that constitute tacit agreement to membership in this full sense. (I explore in part 4 the question of whether anyone in modern political communities actually counts as a tacit consenter in this sense.)

Now Locke himself may well have had both more and less than this in mind in writing about tacit consent (as I suggest in 7.2 below). But this is, in my view, all that a Lockean *should* mean by it. Locke certainly seemed to want to distinguish between tacit and express

---

[14] See my *Moral Principles and Political Obligations*, 89–93.

consent according to the duration of the resulting obligation. But I can see no grounds for supposing that the form of consent uniquely determines anything at all about the duration of any resulting obligation. It is a commonplace for express consent to generate obligations of quite different durations. The obligations based in a wedding vow may last until the union is dissolved, but those based in a promise to babysit for two hours last (we hope) for a considerably shorter time. And it is hard to see why *tacit* consent could not similarly ground either long-term or short-term obligations, depending on the understood significance of one's (tacitly consenting) acts. That, then, is what I believe Locke *should* have said in the relevant sections of the *Second Treatise*.

In fairness, I should mention here an alternative reading of the passages in Locke on express and tacit consent that has enjoyed wide support. It maintains that inheriting land is really a (or the) way of giving express consent, not tacit consent as I have claimed.[15] Such an interpretation must employ a very impressionistic understanding of Locke's use of the term "express," and it must ignore his clear claim that the new owner of the land "has given nothing but . . . a *tacit* consent to the government" (II, 121; my emphasis).[16] Further, the reading seems compelling only if we begin by assuming (wrongly, in my view) that tacit consenters could *not* be "members" or "subjects" who were "incorporated" into the community. But most important, this reading pushes us to a conclusion that Locke could not reasonably have desired: that native-born, but nonlandowning, residents are not members of the society.[17] For in the absence of other signs of express consent, if only express consenters are members, the great masses of unlanded Englishmen would be condemned by Locke to the same standing as that of visiting aliens.

This, of course, is precisely the reading of Locke urged by C. B.

[15] Parry, *John Locke*, 104, 107; Seliger, *Liberal Politics*, 270–71; Gale, "John Locke on Territoriality," 478. Of course Macpherson (discussed below) seems to regard property-holding as the *only* form of express consent.

[16] I, of course, must also ignore a clear claim by Locke—that only express consenters may be members (II, 122). I take this claim to be contradicted by his calling the tacit consenters of II, 120–21 "members" in II, 116–17. Den Hartogh agrees that II, 122 is the passage that cannot be rendered consistent with the rest of Locke's text ("Express Consent," 108).

[17] Here I agree with Dunn that "there is no reason to suppose that Locke can ever have thought native-born Englishmen were not 'subjects of the commonwealth'" (*Political Thought*, 139–40). But I disagree with the "dispositional" account of express consent that he offers as an explanation of how Locke could defend his view ("Consent," 41–42), both for the reasons advanced in 7.2 below and for those offered in the criticisms of Dunn's position in Hampsher-Monk, "Tacit Concept of Consent," 136–37; and Russell, "Locke on Express and Tacit Consent," 305.

Macpherson (who obviously disagrees with my judgment that Locke could not reasonably have aspired to this): "the native with no estate . . . , like the resident foreigner, . . . is simply subject to the jurisdiction of government."[18] According to Macpherson, Locke held that all persons are "members for purposes of being ruled"; but "only those with 'estate' can be full members," only they have "the right to rule" and the "voice about taxation." "The labouring class, being without estate, are subject to, but not full members of, civil society."[19] We can see this, Macpherson claims, because "the only men who are assumed to incorporate themselves in any commonwealth by express compact are those who have some property, or the expectation of some property in land." Tacit consent is introduced only as a device to explain the obligation of laborers and aliens. And it makes sense that Locke should limit membership to those with "estate," for "only they have a full interest in the preservation of property."[20]

Macpherson's interpretation of Locke, however, rests on a variety of false assumptions. First, he mistakenly assumes that inheriting land is a way of giving express consent, in spite of Locke's never saying anything like that.[21] This is, however, a natural mistake, for

[18] *Possessive Individualism*, 249. As Ryan observes, where Locke seems to want to contrast foreigners with members, Macpherson wants to contrast laborers with members ("Locke and the Dictatorship," 248–49).

[19] *Possessive Individualism*, 248–49.

[20] Ibid., 249, 248. Among those who follow the spirit of Macpherson's account are Pateman, *Political Obligation*, 71–72; Parry, *John Locke*, 103–4; Wood, *Agrarian Capitalism*, 83–85, and *Politics of Locke's Philosophy*, 37–39. Seliger argues, by contrast, that Locke clearly intended to include the propertyless as members (citizens) (*Liberal Politics*, 290–92), as does Ashcraft, in the most convincing defense yet offered of the view I accept here (*Locke's Two Treatises*, 166–82). Mabbott seems to think Locke took no stance at all on the question of whether laborers are members of society (*John Locke*, 162–63).

[21] As Hampsher-Monk observes, "Locke is pointing out that express consent is a *precondition* for inheritance, not that inheritance *is* express consent, far less that only inheritors are to be taken as express consenters" ("Tacit Concept of Consent," 136). While I take inheritance to require membership for Locke (as a "precondition"; II, 116–17), I do *not* take it to require express consent (as Hampsher-Monk asserts), but only tacit consent (II, 120–21). See Den Hartogh, "Express Consent," 108. Russell argues convincingly that since Locke's real worry here about inheritance was the possibility of "dismemberment" of the state's territories (II, 117), a tacit submission to the jurisdiction of the government will function perfectly well to avoid that possibility. Russell therefore concludes that Locke's "stronger condition" of express consent and membership prior to inheritance is "a serious mistake" ("Locke on Express and Tacit Consent," 300). I conclude that Locke's real mistake was in saying that one could only become a member by express consent (II, 122). For notice that of the consent that makes *members* in II, 117, "people take no notice of it, thinking it not done at all, or not necessary." How likely is it that people would altogether fail to notice express consent, even if only "given separately in their turns . . . and not in a multitude together"?

if only express consenters are members, where else will Locke find the "multitude" of members he discusses? If, by contrast, we allow that some tacit consenters count as members, no such "creative" interpretation is necessary. Second, Macpherson assumes that only landowners can be express consenters, which entails that even a clear, verbal oath of allegiance by a nonlandowner could not qualify as express consent. This is not a natural mistake, but one flowing only from Macpherson's desire to find in Locke a defense of the class-state.[22] Finally, Macpherson correctly (on my view) depicts Locke as centrally concerned about who has a stake in the commonwealth, but mistakenly assumes that only those with land could have such a stake. It is hard to see why Macpherson would think this, for Locke affirms that *all* persons, landed or not, have property (rights) that they wish to see protected.[23] All persons face the "inconveniences" of the state of nature, the possibilities of anarchic violence or enslavement. And all permanent residents share in the natural rights they retain within civil society, and in the rights granted by the laws that protect them. For the Lockean legislative "is bound to dispense justice, and decide the rights of the subject by promulgated standing laws" (II, 136)—not laws that grant rights to the landed and none to the laborer, but "laws, not to be varied in particular cases, . . . one rule for rich and poor, for the favourite at court, and the country man at plough" (II, 142). All permanent residents have a serious stake in having their rights to protection guaranteed.[24] For this reason, even "the meanest" free person (i.e., nonslave) can be a member of civil society, regardless of property qualification (II, 94).[25]

4.2. Majority Consent

The emphasis on personal consent that dominates Locke's discussion of political rights and obligation may initially suggest to contemporary readers that Locke is a proponent of direct political

[22] Dunn shows decisively that landowning is neither necessary nor sufficient for express consent in Locke, and rightly observes that even Macpherson at one point acknowledges that it is not sufficient ("Consent," 39–40). See also Ashcraft, *Locke's Two Treatises*, 169, 180–82.

[23] Tully, *Discourse on Property*, 154; Ashcraft, *Locke's Two Treatises*, 171–72; McNally, "Locke, Levellers and Liberty," 35.

[24] See Cohen, "Structure, Choice and Legitimacy," 319 (and Cohen's criticism of Macpherson, pp. 306–11).

[25] The language of II, 94 (referring to the "meanest" of subjects) recalls Locke's earlier claims in his 1667 *Essay* on toleration (ECT, 185).

democracy. Locke, however, has no special commitment to democratic government—he is committed to "government by consent" only in a special sense of that phrase (which is not, perhaps, any longer its central sense). Consent for Locke, as we have seen, is the source of a just government's power (authority) and its citizens' obligations. But it does not determine the *form* the government will take.[26] There can be democracies based in consent, for Locke, but there can also be oligarchies and monarchies (hereditary or elective) legitimated by consent (II, 132).[27] Consent is given to membership in the society; the majority then determines the form of government to be entrusted with the society's political power (and subsequent generations of members give *their* consent to that society-with-government). Particular acts or policies of government need not be justified by the particular consent (e.g., by direct participation) of the people on that occasion (their *general* consent to join the society being sufficient to justify subsequent lawful governmental activities)—with two apparent exceptions: the case in which the majority elects *not* to entrust their power to others but to govern themselves and "employ all that power in making laws for the community from time to time" (a "perfect democracy" [II, 123]); and the case of taxation under any form of government, which seems always to require a separate, special consent (II, 138–40). (I discuss this second exception below).

Now the "noble ideal" of government by personal consent may

---

[26] Parry, *John Locke*, 96; Grant, *Liberalism*, 299; Plamenatz, *Man and Society*, 1:231; Dunn, "Consent," 29–30; Cranston, *John Locke*, 211; Farr and Roberts, "John Locke on the Glorious Revolution," 395.

[27] See Kilcullen, "Locke on Political Obligation," 334. Ashcraft argues that Locke in fact intends to deny that there can be a legitimate monarchy (*Locke's Two Treatises*, 118–20, 153–58, 184–86). While conceding that the text is not clear on this point (p. 185), Ashcraft contends that Locke not only favored assemblies (which seems indisputable), but believed that only assemblies could be legitimate wielders of political power. I agree that Locke is extremely unclear on this point, but prefer the reading advanced in the text. As long as the monarchy in question is a *limited* one (with powers sharply defined by the terms of the trust), and not an *absolute* monarchy, none of the arguments cited by Ashcraft seems to tell against its possible legitimacy. Locke clearly believes that monarchy is best suited to poorer, simpler communities (II, 107, 110–11), and it is not clear why he would think it illegitimate in *those* societies. Perhaps his real view is that the standards for legitimacy change with the standard of living, so that monarchy is in fact illegitimate in wealthier communities (it being there inconsistent with the best advancement of public peace and security). Lemos has argued that simple democracy is the only form of government consistent with Locke's doctrines of consent and personal liberty (*Hobbes and Locke*, 114); but his concerns about the liberty of generations living after the state's formation are equally concerns no matter *what* kind of government is instituted (as tyrannous majorities in democracies show quite clearly).

91

seem considerably vitiated by Locke's movement to "majority consent" and even "representative consent"—as when Locke equates one's "own consent" with "the consent of the majority, giving it either by themselves or their representatives" (II, 140).[28] But to suppose this movement constitutes a retreat from personal consent is to misunderstand Locke's argument. Majority consent in a sense *is* the personal consent of each member (i.e., it has the moral weight of personal consent), for each member has personally authorized the majority to act *for* him by the consent he has given to be a member of the society. "Every individual" must personally consent before he is subject to political power (II, 95–96). But this personal consent to be a member just *is* consent to be determined by the majority (II, 96–99)—initially by majority rule in a "perfect democracy," and subsequently by whatever government (if any) the majority entrusts with its power.[29] Thus, while unanimity of personal consent is required to legitimate any society or government, this personal consent entails a right of the majority to rule (a right that may be entrusted ultimately to a single person, should the majority so desire). All members of political society have thus personally consented to majority (and, perhaps ultimately, even monarchical) rule, simply by personally consenting to join a political society.[30]

Unfortunately, Locke's argument that personal consent *must* amount to consent to majority rule is not a very good argument.[31] If his claim were (implausibly) the historical contention that all members of just political societies have consented explicitly to majority rule, he would at least have something that looked like a justification of majority rule (although we would no doubt then question his grasp of empirical reality). But Locke's argument rests rather on the

[28] See Gough's complaint about Locke's alleged retreat from personal consent (*Political Philosophy*, 68–69) and Riley's similar remarks (*Will and Political Legitimacy*, 94). See also Macpherson, *Possessive Individualism*, 253; Lessnoff, *Social Contract*, 65; Herzog, *Happy Slaves*, 185.

[29] Grant, *Liberalism*, 104–6, 116–17.

[30] Macpherson sees this justification for majority rule (*Possessive Individualism*, 254 [final paragraph]), but adds to it an alternative (and, as far as I can see, completely gratuitous) justification in terms of the special interests of the propertied (pp. 253–55). Dunn rejects the reading of Locke (on the justification for majority rule) that I defend here, because "if a *past* consent is adequate to ensure obligation, an absolute monarchy created by the consent of its members would have arbitrary power," and "it seems unlikely that Locke meant this" ("Consent," 44). Dunn's argument, however, seems to be a non sequitur, for (as we have seen in 2.3 and will see again in chapter 5) consent is not sufficient (on independent grounds) to create an obligation to an arbitrary power; but no similar doubts about the sufficiency of consent to create an obligation to majority rule can be raised.

[31] Gough, *Political Philosophy*, 61–63.

logical claim that personal consent to membership *must* be consent to majority rule—that (inexplicit) political consent can have no other content (although it can, of course, have *additional* content). Undoubtedly, part of Locke's aim here is to respond to Filmer's (quite reasonable) contention that no natural authority inheres in majorities (*Patriarcha*, II, 6), and so to avoid Filmer's conclusion that consent theory is impracticable (because of the anarchic consequences of having to seek *unanimous* consent) (*Patriarcha*, II, 5–6). Locke replies that majorities rule "by the law of nature and reason" (II, 96). What he means by this seems to be the following: Locke is not really arguing that majorities have natural authority (i.e., whether or not there has been consent in the first place to be in the body ruled by them). He is arguing rather that an *inexplicit* contract (the agreement to be a member of the body) should be understood as having certain logical consequences, and so a certain understood content. In the case of political consent, the understood content is majority rule.

Why does Locke believe this? He mentions two reasons. First, once incorporated, the people form one body; and if they are to continue as one body, "the body should move that way whither the greater force carries it, which is the consent of the majority." (II, 96). Second, a body needs *some* decision procedure. If each is left the freedom to personally consent to or dissent from any particular policy, each is left as free as "he was before in the state of nature," and the contract to make a body is pointless (II, 97). For unanimous consent on any particular policy "is next impossible to be had" (II, 98). So, barring express (explicit) agreement on "any number greater than the majority," the bare act of uniting into one political society *must* be understood to be an agreement to majority rule (II, 99).

We should note, first, that even if we believe a body must move where the greater force carries it (which seems, implausibly, to deny a majority's ability to control its passions when a minority proposal is enacted), the "greater force" in a body need not lie in the numerical majority. The phenomenon of intense minorities being a greater force in a society than apathetic majorities has been common for too long to excuse Locke from considering it.[32] But second, there are so many decision procedures (short of requiring unanimity) other than majority rule, that Locke's second reason is no reason at

---

[32] Kendall, *Majority-Rule*, 117. Tassi's defense of Locke's argument (as following the procedure of the "new science") makes no response at all to this critical defect ("Locke on Majority-Rule and the Legislative," 34). Similarly, Grant's defense of Locke's position defends it not against the objections I raise here, but only against some relatively simple misunderstandings (*Liberalism*, 115–19).

all (although most of these procedures are admittedly of more recent conception, so that Locke probably *should* be excused on this point). Only if majority rule were obviously fairer and more authoritative than lottery, weighted lottery, votes adjusted for intensity, plural votes for the qualified, and the like, would we be obliged to interpret a commitment to political membership as a commitment to majority rule. Finally, of course, a more recent worry about majority rule— the problem of tyranny by permanent majorities—is one that some of the alternative decision procedures just mentioned address, but which was never discussed by Locke.[33]

What, then, of consent by *representatives*? Again, the authority representatives possess in Locke derives from the initial personal consent given by each individual to join the body politic, although, of course, the selection of representatives requires a separate act of choice by the people. While Locke does not seem to insist that a legitimate government *must* have a representative assembly,[34] he clearly believes that "well-ordered commonwealths" will put the legislative power "into the hands of diverse persons who, duly assembled, have by themselves, jointly or with others, a power to make laws, which when they have done, being separated again, they are themselves subject to the laws they have made" (II, 143; see also II, 138, 142, 153, 159). And Locke clearly believes as well that this representative body should be chosen by means of free election "by the People" (II, 213), for the people have "reserved to themselves the choice of their representatives, as the fence to their properties" (II, 222).[35] But he has none of the familiar worries (e.g., Rousseau's) about representative government diminishing true freedom,[36] nor does he ever explicitly address the question of *who* should vote in the elections of representatives or how the elec-

---

[33] Kendall, *Majority-Rule*, 103; Dunn, "Consent," 44; Mace, *Locke, Hobbes, and the Federalist Papers*, 18; Shapiro, *Evolution of Rights*, 116; Arnhart, *Political Questions*, 238–39. But see my suggestions in 6.3 that Locke's silence on the problem of tyrannous majorities was not due to any simple failure to consider it.

[34] Although Locke does sometimes speak of a *right* to be represented (as in II, 158). This, I suspect, is meant by Locke to be only a *civil* right within an already representative commonwealth, not a *natural* right held by all persons. Grant's claim that "representation is *required as a matter of principle* in any legitimate government, or at least in any government that wishes to collect taxes" (*Liberalism*, 96; my emphasis) thus seems at least overstated. Even in the passage cited by Grant to support her claim, Locke explicitly says that majority consent to taxation may be given "*either* by themselves *or* their representatives" (II, 140; my emphases).

[35] Contrary to Plamenatz's claim in *Man and Society*, 1:231.

[36] As Shapiro observes, "there is no notion of the people participating in government as being intrinsically good or right, as there was to be for Rousseau" (*Evolution of Rights*, 117).

tions should be conducted (beyond his condemnation of various improprieties in II, 222)—issues still loudly reverberating in Locke's day from the Putney debates, where the Levellers' defense of manhood suffrage was hotly contested.[37]

It is often taken as clear that Locke's views on suffrage are intended to embrace the franchise criterion of the "forty-shilling freehold," or some alternative criterion that ties voting to the possession of taxable property.[38] But this is not at all clear. There is, in fact, considerable evidence of Locke's sympathy for manhood suffrage.[39] All I will say here on the subject is that Locke's texts provide no decisive evidence for either view. What Locke *says* is that the people should have "a fair and equal representative" (II, 158), meaning that representation of a district should be proportionate to its "wealth and inhabitants" (II, 157). Locke does stress that "no part of the people" has a right to be represented "but in proportion to the assistance which it affords to the public" (II, 158). But he clearly mentions two standards, including population along with wealth or taxes.[40] Further, Locke is talking here not about criteria for an *individual's* right to vote or be represented, but about the criteria for an *area's* right (the right of a "*part* of the people" [II, 158; my emphasis]). He is advocating electoral reform and the elimination of rotten boroughs, not any specific personal franchise requirement.

What is confusing, perhaps, is that Locke elsewhere argues that "everyone who enjoys his share of protection [afforded by the government] should pay out of his estate his proportion for the maintenance of it" (II, 140). But this individual condition for taxation is *not* said by Locke to be the condition for individual representation or franchise.[41] This may be inferred by some to be the case, but

[37] For an excellent discussion of the Levellers' true position at Putney and its relation to the later Whig platform, see Ashcraft, *Revolutionary Politics*, 145–80.

[38] As we have seen, Macpherson and his followers hold this view. See Wood, *Agrarian Capitalism*, 83–85; McNally, "Locke, Levellers and Liberty," 22–23, 32; Seliger, *Liberal Politics*, 285–87.

[39] As Ashcraft has shown (*Revolutionary Politics*, 164–65, 579, 583–84, and *Locke's Two Treatises*, 175–76, 193–94). Further persuasive evidence for this view is offered in Tully, *Discourse*, 173–74; Richards, Mulligan, and Graham, "'Property' and 'People,'" 39–40, 43–45; Hughes, "Locke on Taxation and Suffrage."

[40] Contrary to Macpherson's view, Locke not only also mentions population here, but never specifically mentions land (but only wealth generally) as the relevant criterion. See Ashcraft, *Locke's Two Treatises*, 176–78. Richards, Mulligan, and Graham correctly take Locke's deafening silence on the question of whether landowning is necessary for membership to be very significant ("'Property' and 'People,'" 50).

[41] Contrary to the claims of Macpherson and, e.g., Andrew, in *Shylock's Rights*, 113, and "Inalienable Right," 541 (although Andrew acknowledges that his reading of Locke ascribes to him a position he should not have held ["Inalienable Right," 542]).

Locke's stated conditions for representation are clearly collective, not individual. Further, even if this individual condition for taxation *were* meant to be the condition for individual voting rights, the poor and the landless *also* often have property (estate) that can be taxed (and often was taxed in Locke's England), pointing not to their exclusion from representation and voting rights, but to precisely the opposite.[42]

It may seem perfectly natural that if a property owner's representative is to consent for him to the taxation of his property, this representative ought to be chosen by him (and his fellow taxpayers) alone. This, however, raises the question of why Locke thought a special consent to taxation was necessary at all, or why only the people or their elected representatives could give it (II, 140). This was, of course, a familiar view based on longstanding practice (and claims similar to Locke's can be found in, e.g., Molina, Suarez, and Bodin). But did Locke have any compelling reasons for simply accepting this practice? Locke's repeated insistence that "the supreme power cannot take from any man any part of his property without his consent" (II, 138; also, e.g., 139–40, 142), suggests the following view: Locke separates the legislative's general right to make law from the right it has to tax property. The first right is granted by each person when he joins society and is subsequently entrusted to the government. But the second right (to tax) requires a separate consent to legitimate it, given by the people or its representatives.

Why should Locke think this? One explanation is that Locke sees a fundamental difference between regulating property and taking it away (by taxation) (II, 139). Only the first right (of regulation) is given to the legislative in joining the commonwealth (II, 120).[43] This line of argument can hardly suffice for Locke, however, since (as we have seen) the right of regulating property is given to society (and the legislative) only as part of the more general surrender of all those rights necessary for society to secure peace and well-being for its members (II, 99, 129). Since "governments cannot be supported without great charge" (II, 140), the right to fairly tax property must also be one of the "necessary" rights surrendered to society and government by *all* individuals on entering society (both by those

---

II, 140 is best read as an argument *for* proportionate taxation of the poor rather than as an argument *against* extending to them the franchise. See Hughes, "Locke on Taxation and Suffrage," 425–26.

[42] See Hughes, "Locke on Taxation and Suffrage," 426–27, 438–42.

[43] This is Tassi's defense of Locke in "Two Notions of Consent."

individuals who submit previously owned property to the government's jurisdiction, and by those propertyless persons who agree that any property they come to own will be subject to that jurisdiction).

But Locke seems to have thought that the right to tax a subject's property was somehow inconsistent with an affirmation of that subject's right to his property (a right Locke clearly wished to defend): "for what property have I in that which another may by right take when he pleases to himself?" (II, 140). This, too, seems confused, however. For if I can have genuine property when another has the right to regulate it (by, e.g., forbidding my sale of it to a nonmember of the commonwealth), I can have genuine property when another has the right to take a reasonable and necessary portion of it (to use in better securing it). It is not as if the right to tax granted to a limited government would be for Locke a right to arbitrary and unreasonable taking of my property ("whenever he pleases").[44] Security for my property is made consistent with the right of government to tax it precisely by the limits on the use of *all* rights entrusted to the government—that these rights may only be used to preserve property and advance the common good. Arbitrary taxation would clearly be *ultra vires*. It seems, then, that there is no sound philosophical reason (but only the obvious political and rhetorical ones) for Locke to insist on the need for a special consent to taxation, given by the majority or their representatives.[45]

The free society that constitutes Locke's model of a just polity, then, enjoys the actual, personal consent (express or tacit) of all of its members, although in practice this consent is normally authorizing actions twice removed from the individual—that is, the actions of the government are authorized by the majority, which has in turn been authorized by each individual to so act. All members of the society enjoy equal protection under standing laws as a right. Which members enjoy more specifically political rights—for example, to vote or hold office—is less clear. There are no good textual grounds for supposing either that Locke obviously intended these rights only to be held by those with "estate," or that he obviously intended them to be held by all members, regardless of property qualifications. But this much is clear: Locke was not plainly defending a class-

---

[44] A point well made by Franklin in "Bodin and Locke on Consent to Taxation," 90.

[45] As others have maintained for different reasons: e.g., Dunn, "Consent," 43–44; Plamenatz, *Man and Society,* 1:229–30.

state in which unlanded laborers were "effectively submitted to [the] jurisdiction" of those with property in land.[46] As much as it is an exaggeration to read Locke as a proponent of modern democratic government, it is an exaggeration to find in his work a defense of the modern class-state.

[46] Macpherson, *Possessive Individualism*, 251–52.

PART 3

THE LIMITS OF SOCIETY

The consent that grounds the political relationship and which makes civil society must be personal and limited to have the moral force utilized by (and to preserve the intuitive appeal of) Lockean consent theory. In part 2 we saw the basic structure of Locke's own theory of political consent and acknowledged that it requires revision in several areas. For instance, while we can allow that either express or tacit varieties of consent can be sufficient to ground political obligations, Locke's own employment of the express-tacit distinction is in certain important ways flawed. And we saw as well that the consent (of either variety) that makes one a member of a civil society *in itself* entails neither consent to any particular form of government (as Locke correctly observes) nor consent to the method of majority rule (contrary to Locke's claims). Only the individual context in which the consent is given, not its very nature as political consent, can determine such specific aspects of the content of political consent as these.

But while Lockean consent theory cannot specify a priori these specific aspects of the political transaction, Locke and Lockeans have defended a certain conception of the more general moral limits on this transaction—that is, a view of what could not be a part of the content of political consent (as we saw briefly in 2.3). We cannot, for instance, give binding consent to be another's slave, nor can we undertake obligations of subjection to absolute government. In part 3, I explore the nature of these alleged limits and the consequences of exceeding them. I turn first (in chapter 5) to the question of the source and extent of the limits, with special emphasis on the most familiar form taken by arguments purporting to establish such limits—that is, on claims that certain rights are in principle *inalienable*. Then (in chapter 6), I look at the moral consequences of societal or governmental transgressions of these limits, and at the resulting Lockean position on dissolution and resistance. Locke's own theory, as we will see, is in large measure a reasonably simple deduction from his views of nonconsensual relations (outlined above in part 1), political consent (part 2), and the limits on consent (chapter 5): resistance is justified as a defensive response to coercion, when those in authority exercise power beyond that legitimated by popular consent. And I will suggest that a great deal of what Locke has to say on this subject is precisely what a sound Lockean political philosophy *should* say.

INALIENABLE RIGHTS

5.1. The Property of Inalienability

That all persons possess certain natural (moral, human) rights that are inalienable is a thesis needing no real introduction. It is still used today, as it was in the great "rights manifestoes" of the eighteenth century, to proclaim the moral inviolability of persons in the face of oppressive government.[1] But it is also a thesis that has been as often questioned as it has been dramatically employed, even by those within the liberal camp who are broadly sympathetic to natural rights theories.[2] Far less often questioned has been John Locke's status as the philosophical father of the tradition in moral and political thought that centrally employs the thesis of inalienable rights. While Locke's direct influence on Jefferson and other American revolutionary writers has been denied in recent years,[3] he is still widely regarded as the clearest example of a political philosopher who presents a systematic defense of inalienable natural rights.[4] The posi-

[1] It is worth remembering, however, that appeals to inalienable rights are not only made in liberal defenses of reductions in government interference, as claims concerning the "right to life" made by conservative antiabortionists clearly demonstrate.

[2] Bentham, of course, was one liberal critic who lacked any such sympathy, regarding natural rights as "simple nonsense," and the addition of adjectives like "imprescriptible" or "inalienable" as merely placing "nonsense upon stilts" (*Anarchical Fallacies*, article 2). More recently, Nozick's strict antipaternalism has included a blanket rejection of inalienable rights (*Anarchy*, 58), in spite of his acceptance of many Lockean principles. See also the arguments against inalienability in VanDeVeer, "Are Human Rights Alienable?" and Stell, "Dueling and the Right to Life."

[3] See, for instance, Dunn, "Politics of Locke"; Wills, *Inventing America*, especially chapter 16; Kendall, "John Locke Revisited," 221–22; Mace, *Locke, Hobbes, and the Federalist Papers*, 9–10, 28–32, 120. But for a contrasting view, see White's argument that "Locke was a powerful influence" on Jefferson and Hamilton, in *Philosophy*, 94 (and *Philosophy, The Federalist*, chapters 1–3). See also Dworetz, *Unvarnished Doctrine*, 5–7; and Pangle, *Republicanism*.

[4] See, e.g., Den Hartogh, "Made by Contrivance," 216; Lessnoff, *Social Contract*, 60, 65; Melden, "Introduction," 3; Benn and Peters, *Social Principles*, 96–97; Stumpf, *Socrates to Sartre*, 273; Friedman, *Legal Theory*, 123–25, among many others. For examples of this view of Locke specifically in recent discussions of inalienability, see

tion that Locke is supposed to defend is that "the majority is to make decisions, but its competence is bounded on all sides by the 'inalienable' rights of individuals and minorities."[5] This reading of Locke has been challenged, of course, but only by regarding numerous prominent passages as mere aberrations, for instance, from a majoritarian position.[6]

One of my aims in this chapter will be to show that Locke's stance on the existence of inalienable rights is far less obvious than is commonly supposed. Indeed, what Locke actually wrote on the subject strongly suggests that he may *not* have had the idea of inalienable rights (in political contexts) clearly in mind at any point in his writings. We saw in chapter 3, of course, that Locke's individuals retain some of their natural rights in the political contract, which is the (sole) source of legitimate political society and government. But it seems clear, I argue below, that not all of these retained rights can be regarded by Locke as *in principle* inalienable; and it is not obvious, at least, that he thought of *any* of them in that way. In addition to clarifying Locke's views, however, I will try to sharpen our understanding of the idea of inalienability, distinguish it from related notions, and examine some currently popular arguments for and against the existence of inalienable rights. This will allow me to comment in closing on how likely it is that the thesis of inalienable rights is true (regardless of Locke's views on the subject) and on the impact that a conclusion on the question of inalienability should be taken to have on Lockean political philosophy.

Advocates of inalienable rights have, of course, normally been concerned with only certain kinds of rights. Legal rights, and institutional rights generally, have not been considered centrally in this context, for the simple reason that such rights can presumably be made alienable or inalienable simply by suitable alterations in institutional rules. Because it is precisely as a bar against institutional encroachments that the inalienability of rights has been af-

---

Stell, "Dueling and the Right to Life," 15–17; Schiller, "Are There Any Inalienable Rights?" 312; Feinberg, "Voluntary Euthanasia," 111; McConnell, "Nature and Basis of Inalienable Rights," 28; Meyers, "Rationale for Inalienable Rights," 139.

[5] Kendall, *Majority-Rule*, 65. Kendall, of course, opposes this understanding of Locke. For a classic statement of the view he opposes, see Sabine, *History of Political Theory*, 525.

[6] This is, of course, Kendall's position; he reads Locke as holding that all natural rights are in principle alienable. I comment below on one of the confusions that I believe leads him to his most peculiar interpretation of the text. I argued earlier (3.1) against the view of (e.g.) Macpherson, Strauss, and Cox that holds Locke's contract of government to involve the alienation of *all* natural rights (and which also thus obviously entails that all natural rights are for him in principle alienable).

firmed, the rights said to be inalienable have been moral rights or, even more commonly, "natural" or "human" rights.[7] Such rights are extrainstitutional, and it is commonly supposed (with Locke) that all persons equally are "born to" such natural rights, regardless of where or when they are born. At least some of the natural rights in question are commonly said to have the properties of being imprescriptible, indefeasible, or inalienable.[8] All of these terms, of course, tell us something about how the rights may be treated, either by the rightholders or by others; and it will be best, as a result, to begin by being more precise about their meanings.

I will start with the characteristic of inalienability. Perhaps because we associate declarations of inalienability with resisting oppression, many believe that an inalienable right is a right that "no man can take away."[9] A different view, held by many philosophers, is that an inalienable right is one that cannot be lost in any way.[10] In Hohfeldian terms, an inalienable right would then be one that incorporates both a disability and an immunity; the possessor of the right would not be able to dispose of it, voluntarily or involuntarily, nor would any other person, group, or institution be able to dispossess him of it. Neither of these interpretations of inalienability, however, is true to the seventeenth- and eighteenth-century employments of the concept;[11] and both distort the significance the concept had for revolutionary authors. More important, though, these interpretations blur philosophically useful distinctions among very different properties of rights, distinctions that are important as well to a proper understanding of Locke's moral and political philosophy.

As we saw in 2.2, Locke writes about three ways in which rights

[7] For a clear discussion of these kinds of rights, see Feinberg, *Social Philosophy*, chapter 6. Curiously, McConnell's discussion of inalienable rights seems to begin with the views of Locke, Jefferson, et al., suggesting that he is concerned (as they were) with the issue of the alienability of *natural* or *moral* rights. But the discussion ends with conclusions that seem relevant only to the properties of legal or institutional rights ("Nature and Basis of Inalienable Rights," 25–26, 53–56). McConnell gives (broadly utilitarian) reasons why "a society is justified in *designating* the right to life as inalienable" (p. 55; my emphasis), rather than reasons why a natural right to life *is* inalienable (regardless of who does or does not designate it so).

[8] See, respectively, the French Declaration of the Rights of Man and of Citizens, the Virginia Declaration of Rights, and the American Declaration of Independence for examples of these claims.

[9] Malone, *Story of the Declaration of Independence*, 88.

[10] See Brown, "Inalienable Rights," 192; VanDeVeer, "Are Human Rights Alienable?" 168; Schiller, "Are There Any Inalienable Rights?" 309; Meyers, *Inalienable Rights*, 2, 9.

[11] See Richards, "Inalienable Rights," especially 398; White, *Philosophy*, chapter 5; Tuck, *Natural Rights Theories*, chapter 7; Feinberg, "Voluntary Euthanasia," 112–13; Ellerman, "On the Labor Theory of Property," 318; Andrew, "Inalienable Right," 533.

can be lost: they can be (a) voluntarily given away or exchanged (*alienated*), (b) lost involuntarily through negligence or wrongdoing (*forfeited*), or (c) taken away by some other party (*prescribed*). Rights that cannot be lost in these ways may be called, respectively, *inalienable, nonforfeitable,* and *imprescriptible.* These Lockean senses of the terms, I believe, give us as well the proper ways to understand them in their later, eighteenth-century uses;[12] and the more precise notion of inalienability specified here (where "inalienable" means "cannot be voluntarily given away or exchanged") will allow us to sharpen considerably our discussion of the thesis of inalienable rights.

While confusion about inalienability has often been generated by a failure to keep carefully distinct the three ways in which rights can be lost,[13] just as often confusion has involved failing to distinguish the property of a right in virtue of which it can (or cannot) be lost, from the quite different property of being (or not being) overridable (which bears only on its *weight*). In a way this latter confusion is understandable, given the ambiguity of words like "indefeasible." On the one hand, "indefeasible" was almost certainly used as synonymous with "imprescriptible" by most eighteenth-century writers; an indefeasible right was simply one that could not be taken away from its owner by others.[14] On the other hand, "indefeasible" is sometimes used as a synonym for "absolute," that is, to identify a right that it is in all cases morally wrong to infringe. The difference, then, between the two notions of a defeasible right is the difference between a right that can be taken away and a right that can, on some particular occasion, be left unsatisfied in the interest of promoting some more morally weighty end (but which remains in the posses-

[12] This was, for instance, clearly how Bentham understood the French declaration's use of "imprescriptible rights," i.e., as rights that "cannot be abrogated by government" (*Anarchical Fallacies,* article 2). See the sources cited in note 11 above for defenses of this understanding of the eighteenth-century uses of "inalienable."

[13] For instance, Kendall's interpretation of Locke suffers from this failure. He concludes that Locke does not defend the inalienability of any natural rights from arguing that: (1) individual rights may be "withdrawn" by the community, and (2) individuals may lose their rights by failing to perform duties (*Majority-Rule,* 69). But not only is (1) false (on Locke's view of the *natural* rights retained in the contract), it concerns only the prescriptibility of rights. And (2) concerns only the forfeitability of rights. Neither point is logically related to any conclusion about inalienability. See the similar confusions in Mace, *Locke, Hobbes, and the Federalist Papers,* 24, 26; and Steiner, "Natural Right," 41n.

[14] Bentham, for instance, says that a right's being "imprescriptible, or, as we in England should say, indefeasible, means nothing unless it excludes the interference of the laws" (*Anarchical Fallacies,* article 2). See also Feinberg, "Voluntary Euthanasia," 113.

sion of its original owner, with all its previous importance). While many eighteenth-century revolutionary authors believed that rights were defeasible in the second sense,[15] few accepted the defeasibility of natural rights in the first sense.[16]

One other confusion we will need to avoid can be dealt with even more quickly. We must be careful to distinguish between rights that are genuinely alienated (even if the alienation is temporary or conditional) and rights that we merely waive in some circumstance or decline to exercise on some occasion.[17] In cases of genuine alienation (as we saw in 2.2), control over the exercise of the right changes hands, even if only for a certain time period or under certain conditions. Rights that we merely waive or decline to exercise in some particular case, by contrast, are rights over which we retain full control. Showing that a right has been waived on some occasion, then, will not suffice to show that the right is alienable in the sense that concerns us here.

In the discussion to follow the application of these distinctions will allow us to ask sharper and more interesting questions, both about

[15] Richards, "Inalienable Rights," 394–99.

[16] One well-known contemporary argument against the inalienability of many popularly acknowledged rights turns precisely on this confusion between conditions for loss of a right and those for legitimate overriding. Brown argued that for many of the traditional human rights, there are clearly circumstances in which we (or the state) would be "morally justified" in refusing to allow a person (or persons) to exercise his (their) rights. Brown concludes from this fact that it is "a mistake to suppose that each man has an inalienable right" in the area under consideration ("Inalienable Rights," 208–9). This argument rests squarely on the confusion of inalienability with absoluteness ("indefeasibility" in our second sense). That a right may be legitimately overriden in no way supports the claim that it may be alienated. Inalienable rights need not be absolute (indeed, there is good reason to believe that no moral right is absolute), nor must absolute rights be inalienable, as Frankena rightly suggests in his reply to Brown ("Natural and Inalienable Rights," 228–29. See also Richards' discussion of Brown's argument [and the similar ones offered by Ritchie and Carritt], in "Inalienable Rights," 392–93).

McConnell disagrees with the second conjunct above: "It seems clear that if a right is absolute, then it is inalienable. If a right may *never* justifiably be infringed, then *a fortiori* it may not be infringed simply because its possessor gives others permission to do so" ("Nature and Basis of Inalienable Rights," 29). This seems to me a non sequitur. If the absolute right *has* been alienated by its possessor's permission (a possibility that cannot be precluded without begging the question), then there is no longer any right to be infringed. This is perfectly consistent with the right's being uninfringeable *while it is still possessed*. The properties of inalienability and absoluteness (indefeasibility) seem to me to be logically unrelated.

[17] The term "waive" is, of course, sometimes used precisely to *mean* "alienate" (see, e.g., Ozar, "Rights," 8; Stell, "Dueling and the Right to Life," 14; McConnell, "Nature and Basis of Inalienable Rights," 25, 27). If we elect this terminology, however, we must simply invent some other term to cover cases of what I here call "waiving" rights.

Locke's theory and about the thesis of inalienable rights generally. But a number of points about inalienable rights (which have often been overlooked) follow so immediately from these distinctions that I will mention them here, as preliminary matters, before proceeding to my examination of Locke's position. First, it is now clear how familiar claims about inalienable rights in certain areas may in fact be compatible with other claims about legitimate government action in those areas. For instance, we have seen that ascribing to an individual an inalienable right does not preclude legitimate infringements of that right by government (say, for the purpose of preventing civil or military disaster). Nor does supposing that all persons possess an inalienable "right to life" conflict with claims that governments may legitimately execute criminals (who may have forfeited, rather than alienated, the right in question,[18]) or even with claims that governments may abrogate (i.e., "prescribe") the right in question.

It is also now easy to see why the claim that *all* natural rights are inalienable, sometimes made by proponents of inalienability (and suggested, for instance, by the wording of the French declaration), is not at all plausible. Nor is it plausible to read Locke as a defender of that view, as some have done.[19] If, as Locke and many others maintain, the right of self-government (that cluster of rights to freely formulate and pursue a life plan, within the bounds of moral law) is a natural or human right, then the inalienability of all natural or human rights would entail that promising (by which the rights we have to freedom of action are voluntarily redistributed) is impossible. And none of the serious defenders of inalienability have thought that the transfer of rights accomplished in promising was not possible. Locke certainly did not think this (as we saw in chapter 3), since his conception of legitimate government relied on the alienation of natural rights in a special contract. Similarly, Jefferson, and other prominent American revolutionary authors, never intended to claim that all of our natural rights were inalienable.[20] Accordingly,

---

[18] See Feinberg, "Voluntary Euthanasia," 112, for further discussion of this point.

[19] For instance, Hacker, *Political Theory*, 270.

[20] This provides a very simple answer to the question that worries Wills—why Jefferson omits the right to property from his list of rights in the Declaration of Independence (*Inventing America*, chapter 16). If Jefferson is mentioning only those natural rights that he regards as inalienable (for the revolutionary argument that flows from claims of inalienability, see below), there is no need to mention property. Both Jefferson and Locke regarded property rights (i.e., "estate") as alienable, so Jefferson's omission gives us no reason to suppose that he was not following Locke on this point. See White's discussion of this problem (*Philosophy*, 213–21). Of course, if

most contemporary advocates of inalienable rights have picked particular natural rights as their favorite candidates for inalienability: for example, the right to life, the right not to be tortured, the right to liberty (or to certain basic kinds of liberty). And the project has then been not to justify sweeping claims of inalienability, but rather to show that some human rights (of an extremely basic sort) are inalienable.

One final point (of largely historical interest) is clarified by the distinctions drawn above. With these distinctions in hand, we can understand more fully the revolutionary employment of the thesis of inalienable rights. As we have seen, what revolutionary authors had in mind was not that the "inalienable rights of man" were rights that no government could take away, but rather that they were rights that no citizen could be understood to have given away. The force of this claim can only be appreciated when we remember that the great rights manifestoes (and Locke's *Treatises*) were written under the influence of contractarian accounts of government authority. According to those accounts, of course, the rights a government (or ruler) has to act in political matters are simply the sum of those personal rights that citizens have transferred to it. So the details of a theory of the loss and exchange of rights were crucial for revolutionary political theory, and the claim that certain rights are inalienable was the main step in the moral justification of revolutionary action.[21] This appears even more clearly in light of the popularity of theories of implied, understood, or tacit consent. The issue of which rights a citizen has transferred to government by an act of consent becomes murky, indeed, when the consent in question is claimed to be tacit only. The champions of arbitrary government, of course, will claim that citizens have tacitly consented to absolute government authority, and consequently that citizens have retained none of the rights that might be "stood on" in resistance or revolution. But if some of our rights simply cannot be alienated, even if we desire to and try to alienate them, then any contract we might have made or consent we might be understood to have given divesting ourselves of these rights must be nonbinding. It no longer matters how past history is interpreted or what is implied by some crafty theory of

---

we think of property not as a set of specific rights in external goods, but rather as a *power* to make such specific rights (e.g., by our labor), the positions of Jefferson and Locke are not as clear as my remarks here suggest (see 5.2 below).

[21] See Nickel, *Making Sense of Human Rights*, 47. Aspects of the theory of rights-transfers other than those stressed below were, of course, also important to the justification of revolution. See 6.1 below.

tacit consent.[22] If certain of our rights are inalienable and our governments nonetheless act as if we lack these rights, the moral justification of resistance has its solid foundation. The thesis of inalienable rights, then, has its most important revolutionary implications when conjoined with the consent or contract account of political authority. And given that Locke defended both a consent theory and a "right of revolution," it is natural to suppose that he defended the thesis of inalienable rights as well.

5.2. Locke on Inalienability

Two of the clearer features of Locke's theory of rights are his views on forfeitability and prescriptibility. While he is never very specific about which rights are forfeited by commission of which crimes (i.e., violations of natural law), it is clear throughout the *Treatises* that all natural rights are forfeitable. As we saw in 2.1, Locke affirms that a person who performs an act that "deserves death" (or who initiates a state of war) is no longer under the "Law of Reason," and thus forfeits all the rights defined by this law: he is "stripped of all property" (II, 173). He has no rights and no persons have toward him duties of forbearance.[23]

We have already seen as well Locke's views on the prescriptibility of natural rights: "no power of man can limit, nor make any law of prescription against" our natural rights (I, 63); "the ties of natural obligations are not bounded by the positive limits of kingdoms and commonwealths" (II, 118).[24] Our natural rights are, for Locke, im-

---

[22] As a result, theorists using the idea of inalienable rights are able to avoid relying on a "principle of interpretive charity"—i.e., they need not argue (with, for instance, Grotius) that while all rights are in principle alienable, charity requires that we interpret actual contracts and consents as not involving the surrender of all rights. Charity seems too fragile a principle for revolutionary appeals to rest on. See Tuck's discussion of interpretive charity in *Natural Rights Theories*, 80, 143. I argue below (5.4) that a part of Locke's arguments about the limits on government power relies on such a notion of interpretive charity (although another part relies, as Tuck sees, on the quite different strategy I summarize in 6.2).

[23] For a much more detailed account of Locke's views on forfeiture and punishment, see my *Lockean Theory of Rights*, chapter 3.

[24] In I, 148, Locke comments on those who try to seize "the rights of fathers over their children, which paternal authority, if it be in them by right of nature . . . nobody can take from them without their own consents." See also II, 83, 135. Whether Locke believes that natural rights can be "limited" in the rather different sense of "overriden" or "justifiably infringed" is less clear. While the *Treatises* sometimes give the impression that Locke regards all rights as absolute (i.e., as final moral claims, or "trumps"), he does allow for the possibility of conflicts of rights (most prominently in II, 183). I discuss Locke's views on this topic below in Chapter 6 and in *Lockean Theory of Rights*, 93–94.

prescriptible. While this reading of Locke may seem to be muddied by noting his sometimes puzzling majoritarian remarks,[25] it would be hard to argue for any other view. Locke repeatedly stresses that nothing but a man's own consent can remove him from his natural condition, that is, limit his natural rights. And after leaving this natural state to enter civil society, the terms of the contract to which he consents in becoming a member must be scrupulously honored. This suggests that none of the natural rights a citizen retains in society could be annulled by the state (although the state could, of course, grant and withdraw institutional rights within the limits of its de jure authority). One would, in short, expect Locke to say (and with considerable plausibility) that a prescriptible right (one that can be annulled or expropriated even if the rightholder does no wrong) cannot be a natural or moral right.[26]

If Locke's reader is treated to some clarity on the questions of forfeitability and prescriptibility, that clarity surely dissolves on the question of the alienability of natural rights. Even discussed in general terms, Locke's position seems to tend in two directions at once. On the one hand, the idea of a strict moral limit on government authority is distinctively Lockean; and many of the best-known defenders of inalienable rights knew and were strongly influenced by Locke's work. On the other hand, I can find nowhere in Locke's writings any use of the term "inalienable" (or "unalienable").[27] Locke's early view, as we saw in 3.1, was precisely that *all* rights are alienable (and, indeed, that they must be alienated for sound government).[28] And while Locke clearly abandoned parts of this early

---

[25] Kendall, of course, builds his entire interpretation of Locke around these passages.

[26] Indeed, as we have seen, natural rights' imprescriptibility seems to necessarily follow for Locke from his account of property—natural rights being property and a constituent right of property being the right not to have it taken without the rightholder's consent. See Skinner, *Foundations of Modern Political Thought*, 1:xiv.

[27] A fact also noted by Kendall (*Majority-Rule*, 68) and Glenn ("Inalienable Rights," 80–82). Glenn believes that while Locke does in fact intend to defend inalienable rights, he deliberately refrains from using the term because its radical implications (the fact that inalienable rights "subvert" the authority of existing governments) would prejudice his acceptance of the Whig revolution and settlement (p. 102). This seems to me an implausible hypothesis, given, first, that the radical language elsewhere in the *Treatises* surely reveals clearly to his readers Locke's intentions (see 6.1 below), and, second, that the settlement was supposed to be one that *respected* the rights Glenn defends as inalienable (and so could hardly be subverted by appeal to them).

[28] See, e.g., First Tract, 124–26, and "On the Difference between Civil and Ecclesiastical Power," 109–10. We have seen as well that some (e.g., Kendall, Strauss, Macpherson, Cox) take Locke's mature position to also maintain the alienability of all rights. On this question, see Polin, "Rights of Man," 24–25.

view, his later antipaternalist sentiments still sit uncomfortably with a theory of inalienable rights, which seems to rest on a concern to protect persons from the consequences of their own voluntary choices. While we might all agree that many attempts to alienate fundamental human rights will, as a matter of fact, fail (being the result of voiding conditions such as duress or insanity), it is quite another matter to argue that these rights are (in principle) inalienable, and an even more difficult matter to argue in this way while staunchly defending our natural moral freedom to control the course our lives will take.

As far as I know, there is only one place in his writings where Locke talks clearly about what we might call an inalienable natural right; and that is in the passage quoted earlier: "a father cannot alien the power he has over his child; he may perhaps to some degrees forfeit it, but cannot transfer it" (I, 100). In fact, this passage does not capture Locke's fully stated views accurately. For Locke paternal (or as he occasionally insists, "parental") power consists of two parts: "the right of tuition" and "the right of honour." Only the second part of parental power is regarded by Locke as inalienable (II, 69) (and even on that point he hesitates [I, 65]). We may give over to another the right to care for and educate our child; but that child remains perpetually bound to honor and assist us as parents.

Now whatever else we may wish to say about this claim of an inalienable natural (parental) right, several points of rather general significance must be made. First, it is clear that the kind of position on inalienable rights that Locke takes here will not entail the kinds of broad claims of inalienability, and strict limits on government authority, which we associate with the Lockean tradition in political philosophy (the only political implication of an inalienable paternal right would appear to concern limits on the parents' ability to turn over to the state their right of honor from their child). More important, however, the argument by which Locke reaches this very limited claim of inalienability is a very bad argument for his purposes (and, indeed, in its own right). Essentially, Locke argues that paternal power over one's child cannot be transferred (alienated) because that power (right) is based on begetting the child; and that is something that only the natural parents have done. No one else, therefore, could satisfy the condition that grounds the right and so have it successfully transferred to him: no one can acquire from another any right "without doing that upon which that right is solely founded" (I, 74).[29] The problems with this argument are quite ap-

[29] Locke later repeats this argument, claiming that when a right is "consequent to,

parent. First, of course, the argument as stated could show only that the right in question cannot be *transferred* to another person; the right could still be *renounced* (voluntarily given up, but not to anyone else) by its possessor, and so would not be strictly inalienable.[30] Second (and considerably more important), if the right in question is tied necessarily to the act of begetting the child, it ought to be impossible not just for another to have it voluntarily transferred to him, but for him ever to hold the right at all. Unhappily, Locke is quite prepared to admit that others can acquire the right if it is forfeited by the parent (e.g., I, 100; II, 65),[31] and this immediately undercuts his argument for inalienability. Finally, we can also perform a rapid *reductio* of Locke's claims by noting the conclusion he seems committed to by following this style of argument for property rights (i.e., property rights in the narrow sense—rights to external objects). Remember that Locke is arguing here (I, 74, 100, etc.) about general limits on inheritance, and the possible objects of inheritance include not only parental power over children (according to Filmer), but also the parental estate (according to Locke). But original property rights are based on the purely personal act of laboring on some unowned object (II, 27), and this is something that only the laborer himself has done (i.e., taking the object "out of the common"). It ought, on the principles Locke espouses, to be impossible for such property rights ever to be alienated. But, of course, Locke is completely unwilling to accept any such conclusion concerning property, and is therefore committed to discarding his claims about the inalienability of parental or paternal rights to honor, as well. We can, I think, put Locke's difficulty here in more general (and more useful) terms: he has confusedly supposed that the conditions for the generation (or first possession) of a right must be mirrored in the conditions for legitimate transfer (and subsequent possessions) of that right. But

---

and built on, an act perfectly personal, . . . that power is so to, and impossible to be inherited [or alienated generally]" (I, 98). See also I, 85, 95–96, 98, 101–3.

[30] The argument also seems to make inalienable exactly those rights that we would expect *not* to be inalienable—i.e., the special rights that are based on personal acts. It is the general rights (e.g., to life, liberty, etc.) that we would expect (and want) to be inalienable. But they are not based on personal acts the possessor has performed; they are based rather on the rightholder's status as a rational being made by God. The argument considered here, then, could not show any of our general rights to be inalienable, and hence could not play the role in Locke's political philosophy that his alleged arguments for inalienability have been supposed to play. This argument serves only to make a point against Filmer.

[31] In II, 65 Locke seems to abandon his claim (made in the *First Treatise*) that parental rights are based merely in begetting the child.

there is no good reason to suppose that this is true, as the case of property rights clearly illustrates.

Put in this way, Locke's argument for inalienable parental rights has much in common with a widely used contemporary argument for inalienability. If we are asking whether any human rights are inalienable, the argument runs, the answer is obvious. Insofar as a human right is one that every person possesses simply in virtue of being human, a person would have to cease to be human in order to alienate (or otherwise lose) a human right. All human rights, then, are necessarily inalienable.[32] But this line of argument suffers from the most general weakness we saw in Locke's approach. The argument turns, of course, on how one understands the claim that every person has human rights simply because he or she is human. If we understand this to be the statement of a sufficient condition for the possession of all human rights, then the conclusion obviously follows (although the premises are implausible). If, however, this claim is taken to mean that every person is "born to" (or with) certain rights, simply because he or she is human, the conclusion is a non sequitur. Locke maintains that all persons are "born to" that collection of rights that constitutes their "natural freedom." They are born to these rights just because they are God's creation, and they receive this birthright at that time (if ever) when they achieve sufficient rational development to be able to competently care for and control themselves and to know the law of nature. Surely the rights of which Locke writes would be properly called "human rights"; yet he never claims, nor would it be sensible to claim, that none of these rights can be alienated. That would be to confuse the conditions for the loss of a right with the conditions for its initial possession. And it is on precisely this confusion that the argument for the inalienability of all human rights, considered above, seems to rest (as well, of course, as Locke's own argument for inalienability).[33]

To return to Locke, we can conclude that even if Locke believed

[32] This style of argument is employed, for example, in Mayo, "What Are Human Rights?" 68–69; Bayles, "Limits to a Right to Procreate," 42; Melden, "Introduction," 3; Lemos, "Concept of Natural Right," 140, and *Hobbes and Locke*, 105, 171–72; Machan, "Reconsideration," 68, and *Individuals and Their Rights*, 202.

[33] Another worry about the argument might be that it seems to preclude not only alienation of human rights, but forfeiture as well (meaning that a criminal retains all of the same human rights as one innocent of wrongdoing, and hence must presumably be respected in the same ways). But I will not pursue that worry here. There is, as we have seen, a sense in which those who forfeit rights in Locke do cease to be human—being no longer under the law of reason, they are (morally) no more than animals.

firmly in an inalienable natural right to honor (held by all parents), his grounds for this belief are shaky, at best; nor will that belief have the interesting political consequences that we tend to link with Lockean positions on inalienability. There are, of course, much better known Lockean views that are traditionally associated with the thesis of inalienable rights, and any serious discussion of Locke's stance on inalienability must surely treat these views as well. I have in mind here several areas of Locke's thought. First, we have seen (in 2.3) that Locke argues against both the possibility of voluntary enslavement and the possibility of absolute or unlimited political power (i.e., political enslavement). It is widely believed that the limit on our voluntary transactions that precludes these possibilities is for Locke a set of inalienable rights held naturally by each person.[34] Second, Locke's name has long been associated with an allegedly inalienable "right of revolution."[35] An inalienable right of revolution or "resistance of oppression" is mentioned in such "Lockean" documents as the Virginia and French declarations of rights, so we may be inclined to suppose that this is another inalienable right in which Locke believed. Third, Locke is often said to have believed that the right to property, at least when this is understood as the right to *make* property (rather than specific property rights in external goods), is an inalienable right.[36] Again, the affirmation of this right's inalienability in later documents (such as the French declaration) encourages this belief. Finally, there is the right to religious toleration (to which I devote section 5.4). Locke's writings on toleration were extraordinarily influential, and many writing in this Lockean spirit later argued explicitly for the inalienability of rights concerned with religious worship (I refer below, for instance, to James Madison's arguments). It is, as a result, perfectly

[34] See, for instance, Andrew, *Shylock's Rights*, 104: "Locke thought one's life and liberty are inalienable rights"; Grant, *Liberalism*, 73: "Locke argues that because the right to life is an inalienable natural right, no man can consent to be a slave"; and the similar views in McConnell, "Nature and Basis of Inalienable Rights," 45; and Polin, "Justice in Locke's Philosophy," 270.

[35] "The last-mentioned supreme power, which is the ultimate sanction in Locke's political system, is the famous right to 'appeal to Heaven', or in other words, the right of revolution. This is an inalienable right, which belongs to the people 'by a law antecedent and paramount to all positive laws of men'" (Gough, *Political Philosophy*, 43). Others who have found (differently described) inalienable rights in Locke's arguments for the right of resistance include Grant (*Liberalism*, 173–74, 179), Andrew (*Shylock's Rights*, 106), Glenn ("Inalienable Rights," 91–92), Dworetz (*Unvarnished Doctrine*, 30), Goldwin ("John Locke," 505), Pangle (*Republicanism*, 255), and Cox (*Locke on War and Peace*, 125, 166, 169).

[36] See Tully, *Discourse*, 113–14, 142; Parry, *John Locke*, 56; Glenn, "Inalienable Rights," 95; Rapaczynski, "Locke's Conception of Property," 306.

plausible to claim that toleration, for Locke as well, was morally guaranteed by a right that could not be alienated.[37]

Despite the weight of these opinions, however, I believe a strong case can be made that Locke was not in any of these instances thinking (or, at least, was not thinking clearly) in terms of (in principle) inalienable rights that citizens retain even in political society. The second alleged inalienable right, the right of revolution, can be quickly disposed of by a careful look at the text (to which I will return in chapter 6). There is no right to rebel, according to Locke, for a rebellion is (by definition) a morally impermissible use of force (II, 226). When a government acts ultra vires, the trust that gives government its power is forfeited, the government dissolves, and the people again possess those same rights (e.g., to preserve themselves and punish wrongdoers) that they possessed prior to their having empowered their government with those rights. The right people exercise in resisting tyrannical government is not an "inalienable right of revolution," or even an inalienable right to "judge for themselves,"[38] but rather only the (perfectly alienable) natural right to be free of (unauthorized) interference by others, which has been returned to them by the government's failure to respect the people's trust.[39] There is no right to resist legitimate governments (which respect the trust that gives them their power), and there is no reason, on Locke's account of the matter, to suppose that an inalienable right is involved where revolution is justified.

The first alleged inalienable right (that which limits our ability to enslave ourselves), however, is not so easily dismissed as having no role in Locke's theory. It is undeniable that Locke argues for limits

[37] As is maintained, for example, in Richards, *Toleration and the Constitution*, chapter 4; Andrew, *Shylock's Rights*, 104–5, and "Inalienable Right," 538; Ashcraft, *Revolutionary Politics*, 500.

[38] Grant, Andrew, and Glenn (see references above) seem to locate the inalienability in the fact that the people retain the right to judge when their trust is violated. But to take this fact as an indication that inalienable rights are involved is confused. The retention of the right to judge is a simple function of the fiduciary nature of the relationship between a people and their government (i.e., *all* trusts involve retention of the right to judge [see 3.2 above]). Notice that this right to judge, held by the people, was previously held by each individual in the state of nature, and alienated by individuals to the society. Far from being in principle inalienable, the people's right to judge has already been alienated once (by the individuals who make up the commonwealth). There is a constant danger we must try to avoid (discussed below) of confusing the fact that a right is retained by individuals or the people in Locke, with that right's being in principle inalienable.

[39] It is not always clear in Locke whether the rights the government forfeits by breach of trust return to individual citizens or to the community considered as a whole (which may then "reinvest" those rights). But in neither case would it be true that any inalienable rights were involved. I return to this issue in 6.3.

on government authority (and on the authority of slaveholders) by an appeal to the moral law. But whether these limits are set in Locke's view by the inalienable rights of citizens (or persons) is questionable.

Recall (from chapter 1) that the natural condition of all persons, for Locke, is "a state of perfect freedom to order their actions and dispose of their possessions and persons, as they think fit, within the bounds of the law of nature" (II, 4). Each person is at liberty to lead his life as he will, and has a right not to be interfered with in his pursuits, to that point at which his duties (under the law of nature) bind him to specific performances. Locke's most general characterization of the law of nature that "bounds" our rights is as a "law of preservation"; the "fundamental law of nature and government" is "that as much as may be, all the members of society are to be preserved" (II, 159). All of the restrictions of natural law are derived from this basic principle (and, consequently, all of the limits on our rights). Our primary duties are duties not to destroy life or to do what tends to its destruction, and we have a right not to be interfered with unless we are breaching a duty.

When we come to the alienation of rights, Locke operates on an eminently sensible rule: "Nobody can give more power [rights] than he has himself" (II, 23). We cannot alienate rights to destroy or endanger life, for we have no such rights.[40] Locke seems to be saying that we can only alienate rights that are not intimately connected with the preservation of ourselves or others. Thus, "no man or society [have] a power to deliver up their preservation, or consequently the means of it" (II, 149); we cannot alienate rights we do not possess.

If this account of Locke is correct, it should be obvious what Locke is saying in the passages that concern slavery and the "right to life." When Locke denies that we can enslave ourselves by voluntary compact, he is not affirming that we possess certain rights that are inalienable. We cannot enslave ourselves because we do not have the appropriate rights to transfer.[41] Even if we transferred *all* of our

[40] Ashcraft rightly notes that this view (that we have no right to dispose of our lives, and hence cannot transfer this right to others) was a frequent theme in the exclusion literature (*Revolutionary Politics*, 294n).

[41] McConnell sees that for Locke "people may not transfer their rights to life and liberty because in some sense these are not theirs to transfer," but nonetheless maintains that Locke holds each person to have inalienable rights to life and liberty ("Nature and Basis of Inalienable Rights," 45). Rights we lack can hardly be inalienable rights we possess. (On the sense in which we *do* have a right to life and liberty, see note 42 below.) McConnell may be thinking in terms of these rights being held in trust (pp. 45–46). But, as I argue below, this view also in no way entails that the rights at issue are held by individuals and are inalienable.

rights to another, we would not become slaves; to become our lords others would need rights over us that we do not ourselves possess. No claims of inalienability are required, and Locke quite clearly does not make any: "For a man, not having the power of his own life, cannot, by compact, or his own consent, enslave himself to any one, nor put himself under the absolute, arbitrary power of another to take away his life when he pleases. Nobody can give more power than he has himself, and he that cannot take away his own life cannot give another power over it" (II, 23).

The same point is made much later in II, 172, and several times between (e.g., II, 135, 149, 168). Our rights end where natural law imposes duties (so the "right to do as we will" is only a "right to do as we will if doing so neither destroys nor endangers ourself or another"). We therefore have no right to "arbitrary control" over our own life, which we could transfer to another in order to become his slave. This entails that we have no right to (and consequently, for Locke, a duty not to), for example, give away property we need to survive, or otherwise do what puts our life in jeopardy.[42]

If we recall one important aspect of Locke's view of our relationship with God, these conclusions will perhaps seem more natural. I have argued elsewhere that we should view Locke's conception of our rights over our own lives as involving a kind of trust from God.[43] God gives us our lives to use in certain ways, but fully retains his property in us in other areas. He entrusts to us, for instance, no rights to destroy or endanger our lives.[44] Within the terms of this trust, we may use our own discretion and are free to pursue our own private life plans. But God remains the final judge of when we have exceeded the terms of this trust and retains always the sole right to destroy life. (We have seen, in 3.2, how closely this rela-

[42] Andrew mistakenly ascribes to me the view that in Locke there is no right to life and liberty, since natural law prohibits the alienation of life and liberty ("Inalienable Right," 532–33). My actual claim is only that in Locke there is no right to destroy (or seriously endanger) life or liberty; other "parts" of the "right to life and liberty" *are* possessed (and *are* alienable). When Locke says (in II, 23) that man lacks "the power of his own life," he means that man lacks the *absolute* right to destroy his life, not that man has *no* rights over his life and liberty.

[43] *Lockean Theory of Rights,* especially 260–64.

[44] Our duty to preserve our own lives (like our duty not to take another's) must be understood to be only a duty not to endanger our lives arbitrarily or frivolously (this is the limit of the trust). We thus have a right to risk our lives in order to better preserve them (e.g., by seeking hazardous medical treatment in the face of serious disease, or by going to war in order to preserve our society), and we may have as well the right to sacrifice ourselves for noble causes (i.e., I may give my life "where some nobler use than its bare preservation calls for it" [II, 6]). The trust gives us the right to endanger or give up our lives for certain kinds of reasons, but not for others.

tionship mirrors that between a people and their government, for Locke.) Notice that on this model we do not possess inalienable rights over our lives. Within the terms of the trust, we may do as we please; our rights there are perfectly alienable, for we have a trustee's right to use discretion in the employment of entrusted rights, consistent with the point of the trust. Beyond the terms of the trust we simply have no rights (those having been retained by God).[45]

The position on voluntary enslavement that flows from this reading of Locke runs roughly as follows: we can give away all our rights, becoming "slaves" in this limited sense (i.e., "rightless"), but we cannot give another the right to kill us or endanger our lives, not having such a right ourselves. Our "master" cannot rightfully starve us, maim us, confine us (in certain ways), or deprive us of property (e.g., clothing) we need to live. In short, as Locke seems to allow, we can sell ourselves into "drudgery" (II, 24), but not into slavery in the strict sense (where another has the right to use us as he will or take our lives).

These same considerations would seem to apply to contracting ourselves into a state of political slavery, where our political superiors have absolute or arbitrary power over us. We lack the rights that it would be necessary for us to alienate (transfer to government) in order to enslave ourselves politically. But could we create for ourselves a state of political "drudgery," that is, a state in which all of the rights we do have are alienated? Contrary to familiar interpretations, there seems to be no clear indication in the *Treatises* that this is not possible, that there are inalienable rights that make such "drudgery" impossible.

Our remaining two candidates for inalienable rights in Locke (the right to make property and the right to toleration) seem initially to be better possibilities. They are at least rights that Locke clearly thinks we possess out of society and we retain in society (unlike the first two candidates we considered).[46] But many of the other rights

[45] Stell argues that this trust is inalienable, and hence that Locke is defending inalienable rights ("Dueling and the Right to Life," 16). But the inalienability of the trust (if that is a proper use of the term) follows for Locke simply from what a trust is—a personal granting of right (i.e., a granting for one person's use only, and so not transferrable to another). The entrusted *rights*, however, which are what is at issue here, need not for that reason be inalienable, provided that alienation is consistent with the point of the trust (as I suggest that it is, for Locke, in the case of rights whose exercise does not endanger life).

[46] It would be possible to argue as well in the case of rights to property and toleration, of course, that aspects of these rights are so intimately connected with our

that Locke thinks we possess in the state of nature and retain in civil society are clearly regarded by him as alienable. The mere fact that a right is retained in the contract that creates society does not show the right to be in principle inalienable. It shows only that transfer of that right is not necessary to the ends for which society is created. I have argued above (in chapter 3) that both specific property rights in external goods and the right of innocent delights are retained by citizens in the Lockean contract. But both are clearly *alienable* as well (as the phenomena of gifts and promises illustrate). Unless we can show more than that the right to make property and the right to toleration are natural rights that citizens retain in civil society, then we will not have advanced the case for Locke's use of the idea of inalienable rights in his arguments.[47]

According to all the indications given by Locke that we have thus far considered, however, all of the rights that we have are in principle alienable. The only limitations Locke ever suggests on the transfer of rights are those set by the law of nature, and he appears to believe that this merely amounts to restating the claim that we cannot transfer rights we do not possess. No transfer of a right we do possess could violate a law of nature. Within the bounds of the law, we enjoy "perfect freedom" to dispose of our possessions, rights included.

Similarly, the only limits on government power that Locke stresses (in chapter 11 of the *Second Treatise*) are entirely derived from the "law of preservation." Government cannot have the power to take our lives (unless we commit an appropriate crime), to deprive us of property at will, to rule by "arbitrary decrees," or to tax us without our consent, because all of these amount to arbitrary powers that might endanger our lives if exercised with malice. Each such transfer of power would be contrary to the natural law of preservation, "which stands as an eternal rule to all men, legislators as well as others" (II, 135). But natural law being also what limits our rights, it seems to follow for Locke that these limits on government power in no way imply that any of our rights cannot be alienated in a contract of government. Locke's limits on government power show only that we cannot transfer to government rights that we lack. This is

---

preservation that they are also rights we do not possess (and so could not transfer). While there is no indication in the relevant texts that Locke thinks precisely this, I consider below (5.4) parallel arguments Locke offers concerning the right to toleration.

[47] I consider the right to toleration in 5.4. below. I will say no more here about the right to make property, having already argued elsewhere for its alienability. See *Lockean Theory of Rights*, chapter 5, especially 231–33.

why Locke, in introducing his list of limits on legislative power, explains the reason for these limits as follows: because a person has only so much power "as the law of nature gave him for the preservation of himself and the rest of mankind, this is all he doth, or can give up to the commonwealth, and by it to the legislative power, so that the legislative can have no more than this" (II, 135). But it seems we can give the commonwealth all the rights we do have, for doing this violates no natural law, and within those bounds we are perfectly free. If this reading of Locke is accurate, it strongly suggests that he did not think of the moral limits on government as limits set by the citizens' inalienable rights; and in the absence of evidence from other aspects of Locke's arguments, it would seem to establish a strong prima facie case against regarding Locke, at any point in his writings (except for his position on paternal power), as a conscious defender of the thesis of inalienability.

5.3. Locke's Commitments

We have seen a distinct lack of evidence in Locke's words that he took himself to be defending a thesis of inalienable rights. Now, however, I would like to step back a bit from the texts and examine them from a different angle. Forgetting for the moment about what Locke says (or, rather, does not say) on the question of inalienable rights, we can ask instead what he *ought* to have said, given the overall position he is defending—that is, to what is Locke committed by his various claims concerning rights? In order to approach this question, we will have to begin by briefly discussing the kinds of rights that are operating in Locke's arguments.

There are, I believe, four kinds of rights (or "powers") that do work in the *Treatises*. There are first the simple moral "liberties" or "liberty rights" (see 1.3). More central in Locke's moral theory, however, are those rights that (unlike liberties) correlate with and are protected by the duties of others. One class of right in this latter category can be referred to (following Hohfeld's classification of legal rights) as moral "powers," a good example of which is the higher-order right to make specific property rights (just mentioned in 5.2). But the most basic class in this category is the "claim right." And within the claim rights, we can distinguish two types. The first type we can call "optional claim rights" (i.e., those rights whose exercise is protected by duties of noninterference on others, but whose exercise is optional for the rightholder), to distinguish them

119

from the second type—what we can call "mandatory claim rights" (i.e., those rights that we have to do our duties).[48]

These simple distinctions may seem sufficient to show that Locke is committed to many kinds of inalienable rights. For if the law of nature is an "eternal rule to all men" (II, 135), then the duties it defines are eternal, as well. And if so, the mandatory rights for the agent that these duties imply and the rights of others with which these duties correlate must also be eternal (hence, inalienable).[49] But while this argument strikes close to the mark, it still proceeds too fast. For whatever else Locke may mean by calling the laws of nature "eternal rules," he clearly does *not* mean that the rights and duties that the laws define (and which we have in our natural condition) are the same rights and duties we will always have (as we saw in 1.2). There is a very clear sense in which natural law is modifiable by consent. The duties that others have not to interfere with us in various ways (and hence the rights we hold against them) can be altered or removed by our promises, agreements, and so on; the boundaries of our "moral space" change shape as our consent carves out rights for others.

It is not clear to what extent our natural moral condition is modifiable by consent in Locke (or whether we can, for example, make another's lying to us or breaking his promises permissible by giving our consent).[50] The only limit to this process that Locke explicitly mentions is our inability to alienate rights intimately associated with our own preservation. And here, of course, we have simply returned to the impasse faced earlier. Locke appears to want to say that we cannot alienate rights intimately associated with preservation because we have no such rights. The limit to the process is set not by inalienable rights, but by our rights' limited extent.

Here, however, we can point to a confusion in Locke's argument

[48] For a full discussion of these kinds of rights and their roles in Locke's moral theory, see *Lockean Theory of Rights*, section 2.1.

[49] Tully's conclusion that Locke is defending inalienable rights is a good example of one drawn from this style of argument: "these rights are inalienable because they result from positive duties to preserve oneself and others" (*Discourse*, 114). Kendall also argues that in Locke "rights are inalienable only in the sense that duties are inalienable—thus, as any man knows who has failed at some time to perform a duty, not inalienable at all" (*Majority-Rule*, 69; see also pp. 79, 113). I have no idea *what* Kendall is up to in this passage, since mere failure to perform a duty obviously has nothing at all to do with alienating it. White is the clearest and most explicit of those who argue that the inalienable rights in Locke are the *mandatory* rights to do one's duty, as suggested by the argument in the text that I am currently considering (*Philosophy*, 211).

[50] Kendall suggests that *all* aspects of natural law are modifiable by consent, for Locke (*Majority-Rule*, 82, 85).

that may be responsible for his failure to recognize (or, at least, explicitly acknowledge) that he is committed to the existence of certain inalienable rights. In Locke's argument against the possibility of voluntary enslavement or political absolutism, the conclusion that he wishes to prove is that one person can never (except in cases of forfeiture) have a right to kill another at will. Locke could, of course, have tried to reach that conclusion by arguing that each person has a (claim) right to kill himself, but that this right is inalienable (so that no other could acquire the right to kill him). Such a line would, however, have run directly counter to the foundations of his moral philosophy, so Locke argued instead that we simply have no right to kill ourselves. He thus consistently (if not convincingly) maintained that no person can receive from another a claim right to kill him at will. But that is only half of the conclusion Locke wants (and uses in his other arguments). Locke also wants to affirm the different and stronger conclusion that it is never *permissible* to kill another at will (i.e., arbitrarily), that one cannot have a right (in the weaker "liberty" sense) to kill another at will, that each person always has a duty not to kill arbitrarily. That conclusion, however, does not follow at all from Locke's claim that I cannot give another a strong (claim) right to kill me. His having no claim right to kill me is entirely compatible with its being permissible for him to kill me. To establish the stronger part of his conclusion (that arbitrary killing is never permissible) Locke must argue that each person has a right not to be killed, and that this right cannot be alienated (renounced or transferred). This right not to be killed is the logical correlate of others' duty not to kill me, and must be "eternal" if that duty is to be eternal.

Let me put the point slightly differently. Transferring to another my right to kill myself would give him the right to kill me. Laying down my right not to be killed would make it permissible for another to kill me (i.e., give him a liberty right to do so). Locke must block both of these possibilities to complete his rejection of absolutism. But he tries to block both simply by denying that I have a right to kill myself, which quite clearly blocks only the first. Given that he is committed to an eternal natural duty not to (arbitrarily) kill another, he is obviously committed to an inalienable right not to be (arbitrarily) killed, as well (which is necessary to block the second possibility). Here, then, is an inalienable right to which Locke is committed. And he is presumably committed, as well, to further inalienable rights not to have those things done to one that "tend to" one's destruction. Finally, although less interestingly, Locke must also be committed to inalienable mandatory rights—that is, inalienable rights to do what is required by the "eternal" duties of natural law. It is not true, then, that the foundation of Locke's moral theory entails the absence of rights in areas intimately associated with our preservation. On this point Locke's words and his theoretical commitments seem to diverge. Locke's own rejection of absolutism could consistently proceed (although it does not in fact do so) precisely by appeal to the inalienability of rights in that area.

All of these conclusions have been dictated, thus far, only by observing what would be necessary to render Locke's various claims complete and consistent. But we have not yet asked whether Locke has any grounds from which to argue that there are inalienable rights—that is, given the moral foundations from which Locke is reasoning, can we show how he might argue from those foundations to a conclusion about inalienable rights? We have seen that according to Locke the fundamental law of nature is that mankind is to be preserved, and that all specific rights and duties are derivable from that more basic principle. The derivation of this specific content of natural law is best understood to proceed through a kind of rule consequentialism, with the preservation of mankind serving as the ultimate end to be advanced. The fundamental law specifies this end, and all other rules of natural law are members of that set of specific rules that best promotes the preservation of humankind. Our duty is to follow these rules, respecting the rights that they entail.[51]

Our question now becomes: Could such rule-consequentialist reasoning lead to the conclusion that some rights are inalienable?[52] The answer must be that if rule-consequentialist reasoning can detail which rights each of us possesses, there is no reason to suppose that it cannot similarly lead to conclusions about the properties (such as alienability) that these rights have. Some rights might be good ones for each of us to have (from the point of view of the purpose of preserving us, in accordance with God's will), without its being crucially important that these be exercised. Such rights would

[51] See *Lockean Theory of Rights,* section 1.4.

[52] I will not address here any more general questions about consequentialist stances on the inalienability of rights. Much of the literature in social choice theory treats inalienability as a property of rights that leaves unsatisfied opportunities for cooperation that all parties would have welcomed (and so as *inefficient* in this special sense). Some consequentialists have argued, however, that certain rights being inalienable would solve serious collective action problems (see, e.g., Hardin, "Utilitarian Logic of Liberalism"; see also Kuflik's reply to Hardin, in "Utilitarian Logic of Inalienable Rights").

then be alienable, and natural law would be modifiable in these areas by consent. Other rights (such as the right not to be killed) might be more intimately related to the effective preservation of persons, in that the failure to respect such rights would work directly against that end. This might constitute the start of an argument for inalienability of certain rights. Finally, the mere possession and observance of some rights (quite apart from questions of alienability), such as the right to kill oneself, could be regarded as directly contrary to the end of preservation. Persons would not possess such rights at all. These are, of course, hardly arguments; indeed, they are barely suggestions of how arguments might proceed. But, if at all plausible, they do point to a way in which Locke might be able, within the basic framework of his moral theory, to argue for the conclusions concerning rights to which his views in the *Treatises* commit him. The machinery for an internally consistent argument for inalienable natural rights does exist within the text.

Even more clearly, however, if we take seriously other strains in Locke's moral thinking, there will be available to Locke arguments for the existence of inalienable rights that seem (at least at first blush) quite straightforward and uncomplicated. If we must not use humanity (including, importantly, ourselves) as mere means (as Locke seems to suggest in II, 6), but must respect the personhood and dignity of each rational agent (including ourselves), then it seems plain why some rights must be inalienable. Certain rights seem so central to our personhood that to be without them is to be less than a person. Respecting our own personhood, then, would seem to require of us that we not surrender these rights under any circumstances (and to require of others that they not deprive us of them). And it seems but a short step from that acknowledgment to the conclusion that these rights are inalienable. Whether this is a good argument for the inalienability of rights, I discuss below. But this at least has seemed clear to many: it is an argument that is importantly similar to arguments advanced by Locke, not only in the *Treatises* but in his writings on toleration. It is in the latter context that I will examine the argument further.

5.4. Toleration

Locke's views on the right to religious toleration, of course, changed considerably during the course of his thinking and writing on the subject. They changed not only on the question of what one has a right to, but also on how one may lawfully respond to religious persecution (connecting Locke's changing views on toleration to his changing views on the right of resistance, the subject of chapter 6). Sometimes Locke seems to treat the right to religious toleration as a special kind of right, to be considered separately from his treatment of other, ordinary rights (there is, for instance, not even a passing reference to this right in the *Treatises*, where rights are far more central than in any of Locke's other writings[53]). At other times, however, the right to toleration seems to be treated by Locke as just one more particular case falling under his quite general arguments for political liberty. What seems clear, in any event, is that Locke's shifting views on toleration correspond precisely to his shifting views on the fundamental political question we considered above (in chapter 3): what are the ends of civil society and what is necessary to those ends? And because of this correspondence, a brief examination of Locke's views on toleration seems likely to cast some light as well on the alleged arguments for the inalienability of other rights that we have already considered in this chapter.

I earlier (in 3.1) commented briefly on the general character of Locke's views in his 1660 writings on toleration (in the *Two Tracts on Government*). A person, Locke claims there, is perfectly free "to dispose of his liberty and obey another" in all matters that do not "lie under the obligation" of God's law (First Tract, 124–25; Second Tract, 227). We may surrender or transfer to another our rights in all "indifferent" matters (those things neither commanded nor forbidden by God), and this includes indifferent *religious* matters (First Tract, 126)[54]—for instance, the details of religious "rites and ceremonies." Others (e.g., Bagshaw, against whom Locke was writing) argued that matters thus indifferent should be left to each person's conscience. Locke takes a different tack. Since the magistrate *must* have the power to legislate on indifferent matters in general, if anarchy is to be avoided,[55] he must have the power to decide for his subjects on indifferent religious matters in particular. This being necessary, citizens must be understood to surrender to the magistrate all of their liberty in indifferent matters (First Tract, 125); and

[53] In II, 209 Locke does mention that oppression that puts their religion in danger may motivate resistance by the people; but even there he is concerned only with the rights of the majority, not the rights of dissenters to toleration.

[54] Which are here *not* treated as special, or as interestingly different from other (nonreligious) indifferent matters. On Locke's notion of the "indifferent," see Yolton, *Locke*, 75–76; and Kraynak, "John Locke," 56–58.

[55] "Let the multitude be once persuaded that obedience to impositions in indifferent things is *sin* and it will not be long ere they find it their *duty* to pull down the imposer" (First Tract, 154).

they are obliged to obey even those laws "which it may be sinful for the magistrate to enact" (First Tract, 152). Even in 1660 Locke recognized, of course, that the force of a magistrate's laws cannot compel religious belief; but force *can* compel outward religious conformity (which is enough for the magistrate's purposes), and the right to do so is in any event a necessary part of the magistrate's quite general power over indifferent things (First Tract, 127–30).

By the time Locke wrote his drafts of "An Essay Concerning Toleration" (in 1667), however, his opinions on these matters had changed dramatically and had largely assumed the form they would ultimately take in his *Letters Concerning Toleration*. This shift in Locke's thinking is often (although not always[56]) attributed to his new association with Shaftesbury. But Locke did not centrally employ Shaftesbury's favorite arguments for toleration (which were economic in character[57]); he offered instead a primarily philosophical defense of the right to toleration, and one that turned on a small but enormously important modification in his previous treatment of indifferent things. Locke still holds in the 1667 *Essay* that "there will be no law nor government if you deny the magistrate's authority in indifferent things" (ECT, 179), but he no longer stresses our power and need to dispose of our liberty in *all* indifferent matters. Now Locke instead divides indifferent matters into those with which the magistrate ought to be concerned and those that are none of his proper business. Regardless of the source of the magistrate's legitimate power (whether it be divine right or popular consent), the sole purpose of this power (and so the limit of its rightful extent) is "the good, preservation and peace of men in that society over which he is set" (ECT, 174), in short, "their own preservation" (ECT, 175). This being so, "purely speculative opinions" and matters of "divine worship" are beyond the right of the magistrate to control (or "meddle" in), since "in themselves [they] concern not government and society at all" (ECT, 175). Religious worship being "only between God and myself," different manners of worship cannot "make me either the worse subject to my prince or worse neighbor to my

[56] On the circumstances surrounding Locke's composition of the 1667 *Essay*, see Cranston, "John Locke and the Case for Toleration," 102–3. Cranston elsewhere maintains that Locke's views had already changed before Shaftesbury's influence on him began (*John Locke*, 111).

[57] Shaftesbury argued that religious persecution both produces conflict and discord at home (which is bad for business) and drives away perfectly productive dissenters (which both deprives the nation of their industry and supplies it for competitor nations). See, e.g., the discussions of these arguments in Cranston, *John Locke*, 107; and Gough, *Political Philosophy*, 173–74.

fellow-subject" (ECT, 177). In these areas, "every man hath a perfect uncontrollable liberty which he may freely use without, or contrary to, the magistrate's command, without any guilt or sin at all" (ECT, 178). Speculative opinions and religious worship have, as a result, "an absolute and universal right to toleration" (ECT, 176), "a clear title to universal toleration" (ECT, 186). Those indifferent matters that *do* "concern society," "have a title also to toleration; but yet only so far as they do not tend to the disturbance of the state, or do not cause greater inconveniences than advantages to the community" (ECT, 178).[58]

Should the magistrate meddle in areas over which he has no authority, persons should follow their consciences "as far as without violence they can"; but they must passively submit to even unjust punishment for their disobedience, as they owe allegiance to both God and their king (ECT, 180–81). Locke's views on resistance have thus shifted from the *Tracts'* doctrine of absolute obedience to one permitting passive disobedience, just as they have shifted from the ruler's authority in all indifferent things to his authority only in those indifferent things that affect adversely the temporal well-being of society and its members. But one point on which Locke's views on toleration never changed was that certain classes of persons were not entitled to toleration of their opinions and practices: those persons whose religions (or opinions) include "doctrines absolutely destructive to the society wherein they live" (ECT, 183). Locke's "liberalism" did not extend to Roman Catholics[59] or to athe-

[58] Kraynak argues persuasively that Locke's shift from absolutism to toleration should be viewed as a change in his conception of the best strategy for securing civil peace. Religious conflict can be managed either by imposing religious uniformity or by requiring liberal toleration. Locke's preference for the latter strategy reflects in part his increasing skepticism about the possibility of widespread acceptance of uniformity and about the king's ability to refrain from imposing his own prejudices on the people ("John Locke," 53–60).

[59] Locke's worries about tolerating Catholicism dated from long before the Exclusion Crisis. (See Cranston, *John Locke*, 45, 129–30, and "John Locke and Government by Consent," 69–70; Mabbott, *John Locke*, 172; Gough, *Political Philosophy*, 176.) Catholics are said by Locke not to be entitled to toleration because: (a) they are intolerant themselves (ECT, 187–88)(although Locke never adequately explains *why* this should defeat their claim to toleration), and (b) "they owe a blind obedience to an infallible pope" (ECT, 188) and thus deny (in practice and in teaching) their essential duties to their lawful sovereigns. To tolerate them would be for the magistrate to "give way to the settling of a foreign jurisdiction in his own country" (L, 155). As Richards has pointed out, even in Locke's day these claims about Catholics were in many cases just empirically false, quite apart from questions about the (dubious) philosophical merits of Locke's stance (*Toleration and the Constitution*, 95–96). Compare Locke's claims with those sometimes made today about the allegiance of non-Israeli Jews to Israel.

ists.[60] Because both supposedly teach doctrines that undermine civil society, Locke was throughout his life opposed to toleration for either.

A Letter Concerning Toleration follows the main lines of argument Locke developed in the 1667 *Essay*, with some changes in emphasis and only a few changes in substance.[61] He continues to emphasize the sharp boundary between what is and what is not the proper business of government. Commonwealths being for "the procuring, preserving and advancing" of the civil interests of their members (where "civil interests" are "life, liberty, health, and indolency of body; and the possession of outward things"), political power ought to be "directed" at and "bounded" by "the temporal good and out-

---

[60] Since belief in God is "the foundation of all morality," atheists can be counted as practicing and teaching a view that makes persons "the most dangerous sorts of wild beasts, and so incapable of society" (although Locke gives no indication that atheists should be treated like *warmakers*, who are also compared to wild beasts). Thus, atheistic opinions are not to be considered "purely speculative" and hence entitled to absolute (or any) toleration (Gough's "Addenda" to the 1667 *Essay*, in *Political Philosophy*, 197). Atheism is forbidden in *The Fundamental Constitutions for the Government of Carolina*, articles 95, 101 (in the composition of which Locke played a significant part), all standing in the colony being made by that document (whose proposals were never in fact implemented) contingent on a belief in God. In the first *Letter*, atheists are not to be tolerated because "promises, covenants, and oaths, which are the bonds of human society, can have no hold upon an atheist" (L, 156). Atheists also "can have no pretense of religion whereupon to challenge the privilege of toleration" (ibid.), although this point seems a non sequitur, since having a religion is on Locke's own account neither necessary nor sufficient for a right to toleration. Locke's position on atheists (and Catholics) *should*, I think, be the same as his position on the "innocent pagans" of America (most of whom, remember, were polytheists at best), who must be tolerated because they are "strict observers of the rules of equity and the law of nature, and no ways offending against the laws of society" (L, 147; compare Locke's remarks on the great atheist nations, in E, 1.3.8). Since both atheists and Catholics are clearly capable of doing as well as pagans in these departments, and since there were many of both even in Locke's own day who neither (respectively) denied the existence of moral and social bonds nor believed they owed no allegiance to their king, the appropriate position for Locke (although not, of course, for us) is to deny toleration only to those who are in fact dangers to society, who express their opinions with the dangerous beliefs (instead of prejudging whole classes of persons). Thomas Jefferson, in his *Notes on the State of Virginia* (17:152), expressed views more suitable than Locke's own to the principles of Locke's *Letters*: "it does me no injury for my neighbor to say there are twenty gods, or no God. It neither picks my pocket nor breaks my leg" (compare with Locke: "no injury is thereby done to anyone, no prejudice to another man's goods" [L, 145]). See, however, Herzog's argument that unbelievers *can* do substantial harm without doing violence—e.g., by leading others out of the true church and so away from salvation (*Happy Slaves*, 163).

[61] I do not discuss here a manuscript on toleration produced by Locke and James Tyrrell (in 1681) between the 1667 *Essay* and the *Letter*. Its argument is very fully summarized elsewhere by Ashcraft (*Revolutionary Politics*, 490–98) and does not seem to depart in its principles from the position advanced by Locke in the *Letter*.

ward prosperity of the society" (L, 126, 153). But "the care of souls does not belong to the magistrate," and anyone who supposes it does "jumbles heaven and earth together" (L, 137, 135). The "end" of civil society and what is necessary to that end set for Locke the limits on the rights of government (as they do in the *Treatises*); and (again as in the *Treatises*) "the sole reason of men's entering into society, and the only thing they seek and aim at in it" is their temporal good (L, 153). The salvation of the soul is each individual's private concern and no part of the end of society (although, of course, society facilitates this process by overcoming the most pressing problems of this life). Locke thus continues to "grant that indifferent things . . . are subjected to the legislative power," but denies that this entails "that the magistrate may ordain whatsoever he pleases concerning anything that is indifferent." Rather, "the public good is the rule and measure of all lawmaking," and in those indifferent matters (such as the details of religious rites and ceremonies) that do not affect the public good, the magistrate has no authority (L, 142–43). What if the magistrate should exceed his authority? In that case, citizens are not "obliged by that law, against their consciences," and each should care first for "his own soul" (L, 153–54). Indeed, it would hardly be surprising if such oppressed citizens thought it just "to resist [the magistrate's] force with force, and to defend their natural rights (which are not forfeitable upon account of religion) with arms as well as they can" (L, 161).

The argument of the *Letter* seems to depart interestingly from the spirit of the 1667 *Essay* primarily in its willingness to consider violent resistance as a remedy to governmental intolerance.[62] In most other areas it simply reiterates (more completely and more elegantly, for the most part) the main elements of the earlier work. But in doing so it also preserves a certain tension that first appeared in the 1667 *Essay*. On the one hand, it is easy to read the *Letter* as (an unincorporated) part of the argument of Locke's *Treatises*. The right to toleration in religious worship is just one of those rights that all persons retain even under legitimate government.[63] It, like other protected liberties, falls outside the area of control that a government needs to exercise in order to fulfill its trust (and accomplish the aims of

[62] A willingness that was already displayed in the 1681 manuscript. See Ashcraft, *Revolutionary Politics*, 496.

[63] Ibid., 476. Mabbott claims that "this liberty of religion is only one particular case of the general right of every individual to be left alone in what concerns his own welfare" (*John Locke*, 177). See also, McClure, "Difference, Diversity, and the Limits of Toleration," 366, 369–70, 379, 381; Baldwin, "Toleration and the Right to Freedom," 36; Mendus, *Toleration and the Limits of Liberalism*, 25–27.

civil society). Since "care of the soul" is not a right that is "necessary to the ends for which [people] unite into society" (II, 99), it is not a right that can be understood to be surrendered in the consent by which persons enter civil society. But in this regard, the right to toleration is no different from other rights citizens retain. This reading of the *Letter* is strongly encouraged by the (antipaternalist) passages in which Locke compares the ground of the right to religious toleration with the ground for a person's liberty "in private domestic affairs, in the management of estates," and so on, where each must be left free to "follow what course he likes best" (L, 136).[64] "The care, therefore, of every man's soul belongs unto himself. But what if he neglect the care of his soul? I answer: What if he neglect the care of his health or of his estate, which things are nearlier related to the government of the magistrate than the other? . . . No man can be forced to be rich or healthful whether he will or no" (L, 137). And, of course, Locke's early view (in the *Tracts*) was also precisely that *religious* indifferent things were to be treated the same as nonreligious indifferent things—a view which, on this reading of the *Letter*, Locke could be said to have kept, changing only his views about what kinds of control by the magistrate are necessary to securing the public good (religious conformity now being seen *not* to be necessary to that end).

On the other hand, Locke also writes at other times as if religious worship belongs in a special class of essentially private matters, which must necessarily be left to the individual. The 1667 *Essay*, remember, carefully separates "purely speculative opinions and divine worship" from all other matters, treating them as a special class. And the fact that the right to toleration is not even mentioned in the *Treatises* might easily lead one to believe that that right is somehow beyond all possibility of political transfer and governmental control, in a way that none of our other rights can be said to be.[65] Indeed, Locke sometimes seems to want to separate altogether all matters of religious worship (including the details of rites and

[64] Note that toleration is here characterized as "leaving one alone" to pursue one's own course, *not* as encouraging or supporting that course. Locke is interested not in the state's positively promoting religious diversity, but only in the state's securing a right to noninterference with worship. See Mendus, *Toleration and the Limits of Liberalism*, 7, 36–37.

[65] Ashcraft, *Revolutionary Politics*, 495–500. Others have speculated that Locke's silence in the *Treatises* about religious toleration can be attributed to (a) his wanting to make a *Christian* case for toleration (Cranston, "John Locke and the Case for Toleration," 105), (b) his views on toleration not having been settled when he wrote the *Treatises* (Waldron, "Locke," 73), or (c) his having regarded toleration not as a natural right, but only as a political device (Windstrup, "Freedom and Authority," 253–57).

ceremonies) from the more general class of indifferent things.[66] If we are forced to worship in ways contrary to our sincere convictions, we cannot fulfill our fundamental duty of (sincerely) worshiping God. Religious toleration is thus essential in allowing us to do our duty (we have a "mandatory right" of toleration),[67] and is in this respect a right different from the others that citizens retain.

This second reading seems less persuasive if we note two points. First (as we saw in 5.3), religious toleration is not special in being necessary for doing our duty. All of our mandatory rights (not just those pertaining to worship) must be retained if we are to do our duty. Second, and more important, if the right to toleration is somehow altogether outside the sphere of politics (unlike our other, nonetheless also retained, rights), how can Locke steadfastly acknowledge that this right is limited by considerations of public good? If persons can be restrained from sincere practice and expression of their religious beliefs on the ground that they are a danger to civil society (as in the case of Catholics and others[68]), religious worship is not outside the sphere of politics. Religion just normally makes no contact with that sphere. But that, of course, is true as well of the other areas of liberty we retain in the Lockean contract. I believe that ultimately Locke never satisfactorily resolved this tension in his thoughts on toleration (i.e., the tension on the question of whether the right to toleration requires or permits a special defense *beyond* what is presented for liberties generally in the *Treatises*). And this fact causes serious difficulties for our task of exploring Locke's views on the inalienability of rights.

On the first reading of the *Letter*, the right of toleration is just one of the rights that citizens retain (because its transfer is not necessary to the ends of civil society). There will be good reason for regarding the right of toleration as inalienable only if all of the retained rights

[66] Locke says that "in religious worship nothing is indifferent," although he seems to mean only that because the worshiper does not regard his behavior as indifferent, his obligatory worship is affected (since Locke allows that the worshiper's acts are "in their own nature perfectly indifferent")("Addenda" to the 1667 *Essay*, in Gough, *Political Philosophy*, 197). I believe Locke is making the same point in the *Letter*, when he claims that indifferent things cannot be imposed on religious assemblies "because, in the worship of God, they wholly cease to be indifferent" (L, 144). Insofar as indifferent matters are not regarded by worshipers as indifferent ("every church is orthodox to itself" [L, 133]), forcing them to worship in ways contrary to their consciences is to require them to worship wrongly and insincerely, thus provoking God (and *that* is not an indifferent matter).

[67] Ashcraft, *Locke's Two Treatises*, 251.

[68] Religious intolerance is always acceptable to Locke when it is necessary as a means of preserving civil peace; the right to toleration is only a right not to be interfered with for *religious* ends (see Waldron, "Locke," 77).

are inalienable; and we have seen that while Locke may be logically committed to an inalienability thesis in the case of some of these other rights, he never seems clearly to say or otherwise directly indicate that he takes them to be inalienable. That rights are retained in a contract of government does not show that they cannot be alienated (for instance, in some nonpolitical context). Indeed, it is in some ways attractive to read Locke as never having changed his views on what rights *can* be alienated, but only on what rights *need* to be alienated for effective government. Locke could, it seems, hold in the *Treatises* and the *Letter* (as he did in the *Tracts*) that *all* of our rights are in principle alienable, but now (departing from the *Tracts*) maintain that only some of our rights are in fact alienated by citizens (because no more than this is necessary to civil society).[69] The retained rights, including the right to toleration, *could* be alienated (in some other kind of agreement or to some other kind of society).[70] There would be, on this reading of Locke, no inalienable rights.

But while this reading makes sense of much of what Locke says, it cannot (because of the unresolved tension noted above) make sense of all of his claims (nor, I think, can the second reading, for reasons already mentioned). Most important, the first reading cannot account for the centrality in Locke's writings on toleration of the thesis that *force cannot compel belief*: "to believe this or that to be true does not depend upon our will" (L, 150).[71] Over and over Locke

[69] We must be clear on the full nature and force of this claim. Locke is, I believe, concerned with how we should *understand* the inexplicit consent given by citizens to their societies (see chapter 7 below). Where the content of our consent is unclear (as it typically is), it should be taken to be what is rational in the context (see Den Hartogh, "Made by Contrivance," 204). In the political case, it is rational to surrender only those rights that are necessary to secure what civil society aims at; so this is what our consent is understood to be consent *to*. But if we explicitly consent to more (e.g., to the political "drudgery" discussed in 5.2), all that can be said is that this is not sensible, *not* that it is morally impossible (see 5.5 below).

[70] Locke's remarks in the *Second Treatise* on early patriarchal monarchies, for instance, seem to suggest that more rights were transferred to these monarchs than are transferred later to the governments of wealthier, more advanced societies (see Grant, *Liberalism*, 86–87). With regard specifically to *religious* rights, Locke's language in the *Letter* often suggests that some of the rights pertaining to worship can be at least conditionally alienated—to churches. We are said to "consent to observe some order," to "authorize" and give "the right of making its laws" to some persons in the church (L, 129–30). The church takes collective care of "what is lawful for every man in particular to take care of" (L, 142).

[71] This claim is made frequently in the *Letter*, as it is in the 1667 *Essay* (for instance, in the long argument that force cannot convert dissenters [ECT, 190–93]). Even in the First Tract, Locke explicitly notes this point, arguing that God has reserved the "disposure" of man's "understanding and assent" to himself, "and not so much as entrusted man with a liberty at pleasure to believe or reject" (First Tract, 127). For an assessment (in Locke's own terms) of these kinds of claims, see Passmore, "Locke and the Ethics of Belief."

gives this as the reason why the jurisdiction of the magistrate does not include the care of our souls. "For no man can, if he would, conform his faith to the dictates of another" (L, 127).[72] It is this fact that is supposed to explain why religious matters are a special case and why the right to toleration is "absolute."[73] But the first reading of the *Letter*, sketched above, makes no contact at all with such arguments. What, then, is the force of this new argument and how should its prominence in the texts alter the interpretation offered in the first reading?

We should note first that Locke's employment of this argument seems a bit shaky on the distinction between religious *belief* (and the inner worship of God) and religious *practice* (i.e., the outward activities of worship). The two are clearly intended by Locke to be connected somehow, but Locke is very far from clear on just *how* he thinks of this connection.[74] Locke argues that we cannot believe at another's command and gives this as the reason why others cannot have authority in the care of our souls. But, of course, no magistrate (in Locke's experience, at least) ever claimed the right to control religious belief—indeed, it is unclear what claiming such a right could mean, if belief is not even under each person's own control (as Locke insists).[75] Magistrates *have* claimed, by contrast, the right to demand

[72] Locke's basic argument seems to be that coercion works on the will, but that belief is not subject to the will. Legal coercion is thus not capable of producing sincere religious belief (which is what is necessary for salvation), making religious toleration the only rational policy for government to adopt. See Waldron, "Locke," 66–67.

[73] Compare the case in Locke thus far presented with James Madison's 1785 defense of his contention that the right of every man to exercise his religion is "an unalienable right." Madison offers two reasons for the inalienability claim (*Memorial and Remonstrance Against Religious Assessments*, 300): (a)"because the opinions of men . . . cannot follow the dictates of other men," and (b) "because what is here a right towards men, is a duty towards the creator." Argument (a) is the one we are presently considering; argument (b) is one (I claimed in 5.3) to which Locke is committed. But whether Locke, like Madison, regards (a) as an argument for inalienability remains to be seen (and I have already suggested that Locke nowhere explicitly employs [b] for any purpose).

[74] Conscience is obviously meant to have a public dimension, related to the rites and ceremonies of institutionalized religion (see Andrew, *Shylock's Rights*, 104). *Public* worship, for instance, seems to be required in *The Fundamental Constitutions*, articles 95, 100 (although Locke seems not to have had in mind requiring any very complicated professions of faith). But Locke never offers any *philosophical* grounds (in his writings on toleration), beyond those considered below—i.e., for a belief in an essential connection between inner and outer worship (see Richards, *Toleration and the Constitution*, 97–98).

[75] The claim could mean, I suppose, that the magistrate has the right to brainwash his subjects or to perform innovative neurosurgery on them and thereby control their religious beliefs. More reasonably, it could be taken to mean that the magistrate has the right to require things (e.g., religious practice) or ban things (e.g., books) that

outward conformity. But outward conformity *can* be given by each (however unwillingly) at another's command (as Locke correctly argued in the First Tract). What, then, has become of the argument? Is it only an argument that the magistrate cannot have the (very strange) right to compel *belief* (which is far short of the conclusion Locke draws in the *Letter*)?

The argument can, of course, be extended in the ways suggested above (ways Locke at least seems to have had in mind). If sincere worship involves the belief that one is worshiping properly (in the way that will please God or is required by God), and proper worship is believed (however falsely) by the dissenter to involve a certain outward performance, then compulsory conformity makes sincere worship impossible for the dissenter (even if the details of his favorite ceremonies are in fact indifferent). So the dissenter could not surrender the right to free religious practice without making impossible fulfillment of the duty to sincerely worship God. Two points need to be made about this "extension" of the argument. First, the "extension" seems to render the original argument largely irrelevant. The problem is not now that belief cannot be commanded by another (no one is "commanding belief" by demanding conformity); rather, the problem is that a *certain* belief (that one is worshiping properly) cannot be achieved in the presence of certain obstacles (required outward conformity).[76] But, second, this first point reveals the critical weakness of the extended argument. It is simply false that one cannot worship sincerely when outward public conformity is required. All the members of the established church, of course, can worship sincerely in such circumstances, as can any dissenters who believe that a particular public outward performance is *not* essential to sincere worship. Locke may believe that proper worship has an essential public dimension; but dissenters need not (and in some cases even in his own day, did not) agree with him. Anyone who believes that private worship is adequate and possible can worship sincerely within a regime of required public conformity. And anyone who believes that the details of outward performance are a *genuinely indifferent* matter (as Locke himself at least often seems to

---

can influence belief. But this latter possibility seems to be precisely the one Locke has forgotten in his main argument. See Waldron, "Locke," 81–83; and Herzog, *Happy Slaves*, 163.

[76] I suppose it might be said that in thus blocking the dissenter's belief that he is worshiping properly, the magistrate is commanding him to believe that he is worshiping improperly. This, however, would both seem a very odd way of expressing the point and be a counterexample to Locke's own insistence that it is impossible to compel belief in another.

maintain), that sincere worship requires only certain inner convictions and mental acts, can worship sincerely even in public (while performing outward acts that for him have no religious or moral significance at all). Any individual falling in any of these categories *can* surrender his rights to free religious practice, without failing in his duties to God (suggesting that these rights cannot be, at least for the reasons Locke gives here, *in principle* inalienable). That these individuals should not *have* to surrender their rights, even if they can do so, is a conclusion to be reached not by this argument, but by the argument of the *Treatises* (and of our *first* reading of the *Letter*). The point is not meant to turn on how many people did or did not fall into the categories noted above. The point is only that the Lockean argument considered here is too weak to establish his desired conclusion—a *strict* limit on the magistrate's powers that absolutely precludes his having the right to decide for anyone else on matters of religious worship. The argument offered in our first reading of the *Letter* seems better suited to yield this conclusion. Perhaps the best way to read Locke, then, is as relying principally on the argument of the *Treatises* to establish the limits that protect freedom of religion, with the argument just considered as a secondary reason why (most) dissenters cannot be legitimately coerced in religious matters.

We have seen, however, that there is no compelling reason to take the argument of the *Treatises* as involving an appeal to inalienable rights. And even if the "secondary" argument were more successful (i.e., of more general application) it would still not be clear that Locke intended *it* as an argument for an inalienable right (of toleration) either. For the argument Locke uses to *reinforce* the "secondary" argument has a form we have seen before (in discussing Locke's views on slavery contracts): no man can give another more power than he has himself. And *that* argument, remember, was not an argument for inalienability, but only an argument that the magistrate could not get certain rights over us because we lack them ourselves (all of his rights necessarily coming from us). Locke can thus maintain (as he does consistently in his writings on toleration) that the magistrate's powers are strictly limited, *without* defending any inalienable rights as the source of this limit.

Locke employs this style of argument (for the limiting to purely civil matters of the magistrate's rights) both in the 1667 *Essay* and (although less directly) in the *Letter*. In the former, he argues that "no man can give another man power (and it would be to no purpose if God should) over that over which he has no power himself";

and since it is "evident" that "a man cannot command his own understanding," he cannot give another the right to decide for him in religious matters (ECT, 176). This argument uses the claim that force cannot compel belief as a *premise* in an argument that claims that we have *no* power in a certain area (not that we have an inalienable power). In the *Letter*, Locke says that power to care for souls cannot "be vested in the magistrate by the consent of the people. . . . For no man can, if he would, conform his faith to the dictates of another" (L, 127). There is here (again) the appearance of an equivocation on the word "power," which sometimes seems to mean "right" and sometimes "ability." It is the fact of our *inability* to control our beliefs and understanding that Locke seems to be using here to deny that the magistrate can acquire a *right* over us (we cannot believe on command, therefore we cannot give another the right to command our beliefs). But what Locke seems almost certainly *not* to be trying to say here is that we have certain rights over ourselves that are inalienable. We simply have no power (ability *or* right) over our religious *beliefs*.[77]

I do not pretend that Locke's stance on an inalienable right of toleration is especially clear. On the contrary, I am not at all sure that Locke knew exactly *what* he thought on this question. All I care to claim here is that there is no *obvious* use by Locke of the idea of inalienable rights in his writings on toleration. Now Locke *does* seem to have thought that certain *things* are "inalienable"—some things cannot be given away, such as our lives and liberty, our understanding or belief, and so on. These things cannot be given to another (although some of them may be forfeited) either because such a transfer is unintelligible or because the things are not ours to give in the first place (belonging instead to God). The belief that some things are inalienable can be traced at least as far back as Grotius, who wrote that "inalienable things are things which belong so essentially to one man that they could not belong to another, as a man's life, body, freedom, honour."[78] But Grotius recognized, as did Locke after him, that this is *not* to say that we must have a complete

---

[77] Notice that Locke at one point says of our understanding (as he says of our lives, in the *Second Treatise*) that God has reserved control (and right) over it for himself (First Tract, 127). White discusses the parallel arguments of Hutcheson and Jefferson that the "right of private judgment" is inalienable because we cannot believe on command. He concludes that they *should* have said that there is no such right, not that there is a right that is inalienable. And he concludes as well that Locke *would* have said this, as I have argued (*Philosophy*, 198–200, 210).

[78] Grotius, *Inleidinghe tot de Hollansche Rechts-gheleertheydt*, II, i, 42.

right over that thing that is inalienable.[79] On the contrary, a thing's being inalienable (in this sense) does not entail the existence of an inalienable right over the thing, or even a right over the thing at all. If, for instance, my life is inalienable and I have it (as I have suggested Locke believes) only in trust from God, it does not follow from my life's inalienability that I have an "inalienable right to life." Rather, Locke seems to have thought, we have alienable rights within the limits of the trust, and *no* rights over our lives (to dispose of or endanger them) beyond the limits of the trust.[80] If I have *no* rights in a certain area, I can hardly have *inalienable* rights in it (however inalienable the thing in question may be).[81]

Before leaving Locke's views on toleration, one last argument of his should be mentioned, both because it is closely connected to claims about inalienable things (and so could be used by Locke to extend those claims), and because arguments like it have seemed to many contemporary authors to be plausible arguments for inalienability. In the 1667 *Essay*, Locke writes that liberty of opinion is that "wherein lies the dignity of a man, which could it be imposed on, would make him but little different from a beast" (ECT, 189). This appears to be a claim that certain freedoms or rights (in particular, liberty of conscience) are essential to or constitutive of humanity and human dignity. To surrender these rights would be to degrade that dignity, to cease to be fully human. This would be wrong (or impossible) to voluntarily bring about, the argument might conclude, and so these rights are inalienable. While Locke says little of this, what he does say looks like at least an important premise in such an argument, and some have attributed this (or a similar) argument to him.[82] The argument is also, of course, closely related to the Kantian argument for inalienability, mentioned at the close of 5.3. On the question of whether it is a *good* argument, I say more below.

[79] See Tuck, *Natural Rights Theories*, 70–71, for fuller quotation of the relevant passages.

[80] It may be true that if a thing is inalienable and we have complete rights over the thing, then at least some of those rights are inalienable. But this is not Locke's view, for he denies that we have complete rights over inalienable things. Rothbard, by contrast, has recently argued for what appears to be precisely this view (*Ethics of Liberty*, 134–35).

[81] Andrew falls into serious confusion on this point. He begins with the perfectly unobjectionable claim that for Locke "life and liberty are inalienable precisely because they are not our own to alienate," but he ends by claiming that "Locke thought one's life and liberty are inalienable *rights* precisely because they are not owned by the individual" (*Shylock's Rights*, 93, 104; my emphasis). Nothing in the pages between justifies this transition from inalienable *things* to inalienable *rights,* nor does Andrew ever distinguish those aspects of our lives over which we do and do not have rights.

[82] For instance, Grant, *Liberalism*, 71; Richards, *Toleration and the Constitution*, 99.

5.5. *Inalienability and Absolutism*

Before asking whether any of the arguments we have examined thus far is a good argument for inalienability, we will need to examine one last line of reasoning on the subject, one that is again a line that an eager interpreter might try (unsuccessfully, in my view) to attribute to Locke. It is, in a way, the simplest argument for inalienability and has been one of the most popular historically. There are, the argument begins (and as we will see in some detail in chapter 8), certain "defeating conditions" that will void promises or contracts (thereby keeping the rights at issue from being transferred). Such conditions include duress, unfair bargaining position, fraudulent misrepresentation, and insanity. Some kinds of contracts, however, are *necessarily* defeated, that is, necessarily involve one of these defeating conditions—specifically, any attempt to alienate (transfer) certain kinds of rights is necessarily and profoundly irrational, bringing into play the defeating condition of insanity (or some related notion). Hence, certain kinds of rights (those whose surrender would be an utterly irrational act) are in principle inalienable. This style of argument for inalienability has been used by Hobbes,[83] Rousseau,[84] and many others, including a number of authors whose work may have directly influenced Locke.[85] And hints of this kind of argument may seem to be present within the *Second Treatise*. It might, then, be taken to be an alternative (and possibly more interesting) Lockean route to inalienable rights.

Locke's most direct references to the irrationality of certain kinds of contracts occur, of course, in his discussions of the limits on legislative power. There he says, for instance, that allowing the Legislative arbitrary power to take the citizens' property would be an agreement that involved "too gross an absurdity for any man to own" (II, 138); persons would have to be "void of reason, and brutish" to enter into such agreements (II, 163). As a rule, Locke's

---

[83] Hobbes writes: "of the voluntary acts of every man the object is some good to himself. And therefore there be some rights which no man can be understood by any words or other signs to have abandoned or transferred" (*Leviathan,* chapter14, paragraph 8). The idea seems to be that attempts to transfer certain rights are a conclusive sign of nonvoluntariness or insanity.

[84] Rousseau argues against political absolutism in this way, in *The Social Contract,* I, iv.

[85] For instance, several of the Levellers. See Tuck's discussion of "the radical theory" (in *Natural Rights Theories,* chapter 7).

claims tend to be slightly weaker than this: for instance, "a rational creature cannot be supposed when free to put himself into subjection to another, for his own harm" (II, 164; similar points are made in II, 93, 131, 137). It is natural to suppose that in these passages Locke is arguing that some political contracts are irrational, and that for that reason one who attempts to enter by contract into a society with a more extensive government (than the limited government for which Locke argues) will fail. Such an attempted contract would be void by reason of irrationality (the extra rights that one attempted to transfer being in principle inalienable, since all attempted transfers would be thus irrational).

Whether this should be taken to be the argument Locke intended to use seems to depend on how we understand the "irrationality" that is involved in efforts to exceed the Lockean limits on authority. The only plausible reading, I think, is this: the irrationality of attempting to contract into a more extensive government consists in such an attempt's being clearly contrary to the agent's best interests. This is plainly the sense of *all* of the passages cited above. Locke is not arguing even for a position so complicated as to claim that the threat of God's sanction is what makes such attempts contrary to the agent's best interests. He is trying only to make the exceedingly simple, straightforward claim that, from the point of view of our temporal interests, arbitrary government is worse than any alternative arrangement (no government at all included). Contracting into a society that is governed arbitrarily is irrational in this simplest of senses: "no rational creature can be supposed to change his condition with an intention to be worse" (II, 131).

But two points need to be noticed here. First, Locke's language makes it clear that he is talking about how we should *understand* the content of an inexplicit consensual act: no person "can be supposed" to have intended to consent to make himself worse off. (As we have seen, how we should interpret the content of vague consent is a major theme in the *Second Treatise*.) In the absence of explicit indications otherwise, we must assume that vague consent is given only to rational terms (i.e., those that advance the consenter's interests). It is not rational to alienate more rights than those required by limited government, when this limited alienation is sufficient to achieve the ends of civil society (what persons aim at in making the contract). "Interpretive charity," then, requires that we suppose all inexplicit consent is given only to limited government. But this is not at all an argument that any contract that makes us worse off (or even badly off) is for that reason void, or that the rights whose transfer is attempted in such a contract are inalienable. An explicit, informed contract with bad consequences for one party might be perfectly valid (if hardly to be recommended). We may not endanger our survival by contracts we make, but that is because we lack the rights to do so. "Political drudgery," however, remains a moral possibility, if not an option that it is sensible to pursue.

Second, it seems clearly false that only those rights that can be transferred without worsening one's position are alienable. When I sell my house too cheaply, surely the "irrationality" of this action does not void the contract, nor would we want to say that my property rights in my house are thus inalienable. Among other things, there is no right the transfer of which necessarily makes one better off or worse off. Which transfers will do this depends entirely on the context in which the transfer occurs[86] (e.g., giving another the right to punch me may bring forth from him only grateful benevolence). Locke could not, then, show in this way that particular rights are inalienable; rights would change status from alienable to inalienable as circumstances changed. But it is not, I think, Locke's intention to argue in this way for inalienable rights. He intends only to make the quite harmless point that if we are sensible, we will not create or support more than a limited government (i.e., we will not create political drudgery), more limitation of our liberty than our purposes in creating or joining a civil society require—and that for that reason we cannot justifiably interpret tacit or vague agreements to be ones that allow more than limited government. Given that we all have a natural desire to preserve ourselves as well as possible, it is simply stupid to accept such arrangements. The argument that we cannot create absolute or arbitrary government (that it is necessarily illegitimate) is the argument we examined in 5.2: we cannot transfer to government the rights that would make it absolute over us, lacking those rights ourselves. The argument from irrationality concerns not so much the moral illegitimacy of certain forms of government, as what an intelligent agent will freely pursue, and can thus be supposed to have consented to. Locke does not, then, intend this argument to be an argument for inalienable rights. Locke intends to show that not only does God's law prohibit *absolute* government, but a rational concern for one's own well-being rules out *any* government more extensive than the one he recommends.

[86] Meyers, *Inalienable Rights,* 12.

139

We have now seen four arguments for the inalienability of some natural rights that might with limited plausibility be attributed to Locke (although I argued that in none of these cases is there adequate evidence to support a confident attribution, and that in all four there is actually better evidence for denying it):

(1) Insofar as we have certain "eternal," unchangeable moral duties (such as the duty not to arbitrarily take life), we have (mandatory) rights to perform these duties and others have correlative claim rights, both of which are inalienable. (Locke, I have suggested, is logically committed to this argument, but there is no evidence of his awareness of that fact).

(2) Some rights are such that, as a rule, their possession advances the preservation of humankind, but their surrender works contrary to that end. These rights are as a result inalienable.

(3) Some rights we cannot surrender without becoming less than fully human or degrading human dignity; these rights are as a result inalienable.

(4) Some rights it would always be profoundly (prudentially) irrational to transfer or renounce; these rights are as a result inalienable.

Supposing that I am correct in my speculation that Locke did not intend any of these arguments to establish the inalienability of (any of) our natural rights, we may ask, in closing, whether he *ought* to have attempted so to employ them. Are any of these popular arguments for inalienability good ones? I suggest the following brief responses to these arguments:

(1) The problems faced by the first argument for inalienability seem clear, for it is not really a free-standing argument at all. It relies on our belief that our eternal duties entail eternal mandatory and correlative rights. But, in the first place, our duties do *not* entail (mandatory) rights to perform them, as Locke assumes.[87] Far more important, however, is the fact that correlative rights are only eternal if the duties that entail them are eternal. Locke has merely *asserted* that our duties are eternal, when this is precisely the point at

---

[87] See the discussions of this claim in *Lockean Theory of Rights*, 74–75, 182.

issue; and even the meaning of his own assertion is unclear, since (as we have seen) he allows consent to modify our rights and duties in *some* areas. We could, of course, simply accept the assertion that God has made our duties in some areas eternal, perhaps on the basis of scriptural evidence. Most of us, however, will at least want to try to understand *why* God should have privileged some duties in this way, but not others. That concern, of course, points directly to the need for *other* arguments for the inalienability of certain rights (and the duties with which they correlate).

(2) The second (rule-consequentialist) argument for inalienability, however, seems unlikely to succeed either. For first, there are good grounds for doubt (well-documented in recent literature[88]) about *any* form of rule-consequentialist theory. Why the favored end (in Locke's case, the preservation of humankind) should be advanced indirectly, by following rules, rather than directly, in an act-by-act fashion, is a question such theories have never (in my view) adequately answered.[89] Second, the calculations required to establish the binding rules in such theories would be so monstrously complex that it is hard to be certain of anything, let alone of a point so subtle as the inalienability of some right. Finally, since whether the alienability of certain rights would have bad consequences within a community seems likely to turn very much on the nature of the community, the tenor of the times, and the number of people who will actually try to alienate the rights, it is hard to believe that rule-consequentialist arguments could in any event produce a defense of those rights as *in principle* inalienable.[90]

[88] See the works cited in my *Moral Principles and Political Obligations,* 52.

[89] Recent developments in utilitarian theory that emphasize the utility of cultivating in oneself certain dispositions to follow rules, merely raise questions about (1) the psychological possibility of assuming such a "schizophrenic" stance (can one maintain utilitarian commitments while being disposed to act on nonmaximizing rules?), and (2) the theoretical issue of whether such a position continues to count as consequentialist (in light of its advocating mechanically noncalculating behavior).

[90] This style of argument may also have an impact on some nonconsequentialist defenses of inalienability. Meyers, for instance, argues (in *Inalienable Rights*) that moral agents and normal children (p. 140) have certain inalienable rights because adequate moral systems "must sustain moral agency" (p. 115). Inalienable rights are those whose surrender would be "antithetical to moral relations" (p. 185), whose surrender would destroy, usurp, or undermine moral agency (pp. 54–68). But if (as Meyers herself recognizes [p., 12]) the consequences of alienation *may* be anything at all (including "business as usual"), it is hard to see how she can defend the view that certain rights *must* be inalienable because of the effect alienation would have on moral relations and agency. That a right "protects something essential to moral agency" (p. 54) does not seem to entail that the right's alienation endangers moral agency (except in the trivial sense of removing rights), without additional empirical assumptions about the likely consequent behavior of others. But then the rights in

(3) The third (Kantian) argument for inalienability strikes me as by far the most promising. Again, however, there are serious grounds for concern. Kant's own position on these matters is in some respects ambiguous,[91] so let us consider instead the very general Kantian style of argument mentioned above: some rights are essential to one's humanity or dignity; their alienation would involve a person's being used as a mere means, degrading the person or reducing him to something less than a person. Since doing these things is always wrong, the rights in question are inalienable.[92] What is hard to understand about such arguments is not the claim that alienation of some rights *can* be (or even, is normally) a way of degrading or using oneself (which seems perfectly correct), but rather that, for any particular right(s), alienating it (them) *must* be a way of degrading or (objectionably) using oneself. Since one may agree to be, say, killed, tortured, or enslaved for good and noble reasons, it is hard to believe that such agreements *must* be, by the very nature of the act, degrading, or that they would necessarily involve treating ourselves as mere means.[93] I may certainly without difficulty regard myself as a free and rational (indeed, praiseworthy) person, even while making such agreements; so it seems it cannot be said, for instance, that in doing so I treat a person (myself) as a mere object. If the idea is instead that the condition to which one would be reduced by loss of the right(s) in question is a degraded or subhuman (i.e., subperson) condition, the claim seems more plausible. Those who lack rights in an area lack the capacity to make *claims* in that area, and this capacity is importantly related to how we think of and why we respect persons. But in the case of a fully voluntary, well-informed surrender of a right for good or heroic reasons, surely the fact that one's condition was thus chosen bears importantly on whether one continues to be worthy of respect once the

---

question will not be necessarily inalienable. At times Meyers seems to want to claim that some rights are necessary for moral agency in a stronger sense than my remarks above suggest; but unless this sense is the (Kantian) one discussed below, I am not sure what it is intended to be.

[91] See Stell, "Dueling and the Right to Life," 20–22.

[92] Meyers argues that sacrificing the object of an inalienable right "degrades the rightholder" and involves "renouncing the basis of the rightholder's dignity"; so promises involving the transfer of such rights cannot be binding (*Inalienable Rights*, 75).

[93] I confess to uncertainty as to exactly what is required to treat *ourselves* as ends. Treating another as an end involves valuing that person and his ends, taking his ends to set both negative and positive demands on our actions. If treating ourselves as ends requires only that we do the same for ourselves, it seems clear that we can do so even while surrendering very basic rights (e.g., for a cause to which we are deeply committed).

right is no longer possessed. One thus deprived of the right could not make claims in that area, but whether this will impair the capacities to act freely, pursue value, or interact productively with other moral agents seems to be a purely *contingent* matter (depending as it does on the behavior of others—i.e., on whether they choose to take advantage of one's rightlessness). This makes the alienability of the right seem a contingent matter as well. If the response is that it is always wrong or degrading to reduce oneself in this way to moral dependence on the good will of others (regardless of one's reasons for doing so), or that no satisfactory moral system could allow such a status even to one who uses his standing as rightholder to *create* such a status for himself, I contend that it has not yet been shown (within the parameters of the theory) *why* this must be the case.

(4) Related points can be made about the fourth argument for inalienability, which appeals to the necessary irrationality of certain right-transfers. Surely it would be very difficult to think of any right whose transfer was *necessarily* a sign of profound irrationality, insanity, or loss of control (lack of voluntariness). None of the favorite candidates in the contemporary or classical literature can qualify in this way. Take, as above, the rights not to be killed, not to be tortured, or not to be a slave. We can surely, for each of these rights, imagine cases in which laying down the right was not only not a sign of insanity, but was eminently rational (in the sense of producing clear benefits for the agent).[94] Facing a painful and incurable disease, or brutal torture with inevitable death, can laying down my right in order to allow another to kill me (if, say, I am unable to dispose of myself) really be said to be "contrary to reason"? Similarly, if I may submit myself to painful medical treatment by placing myself entirely in my doctor's hands (and may thus transfer certain rights without charges of insanity being made, even where others regard the treatment as of dubious value), how can it be maintained that I may not rationally give another the right to torture me (in order to build my character or demonstrate my great courage)? And where, because of my own practical and emotional shortcomings, my life promises only continuous economic hardship and a despair born of lack of direction, but I have found a kind and generous potential master, can it be seriously argued that voluntary enslavement is *clearly* irrational? (Consider here cases of lifelong military or religious commitments.) It is tempting to claim that such examples must

---

[94] VanDeVeer, "Are Human Rights Alienable?" 171.

involve coercive or unfair bargaining, so that the resulting agreement will be morally unconscionable (see 8.3). But all that it is really necessary to imagine is sufficiently unorthodox tastes, which should not be lightly taken as a sign of insanity. To this point there has been no adequate demonstration, for any particular right, that an attempt to alienate that right could not be a sane, uncoerced act. This establishes a strong presumption against inalienability, for in the absence of such a demonstration it cannot be shown that such attempted alienations are *necessarily* irrational or less than fully voluntary (so that the attempted transfer or renunciation of the right is void).

Any conclusion about the inalienability of natural rights, drawn from a discussion like that offered in this chapter, must of course be strictly provisional. Without deeper exploration of the foundations of other moral theories, no conclusion on this subject can be advanced with real confidence. But suppose for a moment that I am correct in suggesting that the proper position for a coherent Lockean political philosophy to embrace is a denial that any of our natural rights is in principle inalienable. Will such a conclusion prove disastrous for the Lockean project in political philosophy or force political philosophers to quite "unLockean" positions? I maintain that it will not.

Lockeans have, as we have seen, used arguments from the inalienability of rights primarily to assert the impossibility of morally legitimate slavery and absolute political power. Locke himself asserts this moral impossibility not by appealing to inalienability, but rather by claiming that we lack the rights over ourselves that would be necessary to create such institutions by alienation. Contemporary secular Lockeans may wish to reject both styles of argument, contending both that no right is in principle inalienable and that persons do (at least in some circumstances) have rights to destroy or seriously endanger themselves. What, after such a purge, can remain of the Lockean case against institutionalized slavery and political absolutism?

Lockeans can, I believe, still mount a powerful argument against these institutions. First, of course, they can still reject these institutions wherever they are imposed by force and wherever they impose hereditary subjection (as is typically the case). The Lockean arguments questioned above concern only the voluntary, consensual establishment of slavery or absolute government by one generation of persons. Locke and Lockeans have many other persuasive arguments showing the illegitimacy of nonconsensual, hereditary despotism. Second, however, even voluntary establishment can still be opposed by claiming (with Locke) that the creation of these institutions is profoundly imprudent, that persons advance their interests far more effectively by pursuing free interaction and limited government. Finally, and most important, Lockeans need not claim that any rights are *in principle* inalienable in order to argue that attempted alienations of certain rights will *routinely* fail. My rejections above of the Lockean arguments for inalienability maintained only that there are no rights whose voluntary transfer is *necessarily* a sign of insanity, *necessarily* degrading, *necessarily* suboptimal, and the like. This is perfectly consistent with maintaining as well that attempted alienations will often fail for one or more of these reasons. Indeed, my case against inalienability relied on the possibility of highly individual circumstances in which alienation seemed morally possible.

Any defense of voluntary institutions of slavery or absolute government, however, must rely on the claim that large numbers of persons have *all* alienated very basic rights. But an entire *people's* finding themselves in the circumstances that permit the rational alienation of basic rights seems unlikely to occur in any but the most unhappy or bizarre variations on the human condition. An admission that in such circumstances (but only then) consensual absolute government is morally possible would not amount to a very interesting weakening of the Lockean position. Indeed, it seems perfectly reasonable to claim (and odd to deny) that if circumstances in a society are horrible enough, *any* political arrangements on which people voluntarily settle may turn out to be morally legitimate. The Lockean can still argue, without affirming either the inalienability of rights or the nonpossession of rights to destroy or endanger ourselves, that legitimate, consensual absolute government and institutionalized slavery are under all *normal* conditions morally impossible.

Chapter 5 has concerned the nature and extent of the Lockean limits on political consent, and hence the moral limits on societal and governmental power. In chapter 6 we turn to a closely related problem: when should society or government be understood to have *exceeded* the limits of their legitimate power, and what are the moral consequences of such transgressions? In what respects and to what extent is Lockean political philosophy committed to a revolutionary stance? Once we have clear answers to this set of questions, we will have before us the final components of the basic structure of Lockean consent theory and all of the essential elements of the Lockean conception of the political relationship.

S I X

DISSOLUTION AND RESISTANCE

6.1. The Revolutionary Stance

It has been said that "the *Two Treatises* is a work principally designed to assert a right of resistance to unjust authority, a right, in the last resort, of revolution."[1] While such a claim may perhaps not give Locke's other ambitions in the *Treatises* their due, it is impossible to deny that the *Second Treatise* is, in several clear senses, a revolutionary work. First, of course, Locke's own practical and rhetorical purposes in composing the work were directly connected to the encouragement and justification of active, armed resistance to an established government. Second, the influence of the work on later revolutionary authors was substantial. And third, the philosophical structure of the work is specially and deliberately developed to leave theoretical space for (and, indeed, to entail) moral limits on the political relationship and consequent moral rights of resistance to tyrannical government. It is primarily on the last of these senses in which Locke's theory is revolutionary that I will concentrate in this chapter.

Our more general purpose here, of course, is to try to understand the Lockean response to a slightly broader question: what are the moral consequences of societal or governmental transgressions of the moral limits on political consent, political power, and political society? I will suggest in this chapter that a proper reading of Locke's text reveals that he defends in many instances the most plausible positions for a Lockean theorist to take on this question. But I should note here as well the limits of the question, as Locke addresses it. Locke is primarily concerned in presenting his theory of political resistance (in chapters 18 and 19 of the *Second Treatise*) with the case of resistance within a flawed, but consensually established polity. His concentration on trust and dissolution makes no

[1] Dunn, *Locke*, 28.

147

sense in any other context (since both presuppose a prior consent by subjects). We must look to other parts of Locke's work for his views on justified resistance within other sorts of (not strictly "political") communities. It will not be until chapter 8 that we deal with the question of "political" resistance within merely de facto, illegitimate states (i.e., those that have not been licensed by popular consent).

One might reasonably expect a discussion of Locke's views on political resistance to begin with a bit of biography and history, telling the story of Locke's own revolution. But on the question of Locke's personal involvement in the revolutionary activities of his day, I can add little to what has been so carefully documented by others in recent years. I will thus not here try the reader's patience with what would inevitably be unoriginal commentary. A few simple facts will have to do to set the stage for the philosophical explorations to follow.

We have known for some time, of course, that the *Treatises* were written considerably prior to the Revolution of 1688, with an eye to encouraging resistance to the Crown. They were not penned after the revolution in an effort merely to justify it.[2] And while there is a sense in which Locke's doctrine of revolution is "conservative" in nature, it was at the same time quite a radical view in its day. For, on the one hand, the purpose of general (i.e., majority) resistance in Locke's theory is to restore the original legitimate condition of civil society (which has been destroyed by usurpation or tyranny), to satisfy the people's right to be governed according to the will of the majority (II, 176).[3] Locke takes great care to reassure his readers that his doctrine is not dangerous or anarchic; indeed, William is described in the preface to the *Treatises* as "our Great Restorer."[4] On the other hand, however, there are good grounds for believing that

[2] Laslett's influential analysis and dating of the texts allowed him to conclude that the *"Two Treatises* is an Exclusion Tract, not a Revolution Pamphlet" ("Introduction," 74–75). But see Ashcraft's argument for dating the *Second Treatise* not in 1679 and *before* the *First Treatise* (as Laslett argues), but in 1681–1682 and after it (*Locke's Two Treatises*, 286–95). On the practical revolutionary appeal of the *Treatises*, and on the relation of the arguments to specific events and problems in Locke's England, see Ashcraft, *Revolutionary Politics*, especially 314–15, 330, 575, and *Locke's Two Treatises*, 215–16; and Dunn, "Politics of Locke," 63–64.

[3] This "conservative" aspect of Locke's theory is stressed in Cranston, "John Locke and Government by Consent," 75; Andrew, *Shylock's Rights*, 108, 111; Parry, *John Locke*, 140–42; Trevelyan, *English Revolution*, 5. Dunn emphasizes both aspects of Locke's theory ("Politics of Locke," 56–60, and *Locke*, 55–56), as does Grant (*Liberalism*, 204).

[4] And elsewhere as the "recoverer" of "oppressed and sinking laws, liberties, and religion" ("Call to the Nation for Unity," 397).

the theory of political resistance espoused by Locke conformed to the thinking not of the more conservative, moderate Whigs of Locke's day, but rather to that of the radical Whigs from whom these moderates deliberately tried to distance themselves. For, as we will see, Locke defended not only a right of revolution for the people as a whole, but rights of individual resistance as well for abused persons or minorities. And Locke's language is often the language of the more radically democratic proponents of social revolution, suggesting that perhaps the right of the majority to self-determination may be exercised in the interest of not only political, but social and economic change.[5]

Philosophically, Locke's defense of a "right of resistance"[6] also occupies an interesting position (although it was, of course, only the most prominent and philosophically sophisticated of a number of very similar defenses that preceded and followed it). We will see, for instance, that it is philosophically interesting that the "appeal to heaven"[7] is uniformly spoken of by Locke as a *right* "which belongs to mankind" (e.g., II, 168), and almost never as a *duty*.[8] It is also

---

[5] See Franklin, *John Locke and the Theory of Sovereignty*, 98–105; and Ashcraft, *Revolutionary Politics*, 196–97, 207, 326–30, 392 405, 550–51, 572–79, 582–83, 590–91, 599–600, and "*Two Treatises* and the Exclusion Crisis." Others who have stressed the radical character of Locke's theory of resistance include Shapiro (*Evolution of Rights*, 113–17), Dworetz (*Unvarnished Doctrine*, 30), Pocock ("Myth of John Locke," 8), Tully ("Political Freedom," 520), Den Hartogh ("Express Consent," 112), Thomas (*There to Here*, 45–46, 53–54, 139), and Richards, Mulligan, and Graham ("'Property' and 'People,'" 51). On the right to resist specifically *economic* oppression, see Seliger, *Liberal Politics*, 173.

[6] I will mostly use this characterization of the relevant Lockean right (rather than "right of rebellion" or "right of revolution"). Locke seems to want to use "rebellion" to mean "unlawful use of force against authority" (e.g., II, 226), reserving "revolution" for describing lawful resistance. But he is not entirely consistent in these uses, as Seliger rightly notes (*Liberal Politics*, 316–20). The expression "right of resistance" better captures the spirit of Locke's right; for it is both neutral with regard to "rebellion" and "revolution," and covers cases of *individual* resistance (which cannot properly be called "revolutions").

[7] The "appeal to heaven" in question here refers, of course, not to the traditional appeal in prayer, but rather to taking up arms to resist oppression (as Jephtha did against the Ammonites [II, 21]). See Tarcov, "Best Fence," 216n. Jephtha's reported appeal seems to have been for God to judge by determining a victor in the combat (as in the idea of trial by combat). And this idea of trial by combat is often taken to be what Locke has in mind (see, e.g., Mace, *Locke, Hobbes, and the Federalist Papers*, 19–20; and Lessnoff, *Social Contract*, 64). Locke, however, really seems to think less in these terms and more in terms of God being the *eventual* (and only possible) true judge of the lawfulness of resistance.

[8] Skinner takes this to be a particularly important feature of Locke's theory (*Foundations of Modern Political Thought*, 2:338). I address in 6.4 the question of whether citizens also have, in Locke's view, a duty to resist tyranny, as was urged in the earlier writings of radical Calvinist authors.

important that the right of resistance is said to be a right of self-defense and a part of our natural freedom to resist unlawful uses of force (e.g., II, 239, 205). And it is crucial that the right of resistance is as a result, for Locke, a strong (claim) right, not a mere competitive liberty right.[9]

That these were not always Locke's views we have seen already. In the *Two Tracts*, for instance, he argued that "the subject is bound to a passive obedience under any decree of the magistrate whatever, whether just or unjust, nor, on any ground whatsoever may a private citizen oppose the magistrate's decrees by force of arms, though indeed if the matter is unlawful the magistrate sins in commanding" (Second Tract, 220). By the time of his 1667 *Essay* on toleration Locke allowed passive disobedience in matters of conscience (ECT, 180–81).[10] And when he composed the *Letter* and the *Treatises*, Locke's thinking had shifted far enough to allow not only violent resistance, but resistance for a much broader range of reasons than he had earlier contemplated. There were, no doubt, many sources of these changes in Locke's view, some of which I have mentioned already (in 3.1 and 5.4).[11] But a philosophically illuminating view of the changes can be acquired by abstracting from Locke's personal and political motives, concentrating instead on the ways in which Locke's development of his mature theory of rights and right-transfer allowed (and perhaps even required) the shift in his views on lawful resistance. And when we understand Locke's shift we will also understand something important about how moral thinking generally began to accommodate a "revolutionary" stance in political philosophy.

It is easy to see, first, why it was unlikely that a doctrine of lawful resistance would flow from any individualistic moral theory that did

[9] Compare with Nickel's claim that "the right to rebel against oppressive governments, much emphasized by Locke and Jefferson, seems primarily to be a liberty right" (*Making Sense of Human Rights*, 31).

[10] On this point I disagree with Dunn's reading of the 1667 *Essay*. Dunn finds in that essay only the same doctrine of passive obedience that Locke defends in the *Tracts* (*Locke*, 29).

[11] These included Locke's personal and political reasons (probably largely motivated by his association with Shaftesbury and other influential Whigs) and his abandonment of earlier theoretical goals (e.g., concerning toleration). A reason I have not yet mentioned is that an extremely pessimistic fear of what a disobedient rabble might accomplish "pervades the *Two Tracts*" (Colman, *Moral Philosophy*, 12), no doubt a result of Locke's feelings about the civil war. But Locke seems later to have arrived at a belief in the stability and solidity of social and political institutions, perhaps only as a result of passing (peaceful) time; and this change of mood permitted him to propose less authoritarian views (Dunn, *Political Thought*, 237–38).

not at least implicitly recognize the existence of moral rights.[12] The revolutionary stance normally presupposes moral ground to stand on; and in a world without rights, it is hard to see what ground is available. Your having a right to resist involves the idea that a wrong has been done to you; there is a claim to be pressed, a debt to be paid. Where there are no rightholders (other than God), there are no justified complainants (except God). Injustice and tyranny on the part of our governors are (at most) an affront to God on that model. The moral participation of citizens (individually or collectively) in the picture is distinctly secondary.[13] It seems natural to argue that the role of citizens should be to pray for deliverance and to obey God's laws (and those civil laws consistent with divine law). This was (roughly) the official doctrine of the Anglican Church during the development of Locke's theory of resistance: absolute political nonresistance, with passive disobedience justified only in cases of laws or commands contrary to God's law.[14] Where the moral emphasis is instead on individual rights (as in Locke's theory), however, we have the basis for claims that may be pressed in one's own name against others, those others importantly including our political superiors. Governments are as capable of violating my rights as are private persons, so they are as vulnerable to forceful resistance, punishment for wrongdoing, and the demand for just reparations.

But if the idea of individual moral rights facilitated the revolutionary stance, it certainly did not necessitate it. For most of the theories of rights advanced prior to the eighteenth century were not taken by their proponents to have revolutionary implications. This was true of many of Locke's most noteworthy predecessors, whose theories of rights were conjoined with political theories that were conservative and even absolutist in character. Suarez and Grotius on the Continent and Selden and Hobbes in England all serve as good examples of this point.[15] If we ask *why* these theories of rights

---

[12] Duties to resist are usually taken to imply rights to do one's duty; and individualistic virtues that resistance might exemplify (such as integrity or solidarity) seem to either (a) imply rights to act virtuously, or (b) be too weak to justify resistance in the first place.

[13] This secondary role might, of course, still involve some sort of individual right. Your right to resist might be the mandatory right to do your duty to God, as in radical theories that affirmed a duty owed to God to remove tyrants (and thus asserted primarily wrongs to *God*, not to *you*). I suggest below (6.4) that this is not the best way to understand Locke's right of resistance.

[14] Dunn, "Politics of Locke," 55. Trevelyan notes that in 1683 Oxford University proclaimed unconditional obedience "the badge or doctrine of the Church of England" (*English Revolution*, 20).

[15] See Tuck, *Natural Rights Theories*, 50–57, and chapters 3, 4, and 6.

should have led their authors to conclusions so different from Locke's, no simple answer will do full justice to any of the authors I have mentioned. But the following general points suggest an answer sufficiently precise to satisfy our primary concerns:

(1) Most theories of rights prior to those of Pufendorf and Locke employed exclusively or primarily a weak conception of rights as moral *liberties* or permissions—that is, the mere absence of obligations. The idea of a right as an area of moral sovereignty, protected by the logically correlative obligations of others, is only fully self-consciously employed beginning (roughly) in the second half of the seventeenth century. But this fact, of course, is very important to the development of doctrines of political resistance. To assert a claim right is to assert that one enjoys not just a moral liberty, which may be in competition with the similar liberties of others (as in Hobbes' famous "right to every thing"), but rather a *protected* liberty, an area of moral control immune to legitimate invasion by others. Asserting a weak liberty right, by contrast, says nothing about whether others act wrongly in interfering with my exercise of my rights. Lacking any correlative duty to respect my liberty right, another may be perfectly within her own rights in interfering with me.[16] Weak theories of rights will provide only weak justifications for resistance. Even if I can truly claim that my rights are being violated by my government, this in no way entails that my government is acting wrongly in doing so. Revolutionaries (or individual resisters) cannot claim the moral high ground they seek, for even tyrants may also be within their rights in opposing the revolution. The Lockean employment of strong claim rights, however, *does* allow the revolutionary a moral high ground to stand on in resisting government. When Locke's citizen defends his rights, those who oppose him also *wrong* him in their opposition (for they breach their correlative duties to respect his rights). The strong theory of rights thus provides the theoretical base needed for a convincing defense of a right of resistance.

(2) Again, however, the strong theory of rights alone hardly necessitates any revolutionary stance, for such a theory is still logically compatible with authoritarian political theories (witness the conclusions drawn by Pufendorf from his strong theory of rights). It is only when the strong theory is conjoined with certain views about the

---

[16] Thus, a Hobbesian subject has a right to defend himself against life-threatening attacks by his sovereign (the right of self-defense being inalienable for Hobbes), but the sovereign *also* has a right to kill him if he wishes to do so (enjoying, as the sovereign does, the right to every thing).

transfer of rights that the theoretical necessity of a Lockean right of resistance is apparent. The idea of the inalienability of natural rights, for instance, was centrally important to later (eighteenth-century) justifications of revolutionary activity. But Locke's theory (as I argued in chapter 5) seems not to centrally employ that idea. Locke does, however, insist on several other limits on transfer, which are crucial to understanding how his theory of rights necessitates a revolutionary stance.

(a) First, of course, Locke holds that rights can only be alienated by those who possess them; the consent that transfers rights must be personal consent. Our ancestors or parents cannot bind *us* by their promises and thus deprive us of our rights: a person "cannot by any compact whatsoever bind his children or posterity" (II, 116).[17] Nor can another forfeit our rights by his misconduct (II, 182–83). These simple (and, today, uncontroversial) claims played an extremely important role in Locke's theory, for they undercut any opposing theory that employs either (1) the idea of a historical contract of government that binds subsequent generations, or (2) the idea that present political power and obligations are based on past just conquests. It was, of course, extremely common before Locke to rely on both of these ideas. The idea of a permanently binding historical contract, for instance, was used by Grotius, Hooker, Cumberland, and many others. Such theories, however, left everything to the interpretation of historical facts and traditions (including covenants that were vague at best, and possibly only tacit or implied), making conservative or absolutist views of political power relatively easy to fashion. For Locke, by contrast, it makes no sense to think of rights as personal unless control over the *disposition* of those rights is personal as well (a view with which it is hard to argue). While one can, of course, authorize another to act for one and to dispose of (certain of) one's rights, one can hardly be supposed to have authorized one's *ancestors* in this way. The foggy history of our nations need not be interpreted (charitably or not) in order to know the substance of our rights.[18] Those rights we have not personally forfeited or transferred remain in our possession, and their violation by gov-

[17] Compare with the claim in the Virginia Declaration of Rights that all men "have certain inherent rights, of which, when they enter into a state of society, they cannot by any compact deprive or divest their posterity"; or with Paine's argument that the English Parliament of 1688 could not have subjected by consent their "heirs and posterity, to the end of time," for "every generation is equal in rights to the generations which precede it" (*Rights of Man*, 66, 88).

[18] Although our *personal* consent and contracts may also be sufficiently vague to require extensive interpretation of their contents (as we saw in chapters 3–5).

ernment may justify political resistance (regardless of what our ancestors may have done).

(b) A related limit on transfer that plays a similar role in Locke's theory is the *imprescriptibility* of natural rights (see 5.2). No person's moral rights can simply be taken from him, either in a particular act of expropriation, or by long passages of time during which the rights are denied or go unexercised. Prescription being thus denied as a valid method of transfer, governments cannot justify invasions of rights by appeal either to their power to rescind those rights or to a longstanding practice of invading them. Again, if I have not *personally* acted to forfeit or alienate my right, I may "stand on" it in lawful (i.e., morally permissible) resistance to government.

(c) Another related, equally simple, and equally important Lockean limit on transfer is the requirement of *voluntariness* in the alienation of rights. Coerced agreements transfer no rights. Locke asks "whether promises, extorted by force, without right, can be thought consent and how far they bind. To which I shall say, they bind not at all; because whatsoever another gets from me by force, I still retain the right of" (II, 186). The mere submission of persons, the coercive suppression of their ambitions, conquering them or exacting from them by force a promise of obedience, can never deprive them of their right of resistance. Against a philosopher like Hobbes (who assumes an understood, binding agreement to obey any other who has the power to take one's life at will), this limit on transfer is crucial in maintaining a revolutionary stance.

(d) Finally, I should mention again a limit stressed by Locke that is a limit on transfer only in the sense that it is the limit on our *possession* of rights. As we have seen (in chapter 5), Locke insists that we cannot give another the right to kill us, endanger our lives, enslave us (etc.), because we ourselves lack the rights to do these things. This argument is the Lockean analogue of revolutionary arguments from inalienability, for it identifies certain rights that government simply cannot obtain from us (i.e., cannot obtain at all). Governments cannot have the rights to arbitrarily kill, endanger, or enslave their subjects, and any government that attempts to implement policies with those consequences cannot but wrong its subjects in so doing. Such violations of the rights of subjects will thus always provide moral grounds for the revolutionary stance, regardless of any agreements to surrender those rights that may be claimed to have occurred.

Locke's theory of rights, then, permits him to move at once against several kinds of opposing views concerning resistance. It allows Locke to attack the conservative defense of passive obedience that rests on a weak theory of (liberty) rights. And it counters various kinds of "full-transfer theories," which allow either impersonal transfers, coerced transfers, or the alienability of all possible control over one's life. We should remember that it is only within the context of Locke's strong theory of rights (and his strong position on rights-transfer) that his argument for a right of resistance unfolds, and the plausibility of Locke's case is, as a result, highly dependent on the appeal of that theory. We feel more keenly than did many of Locke's contemporaries the force of his arguments for a right of resistance precisely because we accept more willingly those aspects of the Lockean theory of rights on which the arguments rest.

6.2. The Right of Resistance

It is seldom noticed that Locke in fact employs two distinct lines of argument in justifying a general (popular) right of resistance to oppressive government, either of which would be sufficient by itself to justify resistance in some kinds of cases. The two lines are run together and intertwined in the text, a fact that is easy to understand when we see that both appeal to moral limits on the use of force and both centrally utilize the idea of forfeiture. But while there is no logical inconsistency involved in using both styles of argument, we (and Locke) would do well to distinguish them more carefully. For their forces and implications seem quite different.

(1) *First line: State of war.* Locke frequently justifies general resistance on the ground that under certain conditions a state of war exists between the people and their government. Here Locke most often has in mind the case of a tyrannical executive power (such as Charles II or James II), but the legislative may also introduce a state of war with the people: "using force upon the people without authority, and contrary to the trust put in him" creates "a state of war with the people" (II, 155; see also, e.g., II, 222, 227).[19] Remember, however (from 2.1), the causes and consequences of the state of war. Warmakers are those who kill or enslave innocents (or demonstrate

---

[19] Von Leyden distinguishes those events that create *a* state of war from those that create *the* state of war, and takes this distinction to be important to understanding Locke's views on dissolution (*Hobbes and Locke*, 183–84). I do not really understand the distinction Von Leyden has in mind, nor does he cite any evidence from the text in support of his claim that Locke intends to draw it. In my view, keeping in mind that the state of war is a *relational* concept for Locke (2.1) adequately explains Locke's use of "a" (to refer to a particular relation of war) and "the" (to refer to more widespread relations of war).

the intention of doing so). They straightforwardly breach the most basic requirements of the law of nature, and in thus committing crimes deserving death, they forfeit all rights under that law (and may themselves be lawfully killed or used at will by any other person). Lesser criminals (e.g., pickpockets or muggers) are *not* warmakers and forfeit only some of their rights by their wrongdoing.

(2) *Second line: Breach of trust.* While Locke often writes as if breach of trust and creating a state of war are one and the same (e.g., II, 222), the two ideas are clearly quite different. The government is entrusted with certain rights for the pursuit of a particular end. When governors act contrary to the terms of this trust, "by this breach of trust they forfeit the power the people had put into their hands" (II, 222). But a breach of trust need not involve either a basic breach of natural law or the (consequent) forfeiture of all natural rights. The forfeiture at issue is only the forfeiture of the *entrusted* rights, not any others; and the act by which this forfeiture is accomplished can be *in itself* quite innocent. If you trust me to manage certain funds, and I merely invest them in a way that is specifically forbidden by the terms of the trust, I may forfeit the entrusted rights. But by my act I neither create a state of war between us (I only break a sort of promise), nor make lawful your killing or enslaving me (or perhaps even imposing any serious punishment at all). If I *subsequently* (i.e., *after* the trust is withdrawn) continue to use the funds, you may be justified in using force to recover them. But this subsequent crime is logically distinct from the mere breach of trust itself (which forfeited only the trustee's entrusted rights, not necessarily *any* of those rights to which the trustee was born).

There are, then, two conceptually distinct kinds of forfeiture at issue in Locke's justification of general (popular) resistance. Governors who act to kill or enslave their subjects forfeit their rights to be dealt with as persons under the law of nature. Governors who breach their trust forfeit those rights entrusted to them by their subjects, and reduce themselves to the status of ordinary persons without authority (II, 239). But the second kind of forfeiture does not necessitate the first. It brings about the first only if it is a particularly vile sort of breach of trust, or if it is followed by acts of aggression without authority (perhaps in an attempt to retain or regain the previously enjoyed position of lawful power).

Now Locke seems to believe that the second kind of forfeiture, in the case of governments at least, *does* necessitate the first. The trust a government enjoys is an especially vital kind of trust, since it concerns the people's freedom and well-being. Any breach of this trust, any hindering or altering of government functions intended by the people, threatens the "safety and preservation of the people" (II, 155). Such breaches are identified by Locke with attempts to wield absolute power, to reduce the people to slavery (II, 222). Even the lesser breaches of trust can be read as signs of "ill designs" by government (II, 149, 225, 230, 239),[20] designs that we are presumably supposed to equate with the "sedate, settled design" (II,16) that initiates a state of war.

These claims by Locke, however, are not very plausible as they stand, even on his own terms. For if a state of war is only begun by a sedate, settled design on another's life or freedom (as we saw in 2.1), breaches of trust that are passionate and ill-planned, breaches that are minor or isolated, and even major breaches that are just the result of hopeless incompetence,[21] should not be taken to begin a state of war between governor(s) and governed. Such breaches will forfeit the trust and will perhaps forfeit other rights as well (justifying punishment of the governor[s]); but they will not entail a forfeiture of all rights by those who govern, nor will they initiate war. Strictly speaking, Locke's justification of resistance does not require his central use of the concept of the state of war at all. Breach of trust will justify withdrawing the trust and recovering the entrusted rights; wrongful coercive acts by governors subsequent to the trust's withdrawal will justify resistance and punishment (as between equals in the state of nature); and wrongs done by governors in breaching the trust (both including and beyond the wrong of the breach itself) will be punishable in proportion to their seriousness (which may include the death penalty, for those governors who make war on their subjects). Notice that nothing in this argument gives the state of war a central place in the justification of popular resistance. It seems reasonable to conclude that it was Locke's *rhetorical* needs and practical political ambitions that caused the state

---

[20] Although Locke seems to say that only if lesser breaches occur in "a long train of actings [that] show the councils all tending that way" (II, 210) can we conclude from them a design to attain absolute power.

[21] Incompetent breaches, not resulting from any settled design, cannot consistently be said by Locke to initiate war. Locke says that the people will tolerate "great mistakes," "slips of human frailty," "wrong and inconvenient laws" (etc.), provided there is no "design" visible to them (II, 225). This suggests, as I have suggested in the text, that even significant breaches of the trust may not introduce a state of war, although they will certainly justify withdrawing the trust and placing it in abler hands (even if the patient people opt not to exercise that right in their role as settlor of the trust). Von Leyden, incorrectly on my view, specifically mentions incompetence as a possible source of a state of war between government and governed (*Hobbes and Locke*, 181).

of war to appear in its starring role in his arguments for the right of resistance. If a state of *war* exists, of course, it is eminently clear that we may not only oppose, but oppose with arms those who oppress us (II, 155, 204).[22] And if a state of war exists, we need not debate the question of how serious a punishment the oppressors deserve. Their crimes clearly merit death. The state of war's unnecessarily large role in Locke's argument clearly reflects his view of the specific nature of the breaches of the trust in his own England, and it appears on its face to be an effort on Locke's part to justify tyrannicide.[23]

If the preceding analysis is correct (or even nearly correct), it should be reasonably clear what Locke's right of popular resistance ("revolution") is. It is simply that "right of self-defense" that all persons possess naturally (as part of their "natural freedom" or right of self-government) (II, 205, 239), that right that each possesses in a state of nature to be free of and to actively resist invasions of life, liberty, health, and estate. This individual right is for each citizen limited by his entrance into civil society, since some of each person's rights are given up to society and can no longer be exercised or defended by the individual. Society then possesses the right to resist

[22] Locke says very little about the justifiability of the use of violence, either in this context or in general. But his view that unjust war justifies violence by those attacked seems consistent with all but the most ardently pacifist positions on the subject; so his appeal to the (unjust) state of war at this point in his argument serves well his practical aims. In general (and as we saw in chapter 2), Locke's position on the use of violence seems to be that it is permissible only in response to rights-violations and only then in proportion to the severity of the violation (since it is the forfeiture of the violator's own rights that makes permissible the use of violence against him). Violence (in varying degrees) will thus routinely be morally permitted to defend against rights-violations, to punish them, or to secure reparations for them. Locke's chief problem in applying this view to his theory of resistance is this: if governors do *not* always initiate a state of war when they breach the people's trust, the unlimited violence against them that war would justify may *not* always be justified. Violence against them is permissible only in proportion to the moral seriousness of their offenses.

[23] See Ashcraft's different, but also convincing, argument to this same conclusion (*Locke's Two Treatises*, 220–24), as well as Ryan's remarks on the subject ("Locke and the Dictatorship," 252). Locke scholars have frequently taken II, 205–6 as evidence of Locke's prohibition of violence against the king. Even Franklin, whose reading of Locke's *Treatises* is rare in acknowledging that work's radical implications, takes Locke to be opposed to tyrannicide (*John Locke and the Theory of Sovereignty*, 95). But as Ashcraft observes (ibid., 222), the passages in question seem clearly to allow that if a state of war exists between a king and his people, all bets are off ("who can tell what the end will be" [II, 205]). It is impossible to read (e.g.) II, 235 and 239, and all of Locke's colorful remarks on the state of war, without concluding that his audience would certainly have *taken* Locke's argument to sanction tyrannicide ("what shall hinder them from prosecuting him who is no king, as they would any other man who has put himself into a state of war with them" [II, 239]).

invasions of *its* rights (i.e., those rights transferred to it by individual members), a right that is again transferred by the entrusting of society's rights to government. When this trust is breached, the entrusted rights are returned to society (and perhaps to individuals, as we will see in 6.3), which can again defend itself against violations of them by removing its oppressors from power and installing a new government (chosen by the majority) designed to better secure those rights (II, 222, 227, 239, 243).[24] The right of resistance, then, is neither an inalienable right (5.2) nor a "right of war" (since war is not necessarily involved in such a breach of trust). It is not even the *executive* right, although that right to punish may also be exercised against deserving tyrants (the executive right having been returned to the people by the breach of trust). It is rather the simple right to freely determine the course of our lives (within the bounds of morality) and to resist encroachments upon it, a right entrusted in part to government, and returned (along with the executive right) by government's forfeiture of its trust.[25] This forfeiture occurs not just on the occasion of an actual, completed breach of trust, but also in the event of a planned breach, anticipated by the people.[26]

[24] That Locke thus espouses the right of the *people* to change their government, rather than a right for inferior magistrates or the people's representatives (in Parliament generally, or in Commons) to do so, constitutes an important departure from many earlier views (which were developed in fear of democratic revolutions) (see Franklin, *John Locke and the Theory of Sovereignty*, 1–2; and Lessnoff, *Social Contract*, 31, 34, 38). That Locke (as I argue below) allows for *individual* rights of resistance makes his theory of resistance even more radical.

Locke is often taken to be attacking the very idea of sovereignty in his work (e.g., Barker, "Introduction," xxv–xxvi; and Aaron, *John Locke*, 281); but there is a fairly clear sense in which he takes the people (society) to be sovereign. While the legislative acts within its trust, it is the "one supreme power"; but the people retain "a supreme power to remove or alter the Legislative," so that "the community may be said in this respect to be always the supreme power" (II, 149, 150). The sovereign power possessed by the community is simply the power of a settlor to judge the performance of and withdraw the authority of his trustees. Franklin argues that this is the only adequate solution to the problem of resistance in a mixed constitution (ibid., ix–x, 123), and that Locke is in this offering a theory that corresponds to Lawson's view of sovereignty (ibid., 89–95). See also Gough, *Political Philosophy*, 109–13.

[25] The power of society to withdraw its trust is *not*, of course, equivalent to the power of individuals to withdraw their consent to society. Locke thus avoids the concern of Filmer: that the people's right to judge would lead straight to anarchy and discord (*Patriarcha*, II, 17). Locke also argues, of course, that the people will in any event be slow to act against their government (see below).

[26] Persons "have not only a right to get out of [tyranny], but to prevent it" (II, 220; see also II, 210, 239; and Grant, *Liberalism*, 150–1). Andrew argues that since the public trust can dissolve before actual violation of rights by the government (i.e., even when the people merely judge such a violation to be part of government's designs), "Locke's argument that the government not the people initiates rebellion seems questionable" (*Shylock's Rights*, 110). This criticism of Locke is hard to accept, for criminal

I have thus far characterized Locke's justification of popular political resistance simply in terms of the government's breach of the trust that gives it political power. But capturing the full content of Locke's account of the right of resistance requires that we complicate considerably this simple picture. For individual and minority rights of resistance are not based simply on governmental breach of trust (as we will see in 6.3). And the justification of *majority* resistance turns importantly on the idea of a moral collapse by government that can occur in a variety of ways.

Locke's account of the justification for resistance, then, is in fact considerably more complex than my initial discussion has suggested. Locke prominently distinguishes, for instance, between external causes of the dissolution of government (such as conquest) and internal ones (altering or hindering the legislative, exceeding the trust, etc.). And we will see below that the idea of "dissolution" is useful in understanding both individual and majority rights of resistance. But Locke also gives several other quite general formulations of the conditions that justify resistance, formulations that apply to both individual and majority resistance. First, Locke frequently subsumes justified political resistance under the general heading of justified responses to the use of "force without right" (e.g., II, 168, 202). Any time another employs force against us without the right to do so, we may lawfully resist, and this includes occasions when our political superiors exceed their rights (or act as authorities subsequent to the dissolution of government).[27] This

---

conspirators can surely be said to have initiated conflict with society, even when society's agents apprehend them prior to any criminal attempts. If the question is instead about a dissolution of government where the people have *wrongly* judged the government to have "ill designs," see 6.4 below.

[27] Locke sometimes goes further, claiming that "whosoever in authority exceeds the power given him by *law* . . . may be opposed as any other man who by force invades the right of another" (II, 202; my emphasis). This cannot be correct, since Locke allows that prerogative may sometimes be legitimately used "against the direct letter of the law" (II, 164). (On the necessity of prerogative, Locke and Filmer seem to be largely in agreement [see *Patriarcha*, III, 8].) Political power (right) or authority is not strictly, but only largely, limited by *law*; its strict limit is set by the terms of the trust.

Locke distinguishes two ways in which our governors may use "force without right": "*usurpation* is the exercise of power which another hath a right to; . . . *tyranny* is the exercise of power beyond right, which nobody can have a right to" (II, 199; my emphases). I will not discuss this distinction further, beyond noting two of the complications raised by it: (1) Are acts of tyranny really confined to exercises of power that nobody (i.e., no *legitimate* authority) could rightfully perform (as Locke seems to say), or do they include *all* exercises of power beyond the rights of the individual governor (which could be all that Locke means here, if the second clause in the quoted definition of tyranny simply means [redundantly] "nobody can have a right to the

general formulation, conjoined with a flawed and wishful definition of the state of war, allows Locke to claim that any breach of trust by government begins a state of war.[28] Second, Locke suggests that cases of justified resistance are ones where the possibility of legal redress for wrongs done is absent: "where the injured party may be relieved and his damages repaired by appeal to the law, there can be no pretence for force, which is only to be used where a man is intercepted from appealing to the law" (II, 207; see also II, 168, 176). The problem to which Locke points, of course, is that where the legislative body is not allowed to serve as court of appeals for wrongs done by the executive, or where the legislative (or the people) is itself the culprit, the people (or individuals) have no appeal but to heaven. Their "umpirage" is taken from them and avenues of peaceful conflict resolution disappear (II, 227).

Being deprived of their umpire, the common judge over them all, the people might seem (given the point of leaving the state of nature for civil society) to be returned to the state of nature by their government's misconduct. On the other hand, Locke quite explicitly and prominently distinguishes between the dissolution of government and the dissolution of the political society it governed.[29] "The usual and almost only way" the political society itself is dissolved "is the inroad of foreign force making a conquest upon them." Such conquest dissolves the union of the people, so that "everyone return[s] to the state he was in before, with a liberty to shift for him-

exercise of power beyond right")? If the former, Locke needs a third class of uses of force without right (i.e., uses of power that a person *could* have a right to, but which happen to be beyond the rights of the governor in question). If the latter, usurpation is logically a subclass of tyranny (any usurper exercises power beyond *his* rights). Locke's ambiguity on this point is merely one reflection of his more general tendency (noted in 6.2 above) to equate all uses of force beyond right (including relatively harmless breaches of trust) with morally monstrous acts of war (which are beyond the rights of any person). (2) Some acts that dissolve government seem to be neither acts of usurpation nor of tyranny (however one defines tyranny), although Locke writes as if he intends the dichotomy to exhaust the possibilities. The failure of the executive to enforce the laws (II, 219), for instance, seems to involve neither exercising power that by right belongs to another nor acting in excess of one's (anyone's) assigned rights. It involves rather the failure to perform an assigned (entrusted) duty.

[28] As we have seen before (in 2.1), Locke (unconvincingly) tries to define the state of war in terms of "any use of force without right" (II, 155, 181, 227, 232). Since many minor crimes, intended neither to kill nor enslave their victims, involve the use of force without right, I take this definition to be dramatically inconsistent with Locke's earlier account (in II, 16). His use of the new definition in these sections thus seems to be more for rhetorical than philosophical reasons.

[29] And it is hard to see what the point of Locke's central presentation of the distinction could be except to maintain that in some cases governments are dissolved by misconduct *without* the destruction of society and the return of each to the state of nature. I return to this issue in 6.3.

self" (II, 211). The dissolution of society (and the return of each person to the state of nature [simpliciter]), in this case, causes as well the dissolution of the society's government. Each person has returned to him his full natural freedom (including his natural right of self-defense), and may lawfully resist the conqueror's use of force against him (provided this force is not an imposition of just punishment) (II, 192). But "besides this overturning from without, governments are dissolved from within" (II, 212).[30] This "dissolution from within" occurs when the legislative is altered—by the executive substituting his arbitrary will for the laws (II, 214), by the executive hindering the legislative from assembling or acting freely (II, 215), by the executive changing "the electors or ways of election" contrary to the people's interest (II, 216), or by the people being delivered "into the subjection of a foreign power" (II, 217).[31] Similarly, dissolution from within occurs when the executive power fails to enforce the laws (II, 219),[32] or when either branch of government acts contrary to its trust (II, 221). Actually, the last listed cause of dissolution (breach of trust) includes all of the others, since all of the other causes are either contrary to the executive's "double trust" (II, 222) or more generally contrary to the general good (which is in all instances the limit of the people's trust). Internal dissolution, then, can without distortion be said to occur as a result of governmental breach of trust.[33]

When the people resist the efforts of a dissolved government to retain its power, then, they cannot properly be said to be resisting civil government at all. Civil government has authority entrusted to

[30] This aspect of Locke's theory of resistance involved his embracing yet another radical position. As Franklin observes, among Locke's contemporaries the Tories tended to favor theories of "constructive abdication" while the moderate Whigs favored views that regarded the tyrant's throne as "vacant." It was the radicals who argued that tyranny resulted in the dissolution of government (*John Locke and the Theory of Sovereignty*, 98–105).

[31] Each of these causes of dissolution, of course, was exemplified (Locke believed) in the recent behavior of England's own executive. For summaries of the relevant historical events, which explain the ways in which Locke's theory of resistance constituted a practical political recommendation to his contemporaries, see Ashcraft, *Revolutionary Politics*, 192–93, 314–21, 546–47, and *Locke's Two Treatises*, 215–16; Seliger, *Liberal Politics*, 354–59; Parry, *John Locke*, 138–39.

[32] Locke has in mind here a systematic failure of execution, which creates virtual anarchy. Executive prerogative may allow the failure on some particular occasions to enforce the law, where the common good can in those cases be advanced by acting contrary to law.

[33] One other cause of dissolution of government, mentioned only in passing by Locke, is neither "from within" the government nor "from without" the political society. This is where the people "have set limits to the duration of the legislative" (II, 243).

it by its citizens; a dissolved government, by breach of its trust, has forfeited its authority. Since "rebellion" is "an opposition, not to persons, but authority" (II, 226), those who resist a dissolved government are not "rebels" in the strict sense. They are only free persons, exercising their natural rights. It is rather those in government who betray their trust who "are truly and properly rebels" (II, 226); for they use force against the people without any right (having forfeited their authority), and thus oppose the "authority" that the people have to secure their rights (e.g., II, 204, 227–28, 230). Indeed, such governors are far more guilty than any ordinary person who uses force without right. They not only do *this* wrong, but they breach a trust and they show themselves to be "ungrateful" for the "greatest privileges and advantages which the people have given them" (II, 231). There is a sense, then, in which it is not the people who dissolve their tyrannical governments at all. These governments actually "dissolve themselves," leaving the people morally free to seek new avenues for securing their rights.[34]

Since Locke employs the notions of dissolution of government and society in order to explain his view of the moral and social consequences of revolution, we should try to understand precisely what he means by them. This is not as easy as at first blush it seems. Dissolution of government seems a reasonably clear notion: it is the loss of a government's authority, its entrusted rights, its political power. Dissolution is thus a *moral* idea. Locke could hardly have had in mind that "dissolution" referred to the *physical* demise of government, its loss of the physical power to control society or a breakdown of its organization or internal coherence. For none of the causes of dissolution he mentions, save one, is a cause of physical dissolution (indeed, Locke's view of his own government was that it was dissolved, in spite of its continuing to function and wield physical power). But the one exception just noted is troubling. Conquest causes a dissolution of government (II, 211). Here, however, Locke must mean by "dissolution" the *physical* demise of the gov-

[34] Locke is in fact not as clear on this point as one would like him to be. Does a government dissolve when it *actually* breaches its trust or only when the people somehow (performatively) *judge* it to be in breach? The former view suggests that governments can dissolve themselves and become illegitimate even when the people are uninterested in their transgressions and continue to freely obey them. The latter view suggests that the people may be patient and keep a government in (lawful) power even when it frequently breaches its trust (as Locke may have in mind in II, 225). Both views have their attractions, since Locke may want to affirm both the power and options of the people as settlor of the trust and the illegitimacy of tyranny even where a sluggish people seem unconcerned about it. I return to this question in 6.4 below.

ernment, for a conqueror cannot by force deprive a just government of its *rights*, but only its physical power (and Locke nowhere suggests that only a lawful conquest dissolves government). Similarly, the dissolution of society appears to be a nonmoral notion. For conquest also dissolves society, by which Locke seems to have in mind the physical "mangling to pieces" of a society which follows conquest (II, 211). Civil society is a *moral* notion (as we have seen); but the dissolution of civil society appears not to be, since a conqueror cannot by force sever the moral bonds (political obligations) by which members of a legitimate society are connected.

We can try to deal with this problem in a variety of ways. It could, of course, be dismissed as just one more case of Locke's having become muddled about the concept of "power," confusing the loss of moral right (political power) with the loss of physical capability. Or we could rewrite the text a bit, saying that Locke must have meant that society and government are dissolved only by a *just* conquest, where the conquered society has forfeited (by warmaking) its rights (political power), and can thus no longer persist as a moral body. But the likeliest reading of the text, and one that makes perfectly good sense in its own right, is that Locke believed that certain kinds of "physical dissolution" *cause* "moral dissolution" to occur. If we understand the contract (or consent) that binds persons together in civil society to be an agreement "with other men to join and unite into a community, for their comfortable, safe, and peaceable living one amongst another . . . and a greater security against any that are not of it" (II, 95), then (a la Hobbes) when the body is no longer able to provide domestic peace or security against invaders (at a level superior to what could be enjoyed *without* civil society), the contract no longer binds persons together. The society's physical demise breaks the moral bond among its members (i.e., effective power is necessary but not sufficient for political legitimacy[35]). Similarly, a government is entrusted with the task of securing its citizens' rights. When it can no longer do so (at an acceptable level), the trust is breached (albeit, perhaps, unintentionally), and the government dissolves. Even conquest, then, may cause dissolution of government only through the government's breach of trust. In this way, it is possible to read Locke's notion of dissolution as throughout a moral notion (equivalent to loss of right or authority—i.e., "power" in its moral sense), even though the conquests that cause it are only brute, physical takings that *in themselves* cannot deprive society or government of their rights.

[35] Raz, *Morality of Freedom*, 76.

If this reading of the idea of "dissolution" is correct, the dissolution of government always occurs as a result of its failure (from inability, incompetence, ambition, or corruption) to carry out its trust to secure the rights of its citizens (better than they could secure those rights themselves). And the dissolution of society likewise results from *its* failure to do better for its members than they could do in fending for themselves. (This parallel is hardly surprising, given that the political power given up by each member to society is identical to the power entrusted to government.) Locke never discusses the possibility that society *itself* (rather than just its government) might be so corrupt or effete as to cause its own dissolution ("from within"), but I take it that this must be allowed by Locke as a possibility. Popular accounts of the fall of Rome might count as an example of such a dissolution. Similarly, natural disasters (earthquakes, famines, floods, etc.) go unmentioned by Locke as possible sources of a society's dissolution, yet they can clearly have as dramatic an effect as foreign conquest on a society's ability to "maintain and support themselves as one entire and independent body" (II, 211). Locke's allowing that conquest is "the usual and *almost only* way" in which society is dissolved (II, 211; my emphasis), of course, leaves logical space for the kinds of causes of dissolution I have just mentioned. He seems also to have believed that dissolution of government is likely to cause dissolution of society in some cases—more likely in cases of alteration of the legislative (II, 212) than otherwise. But I doubt that he thought this a *necessary* consequence of the dissolution of government in *any* kind of case.[36]

It was important to Locke that this doctrine of dissolution be seen not to be a dangerous doctrine, one that "lays a ferment for frequent rebellion" (II, 224) when preached. It was important to him not only as part of his response to Filmer,[37] but also because of his constant concern for consequences (see 6.4). In fact, Locke contends, his doctrine "is the best fence against rebellion, and the probablest means to hinder it" (II, 226), and he offers a set of considerations in support of this claim. First, the people are slow and averse to change (II, 223,

[36] Contrary to the view of Grant, who argues that for Locke alterations of the legislative dissolve not only government but society as well, while simple breaches of the trust (Locke's "second way" [II, 221]) dissolve only government (*Liberalism*, 151–54). Tarcov also reads Locke in this way, and suggests that Locke's "usual and almost only" remark about conquest is intended to leave room for cases where the legislative is altered ("Best Fence," 206–10). I suggest in 6.3 some reasons for being unhappy with such an interpretation.

[37] Filmer, of course, had contended vigorously that such a doctrine would encourage anarchy (see, e.g., *Patriarcha*, II, 14–17).

230), and they will not rise up except when government creates great inconveniences (II, 168) and "a long train of abuses, prevarications, and artifices" (II, 225; see also II, 208–10). Second, no matter what doctrine is preached, "the people generally ill treated, and contrary to right, will be ready upon any occasion to ease themselves of a burden that sits heavy upon them" (II, 224). Neither of these reasons, of course, really has any special connection with *Locke's* doctrine, regardless of what his remarks suggest. They could be offered equally plausibly on behalf of *any* doctrine of resistance, including Filmer's (since they really only consist of social facts that include no consideration of what doctrine of resistance is being preached).

A third consideration Locke advances, however, is more closely tied to the virtues of his specific position: the best ("properest") way to prevent tyrannical excesses by government is to let government see "the danger and injustice of them," by openly acknowledging the people's right to remove tyrants by force (II, 226).[38] The problem with this third argument, however, is that it seems inconsistent with the first two. If those in power know the people are slow to resist, and know they *will* resist at a certain point no matter what doctrine is preached, then those in power are unlikely to be specially deterred by advocacy of Locke's doctrine. The argument makes sense only if Locke means that preaching his doctrine will make the people less slow to resist than they would otherwise be. And since Locke's practical political aims were (in part) precisely to rouse a sluggish people to resist tyranny, we can safely suppose this is what he had in mind. This will mean, of course, that preaching Locke's doctrine may make resistance likelier than preaching a doctrine like Filmer's, at least until those in power get the message and are deterred by it (making necessary resistance less likely in the long run than were Filmer's doctrine believed). But the temporary "trouble" this would cause would be no more trouble than justice generally causes (and is worth) (II, 176). I think, finally, that an important point of Locke's distinction between the dissolutions of society and government is precisely to counter Filmerian fears about the anarchic consequences of Locke's doctrine of popular resistance. For if the dissolution of government still leaves *society* intact, Locke's doctrine cannot be read as promoting the chaos and anarchy of a state of

[38] See Grant, *Liberalism*, 165; Parry, *John Locke*, 145. Von Leyden offers a slightly different list of Locke's arguments for the "efficiency" of his doctrine of resistance (*Hobbes and Locke*, 188); the one I offer here seems to me more concisely to capture the force of Locke's claims.

nature (which Locke's contemporaries were still prone to think of in terms of a Hobbesian war of all against all). Since the order of society remains even after its government is removed, degeneration into life at the mercy of the mob is not to be feared whenever resistance to tyranny is urged.

6.3. The Consequences of Dissolution

I have suggested one way of reading the relation in Locke between the dissolution of government and the dissolution of society (and thus one way of understanding Locke's view of the moral and social consequences of revolution). As Leo Strauss plausibly observes, however, Locke at least appears to teach both "on the one hand, that society can exist without government (ibid., secs. 121 and 211) and, on the other hand, that society cannot exist without government (ibid., secs. 205 and 219)."[39] The result of this tension in Locke's text is that the text can be plausibly interpreted in three different ways: (1) the dissolution of government returns persons to the state of nature;[40] (2) the dissolution of government leaves society intact, and so does not return persons to the state of nature;[41] (3) the dissolution of government sometimes dissolves society and sometimes does not, depending on the kind of dissolution in question.[42]

Locke's early view appeared to be that society required government for its survival, that without the state or government "every community among men falls to the ground" (ELN, 119).[43] This implies that the dissolution of government involves the dissolution of society and a return to the state of nature. And in a *technical* sense, this may be Locke's mature view as well; for if "perfect democracy" (in which the community as a whole simply directs itself) counts as "government" (as Locke suggests in II, 132), then wherever society exists there is at least this minimal form of government as well.[44]

[39] *Natural Right*, 232n.

[40] The best recent defense of this view is in Ashcraft, *Revolutionary Politics*, 162n, 193, 315, 330n, 332, 484, 569–70, 575–77, *Locke's Two Treatises*, 202–5, 216–19, and "Locke's State of Nature," 902. See also Cox, *Locke on War and Peace*, 59.

[41] Franklin, *John Locke and the Theory of Sovereignty*, 107; Tully, *Discourse*, 160; Laslett, "Introduction," 128–30; Seliger, *Liberal Politics*, 105–6, 124, 127.

[42] Tarcov, "Best Fence"; Grant, *Liberalism*, 148–50.

[43] Since Locke only says that community falls when both government and "the fulfillment of pacts" are abolished, my use of this quotation is slightly misleading. But the text immediately following the quoted passage makes it clear, I think, that Locke believed the abolition of *either* to be sufficient alone to undo society.

[44] Seliger, *Liberal Politics*, 107, 124, 128; Grant, *Liberalism*, 104–5.

Thus, the dissolution of *all* government would entail the dissolution of society (in this technical sense). We need to ask as well, however, the more interesting and practically relevant question about Locke's mature position: Does the dissolution of the *current* form of government (be it democracy, oligarchy, monarchy, or mixed) cause the dissolution of society, and not just a return to society's most basic form of "government" (i.e., perfect democracy)? Does our government's dissolution destroy society as well and return us to the state of nature?

One possible answer is that the question is confused. Perhaps Locke believes that the dissolution of government *does* return the society to the state of nature, but that this is not the same as destroying the society. When one's government dissolves, political power returns to the people, still constituted as a community. But this community should itself be seen as existing in the state of nature, one could argue, for the destruction of its government has removed the authorized judge that existed to settle conflicts within it. And the absence of a common judge defines the state of nature. Further, since the community is in a state of war with its oppressors, it must be in the state of nature as well (since the former entails the latter). So while Locke might seem to be trying to contrast the state of nature with civil society or community (defining the former as the absence of the latter), we could argue, this appearance is misleading. His real intention is to contrast the state of nature with the state of being under legitimate civil government. Whenever government dissolves, the people are returned to the state of nature, even if their *society* in some sense persists.[45]

There is no denying that Locke seems to say in several places that the dissolution of government returns persons to the state of nature. For instance, he argues that an express consenter never returns to the state of nature "unless by any calamity, the government he was under comes to be dissolved" (II,121). "Everyone is at the disposure of his own will" when the legislative is altered (II, 212); and when the prince creates "a state of war with his people," he "dissolve[s] the government, and leave[s] them to that defense which belongs to everyone in the state of nature" (II, 205). Indeed, certain actions

---

[45] This is the reading defended by Ashcraft (*Locke's Two Treatises*, 216, 203, 205, 217). Whether Ashcraft wants to say that *individuals* are in the state of nature after the dissolution of government is unclear. He asserts in one place that the contrary view cannot be sustained (ibid., 217). But in another he argues that dissolution "returns men to the state of nature, but not as separate individuals" (*Revolutionary Politics*, 577).

by the prince produce "effects very little different from foreign conquest" (II, 218) and "reduce all to anarchy" (II, 219).

It is possible, of course, to read these passages without believing that Locke means the dissolution of government *always* returns persons to the state of nature. One might, for instance, argue that only some kinds of dissolution of government have this effect. Locke explicitly distinguishes between dissolution ("from within") in which "the legislative is altered" (II, 212) and that in which "the legislative, or the prince, either of them act contrary to their trust" (II, 221). Only in the first case is it obvious that the dissolution of government causes the dissolution of society (and a return to the state of nature), for only in the first case is the "soul" of the commonwealth destroyed (II, 212). The second kind of dissolution from within, that which involves only breach of trust (as when the legislative or the executive tries to gain arbitrary power), might merely return political power to an intact society, which may then entrust that power again in creating a new government. In the second case, on this reading, individuals would not be returned to the state of nature.[46]

Now I will not try to claim that Locke succeeds in presenting a very clear position on these matters, but I do think it is clear that this latter reading cannot be defended as making the best possible sense of the relevant text. In the first place, Locke's summary of the effects of the first kind of dissolution of government (i.e., alteration of the legislative) suggests precisely that the society is *not* dissolved in such cases. It is *"the People"* who are "at liberty to provide for themselves by erecting a new legislative"; it is *"society"* which "can never . . . lose the native and original right it has to preserve itself" (II, 220; my emphasis). "Society" can hardly retain its rights if it has been dissolved. Further, if we take seriously that it is the removal of the common judge or umpire that makes the dissolution of government return persons to the state of nature, this "removal" occurs as surely in the second kind of dissolution as in the first. And while Locke does seem to emphasize the gravity of causing the first kind of dissolution by calling it "certainly the greatest crime men can be guilty of" (II, 218), he says later that "the greatest crime . . . a man is capable of" is doing *anything* that overturns a just government (II, 230), which clearly includes as well causing the second kind of dis-

---

[46] This is the reading favored by Tarcov ("Best Fence," 207–10). Tarcov contends as well that the first and second cases of dissolution correspond to Locke's distinction between usurpation and tyranny (p. 210). Grant correctly notes that this contention is mistaken (*Liberalism*, 149n), but she follows Tarcov in the essentials of his reading of Locke on this subject.

solution. It is also very hard to believe that Locke would refer to foreign conquest as "the usual, and almost only, way" that society is dissolved, if he intended immediately to suggest another quite common way in which society is dissolved (i.e., alteration of the legislative, which was, of course, one of the problems in Locke's own England, in his own view). It is far more likely that Locke intended the "almost only" to leave room for the kinds of natural disasters or moral collapse of a society to which I earlier referred. Finally, and most important, while Locke *does* say of the first kind of dissolution that it leaves everyone "at the disposure of his own will," he also says (as we have seen) that when the prince creates a state of war, he leaves people "to that defense which belongs to everyone in the state of nature" (II, 205). And it is precisely the second kind of dissolution of government (involving breach of trust) of which Locke most emphatically asserts that it involves "a state of war with the people" (II, 222).[47]

At this point it might seem prudent to retreat to the first position we considered: any kind of dissolution of government returns the people to the state of nature. But there are good reasons to be unhappy with that interpretation as well. For both the first and last paragraphs of chapter 19 of the *Second Treatise* suggest precisely the contrary. II, 211 makes it clear that society almost always remains "out of the loose state of nature" when its government is merely destroyed from within (i.e., in the absence of foreign conquest). And in II, 243, Locke states explicitly that when political authority is forfeited by the rulers, "it reverts to the society" and it "can never revert to the individuals again, as long as the society lasts, but will always remain in the community." Even II, 121, which has often been read as stating that the dissolution of government reintroduces the state of nature, really only claims that the dissolution of government is necessary for express consenters to return to the state of nature. It does not claim that dissolution of government is sufficient (by itself) to bring about this result (for all this passage tells us, further dissolution of society might also be necessary).

There are, in fact, good reasons to suppose that Locke would have been quite uncomfortable with the view that dissolution of government reintroduces the state of nature. As I noted in 6.2, it seems clear that Locke's distinction between the dissolution of government and the dissolution of society is at least largely intended by him to

---

[47] II, 222 actually concerns breach of trust by the legislative, not by the prince. But it is obvious that the same breach of trust by the prince would also introduce a state of war (as the wording of II, 221 makes clear).

counter worries about the possible anarchic social consequences of practicing his theory of justified resistance. These intentions would be ill served by defending the view that dissolution of government reintroduces the state of nature (a state that raised for Locke's audience the spectre of a war of all against all). They would be much better served by maintaining (as Locke appears to maintain) that only (or almost only) foreign conquest will set persons "loose" again in the state of nature. But in fact Locke does not need to (nor, I think, does he intend to) defend either of these positions.

If we remember (from 1.1) the relational character of the state of nature in Locke's philosophy, it is immediately clear that another, quite sensible, stance is available to Locke. And this is, in fact, the position that squares best with what Locke actually says. He appears to be saying both that dissolution of government returns persons to the state of nature and that it does not, because, in a sense, he *is* saying both of those things. Dissolution of government returns persons to the state of nature *with respect to their governors,* but *not with respect to their fellow citizens.* Their governors, by their transgressions, have forfeited their standing within the community and broken their bond with the citizens they were trusted to serve.[48] But the contract that makes civil society is made among the citizens of that commonwealth. That contract remains unbroken, the citizens' obligations to one another remain in force,[49] and hence they remain out of the state of nature with respect to each other. Locke's position thus allows him to claim *both* that oppressed citizens are as free as people ever were to resist those who invade their rights (the natural rights to defend against and punish wrongdoers having been returned to the community by the breach of trust) *and* that this "return to the state of nature" is not a dramatic return (i.e., not one that threatens to bring to all a life that is nasty, brutish, and short). Citizens of commonwealths are always in the state of nature with respect to many people (e.g., all aliens, young children, idiots, etc.).

[48] Actually, Locke ought to have said that only certain kinds of government-dissolving transgressions put governors and their (former) subjects in the state of nature with respect to each other. The governor who breaches the trust in a way that does not create a state of war (see 6.2) and who subsequently peacefully surrenders his power when called on to do so (when the government dissolves), ought to simply be reduced again to the status of a private citizen of the commonwealth (perhaps more like a minor criminal who still enjoys that status). As such, the former governor would still be out of the state of nature with respect to his former subjects. Locke can, however, be excused for failing to mention what is certainly an unusual state of affairs (i.e., one in which the governor peacefully surrenders power after only relatively undramatic breaches of the trust).

[49] Dunn, *Political Thought,* 180–81.

Dissolution of government merely adds their governors to the list of those with respect to whom they are in the state of nature.[50] No Filmerian worries about immediate chaos are called for. Yet this small change in the citizens' moral position (and social condition) makes all the difference in justifying armed resistance and conscientious punishment.

With this understanding of Locke's position, we can see why Locke begins and ends chapter 19 by denying that dissolution of government ends society, but still talks between of the citizen as left by dissolution "at the disposure of his own will" (i.e., with respect to his governors). When our governors initiate with us a state of war, of course they leave us free with respect to *them*, not with respect to each other. We remain subject to the will of the majority of citizens in any conflict between citizens; the governmental judge over us all has been destroyed by that government's abuse of power, but the body of the people still remains a judge over all (in a sense sufficiently strong to exclude the state of nature among citizens, since in such a "perfect democracy" the society as a whole still possesses intact the executive right). It is always possible, of course, that the dissolution (from within) of their government may leave a people unable to act as one body. If so, this physical incapacity will cause society to lose its moral authority over its members (as we saw in 6.2); the contract among the members will be broken, and all will be returned to the state of nature (simpliciter). But II, 211 makes it clear that Locke believes such events to be quite uncommon, and not at all a necessary or expected result of (any kind of) dissolution of government.

If the right to resist and punish tyrannical governors thus (typically) returns on dissolution to the community as a whole, leaving all of the incorporated citizens still bound by the will of the majority, however, another kind of question about Locke's position springs readily to mind. What does Locke think about the rights of abused *individuals* whose complaints are not shared or acknowledged by the majority? Is the right of resistance a right that can be possessed only by the people as a whole, or can it be exercised by individual citizens as well (who are not capable of mounting anything like a revolution)? The standard reading of the text seems to be that Locke's right of resistance can be held only by the body of the people, its proper

[50] Both Ashcraft and Tarcov occasionally make claims that seem to indicate an acceptance of this reading of the text, although neither seems to explicitly endorse it (Tarcov, "Best Fence," e.g., 206, 210; Ashcraft, *Locke's Two Treatises*, e.g., 202). See also Seliger, *Liberal Politics*, 104–5.

exercise to be determined only by the majority of the body politic.[51] When the majority judges the government to have overstepped its proper bounds and breached its trust with the people, only then is the government dissolved, and only then can resistance be lawful (although, of course, the *ultimate* lawfulness of resistance can only be decided by the God to whom the revolutionaries "appeal"—there being no judge on earth authorized to settle the question).[52] Locke did not, it is claimed, consider seriously (or perhaps at all) the problem of a tyrannous majority in society.[53] He either thought the plight of oppressed individuals or minorities was their own problem (which should not or did not interest others),[54] or he assumed that the majority in a legitimate commonwealth would always be "rational and just."[55] Either way, this would seem to represent a fairly serious oversight (moral or factual) on Locke's part.

While supporters of the majoritarian reading of Locke's theory of resistance often acknowledge his occasional lapses into individualist language,[56] they can point to a significant body of text to support their view that these are indeed lapses (rather than indications of Locke's true stance). In one place, for instance, Locke seems to contrast the individual's right to appeal to the law with the majority's right to appeal to heaven (II, 176). In many other passages (e.g., II, 149, 220, 222, 240, 243), he strongly suggests that as settlor of the trust that creates government, the community must be the one to which rights are returned on dissolution (apparently ruling out the possibility that individuals in their private capacities might receive new rights as a result of that dissolution). If the body of the people

[51] Kendall, *Majority-Rule*, e.g., 132–34; Gough, *Political Philosophy,* 37, 39n; Von Leyden, *Hobbes and Locke*, 185; Yolton, *Locke*, 67; Monson, "Locke's Political Theory," 194; Mansfield, "Right of Revolution," 155; Grady, "Obligation, Consent," 288–89; Arnhart, *Political Questions*, 252; Sigmund, *Natural Law*, 83. Parry seems to say both that the right to resist is held by the majority and that it is held by individuals (*John Locke*, 144). Dunn seems to accept the majoritarian reading in his *Locke* (p. 56), but elsewhere he makes clear that his view is more complicated. I discuss Dunn's view in 6.3 and 6.4 below.

[52] Sometimes Locke's position is taken to be even more dramatically majoritarian. It has been claimed, for instance, that the majority not only possesses the right to judge and to resist, but that it determines the *truth* in such political matters. The dissenter who disagrees with the majority is necessarily *wrong* (Grady, "Obligation, Consent," 289).

[53] Kendall, *Majority-Rule*, 103; Gough, *Political Philosophy,* 40; Strauss, *Natural Right*, 233n; Shapiro, *Evolution of Rights*, 116.

[54] Andrew, *Shylock's Rights*, 112. I discuss this view further in 6.3 below.

[55] Kendall, *Majority Rule*, 134; Gough, *Political Philosophy,* 42.

[56] Von Leyden, *Hobbes and Locke*, 239n; Strauss, *Natural Right*, 232–33; Laslett, note to II, 168, in Locke, *Two Treatises*, 426. Others just read Locke as contradicting himself (e.g., Anglim, "On Locke's State of Nature," 88).

is not oppressed by or inclined to resist their government, Locke seems to argue, unfortunate individuals who suffer at the government's hands must suffer without recourse (II, 205, 208, 230).[57]

Even if this were Locke's true stance, it would represent a significant departure from the more usual view in Locke's day: that only the people as a whole can lawfully resist the government (or king), and even they can resist only through their lawful representatives. Locke maintains the more radical view that the right to resist belongs to the people themselves, not just their representatives.[58] But I believe Locke's real position on the right of resistance is more radical still. The right to resist can be exercised both by the people as a whole (guided by the will of the majority) and by abused individuals.[59] This position, I maintain, is not only the one reflected by a careful reading of Locke's *Second Treatise*, but it is also the *right* position for Locke to be defending (i.e., the one most compatible with Locke's own, and any plausible Lockean, theory of rights, the political relationship, and governmental legitimacy). And it is, finally, the least moderate of all the positions adopted by Locke in the *Treatises*.

The passages in which Locke affirms an individual right to resist are simply too numerous to ignore or explain away. He prominently claims that "where the body of the people, *or any single man*, is deprived of their right or is under the exercise of a power without right, and have no appeal on earth, there they have a liberty to appeal to heaven, whenever they judge the cause of sufficient moment" (II,

---

[57] Even of these passages, all frequently cited in support of the majoritarian reading, one (II, 208) clearly affirms the right of "private men" to defend themselves and exact reparation. I suggest below what I take to be the proper reading of such passages as these.

[58] Franklin, *John Locke and the Theory of Sovereignty*, 1–2; Grant, *Liberalism*, 107–8.

[59] Those who most clearly acknowledge an individual right of resistance in Locke include Plamenatz, *Man and Society*, 1:232; Grant, *Liberalism*, 173; Skinner, *Foundations of Modern Political Thought*, 2:338; Mabbott, *John Locke*, 168–69; Tully, "Political Freedom," 518; Kilcullen, "Locke on Political Obligation," 337–38; MacCormick, "Law, Obligation, and Consent," 396; Tarcov, "Best Fence," 215; Anglim, "On Locke's State of Nature," 88; Hampsher-Monk, "Resistance and Economy," 92–95. Dunn also mentions the individual's right to resist in Locke, but argues that the individual's "title to punish the ruler is one which he may only exercise if to do so is unlikely to damage the interests of others" (*Political Thought*, 178–79; see also "Politics of Locke," 60–61). I discuss below the respects in which I differ with Dunn. Ashcraft notes Locke's defense of individual rights of resistance, but then seems to misread II, 242 as claiming that individuals must appeal to the body of the people to judge their cases (*Revolutionary Politics*, 308–309). In fact, II, 242 concerns only those cases of controversy "where the law is silent." Andrew also claims that in Locke "individuals have the right to rebel," but then maintains as well that "the power of the majority is also the right of the majority" (*Shylock's Rights*, 112–13).

168; my emphasis). Later, speaking of acts of tyranny that reach only "some private men's cases," Locke argues that "they have a right to defend themselves and to recover by force what by unlawful force is taken from them" (II, 208). The "innocent honest man" is not to be blamed if he "defends his own right" (II, 228), for *every man is judge for himself . . .* whether another hath put himself into a state of war with him, and whether he should appeal to the Supreme Judge, as Jephtha did" (II, 241; my emphasis). Admittedly, the body of the people is "the proper umpire" in matters "where the law is silent or doubtful" (II, 242), but this covers only a fraction of the possible occasions of abuse of individuals or minorities. Indeed, if Locke were *not* affirming an individual right of resistance in many cases, it would make no sense at all for him to twice assure his readers that individuals' having such rights is not a threat to the order of society (II, 208, 230). It is in these passages that Locke tries to make acceptable to a nervous audience a quite radical doctrine of lawful individual resistance, contending that anarchic consequences will not follow from general acceptance of the doctrine. Locke was, of course, no stranger to governmental and majority abuse of individuals and minorities (abuse particularly for religious, but also for political, reasons). That he does not write more about the problem of tyrannous majorities reflects not Locke's failure to see such problems, but rather his awareness (affirmed in II, 208 and 230) that the political plight of abused individuals and minorities is (more or less) hopeless. The only rational response for these people is patience (II, 176). Such unfortunates have the right to resist their oppression, but they will generally be unable either to overthrow their oppressors by themselves or to "rouse" the sluggish people who are not themselves harmed by the wrong. Here Locke speaks with two voices, both assuring conservative readers that Filmer was wrong about the social effects of popular belief in such a doctrine of resistance, while at the same time expressing what appears to be regret that the body of the people cannot be more easily enlisted in the fight against injustice.

We have seen, then, that Locke defends a right of resistance both for individuals (and minorities) and for the incorporated people as a whole.[60] How can he claim that both possess this right?

---

[60] Again, I am supposing (as in 3.1) that the rights of "the incorporated people" (as well as their duties, to which I will refer below) are analyzable into rights and duties of constituent members—e.g., rights and duties of individual citizens or government officials to contribute to and facilitate centralized or collective action. But I am far from certain that Locke is thinking in these terms. On the (reductionist) read-

The answer is (reasonably) simple once we remember the content of the contract (or consent) that makes one a member of a legitimate civil society. When we enter civil society, we surrender only some of our natural rights to the community (as we saw in 3.1)—specifically, our executive rights and those portions of our right of self-government that are necessary for effective political government. We retain rights to property, to religious toleration, to innocent self-defense, and to many other kinds of freedom of action. When government violates our rights, then, it sometimes violates rights that we hold as private individuals and sometimes violates rights that we have transferred to the community. Depending on which kind of violation is at issue, either the individual or the people as a whole (respectively) will have a right to resist the violation (rightholders always possessing for Locke the further right to defend their rights).

Individual (innocent) citizens can never make it lawful for governments (or societies) to kill them or deprive them of those things they need to live. They cannot give government (or society) the right to do what they themselves lack the right to do (5.2). It follows from this that even in civil society they may (indeed must) resist unlawful infringements of their rights to person and property.[61] Locke also makes a point quite early in the *Second Treatise* of claiming that while the magistrate has "the common right of punishing put into his hands," he has no right "to remit the satisfaction due to *any private man* for the damages he has received. That, he who has suffered the damage has a right to demand in his own name, and he alone can remit" (II, 11; my emphasis). Even in civil society, then, each citizen also retains a private right to reparation for wrongful injuries (the transfer of that right apparently being unnecessary for effective government, in Locke's view). Given these claims, Locke is not only consistently able to, he is obliged to assert that private individuals, even in civil society, "have a right to defend themselves and to recover by force what by unlawful force is taken from them" (II, 208). And this, of course, amounts to a substantial individual right of re-

---

ing I favor, it is possible for individual citizens to do *their* duties, say, without the people as a whole doing *its* duty. But the alternative (nonreductionist) reading leaves it completely unclear (at least to me) how group rights and duties translate (if at all) into *any* permissions or requirements for actual persons (who must, after all, do the acting if the *body* is to act).

[61] Ashcraft rightly notes that "one reason that the radical Whigs' conception of resistance reached down to the level of the individual was derived from their interpretation of the suicide taboo: that is, no one could authorize his own death" (*Revolutionary Politics*, 308n).

sistance, justifying as it does the use of force not only to defend against but to recover from an abusive government (however unlikely it may be that individuals will actually succeed in exercising the right).

On the other hand, the right to punish governors who breach their trust with the people initially seems to be part only of the people's right to resist. Individuals surrendered the executive right to society, which subsequently entrusted it to government. The governmental breach of trust returns the right to punish to the society; but there seems to be no reason to believe that the right must go further (i.e., all the way back to private individuals). Perhaps Locke intends this as an argument against private assassination of governors who tyrannize only particular individuals or minorities, reserving the right of tyrannicide only for the people as a whole. Perhaps not, for there is certainly also room for Locke to argue that "private tyranny" returns the right to punish to the tyrannized individuals—either because the right to punish is necessary for effective self-defense (as Locke argues early in the *Second Treatise*), or because persons only agree to join civil society in order to live "in a secure enjoyment of their properties" (II, 95). If society makes no effort to punish those (such as a tyrannical governor) who make my property insecure, this would seem to violate the conditions under which I gave my consent to join society, breaching (and hence voiding) the contract and freeing me of my obligation to allow society to be the sole punisher of wrongdoers (just as if foreign conquest or natural disaster had made society incapable of securing my property better than I could myself). Worse, of course, the society itself, rather than just society's government, may be the party that is violating the rights of individuals or minorities within it. The majority may not only have ignored the abuse of some of society's members, it may have "actually assisted, concurred, or consented to that unjust force" (II, 179). In such cases it seems clear that the pact between the oppressed individuals and the society that victimizes them is broken, returning those individuals to the state of nature (simpliciter). Where governmental tyranny may in typical cases only put citizens in the state of nature with respect to their governors, then, neglect and tyranny by society itself may return some to that state with respect to all persons (and thus return to them their native full complement of rights to defend their property and to punish those who breach their rights). In this latter case we may say that the society is dissolved, not absolutely, but with respect to oppressed individuals.

6.4. The Duty to Resist

When we see that Locke is committed to both individual and majority rights of resistance, of course, we can easily explain the presence of the passages cited in support of both majoritarian and individualist readings of Locke. But to this point my analysis will seem to many to raise at least as many questions as it answers. If individuals have a right to resist, must others aid them in their cause? Can governmental abuse of individuals or minorities by itself cause a dissolution of that government (with respect to the majority)? Are the only limits on the individual's right of resistance those set by the practical hopelessness of "fighting city hall"? The remainder of this chapter will be occupied with attempts to answer these (and related) questions, and in the process to achieve a clearer understanding of some of the subtler elements of Locke's (and the Lockean) theory of resistance.

It may at first seem a sham for Locke to affirm individual (and minority) rights of resistance, while at the same time suggesting that wronged individuals will normally have no real option but patient acceptance of their situation. It is, after all, not much of a right that one can almost never prudently exercise. But the plight of tyrannized individuals and minorities will seem less pathetic (and Locke's claims less of a sham) when we remember that the body of the people (the majority) *may* choose to help wronged individuals to obtain justice. While Locke seems pessimistic about this possibility in chapter 19 of the *Second Treatise,* his pessimism may be there exaggerated to emphasize that his doctrine is not conducive to frequent rebellion or anarchy. For earlier in that work, he makes clear reference to people aiding injured individuals. One who uses unjust force against another "renders himself liable to be destroyed by the injured person and the rest of mankind, that will join with him in the execution of justice" (II, 172). A person who has been injured by another has "a particular right to seek reparation from him that has done it. And any other person who finds it just may also join with him that is injured, and assist him in recovering from the offender so much as may make satisfaction for the harm he has suffered" (II, 10). Locke's emphasis (in II, 10) on aiding others in securing reparation is especially significant in light of his later clear assertions that wronged individuals even in civil society have the right to use force in repairing their injuries (II, 11,

208). We know, of course, that a wrong done to an innocent person (or minority) is "a trespass against the whole species" (II, 8), and it would hardly be surprising if the people saw deliberate attacks on the few as a precedent, as a sign of imminent attack on the many (II, 209).[62]

The people, then, *may* aid oppressed individuals. But *must* they? It might seem that Locke is committed to an affirmative response, since he has argued that all persons have a duty to preserve mankind, and this seems to entail a duty to aid beleaguered minorities. But this duty to preserve mankind, of course, is severely constrained in Locke, the most central condition being that one is bound to aid others only "when his own preservation comes not in competition" (II, 6). It may well be that Locke took this condition to be applicable in the case of minority oppression, for to ask the people to take up arms and to shake the foundations of government when they (or the majority) are not personally injured might seem to be to ask them to risk their own preservation in order to aid others: "it being safer for the body that some few should be sometimes in danger to suffer, than that the head of the republic should be easily, and upon slight occasions exposed" (II, 205). Such a claim may not be particularly persuasive; but what cannot, in any event, be denied is that Locke uniformly refrains from saying that the people *must* aid individual victims of injustice. Locke's language (like his language with regard to punishment) is always the language of *option*; we have the right to aid the oppressed, but not a duty to do so.[63] Perhaps Locke is worried that such a duty would conflict with the citizen's duty to obey the law and support the society's chosen government. Perhaps he is only concerned that defense of such a duty would open his theory to charges of rabble rousing and invitation to anarchy—"all those mischiefs of blood, rapine, and desolation which the breaking to pieces of governments bring on a country" (II, 230). But it seems clear that Locke expects the people to resist only when government has become "the common enemy and pest of mankind" (II, 230), not when it has become the enemy of only a few.

Indeed, it is not even obvious that Locke takes the people to have a duty to resist injustices done to the body of the people. The people *may* resist "whenever they judge the cause to be of sufficient moment" (II, 168). Locke writes of the slowness of the people to respond to injustice (e.g., II, 225, 230) *not* as if this constitutes a breach

---

[62] Grant, *Liberalism*, 167.

[63] As Andrew argues: "the right of rebellion imposes no duty to aid the victims of governmental oppression" (*Shylock's Rights*, 112).

of duty on their part, a grave moral wrong, but rather as if this is, at the very worst, merely regrettable. The people will bear "great mistakes" and many bad laws "without mutiny or murmur"; they are "more disposed to suffer, than right themselves by resistance." Nor does Locke ever suggest that the people do any wrong in being thus patient and long-suffering. Locke does say, of course, that the people (like individuals) cannot give their governors the right to destroy them; but the people also "reserved that ultimate determination to themselves, which belongs to all mankind, . . . to judge whether they have just cause to make their appeal to heaven" (II, 168). Here Locke seems to suggest that any rightholder, be it the people as a whole or any member of "mankind," has as well the liberty to determine when it is appropriate to resist violations of the right. One may tolerate such violations or resist, repair, and punish them, as one judges acceptable. Elsewhere, Locke seems to argue that it is the people's special standing (*not* shared by all rightholders) as settlor of a trust that gives them the special right to judge when the trust has been breached (II, 240). But again there is no suggestion that the settlor has a *duty* to remove the trustee the moment the trust is breached. It is the settlor's right to judge when the trustee's performance is intolerable and when it is not.

Insofar as this *is* Locke's position,[64] it is not, I think, acceptable. Perhaps individuals have the right to passively accept violations of their own rights, and perhaps settlors have sole discretion where breach of their trust is concerned. But there is another party to the moral transaction between people and government who is forgotten in the analogies with individual rightholders/settlors and their rights to judge. Individual rightholders often do not have a *duty* to exercise their rights. Settlors, insofar as they invest their own property, at least often do not have a duty to exercise their rights over their trus-

---

[64] It is argued by some that Locke *accepts* a duty to resist. Cranston, for instance, finds this duty in Locke (*John Locke*, 211, 303), as does Dunn (see below). Grant argues that in Locke each has a duty to resist injustice that derives from consenting to join a society (*Liberalism*, 131), while Dworetz maintains that the duty to resist in Locke follows from the duty each has to tend to the salvation of his soul (and hence to preserve the liberty necessary for that activity) (*Unvarnished Doctrine*, 174–76). These arguments cannot yield a duty to resist injustice done to others or to minorities. But the real difficulty lies not in believing that Locke *should* have said these things, but rather in finding any textual support for reading Locke as defending them. And there are some (historical) grounds for supposing that Locke might not have wanted to defend a duty to resist. By merely asserting a right to resist, but no duty to do so, Locke reassures a skittish public that while they need not feel duty-bound to take up arms in support of an uprising, they clearly have no duty to *oppose* one. He thus encourages those who cannot bring themselves to actively resist to believe that simply staying out of the way is morally acceptable.

tees. But the *people* (as rightholder and settlor) *do* have a duty to exercise their rights. For the people have made a contract with every member of the community to exercise that member's rights (transferred by the member to the people) for the good of every member. The people promise to use their new power to secure the property (rights) of each citizen. And in light of that promise, the people are *not* morally free to decide to tolerate the oppression of either a few or many of their members. It is as if the settlor had promised some third party to strictly enforce the terms of the trust; the settlor's normal judgment or discretion would surely be constrained by such a promise, as is the people's liberty to judge when the cause is "of sufficient" moment constrained by the contract that created one people from a mass of individual rightholders. The people not only charge their government with "the preservation of every man's right and property" and with seeking "the good of every particular member of that society" (I, 92);[65] the people promise their members to oversee that trust. The people have a duty to resist injustice (i.e., violations of the rights of any of their members or of the people as a whole).[66] Locke seems determined not to acknowledge this consequence of his overall position, perhaps (again) out of fear that such a theory would appear too radical, by encouraging (or being thought to encourage) rebellion on "slight occasions."[67] But Locke need not have worried so about defending a duty to resist, for (as we will soon see) the simple fact of a right or duty to resist is not for Locke sufficient to justify resistance in all cases.

If Locke was determined to deny that the people had a duty to resist injustice, owed to individual citizens, he seems to have been just as determined to deny that the people owed any such duty to

[65] Appeals to the common good are clearly reduced by Locke in this passage to appeals to the good of each individual. See also, e.g., II, 134 ("every person in it"); II, 171 (harming only "corrupt" members); ECT, 185 ("the preservation, as much as possible, of the property, quiet, and life of every individual being [the magistrate's] duty, he is obliged not to disturb or destroy some for the quiet and safety of the rest, till it has been tried whether there be no ways to save all"); King, *Life*, 2:109 ("the end of civil society is civil peace and prosperity, or the preservation of the society and every member thereof in a free and peaceable enjoyment of all the good things of this life that belong to each of them"); L, 126 ("It is the duty of the civil magistrate . . . to secure unto all the people in general, and to every one of his subjects in particular, the just possession of these things belonging to this life").

[66] This seems to be the argument Dunn attributes to Locke (*Locke*, 56). While I agree that Locke is committed to this position, I can find no indication in the text of any real willingness on his part to acknowledge it.

[67] Notice that the authors of the American Declaration of Independence do not share Locke's concerns on this point, for from essentially the same Lockean premises they conclude that the people have both a right and a duty to resist oppression.

God. Locke certainly knew that one could argue on religious grounds for a duty to resist tyranny, owed directly to God, as had, for instance, the author of the *Vindiciae* and earlier radical Calvinist authors.[68] Locke could have argued for a mandatory right of resistance (a right to do our duty). But he quite clearly does *not* choose to argue in this way. Locke's decision to discuss the issue of resistance in the moral context of a trust between the people (as settlor and beneficiary) and the government (as trustee) makes it clear that the moral issue for Locke is between the people and those they trust. God is only the ultimate judge of the lawfulness of resistance (as he is of all things), not an injured party demanding justice. Locke's theory of resistance can thus properly be thought of as a "genuinely political" theory, rather than a predominantly religious one.[69] It is not quite accurate to say with Quentin Skinner that Locke's position is "the classic formulation of a fully secularized and populist theory of revolution,"[70] for the theory of rights on which the theory of revolution rests is itself based on largely theological foundations. But it is certainly true that Locke's arguments about revolution are logically detachable from those foundations, an aspect of Locke's project that is a quite deliberate and largely successful attempt on his part to make his arguments appeal more widely. Locke's theory of rights *could* be anchored on quite secular foundations, resulting in a "fully secularized" theory of revolution. Indeed, Locke appears to approach such a position whenever the consequentialist justifications for his claims are pushed to the fore.[71]

If Locke faces problems of consistency in his apparent denial of a general duty to resist injustice, he seems to face problems just as troubling (and for the same kinds of reasons) in his use of the concept of dissolution of government. We have seen (in 6.2) that dissolution is for Locke a *moral* concept: a government is dissolved when it loses its authority, its entrusted right to govern (its "political power"). And we have seen as well that dissolution (from within) can be characterized in general terms as resulting from breach of trust. But if the trust in question requires government to secure the

[68] Skinner, *Foundations of Modern Political Thought*, 2:240; Lessnoff, *Social Contract*, 33.

[69] Ibid., 335–36, 338–39.

[70] Skinner, "Origins of the Calvinist Theory of Revolution," 309–12.

[71] As in II, 205: "the inconvenience of some particular mischiefs . . . are well recompenced by the peace of the public"; or in II, 229, where Locke seems to try to derive conclusions about the right of resistance from asking "which is best for mankind?" On the secular strain in Locke's moral theory, see my *Lockean Theory of Rights*, chapter 1.

rights of "every particular member" of the society, why is the trust not breached and the government dissolved *whenever* the rights of citizens—individuals, minorities, or the majority—are violated by the government? This question can be given a more precise formulation, for we know that no society can be realistically expected *never* to violate any of its citizens' rights. A society can agree to (and a government be entrusted to) do no more than make an honest, careful effort to secure its citizens' rights. This commitment is consistent with occasional, unintentional injustice and with, for instance, the imperfections of criminal justice systems, the best of which unavoidably harm innocent persons on occasion. The acceptance of the risk of these sorts of injustices, we may say, is implicitly agreed to by all consenting citizens of legitimate polities, for it is simply part of the price of being a member of any society (as is, for instance, the risk of being called on to fight in the society's defense). There is, then, no breach of contract by society, or breach of trust by government, in the event of occasional, accidental wrongs to individuals (it is not possible, Locke might say, to declare war by accident). But regular, systematic injustices against individuals or minorities are a different matter altogether. "For wherever violence is used and injury done, though by hands appointed to administer justice, it is still violence and injury, however coloured with the name, pretences, or forms of law, the end whereof being to protect and redress the innocent, by an unbiassed application of it, to all who are under it" (II, 20). Where governments deliberately abuse the innocent, or where they craft bad laws under which to prosecute the harmless, they breach their trust. Where society does nothing to remedy such injustice, it breaks its contract with those so abused, denying them their final earthly appeal (i.e., to the will of the majority). Our more precise question, then, should be this: why does Locke not claim that the government is dissolved whenever there is deliberate violation by the government of the rights of any of its subjects (including "particular men")?

The difficulty we face is that on our current understanding of the concept of "dissolution," dissolution should be a simple matter of moral fact. If government has breached its trust, it has dissolved itself (forfeited its authority), lost its legitimacy, and reduced the governors to the status of ordinary persons. But this understanding of dissolution is consistent with at least three theoretically troubling possibilities: (1) the government might be dissolved (hence illegitimate) even though none of its subjects believed it to be dissolved or cared about its transgressions; (2) the government might be dissolved although only some individuals (or some minority) believed it to be, the majority remaining convinced of its legitimacy; (3) the government might remain *undissolved* even though its subjects wrongly judged it to have breached its trust (and dissolved itself) and were prepared to remove it by force. At least the third of these possibilities is considered by Locke when he notes that "whoever . . . lays the foundation for overturning the constitution and frame of any just government is guilty of the greatest crime . . . a man is capable of." One possible cause of such unjust rebellion is "the people's wantonness" (II, 230). This makes it clear that it is possible for the people to judge wrongly that their government has dissolved itself. How, then, is the idea of dissolution tied to the idea of the people's "right to judge"? What does Locke mean when he asserts again and again that "the people shall be judge" (e.g., II, 240)?

First, I think it is clear that Locke means that the relevant judgments are those that accord with the will of the majority of freemen incorporated in the society (and not, for instance, the majority of landowners[72]). The "people" of II, 223 could hardly be anything but the full body of freemen in society, and it is the majority of this people whose right it is to judge. Further, the contract that creates civil society is made among all those who consent to join it (and who thereby give up some of their rights to it) (II, 95). Each member "puts himself under an obligation to every one of that society, to submit to the determination of the majority" (II, 97). The majority which, as a result, has "a right to act and conclude the rest" (II, 95) can thus only be the majority of *rightholders* (i.e., freemen) who have joined the society. Every freeman has an equal interest in judging whether his entrusted rights are being employed for the good of all, but each has surrendered the right to judge in this matter to the majority of

---

[72] Macpherson, of course, has argued that Locke allows no right of revolution for the (essentially irrational) laboring class, the relevant "majority" being comprised of landowners (*Possessive Individualism*, 224). Others who share this view of Locke's conception of "the people" (although sometimes for different reasons than Macpherson's) include Andrew (*Shylock's Rights*, 114–16), Wood (*Politics of Locke's Philosophy*, 39), Plamenatz (*Man and Society*, 1:250), Replogle (*Recovering the Social Contract*, 205–6), and Dunn ("Politics of Locke," 60–61). Ashcraft has, I think, convincingly demonstrated that there is no warrant in Locke's texts for such an understanding of "the people," and that there are very good reasons for supposing the contrary (namely, that "the people" are the "freemen" in society). See *Locke's Two Treatises*, 219–20, 225, and *Revolutionary Politics*, 298–311, 560–66, 579–82, 588. See also the persuasive argument to this same conclusion in Richards, Mulligan, and Graham, " 'Property' and 'People,' " 46–47. Others who have argued for the view I urge here include Ryan ("Locke and the Dictatorship," 247) and Drury ("Locke and Nozick on Property," 38).

his fellows (although, as we have seen, each *retains* the right to judge in matters where those rights he has kept are at issue).

Second, Locke seems to intend that the "judgment of the people" be in an important sense *performative* in nature. It is (in part) the people's judgment that a government is dissolved (has breached its trust) that *makes* that government dissolved. Thus, Locke stresses the people's right to resist "whenever they judge the cause of sufficient moment" (II, 168) and their right as settlor "to discard" their trustee (II, 240). But the people's judgment cannot be sufficient by itself for dissolution, since the people may judge wrongly that their trust has been breached (as we have seen). "The power that every individual gave the society" and that society has placed in the hands of government "can never revert to the people while that government lasts"; only when that trust is temporary "or else when by the miscarriages of those in authority, it is forfeited" can political power "revert to the society" (II, 243). There must actually *be* a miscarriage for government to forfeit its authority.[73] This is the warning Locke conveys in the final paragraph of the *Second Treatise*. The position suggested by these apparently conflicting ideas is this: the judgment of the people that the government is acting ultra vires and hence dissolved is a necessary but not sufficient condition for the moral dissolution of government. Merely having a majority judgment that the government is in breach of its trust cannot *by itself* dissolve a government that has in fact done no wrong (although the subsequent *physical* dissolution of government, brought about by unlawful popular rebellion, will accomplish the moral demise of government as well). But neither is an actual breach of the trust by government by *itself* sufficient to dissolve the government, for the people may choose to be patient and to tolerate its excesses (provided they do not threaten its very preservation). Only when there is both an actual breach and a performative judgment of dissolution by the majority of society's freemen is the government morally dissolved. But because for practical purposes the people must also be the judge that decides when an actual breach has occurred, the people's judgment of dissolution is *practically* performative (even if not morally incorrigible).[74]

[73] This view of Locke's position seems to be in agreement with Gough (*Political Philosophy*, 132) and Parry (*John Locke*, 139). Kendall reads Locke as arguing that the majority may exercise its right of revolution "at its own discretion" (*Majority-Rule*, 99–101, 127–28), but even he notes some of the many passages that appear to conflict with his reading. The interpretation I offer here explains both the passages that seem to support Kendall's reading and those that obviously conflict with it.

[74] The freedom of the settlor (the people) to remove the trustee (the government),

We should hardly be surprised to find Locke espousing such a position on the people's "right to judge," for it simply mirrors his view of the individual's right to judge (in the state of nature) in matters of punishment and reparation. When Locke asks "who shall be judge?" in private cases,[75] he answers "I myself can only be judge in my own conscience" of whether another has wronged me (II, 21). But my judgment of wrongdoing is not sufficient to justify my actions (e.g., punishing another), for "if he that judges, judges amiss in his own or any other case, he is answerable for it to the rest of mankind" (II, 13). Actual wrongdoing is necessary to justify punishing; but I may, by deciding *not* to punish a wrong done me, performatively forgive the one who has wronged me (or by judging him guilty, make him liable to punishment).[76] I have the right, but not the duty, to punish every actual breach of my rights. For this reason, once this executive right is transferred to government, the magistrate "can often, where the public good demands not the execution of the law, remit the punishment of criminal offences by his own authority" (II, 11). Just as the magistrate can decline to punish where it seems best, the people can decline to dissolve their government even if it has breached its trust.

A consequence of this view, of course, is that a government can remain legitimate (with respect to the majority) even while it violates the rights of individuals and minorities (or, perhaps even worse, while it violates the rights of an apathetic majority or a majority benighted by ignorance or false consciousness), provided only that the majority never elects to judge it in breach of its trust. Lest this seem a shallow (or even vile) conception of legitimacy, we should try to remember that Locke's position is in fact one not altogether implausible solution to an extremely difficult problem in

---

to which I referred in 3.2, is a *limited* freedom when looked at from an objective moral point of view. The trust at issue is in some ways an irrevocable trust, since it cannot be legitimately withdrawn without just cause. In a legal trust, of course, there is a judge to decide when the trust has been breached. But in the *political* trust, there is no judge authorized to decide controversies between people and government (except God). So the question arises: who is to judge? Locke's answer is that the moral facts of the matter are one thing, and all the parties will ultimately be judged by God. But for *practical* purposes, the people must be accepted as the best judge of when an actual breach has occurred. For the entrusted rights are ultimately theirs, and their interests in seeing those rights properly used are far more important than the trustees' interests in maintaining their positions.

[75] This question, of course, echoes Filmer's similar question "Who shall judge?" in *Patriarcha*, I, 2.

[76] This is, in fact, only one of two positions suggested by Locke. The right to punish is said by Locke both to belong to the victim of the wrongdoing (the criminal's rights are forfeited *to* the victim) and to all persons. See *Lockean Theory of Rights*, section 3.5.

political philosophy. For it is far from obvious what stance to take on the question of the moral status of effective governments that systematically harm some of their subjects. Did the government of the United States in the first half of the nineteenth century lose all legitimacy by virtue of its condoning the systematic and dramatic abuse of a racial minority? Was this government "dissolved" (assuming here that it would otherwise have been legitimate), so that anyone might without wrongdoing disregard its laws and official pronouncements (about otherwise morally neutral matters)? A "yes" answer, of course, would be far from outrageous. But those who oppose such an answer can plausibly appeal to the fact that for the unabused majority (and even, although to a considerably smaller extent, for the abused minority) the government still upheld the rule of law, preserved the peace, and coordinated the provision of many essential benefits.[77] It was still "doing its job," even while breaching its trust to protect equally *all* of its subjects ("one rule for rich and poor," etc. [II, 142]). Locke's solution to this problem is to claim that even a government that deliberately wrongs some of its subjects remains legitimate with respect to the body of the people, until they themselves find its excesses intolerable (and judge it to be in breach). The people may reach this "point of no return" as a result of moral indignation about injustice to others, although Locke clearly believes they will as a rule reach it only when they are made to fear for their own security and freedom. Abused individuals and minorities, by contrast, are *morally* free to resist and repair (and perhaps even punish) the wrongs their governments do them. Every person is judge in the case of his own (retained, untransferred) rights; and where there is an actual, deliberate infringement of those rights by government and a performative judgment by that individual that "the cause is of sufficient moment," the government is dissolved *with respect to that person*. If society does nothing to aid the wronged individual, society also loses its moral authority over him (is dissolved with respect to him), and he is returned to the state of nature (simpliciter). There may be no prudent recourse available to the individual but patient acceptance of wrongs done him. But right is on his side (and, presumably, God pays serious attention to such matters).

The greatest weakness in Locke's position on these questions is not in his denial that the people have a duty to overthrow their gov-

[77] Locke suggests in a journal entry that even illegitimate governments still provide services and are hence owed at least some obligations (see Den Hartogh's discussion of this entry in "Made by Contrivance," 215).

ernment whenever it deliberately abuses individuals or minorities. Few reasonable people believe that they have such a duty. The greatest weakness lies rather in Locke's failure to acknowledge that the people have a duty at least to employ less drastic measures than revolution in defense of their innocent but victimized colleagues. Locke seems able to imagine only violent overthrow or passive acceptance of unjust government as practical political options. Where the injustice reaches only a few, the latter option seems to him obviously preferable to the former. And most of us can accept this reasoning, as far as it goes, for most of us accept with Locke the moral importance of the consequences of our actions (in this case, the preferability of tolerable civil peace to possible anarchy)—some injustices are not worth making the heavens fall. But the limited options Locke considers betray the limits of his imagination. He does not imagine (or, at least, he does not discuss) ways in which a people might without overthrowing their government nonetheless force it to halt unjust oppression of minorities, nor does he seem to see that it is at least *this* kind of aid that the people owe as a moral duty to those of their number whose rights are systematically violated. It is too much to ask that we pull our government down, possibly unleashing a social whirlwind, whenever citizens are abused. But it is *not* too much to ask that we *act* on their behalf.[78] Indeed, Locke is logically committed to the people's duty in this area. For, as we have seen, society has, first, a contractual duty to look to the security of *every* innocent member. And second, *every* person, in or out of society, has a natural duty to help preserve others "when his own preservation comes not in competition." Armed revolution and violent overthrow of government on behalf of another may reasonably be thought to bring my own preservation in competition. But aid to the oppressed of other kinds (e.g., concerted, nonviolent political action) cannot; on Locke's own principles we owe such aid, both as fellow citizens and as fellow persons. Locke may have believed that to embrace such a view would be to make himself too vulnerable to charges of inviting anarchy. But if so, he erred doubly. For his moral (and political) theory demands this view; and the relevant factual

---

[78] Settlors often have the legal power to punish or limit the authority of their trustees, instead of removing them altogether. This constitutes a kind of remedy (for trustee wrongdoing) intermediate between passive acceptance and complete removal. Locke never discusses such intermediate remedies in the political case (although perhaps the efforts by Parliament to assemble without being called counted as a recent historical instance of such a remedy). It appears that Locke's eagerness for revolution either blinded him to or made him reluctant to mention both the theoretical possibility and the historical precedent for intermediate remedies.

judgment (that acknowledgment of the people's duty to oppressed minorities invites anarchy) is demonstrably false.

Just as Locke worries (too much) about the social consequences of a duty on the people to aid oppressed individuals, he also worries about the social consequences of a right of resistance for those individuals themselves. As we have seen, Locke tries hard to assure his readers that a belief in individual rights of resistance will have no dire consequences for society. Although oppressed individuals have a right to resist, "yet the right to do so will not easily engage them in a contest wherein they are sure to perish" (II, 208). Nor are the people likely to rally to the cause of these individuals, for "the examples of particular injustice or the oppression of here and there an unfortunate man moves them not" (II, 230). Locke does not, however, seem able to give his audience the kind of "juridical guarantee" that his doctrine does not threaten the peace that that audience undoubtedly wanted.[79] He gives them only *predictions* about the likely consequences of individual rights of resistance, based on empirical observations about individual prudence (II, 208) and societal motivations (II, 230). It is foolish to exercise a right when doing so will lead to your destruction. But Locke's emphasis on this merely *prudential* limit on individual rights of resistance forces us to confront the question of whether Locke has in mind any moral limits on the exercise of these rights. If an oppressed individual (or minority) is able safely to do so, can he (or they) rightfully overturn an established (undissolved) government, if doing so is necessary to defend himself against and/or secure reparation from government for deliberate violations of his rights?

Locke issues several warnings about our responsibility for the consequences of our acts of resistance. "He that appeals to heaven must be sure he has right on his side; and a right too that is worth the trouble and cost of the appeal, as he will answer at a tribunal that cannot be deceived" (II, 176). The republic should not "be easily and upon slight occasions exposed " (II, 205), and he who wrongly overturns a just government "is guilty of the greatest crime . . . a man is capable of" (II, 230). How should we understand such warnings? One way would be to take Locke to be saying that the right of individual resistance "is one which he may only exercise if to do so is unlikely to damage the interests of others."[80] But this is not exactly

[79] Franklin, *John Locke and the Theory of Sovereignty,* 96, 112.

[80] Dunn, *Political Thought,* 178–79. Dunn is actually speaking here of the right a wronged subject has to punish the ruler, but his remarks seem intended to apply to rights of resistance generally. One may, of course, destroy the legal order for defense

what Locke actually says. Locke affirms the right of a wronged individual to resist (for defense and reparation) *without conditions*. He warns that such a right must be used responsibly—not, for instance, on the occasion of trivial injustices, "slight occasions" of violations of rights that are "not worth the trouble" of resistance. It may sometimes be wrong to exercise the right one possesses. The social consequences must be considered. But Locke never says the wronged individual must not exercise his right to resist if the interests of others (e.g., in keeping unjustly acquired property or in preserving a government that oppresses some minority) will be threatened. On the contrary, Locke makes it clear that an innocent man need not submit to injustice simply because his resistance might threaten the peace or well-being of others. If we assert the contrary, we might as well say

> that honest men may not oppose robbers or pirates, because this may occasion disorder or bloodshed. If any mischief come in such cases, it is not to be charged upon him who defends his own right, but on him that invades his neighbor's. If the honest man must quietly quit all he has for peace's sake, to him who will lay violent hands upon it, I desire it may be considered what kind of peace there will be in the world, which consists only of violence and rapine and which is to be maintained only for the benefit of robbers and oppressors.[81] (II, 228)

What, then, should we make of Locke's warnings about the social consequences of resistance? If individuals have a right to resist injustice in civil society, this means for Locke that they have a virtually absolute moral justification for resistance. But the justification is only *virtually* absolute. The right to resist may be overridden or outweighed by conflicting rights or by dramatic social utilities.[82] By "dramatic social utilities" I mean to refer only to those cases in

---

and reparation, without punishment being an issue at all. Richards seems to me to come close to Locke's actual position when he suggests that for Locke there is a right to resist when (a) one is released from the obligation to obey, (b) resistance is feasible, and (c) the rights of innocent third parties are not endangered by resistance (*Toleration and the Constitution*, 98). But, as we have seen, feasibility does not affect *possession* of the right to resist, for Locke, and condition (c) needs to be expanded to isolate instances of justified resistance (as I argue below).

[81] Similarly, in his writings on toleration, Locke makes it clear that citizens should look to their own souls first and worry about preserving the public peace second (e.g., L, 154).

[82] This seems a better reading of the passages that Dunn summarizes as saying that "consequent (unjust) individual suffering is sanctioned by social expediency" (*Political Thought*, 179n).

which the cost of resistance (in terms of the effective preservation of mankind) is extremely high, or where the difference between the cost of and what is secured by resistance is very large (the right at issue must be "worth the trouble and cost of the appeal"). In cases involving conflicts of right or where utility losses in exercising a right are severe, direct appeal to the first principle of morality ("humankind is to be preserved") resolves the issue.[83]

Both dramatic social utilities and conflicts of right *may* be at stake where individual resistance is contemplated. But they need not be. Individual (or minority) resistance *might* threaten chaos and bloody anarchy. More likely it will threaten either nothing of consequence at all, the awakening of the people's conscience, pressure on the government to reform (or even the violent removal of some unjust governor[s]), and so on. And none of these latter consequences would render resistance unjustifiable in most instances. Similarly, while individual resistance *might* attack the legitimate rights of others, more likely it will threaten *unjust* claims—for instance, my claim to be left in peace by those who are abused at the hands of a government I support. The people have a right "to have such a legislative over them as the majority should approve and freely acquiesce in" (II, 176). But they do *not* have a right to have a government that violates the rights of innocent persons. Indeed, the people have a right to exist as a body in the first place only because in thus incorporating themselves, they "injure not the freedom of the rest" (II, 95). Their incorporation gives them no new right to injure anyone, in or out of society, who has not freely consented to surrender the relevant rights.

Locke tells the individual resister, then, that if the rights he has retained in society are systematically infringed by his government, he has a right to resist and demand reparation for those wrongs, whenever he judges the occasion to be appropriate. He must be careful that he is in the right in exercising his right and that the issue is serious, for if he errs in this, he risks being guilty of the worst possible wrong (II, 218, 230). And he must keep in mind the likely consequences of his acts, making sure that what he can reasonably expect to accomplish will not be disastrous for his fellow men, and that he violates no equally important rights of others in the process. Beyond these concerns, however, he need have only a prudent regard for his own safety, and perhaps not even this if his cause is morally urgent.

[83] See *Lockean Theory of Rights*, section 1.4.

This is, I believe, the *right* message for Locke to send to the person (or group) contemplating individual (or minority) resistance to a government that oppresses him (or them). Only Locke's silence about the people's duty to aid the oppressed sends the wrong message. On balance, then, it may well be that Locke's "doctrine of resistance is . . . the most valuable part of his political theory."[84] For it is in his theory of resistance that Locke presents his most compelling political application of his theory of rights. It is in his theory of resistance that Locke completes his account of the political relationship, applying his views of political consent and of the limits on political consensual transactions to an analysis of injustice and misfortune in actual political life.

[84] Plamenatz, *Man and Society,* 1:234.

PART 4

CONSENT AND THE EDGE OF ANARCHY

We have now explored the three basic elements of the Lockean conception of the political relationship: its accounts of our natural moral condition and nonpolitical relationships (in part 1), of the consensual transaction necessary to the creation of legitimate political society (what I have called the ground of the political relationship) (in part 2), and of the moral limits on this transaction and on the society it creates (in part 3). In each case I carefully examined and analyzed Locke's writings, in an effort to present a clear, coherent, and philosophically sensitive picture of his views. I also criticized, developed, or abandoned Locke's positions, as seemed most reasonable, in ways that I took to be still broadly consistent with the spirit of Locke's political philosophy. Thus, I clarified and supported the basic Lockean conception of the state of nature (in chapter 1), Lockean political voluntarism (in chapter 3), and the broad outlines of Locke's theory of justified political resistance in a consensual society (in chapter 6), while also arguing for the necessity of serious revisions in (among other things) Locke's account of war (in chapter 2), in his application of that account to his theory of resistance (in chapter 6), in his employment of the idea of tacit political consent, and in his defense of majority rule (both in chapter 4). I also urged (in chapter 5) the abandonment of any Lockean reliance on the idea of the inalienability of certain natural rights, and consequently also the rejection of those aspects of Locke's own moral theory that commit him to claims of inalienability (despite this being a commitment of which Locke seemed quite unaware).

I take the arguments of parts 1–3 of this work to have placed before us the strongest possible version of a Lockean conception of the political relationship. This version is not Locke's, exactly, but rather an improvement on Locke's that departs from his version only in ways that permit it still to be considered truly Lockean in its basic commitments. It is, in my view, the core of a presentable Lockean political philosophy—that is, it is the heart of a Lockean program in political philosophy, as it ought to be presented to contemporary political philosophers, to be accepted, used, or rejected as its virtues merit.

I will argue in part 4 that the primary weakness of Lockean political philosophy lies not in its basic voluntarist principles (and concepts), but rather in the way that Locke (with many other subsequent theorists) tries to apply those principles to yield certain desired and intuitively appealing conclusions about rights and obligations in actual polities. To see this, however, we must return to the central Lockean idea of political consent, whose basic role in Lockean theory we examined in part 2. Our (re)concentration in part 4 on political consent is necessitated, of course, by that idea's role as the pivotal concept in all components of the Lockean picture of political relationships. The Lockean conception of nonpolitical relationships, for instance, is the conception of relationships among persons in the absence of a special sort of *consensual* tie. The Lockean conception of the limits on the possible extent of the political relationship is, similarly, just a conception of the moral limits on binding *consent*. And the Lockean account of justified political resistance is an account that applies only within a *consensual* community—that is, it is an account of when others may be understood to have exceeded the terms of individual or majority consent (contract, trust).

The idea of political consent is thus the idea on which rest the other central elements of Lockean political philosophy. If Lockean consent theory is indefensible or if it is misapplied, so will be the Lockean conceptions of nonpolitical relationships and of the limits on (and of the justified responses to others' exceeding the limits on) the political relationship. It is thus to possible attacks on consent theory and to the conclusions warranted by those attacks that I turn my attention in the remaining pages of this study. We must now ask, for instance: to what extent can the ideal of legitimate consensual civil society described by Lockean theory be taken to characterize our actual political lives, or to what extent can we (or must we) alter actual political practice to conform to this ideal? Chapter 7 begins to answer these questions by examining what has come to be the standard critique of Lockean consent theory (and of the Lockean conception of the political relationship) and by evaluating the interpretations of Locke's own consent theory that might allow him to escape this critique. But chapter 8 will bear the main burden of criticism. For its purpose is to ask whether any consent theory, not just Locke's, or any voluntarist political philosophy can deal with the problems Locke's consent theory was designed to solve. The answer, we will see, presses us toward a Lockean philosophical anarchism, the position to which we are driven if we remain true to the best, most defensible elements of Locke's political philosophy.

THE CRITIQUE OF LOCKEAN
CONSENT THEORY

7.1. Hume's Attack

I commented earlier in this study (3.3) on the source of the appeal (and of the plausibility) of Lockean consent theory. We saw then as well, however, the wide range of opposed conceptions of political obligation and authority. And not all of those opponents were collectivist or communitarian (or otherwise anti-individualist) in basic orientation. Indeed, there is a prominent tradition of individualist opposition to Lockean voluntarism in Anglo-American philosophy that can be traced back at least to David Hume's essay, "Of the Original Contract." Hume's critique of consent theory was not in any way gentle or qualified. He wrote that in most parts of the world, one who openly espoused the consent theory of political authority and obligation would undoubtedly be shut up "as delirious, for advancing such absurdities."[1] Since that time considerable philosophical energy has been expended in attempts to revive or revise the Lockean consent theory against which Hume's attack was mounted. But while none of these efforts has been obviously the product of delirium, neither has any been obviously successful as a defense of consent theory. Hume's arguments continue to seem forceful, and I will want to discuss them later in this chapter. But before considering arguments against consent theory, we would do well to get clear on just what would count as a *defense* of consent theory.

It is typically agreed all around that genuine, freely given consent can at least sometimes create de jure political authority and ground political obligations. Few have denied that a promise or contract to obey, express consent to a just government's authority, or at least an ongoing pattern of real political participation in a free society can

[1] "Of the Original Contract," 259.

(assuming suitable background conditions) bind a citizen to obey. Even Hume conceded that consent is "the best and most sacred" foundation of government, that genuine consent (at least within certain limits) is sufficient to ground political obligations and political authority (and is a desirable foundation of political society).[2] The attack on consent theory usually grants this much. But the consent theorist wants to claim more.

The classical defense of consent theory (including Locke's) involves not only claiming that consent (under certain conditions) is sufficient for political obligation, but also establishing three further positions:

(1) That consent is not just sufficient (within the limits described in chapter 5), but *necessary* for political authority and obligation (see 3.3). What is distinctive about consent theory is its insistence that there is no possible source of legitimate government *other* than the consent of the governed.

(2) That both "direct," explicit consensual acts and certain kinds of "indirect" acts or performances can count as ways of giving binding consent, and, in particular, as ways of giving consent to the authority of some government. The most important part of this position concerns the specification of what will be taken to give tacit or implicit (indirect, implied, virtual) consent (as we saw in 4.1).

(3) That a substantial number of ordinary citizens in ordinary states actually do things that count as the giving of consent to their political authorities and institutions. Thus, some actual governments should turn out, on the consent theory account, to be morally legitimate with respect to at least significant numbers of their citizens. While this claim is in no way essential to consent theory, the classical consent theorists (with the exception of Rousseau, but certainly including Locke) all wished to argue for the legitimacy of at least the most reasonable de facto political authorities.[3]

---

[2] Ibid., 262. See also Lessnoff, *Social Contract*, 67.

[3] That is, they wanted their consent theories to be not only "normatively robust," but also "descriptively plausible" (Herzog, *Happy Slaves*, 185). That consent theory can be evaluated by either conservative or critical standards has been noticed by several writers on the subject (e.g., Green, *Authority of the State*, 165–66; Beran, *Consent Theory*, 3, 49–50, 86; Klosko, "Reformist Consent," 676–78). A conservative evaluation would find consent theory a failure if few or no actual states turned out to be legitimate by its standards. A critical evaluation would find the theory a failure only if it exhibited serious internal defects, regardless of its practical implications for the status of existing governments.

Position (3), of course, displays its weakness center-stage. There is simply not much evidence in actual states of ordinary citizens doing things that look very much like giving morally interesting consent to political authorities. The problem for consent theory, then, is not one of intuitive *force*, but rather one of *realism*. And this problem was, of course, Locke's problem as well. Locke, as we have seen, embraced (1) above; and he was also concerned to affirm (as in [3] above) the legitimacy of at least some existing states (including his own, postrevolutionary, state[4]). But hordes of active consenters were no more in evidence in Locke's England than in twentieth-century England. Locke's solution to the problem was to offer a quite distinctive version of position (2) above, his famous theory of tacit consent (which we examined at some length in 4.1).

Because that theory of tacit consent allows Locke to portray residents, landowners, travelers on the highways, and lodgers in the inns—in short, all who enjoy the state's territories—as consenters, he has no problem appearing to show that actual states can be legitimate. But his solution also seems to face a series of devastating objections, which have collectively become the (dismissive) *standard critique* of Lockean consent theory:

(a) Locke's notion of tacit consent is not a plausible notion of real consent at all. Locke either embraces a model on which "consent" may be given without real choice, or he misapplies a more adequate model to actual political cases. If the former, Locke's tacit consent is too weak a form of "consent" from which to derive important obligations and right-transfers; and it allows that persons may, by simply residing or traveling, consent unintentionally, without realizing what they are doing (which is absurd). More charitably, perhaps, we can choose the latter reading (as I did in 4.1), according to which Locke intends a perfectly acceptable notion of tacit consent as genuine choice made by not-explicitly-consensual conduct. But then the criticism must be that Locke wishfully and implausibly characterizes behavior by ordinary citizens that need not constitute the making of a choice as nonetheless giving tacit consent to governmental authority.

(b) Locke's theory of tacit consent (or his applications of that theory) undermines the whole point of consent theory. For Locke al-

---

[4] Locke seeks, of course, to "make good [King William's] title in the consent of the People" (*Two Treatises*, preface). See Waldron's contrast of Locke and Rousseau on the legitimacy of actual governments (*Nonsense upon Stilts*, 20), and Bennett's slightly different formulation of Locke's problem ("Note on Locke's Theory of Tacit Consent," 226–27).

lows that tacit consent can be given by mere residence, for instance, apparently without conscious choice; such a consent theory (or application of consent theory) can in no way be consistent with Locke's affirmation of our natural freedom to choose where our allegiance will lie.

(c) Locke's theory justifies precisely what Locke (along with all consent theorists) wishes to oppose. Tacit consent is so wide a notion for Locke (or is applied by him so widely), that it justifies virtual subjection by birth, since all residents can be taken as obligated consenters. And it seems to justify as well subjection even to oppressive regimes or conquerors, since obedience is virtually equivalent to consent.[5]

Hume, without specifically identifying Locke as his target, offers one form of this standard critique of Lockean consent theory. Indeed, Hume attacks that theory (in "Of the Original Contract") on each of its three central claims ([1], [2], and [3] above). Hume's essay concludes with a "philosophical refutation" of consent theory, designed to show that consent is not necessary to establish an obligation of "allegiance" (against [1] above). This attempted refutation proceeds through Hume's presentation of a roughly utilitarian theory of obligation that is not, in my view, at all convincing.[6] But earlier

---

[5] For contemporary versions of the "standard critique," see Plamenatz, *Man and Society*, 1:227–28, 230, 234, and *Consent, Freedom, and Political Obligation*, 6–7, 169–70, 178–79; Gough, *Political Philosophy*, 64–65; Waldman, "Note on John Locke's Concept of Consent," 45; Pitkin, "Obligation and Consent—I," 995; Kleinig, "Ethics of Consent," 106; Green, *Authority of the State*, 166; Herzog, *Happy Slaves*, 183–85. In *Moral Principles and Political Obligations*, chapter 4, I stress (a) and (b), but reject criticism (c), in my presentation of the obvious first response to Locke's position.

[6] "Of the Original Contract," 267–69. It may be appropriate to make here a brief comment on Hume's central argument—i.e., that the obligation to keep a promise (fidelity) is no more basic or fundamental than political obligation (allegiance), so that it makes no sense to base the latter on the former (as the consent theorist does). Both obligations, Hume claims, are conventional or "artificial," justified by the utility of the relevant conventions in society. So we can "bypass" consent and justify allegiance by a direct appeal to utility.

The Lockean must respond that the obligation to keep a promise *is* more basic, for it is a natural obligation, not a purely conventional one (see Riley, *Will and Political Legitimacy*, 72–73; and my *Lockean Theory of Rights*, section 1.5). While Locke's own arguments for this obligation's being natural may not have impressed modern readers, the view that the obligation is natural is *not* an implausible one, nor is the view that in being natural it is more basic or fundamental than (clearly derivative) political obligations. Contrary to Hume's and (e.g.) T. H. Green's suggestion that there could be no contracts in a Lockean (preconventional) state of nature (*Lectures on the Principles of Political Obligation*, paragraph 52), see Scanlon's very convincing sketch of an argument that "the principle of fidelity to agreements is a natural moral requirement," with conventions serving only as an aid in helping us to create specific expectations ("Liberty, Contract, and Contribution," 244–45; see also the more recent develop-in his essay, Hume had attacked the Lockean defense of consent theory as well on positions (2) and (3). He argued persuasively both that Lockeans have counted as binding acts of consent things that quite clearly are not, and that ordinary citizens in ordinary states seldom do anything that can plausibly be regarded as a way of consenting to the authority of their governments.

The structure and plausibility of Hume's arguments, combined with the intuitive appeal of Lockean voluntarism, jointly suggest the possibility of adopting a position intermediate between the classical defense of consent theory and the thoroughgoing skepticism about consent demonstrated by Hume. If we suppose, with Locke and against Hume, that consent (or at least some voluntary performance) is necessary to bind citizen to state, but allow, with Hume and against Locke, that few people in existing states have done anything that could reasonably be taken as giving such consent, we are pushed to the conclusion of philosophical anarchism.[7] According to the philosophical anarchist, there are no morally legitimate states; few (if any) citizens in existing political societies have political obligations. Some philosophical anarchists, like Robert Wolff, have argued that there can be no legitimate states, rejecting the possibility of legitimacy on a priori grounds.[8] Others, who come to their conclusion from the kind of commitment to voluntarism described above, simply deny on *empirical* grounds that any legitimate states exist. If the political relationship between citizen and state could be rendered genuinely voluntary, citizens would have political obligations and governments de jure authority. But given present political practices, the requirement that the citizen-state relationship

---

ment of Scanlon's position in "Promises and Practices"). For other nonconventionalist conceptions of promissory obligations, see Robins, "Primacy of Promising"; and Fried, *Contract as Promise*, chapter 2. Other discussions of Hume's "philosophical refutation" can be found in Beran, "In Defense of the Consent Theory," 264–65, and *Consent Theory,* 92–95; Green, *Authority of the State,* 179–81; and my comments in *Moral Principles and Political Obligations,* 52–54.

[7] See Green, *Authority of the State,* 166, 189; and my discussions of voluntarism and anarchism in "Voluntarism and Political Associations." Schochet agrees that Locke's voluntarism is *philosophically* anarchic (since individuals need not join the political society), but correctly observes that Locke could take his position not to be *practically* anarchic (since he believed that most individuals do in fact freely join the society to which their parents belong)(*Patriarchalism,* 254). Lessnoff argues that Hume's critique does force consent theory to the anarchist conclusion, but that common sense cannot accept that conclusion. Therefore, consent (contract) theory of the Lockean sort must be rejected (*Social Contract,* 89). I reply to such lines of argument in 8.4.

[8] Wolff, *In Defense of Anarchism,* chapter 1. See my comments on a priori anarchism in "Voluntarism and Political Associations," 21, and "Anarchist Position," 269–70. See also Beran, *Consent Theory,* 86–91.

be fully voluntary is simply not met in existing societies. This is the form of philosophical anarchism that I have myself defended.[9]

In order to defeat this latter form of philosophical anarchism, one of two strategies must be adopted. Either the theorist must, as Hume attempts to do, offer a competing, nonvoluntarist ground of political obligation and authority, in order to show that a voluntary transaction between citizen and state is unnecessary in establishing the moral legitimacy of government. Or the theorist must argue, with Locke, that the behavior of actual citizens at least often includes genuine acts of consenting. I have tried elsewhere to undermine both of these strategies.[10] Here I wish to pursue these arguments further: first, by examining more closely the true nature of Locke's problem (in 7.2), and then by exploring the issue of what a Lockean *ought* to say on these questions (in chapter 8). The defense of political voluntarism in 1.3, 3.3, and chapter 8 argues against the first strategy, while the bulk of chapter 8 is intended to defeat the second.

7.2. The Meaning of Consent in Locke

How might Locke be rescued from the predicament sketched above, saved from the standard critique? For this critique finds in Locke's argument a degree of simplemindedness that we should be reluctant to attribute to a great thinker's work. A range of readings of Locke's consent theory has been offered, designed to show that he is not really so vulnerable to (all or part of) that critique as has been traditionally supposed. I advanced one such reading in *Moral Principles and Political Obligations*, where I argued that Locke at least often seems to confuse two quite different sources of political obligation in his discussion of consent: deliberate, intentional undertakings of obligation, on the one hand, and the willing receipt or acceptance of benefits provided by the government, on the other (the "enjoyment of any part of the dominions of any government" stressed by Locke).[11] While only the former is properly called "consent" (despite Locke's own broader use of that term), the latter seems another reasonably plausible suggestion concerning the source of people's political obligations.

[9] *Moral Principles and Political Obligations,* chapter 8. For other sorts of defenses of broadly anarchistic conclusions, see Smith, "Is There a Prima Facie Obligation to Obey the Law?"; Woozley, *Law and Obedience*; Raz, "Obligation to Obey the Law."

[10] *Moral Principles and Political Obligations.* The entire book can be viewed as an argument against the first strategy. Chapter 4 specifically argues against the second.

[11] *Moral Principles and Political Obligations,* 83–95. A similar view is suggested in passing by Plamenatz, *Consent, Freedom, and Political Obligation,* 24.

Thus, my reading of Locke accuses him not so much of a feeble consent theory of political obligation, as of having conflated two (or more) plausible grounds for political obligation under the term "consent."[12] And because even consent properly construed, in Locke, is not sufficient for obligation (as we saw in chapter 5), Locke escapes, as well, the charge that his account of consent would obligate all residents (visitors, etc.) to obey even unjust or tyrannical regimes. Locke, on my reading, is left primarily with the problems of having abused the term "consent" and of having relied upon a ground of political obligation (benefaction) that may be inconsistent with his apparent commitments to strict voluntarism and to full freedom of choice in one's political ties.

I will not repeat my arguments here, but will only note instead how natural it is for Locke to slide from voluntarily assumed obligations (consent) to not-necessarily-voluntarily assumed obligations (those arising from benefaction) in his account of political obligation. For Locke is searching for an account of our special ties to the states in which we reside, for an account of the particularized obligations that bind us to our countries of residence before all others. General (nonparticularized) duties to promote justice or to advance other desirable ends (such as utility) cannot play this role.[13] But some *nonconsensual* obligations can serve perfectly well to explain such special ties. The kinds of benefits we receive from our own societies, for instance, we generally receive from no others; so our obligations (if any) to repay such benefits might well tie us specially to our own societies over all others, even in the absence of our genuine consent to the authority of our own societies or their governments. Locke is looking, first and foremost, for a source of *created* (i.e., not natural)

---

[12] Others who seem to agree that such a reading of Locke is at least plausible include Pateman (*Political Obligation*, 73–74); Waldman ("Note on John Locke's Concept of Consent," 48); Dunn ("Consent," 36–37); MacCormick ("Law, Obligation and Consent," 407); Den Hartogh ("Express Consent," 108). Among those who find this reading unconvincing, Bennett argues that there is simply "no evidence in the text of the *Second Treatise*" that supports a claim that Locke was interested in benefaction as a ground of obligation ("Note on Locke's Theory of Tacit Consent," 232–33). I take Locke's frequent references (in the central passages, II, 119–21) to "enjoyments" as precisely such evidence. Herzog agrees that the evidence is present, but prefers to take Locke at his word when he claims that "his is a consent doctrine," not a doctrine of obligations to repay benefits (*Without Foundations*, 84–85). Grant takes a similar position, claiming that "Locke argues that obligations to obedience arise from consent rather than from a duty to one's benefactors" (*Liberalism*, 134). I concede, of course, that the general drift of Locke's thought *should* push him to a strict consent theory, but try to explain below (and in my earlier work) why his interests might have turned toward benefaction, construed by him as a kind of "consent."

[13] *Moral Principles and Political Obligations*, 30–35, 143–56.

obligations and rights for citizens and governors (as an answer to Filmer's naturalism).[14] Locke wishes above all to argue that each person is naturally free of political obligations and that political power is artificial (i.e., created by the acts of persons), not natural. Consent may be the most salient source of created obligations, being the vehicle for deliberate creation, but it is natural that Locke's arguments should lead him as well to consider less salient sources of created (special, particularized) obligations, such as willing benefaction. Whether this extension of Locke's "consent" theory actually aids his endeavors, I consider below (in 8.4).

The reading I suggest here, however, is far from being the only interpretation of Locke's consent theory that would avoid the main force of the standard critique. Another approach relies on identifying a second strand of argument in Locke as his true concern. Locke's consent arguments seem primarily concerned with the questions of how society gets authority over particular individuals and how legitimate polities come into existence in the first place. But he quite clearly is interested as well in the quality of governments, independent of any consideration about their origins or about who has consented to them. As we have seen, there is a straightforward sense in which the *Second Treatise* can be described as a defense of limited government—a defense of it as rationally preferable not only to all other kinds of government, but also to life in the state of nature (simpliciter) with no government at all (i.e., anarchy).

Just government, for Locke, operates within certain bounds (II, 142) and aims to promote certain ends (those ends whose promotion by government would make it rational for people to subject themselves to government [II, 137]). More specifically, just government aims at the preservation of its subjects' property (II, 124, 134), that is, their "lives, liberties and fortunes" (II, 137; see also II, 123); it has as its end "the securing of mens' rights" (II, 219).[15] The promotion of this end seems to be meant by Locke to be equivalent to the promotion of the "common good" (e.g., II, 131, 134, 135, 142). And just governments must promote these ends nonpaternalisti-

[14] Snare argues against the view that "consent," for Locke, is just "any sort of act which is said to create obligations, rights, powers, etc.," citing harming others and creating children as acts that create new obligations without counting as consent ("Consent and Conventional Acts," 31–32). I agree with this as a general interpretive point, but I believe that willing benefaction was one kind of obligation-creating "act" that did count for Locke as a form of consent.

[15] And "what was the end of erecting of government ought alone to be the measure of its proceeding" (ECT, 174).

cally (i.e., in accordance with the people's own assessment of what counts as promoting them).[16] When governments have these qualities (and only then), it is rational for all of us to live under them, since they then facilitate the advancement of both our civil and religious interests.[17] But is this not just a way of saying that governments with these qualities are *legitimate* with respect to all persons? Governments that best solve the problem of social interaction are legitimate and hence owed obedience (a la Hobbes), this line of argument suggests.

But now it seems easy to see consent beginning to drop out of Locke's true account of political authority and political obligation. If it is the quality and structure of government that make it legitimate, why should Locke be concerned with the origin of governments' authority or with their subjects' personal consent? What really matters to Locke is that the government is of such a quality that a rational person *would* consent to its authority.[18] Hypothetical consent (as stressed by contemporary contractarians) now becomes the test for legitimacy and political obligation. For what rational contractors *would* agree to is precisely a government that acts in the manner and is limited by the constraints Locke specifies (i.e., a government that is of acceptable quality). The *actual* consent of subjects is necessary for neither their obligations nor their government's authority over

[16] See my *Lockean Theory of Rights*, section 4.5.

[17] It is hard to agree with Dunn's suggestion that society's "essential function" is to allow its members "to execute their religious duties" to "discharge the religious assignments for which God created them" (*Political Thought*, 123, 125). While Locke clearly believed that civil society makes discharging our duties easier (and may even have embraced the Puritan view of government as an antidote to sin), he continuously identifies the end of civil society (its essential function) in terms of our secular, civil interests. This is clear in all of the passages cited above, and is clearer still in *A Letter Concerning Toleration*: "the commonwealth seems to me to be a society of men constituted only for the procuring, preserving, and advancing their own civil interests"; society promotes "the comfort and happiness of this life, leaving . . . to every man the care of his own eternal happiness"; "the temporal good and outward prosperity of the society . . . is the sole reason of men's entering into society, and the only thing they seek and aim at in it" (L, 126, 152–53). It seems obvious from these (and many other) passages that secular justifications for the state are at least as central in Locke's thought as religious ones. They run side by side with his theological justifications. To try to cast these secular concerns (and arguments) as strictly secondary to Locke's religious concerns is to ignore the weight of Locke's own words. Locke's identification of the essential ends of the state with certain secular concerns should not, of course, lead us to conclude that he is trying to "secularize" political society (as Richards rightly observes in *Toleration and the Constitution*, 120). But neither can we conclude that society is for Locke *only* a vehicle for advancing religious ends. See Skinner's discussion of earlier Thomist views that the state is created for the fulfillment of purely mundane ends (*Foundations of Modern Political Thought*, 2:154, 159–61).

[18] Gough, *Political Philosophy*, 70–72; Tarcov, *Locke's Education for Liberty*, 7.

them. All of the consent talk in Locke is just his (misleading) way of emphasizing a hypothetical (rational) consent standard. This interpretation of Locke's consent theory is (roughly) the one offered by Hanna Pitkin (and others),[19] and if adequate it would clearly save Locke from much of the force of the standard critique. For on Pitkin's reading, Locke cannot be accused of resting his case on a weak, virtually "automatic" kind of actual consent, which would bind us to even unjust governments. He is not centrally concerned with *actual* consent at all, and his hypothetical consent standard would clearly rule out obligations to unjust regimes (although on this reading Locke would still face the problem of relying on a nonvoluntary ground of obligation and authority).

But the hypothetical contractarian reading of Locke is *not* adequate, however convincing contractarianism might be as an independent theory.[20] In the first place, Pitkin's interpretation is motivated partly by mistaken beliefs about whether consent in Locke is a sufficient condition for obligation.[21] But more important, that interpretation simply cannot be rendered consistent with the many passages in Locke in which he stresses his interest in the *actual, personal* consent of each individual subject—not the consent of the subject's parents, the majority of subjects, the people as a whole, some ancient historical consent, the hypothetical consent of a rational person, or the subject's disposition to consent.[22] The consent that makes persons subjects is the consent "of *every individual*" (II, 96, 106), it is "his [or their] *own* consent[s]" (II, 15, 95, 119, 138, 139, 189), given *separately*

---

[19] Pitkin, "Obligation and Consent—I," 995–97. Pitkin is followed in this reading by Pateman (*Political Obligation*, 66, and "Women and Consent," 151), Richards (*Toleration and the Constitution*, 99), and Waldron (*Right to Private Property*, 273). Von Leyden seems to find the reading "fairly adequate" (*Hobbes and Locke*, 168–69). Cohen pursues a similar analysis of Locke's problem ("Structure, Choice, and Legitimacy," 311–12). And Zvesper claims that the "utilitarian" (hypothetical contractarian) reading of Locke is truer to the spirit of his texts than the "voluntarist" reading ("Utility of Consent," 55–57). Dunn also stresses hypothetical agreements in a number of places (e.g., *Political Thought*, 129–30, and "Consent," 41–42), although he has more recently claimed that Pitkin's reading of Locke is not completely accurate ("What Is Living and What Is Dead?" 21); and Dunn seems in any event to have had in mind throughout a *personal dispositional* version ("Would he have consented if asked?"), rather than a *rational choice* version ("Would a rational agent have consented?") of the hypothetical contract. Others, as we will see below, accept Pitkin's reading as an account of Locke's views on legitimacy, but not obligation.

[20] See Beitz, "Tacit Consent and Property Rights," 489; Windstrup, "Freedom and Authority," 259; Den Hartogh, "Made by Contrivance," 207.

[21] As I argued in *Moral Principles and Political Obligations*, 84–89.

[22] See Kilcullen, "Locke on Political Obligation," 340; Plamenatz, *Man and Society*, 1:212–13, 216; Den Hartogh, "Made by Contrivance," 207.

in their turns" (II, 117) by *"actually* entering into" a promise or compact (II, 122; my emphases throughout).

Some, perhaps noticing the weight of this textual evidence, but
still impressed by the point that motivated Pitkin, have tried to pry
apart Locke's theories of legitimacy and obligation. Where I have
throughout taken political obligation and political authority (power)
as logical correlates in Locke, others deny this.[23] It has been argued,
for example, that personal consent is for Locke the ground of political obligation, but that Locke's conception of legitimacy makes it
turn on hypothetical consent (quality of government). And "since
legitimacy and obligation are generated by independent mechanisms, by (respectively) the hypothetical behavior of rational creatures and the consent of actual ones, there is a possibility they will
diverge."[24] It has also been claimed, by contrast, that consent is not
the "general ground" of political obligation in Locke; for "political
duty was always discussed as a duty to God," a "conclusion of reason" drawn from simple facts about the human condition.[25] On the
other hand, consent *is* said to be "the sole source of legitimate
authority," the only way that rulers "can have rights to political authority."[26]

In the face of two such diametrically opposed views of Locke's
position, it is perhaps best to note first the content that they share.
Both quite correctly see that Locke is interested both in questions
about the origin of political authority (and obligation) and in ques-

---

[23] As we have seen, Kilcullen denies the correlation in Locke's theory of political
obligation and political power, although he accepts the correlation of political obligation and political authority ("Locke on Political Obligation," 325–26). I have argued
throughout this study that political power and political authority are identical in
Locke's political philosophy; for political power is also (like political obligation and
authority) derived from the "mutual consent" (II, 171) and "voluntary agreement"
(II, 173) of the people. The denial of correlation *outside* Locke scholarship has also
enjoyed increased popularity in recent years. See, e.g., Sartorious, "Political Authority"; Herzog, *Happy Slaves,* 206; Raz, *Morality of Freedom,* 104.

[24] Herzog, *Without Foundations,* 83 (see also pp. 76–80), and *Happy Slaves,* 206. This
also seems to be Beitz's view, in "Tacit Consent and Property Rights," 489.

[25] Dunn, "Consent," 31. Consent "denotes the occasion of incurring political obligations," but does not ground them. See Green's brief summary of a similar view
in *Authority of the State,* 161.

[26] Dunn, "Consent," 33, and *Locke,* 51. Dunn's conception of Lockean consent,
however, is much "thinner" than the usual (see below). At times Dunn overstates
his view, as in claiming that "what constitutes the legitimacy of a political society is
precisely its recognition as legitimate by its subjects" (ibid., 50). This cannot, of
course, be what constitutes legitimacy, since subjects of clearly illegitimate absolute
rulers may (mistakenly) recognize their society as legitimate (as we saw in 6.4). Dunn
means, I take it, that recognition (consent) *within the limits* on morally effectual consent (outlined below) gives legitimacy.

tions about the quality of government (its suitability to human needs and to a rational will).[27] This is hardly surprising, for we too acknowledge many different standards of legitimacy in political life.[28] Indeed, given that Locke almost never uses the language of "legitimacy" at all, it would be odd if we could identify his "true" theory of legitimacy.[29] But if by "legitimate" government or authority we mean one with "political power" over persons (i.e., one with the moral right to command and be obeyed, to make and enforce law), there seems to me to be one view of its ground that clearly dominates the *Treatises*. And that is the view identified above in 3.1: it is a person's own consent, and only his consent, which gives another political power over him (e.g., II, 95, 192). Governments are "legitimate" with respect to individuals *only* by virtue of the actual, personal consent of those individuals. Governments may also be good or desirable in many other ways; they may be the sort to which a rational chooser would give his consent. But without his actual consent, they cannot have legitimate authority (political power) over him. Similarly, it is *"by consenting"* that one "puts himself under an obligation" to society (II, 121; my emphasis). The political obligation anyone is under binds him *"by virtue of"* his performance of consensual acts (II, 121; my emphasis). Actual, personal consent is the ground of both political obligation and political power (authority, legitimacy);[30] they are logical correlates, obligations and rights both generated in accordance with the natural law precept that voluntary undertakings must be respected.

But if consent occupies this central role in Locke's theory of obligation and authority, what role remains for Locke's quite obvious interest in the quality of government, independent of the origin of its rights over individuals? I suggest the following quite extensive and important, but also quite different, roles:

(1) Considerations of the quality of government serve as a crucial limit on consent—that is, a limit on what we may create consensual obligations to do. A political society's being good (and its having good government) cannot make it legitimate with respect to independent persons or ground their obligations to obey it. But it does

[27] Riley takes quality of government to dominate Locke's thoughts in his early works, and origin to dominate in his mature works (*Will and Political Legitimacy*, 70–71). This view is, I think, essentially correct.

[28] *Moral Principles and Political Obligations*, 195–98.

[29] Grant avoids choosing Locke's true theory of legitimacy by choosing three criteria of legitimacy that he employs (*Liberalism*, 65, 88–89).

[30] This seems to be the view of both Parry (*John Locke*, 96) and Von Leyden (*Hobbes and Locke*, 168), although I am not certain in either case.

bring that society into the class to which we may give binding consent; its goodness makes it possible for our consent to it to be morally effectual. Locke's position is that consent is *necessary* for political obligation and authority but not *sufficient* for either.[31] Consent obtained under duress is not binding (II, 175–76, 186, 192, 198), nor is consent obtained by using another's need against him (I, 42–43). Consent (oaths) cannot bind us to disobey the just laws of those to whom we are legitimately subject (II, 134). And most important in this context, consent cannot bind us where it exceeds our rights to give it (i.e., where it is given to arrangements that jeopardize our effective preservation). We cannot give binding consent to become slaves (II, 23) or to subject ourselves to the political slavery of absolute, arbitrary government (II, 93, 131, 137–38) (as we saw in chapter 5). The rational preferability of limited government to its alternatives thus makes it a fit object for consent, one to which we can bind ourselves. But this is not at all to claim that its rational preferability makes it legitimate with respect to those living within its domains, or obviates the need for actual consent.

(2) Considerations of the quality of government (what it would be rational to consent to) also serve to help specify the content of political consent in Locke. Political consent is often tacit, according to Locke, and it is initially unclear just what tacit consent is consent *to*. Indeed, even the express consent of those who form a commonwealth is no more explicit in its content than agreeing "to unite into one political society" (II, 99). To what exactly does this consent bind us? As we have seen, our consent binds us to accept whatever is necessary to the legitimate ends of civil society, and no more than this. But understanding what makes a government good and rationally preferable to alternatives, just *is* to understand what is necessary to the legitimate end of civil society. Locke's emphasis on the quality of government (on the rational preferability of limited government), then, can best be understood as an attempt to elaborate

[31] *Moral Principles and Political Obligations*, 86–88. See also Grant, *Liberalism*, 128; Von Leyden, *Hobbes and Locke*, 130–31; Medina, *Social Contract Theories*, 39. Best argues that consent is "*both* the necessary and sufficient condition of legitimate government" ("Innocent, the Ignorant, and the Rational," 175). Her argument seems to be that true consent must be reasonable, so that (e.g.) "consent" given to an arbitrary government is not really consent at all. This is not what Locke says (e.g., II, 23), but Best's view is extensionally equivalent to my own. Zvesper's argument (that the limits on Lockean consent show that only rational consent in Locke can bind one) ("Utility of Consent," 58, 60, 64) in no way demonstrates (as he believes) that actual consent is not necessary for obligation in Locke; it shows only that actual consent is not sufficient.

the (initially obscure) content of all political consent in his theory.[32] It should be emphasized again here just how central to the arguments of the *Second Treatise* are Locke's views about how we should interpret contracts and other consensual acts. Locke's argument for majority rule turns on such considerations (as we saw in 4.2), as does his understanding of marriage contracts.[33] And we have seen (in 5.5) that other arguments in Locke rely similarly on a particular view of how to interpret vague contracts. It would not be too strong, I believe, to claim (as I claimed above) that this is a major theme in the *Second Treatise*.

(3) Role (1) above, of course, is central in providing Locke with an answer to the defender of absolute government (such as Filmer). Since absolute government is contrary to God's plans for us (and it is thus beyond our capability to transfer rights to it), absolute governments cannot possess legitimate political power. Consent is not sufficient to authorize absolute, arbitrary regimes.

(4) Role (1) above also makes it possible for Locke to respond convincingly to the anarchist, who prefers the state of nature to any possible form of government, and who argues that no rational person should give his consent to any government. It is clear that the anarchist is not a serious opponent in Locke's mind, for he states several times that we all agree that there ought to be government (power) in the world (I, 81, 106). Locke also, of course, makes a point of emphasizing the reasons why government is needed at all and the specific problems of life in the state of nature; but these arguments seem aimed more at revealing the legitimate ends of and limits on government than at convincing anarchist skeptics. Whether intended or not, however, Locke's claims about the rational preferability of limited government provide him with ammunition against opponents at either the authoritarian or the libertarian end of the spectrum.

Yet another way of helping Locke to avoid (part of) the "standard critique" of his consent theory is suggested by John Dunn's analysis of Locke's position. To the criticism of Locke that his notion of consent is too weak to facilitate his ambitions, Dunn responds that Locke intended nothing more than the quite weak notion of consent as voluntary acquiescence, and that we ought to reevaluate the traditional understanding of Locke's ambitions in light of this fact. Locke's aim is not to identify something sufficiently strong to serve

---

[32] See Pitkin, "Obligation and Consent—I," 995–96; Grant, *Liberalism*, 126–28; Parry, *John Locke*, 102–3.

[33] See *Lockean Theory of Rights*, 170–75.

as a convincing ground of political obligation. His primary concern is rather only to distinguish between cases of coerced and uncoerced acceptance of government, between submission and assent,[34] and thus to distinguish conquerors from lawful rulers. Consent must be fully voluntary,[35] but "voluntary" here means only "not coerced"; its voluntariness need not indicate the presence of anything like an intention to consent or a conscious choice to do so, according to Dunn.[36] Political consent, on this reading, is simply what characterizes "not-unwilling" subjects. It is given where people "go along with" (assent to, acquiesce in) political arrangements in a free society (i.e., one that does not coercively compel membership or impose arbitrary laws).[37] Political consent need not flow from a decision, need not be a conscious commitment to or authorization of anything.

Two main textual points seem to provide support for this interpretation of Locke. First, the signs of political consent mentioned by Locke hardly seem good candidates for instances of intentional choice, for they include not only express acts (like oaths), but also "acts" like residing, holding land, or traveling in the state. These signs of consent do, however, look like good examples of "going along with" the political arrangements (or, in my reading above, "willing benefaction" within those arrangements). And it is hard to believe that Locke could have failed to notice this. Second, a few of Locke's other examples of "consent" are perhaps better analyzed as cases of willing acquiescence than as cases of intentional undertaking—the clearest case in point being the "voluntary consent" people allegedly give to the use of money (II, 50).[38]

---

[34] Dunn, "Consent," 34–35, 47, *Political Thought*, 145–46, and *Locke*, 51. See also Medina, *Social Contract Theories*, 37.

[35] Riley, *Will and Political Legitimacy*, 74.

[36] "Consent," 32–33, 35, 48, 51. "Choice" *is* necessary for Lockean consent, according to Dunn, but "choice is not seen as a particular historical event in the mind of the subject." Rather, choice is implied by "certain behavior" in "the absence of compulsion" (p. 48), behavior that indicates "a prima facie disposition to take . . . advantage of the practice" (p., 51). See Hacker's related claim that tacit consent for Locke is "beneath the level of conscious awareness" (*Political Theory*, 279).

[37] See Walzer's related claim that the consent that explains "the rights of states" is simply the willing acceptance of a common life (*Just and Unjust Wars*, 54).

[38] But it should also be noted that these cases are far fewer than is commonly supposed. Notice first that the "consent" given to the use of money has very questionable force as a moral argument and has a peculiar status within Locke's position (as I argued in *Lockean Theory of Rights*, 300–306). "Consent" to the use of money is supposed by Locke to *legitimate* the material inequality that he sees as a part of any money economy. But contemporary persons (as well as Locke's contemporaries) had no choice to refuse to participate in a money economy. Their "tacit consent" has no

There are however, reasons for believing both that Dunn's version of Lockean consent cannot be the only one with which Locke is working and that Locke needs a stronger notion of consent (than Dunn's) for his arguments to be convincing. For, in the first place, Locke's "consent language" is far more often the language of deliberate and conscious choice than the language of passive (voluntary) acquiescence. All persons reach maturity free to "choose" what society to join and what government to "put themselves under" (i.e., what to consent to) (II, 73, 102, 118). We may rightfully resist any government imposed on us that we do not "willingly and of choice consent to" (II, 192). Further, Locke *distinguishes* what the people "of their own free choice" permit their rulers to do, from what they afterwards "acquiesce in" (II, 164), making it clear that their consent is at least not equivalent to mere passive acquiescence (acquiescence being for Locke either only one part of consent, or else itself an active notion involving choice).[39]

In the *Essays on the Law of Nature*, Locke carefully distinguishes

---

apparent binding force, nor is it really even appropriate to call it "consent" at all (see below). More important for our purposes here, the other examples frequently cited of Locke's "attenuated consent" or "consent as acquiescence" are in fact not best described in that way. It is often confusedly supposed that in I, 43, for instance, Locke asserts that the beggar "consents" to his subjection to the lord, and that this is an interesting case for illuminating Locke's passive notion of consent (as asserted in, e.g., Pateman, *Political Obligation*, 62; Herzog, *Without Foundations*, 85–86, and *Happy Slaves*, 226; Ashcraft, *Locke's Two Treatises*, 90–92, 138). But this passage is clearly *not* pointing to a case of binding consent (indeed, the whole point of I, 42–43 is to deny this); Locke is only saying that even if consent *were* a ground for lawful subjection in such cases (which it clearly is *not*), the right of the lord would still not begin in his property, but only in the consent of the beggar. Similarly, it is frequently claimed that the consent given by grown children to continuing paternal authority (II, 74–75) is an example of "consent as acquiescence" (e.g., Gough, *Political Philosophy*, 65–66; Von Leyden, *Hobbes and Locke*, 169). While Locke does say that this consent is "tacit and scarce avoidable" (II, 75), this is clearly meant to convey only that it is "natural" and almost inevitable that the children will give it. This in no way implies that the consent in question is not intentional or the result of conscious choice (see *Lockean Theory of Rights*, 217). Indeed, Locke's language is (throughout the passages on the transition from paternal to political power) the overtly active language of "permitting" (II, 74), "giving" and "making" (II, 105), "joining" (II, 106), "pitching upon," "running into," and "putting themselves" (II, 107), and "entrusting" (II, 110). None of this language is consistent with an interpretation on which filial consent is viewed by Locke as mere uncompelled, passive acquiescence.

[39] Locke appears similarly to distinguish in II, 110 between children "tacitly submitting" to government by their father and their later "acquiescing" in the arrangement when it is seen not to "offend anyone." Since the tacit submission is (later in II, 110) equated with "entrusting" the rulership—and "entrusting" being an undeniably active concept—acquiescence is again seen to be either only part of (or unrelated to) consent (if Locke means to distinguish submission from acquiescence), or else for Locke itself an active notion involving choice (if Locke means to equate submission and acquiescence).

between the "positive consent" that is given in (tacit or express) contracts, and which grounds clear obligations, from the merely "natural consent" that occurs when people simply conform their actions to the customs of social life or "give assent" to prevailing opinions (ELN, 161–165).[40] While this conformity and assent are clearly free (uncoerced), Locke is also quite clear that "natural consent" is "by no means a sufficient reason for creating an obligation" (ELN, 177). And in the *First Treatise,* Locke quite explicitly denies that "common practice" (what people willingly go along with) can be understood as binding "common consent," for you cannot have consent where "that hath never been asked, nor actually given" (I, 88). Notice that the practice in question in this passage (children's right to inherit from their parents) is freely accepted and taken advantage of by all (and so counts as "chosen" by them and "consented to" in Dunn's sense), but that this fact is insufficient to render people's behavior (bindingly) consensual in nature—because the behavior in question is not in response to a choice with which people were clearly presented.[41] I suggested above in 4.1 and will argue further in chapter 8 that morally significant consent must be voluntary and intentional (in the sense that signs of consent must be intentionally used with full awareness of their significance), and that binding inexplicit (e.g., tacit) consent can be given only by behavior that constitutes a free and overt response to a clear choice situation (i.e., even tacit consenters must know what they are doing when they consent). The passages cited above strongly suggest (against Dunn's view) that Locke at least often had similar conditions for consent in mind.[42]

[40] Locke characterizes "natural consent" as "one to which men are led by a certain natural instinct without the intervention of a compact," and he gives three examples: conformity in moral conduct and the practices of social life, assent to opinions, and assent to "first principles," that is, those that "elicit ready assent from any man of sound mind" (ELN, 165).

[41] Locke may in fact be attempting in I, 88 to distinguish *express* consent to common practice (which must be "asked for and actually given") from *tacit* consent to common practice (which need not be) (as Den Hartogh argues in "Made by Contrivance," 211). Even if this is Locke's intention, however, it in no way follows that Locke cannot also intend that even tacit consent must be deliberate and voluntary. For consent's not having been asked for by someone or actually given (i.e., expressed, in Locke's sense) is perfectly consistent with its being a deliberate response to a situation clearly calling for choice.

[42] See Plamenatz, *Man and Society,* 1:222–23; Snare, "Consent and Conventional Acts," 34. Locke uses the same language of consent in his writings on toleration, when he discusses membership in another kind of voluntary association—a church (e.g., L, 130, and the 1661 entry in Locke's commonplace book entitled *Ecclesia,* discussed by Gough in *Political Philosophy,* 185). And, as Ashcraft astutely observes, in the case of church membership Locke certainly intends the "consent" in question to involve a deliberate, conscious choice (*Locke's Two Treatises,* 250–51).

None of this, of course, is meant to argue that consent is equivalent to some mental act or attitude (such as approval)[43] or that a consenter must have more elaborate intentions (such as the intention to actually allow what he consents to). I approve of many things to which I have never consented; and insincere consent (like an insincere promise) may nonetheless bind me (even if I never had any intention of allowing what I consented to). Consent in Locke is clearly a kind of act (as is stressed in II, 120), involving a performance that has conventional (or otherwise contextually determinate) significance.[44] Dunn quite rightly criticizes the view that consent is "a fact about the psychology of the individual," as have many others.[45] But this does not mean that consent has no essential mental component, or that it must be given a purely behavioral or dispositional analysis.[46] And Locke, I have suggested, similarly had in mind a consent that involved deliberate, knowing choice in at least many of the key passages on political (and nonpolitical) consent in the *Treatises*.

A simple explanation of this fact about Locke's position is that Locke clearly needed this stronger (intentional) notion of consent for the case he was trying to make. He needed it even for the distinction between government by consent and government by conquest, which Dunn takes to be the main focus of Locke's theory of consent. For if consent in Locke is so weak a notion as mere acquiescence in a free political environment, then even someone who unjustly seizes power by force and (perhaps after a period of years)

[43] As has been maintained by Siegler in "Plamenatz on Consent and Obligation," especially 258; and Seliger, *Liberal Politics*, 255.

[44] Snare, "Consent and Conventional Acts," 27–29.

[45] Dunn, "Consent," 32. See my critique of the "attitudinal" sense of consent in *Moral Principles and Political Obligations*, 93. See also John Jenkins, "Political Consent," 62–64; Kleinig, "Ethics of Consent," 93–96; Feinberg, *Harm to Self*, 181; Plamenatz, *Consent, Freedom and Political Obligation*, 5, 167; Lemos, *Hobbes and Locke*, 99; Nino, "Consensual Theory of Punishment," 295. One obvious reason why a consent theorist (like Locke) must be concerned with acts (choices) rather than attitudes is that the difference between a free society and a benevolent despotism turns on this concern. A benevolent despot can mold his policies to the concerns of his subjects, producing a happy society of which the subjects approve. But such a society would not be free, for its people could not choose their governors, or make their lives as they chose (as opposed to simply being happy with the lives they were allowed or given). This suggests again the important point, stressed above, that ruling with approval is not the same as ruling with consent, for consent requires background conditions of freedom to choose and to do otherwise, which mere approval does not (II, 192).

[46] Dunn appears to give dispositional analyses of both express and tacit consent in Locke ("Consent," 42, 51). I can find no textual warrant for such a view. For some of the problems Dunn's analysis creates, see Hampsher-Monk, "Tacit Concept of Consent," 136–37; and Russell, "Locke on Express and Tacit Consent," 305.

subsequently enjoys passive obedience from subjects within a free environment, has as legitimate an authority (based on people's consent) as a ruler actually chosen by the people.[47] But this is to give unjust force a moral weight that Locke can hardly want it to have. If, on the other hand, consent requires a deliberate choice, force followed by (free) acquiescence is not enough; some indication of genuine and intended choice would be required.

Far more important for my purposes here, however, is the fact that Locke needs a notion of consent sufficiently strong to serve as a ground of political obligation and authority (as I have argued above). Political rights and obligations, remember, affect quite central and important interests for those who have them; and it is plain that the more important the interests that are at issue, the clearer and less controversial must be the signs of consent that ground obligations that affect those interests.[48] Signs of political consent, then, should be especially clear and uncontroversial if they are to count as grounding political obligations (and rights). But consent understood merely as free acquiescence cannot possibly satisfy this requirement. That I have merely gone along with someone's plans without coercion surely is not a particularly clear sign of my consent to them. If anything, it seems clear that such acquiescence typically grounds no obligation at all with respect to my future conduct. If a group of us come together to play baseball, and one pushy participant steps forward and divides us into teams, assigns positions and batting orders, and so on, we may all go along with him (and even be glad that someone spared us our indecisive efforts to organize ourselves). But willing acquiescence in such a case surely grounds no *obligation* to continue to do as our assertive colleague demands, or grants him any *right* to his role. Consent to his "authority" would have had to be more active and deliberate for any wrong to be done in resisting his will. This conclusion follows even more strongly, of course, in the case of the much more important political rights and obligations with which we are here concerned. That we acquiesce

---

[47] Remember that the "free environment" necessary here can be as minimal as one in which subjects are "allowed their due property" and governed by standing laws to which they have consented (II, 192). But given the extraordinary passivity of the people (e.g., II, 225), it would seem to be a relatively easy matter to overthrow their chosen government, preserve their laws and property, and obtain title to rule by their passive "consent." On Dunn's reading of Locke, then, the alienation of rights by subjects (through consent) can become alarmingly like the prescription of rights by government; but Locke's intention was clearly to emphasize the difference between these two ways of losing rights.

[48] Green, *Authority of the State,* 169.

freely, of course, does confirm the absence of coercion, which is a necessary background condition for binding consent. But it cannot itself *be* binding consent, if consent is to ground rights and obligations.[49]

The conclusions we should draw from the argument of this section are three. First, Locke's consent theory is intended by him to ground both political obligation and political power (rights, authority) in the actual, personal consent of individuals, a consent that is active, voluntary, and deliberate (and which thus involves awareness and free choice). Second, this is the correct position for Locke, or for any Lockean voluntarist, to take, since weaker notions of "consent" cannot ground the important rights and obligations at issue. But third, Locke's consent theory (at least on the strength of what we have thus far seen) cannot fully avoid the force of the "standard critique" with which we began. Even if we suppose (as I urged that we should) that Locke has mistakenly subsumed cases of willing benefaction under the heading of "tacit consent" (and so we do not complain about the implausibility of counting residence as a sign of "consent"), Locke still faces the following objection: his desire for generality in his accounts of political obligation and authority (i.e., his desire to show that many actual citizens have political obligations and many actual governments have political authority) leads him to embrace grounds of obligation that seem inconsistent with our natural freedom to choose where our allegiance will lie. Indeed, neither of the rejected interpretations of Locke (Pitkin's or Dunn's) is able to avoid this problem either, since they would ground obligation or authority either in quality of government (ideal hypothetical consent) or in passive acquiescence, neither of which involves genuine choice by subjects. And consistency with natural freedom seems (as I argued in 3.3) to be the main source of the appeal of consent theory in the first place, both for Locke and for ourselves. We thus seem to face the following dilemma: we must either give up our commitment to our natural freedom (a basic premise of Lockean political philosophy), or accept the anarchist implications of consent theory. If we are to avoid these horns altogether, we must defend (better than

[49] This point seems to tell even against Dunn's account; for while consent is not for him the ground of political obligation, it *is* the ground of political *authority* (rights). And this can no more arise from mere willing acquiescence than can obligations. On the importance of distinguishing binding consent from mere willing acquiescence, see Green, *Authority of the State*, 158–60; and Feinberg, *Harm to Self*, 173.

Locke does) a form of *genuine* consent (or some other appropriately voluntary ground of political obligation) that is sufficiently widespread in genuine communities to justify Locke's claims about obligation and authority within free societies. I explore this possibility in chapter 8.

EIGHT

CONSENT, OBLIGATION, AND ANARCHY

8.1. Consent and Voting

Thinking now about notions of consent sufficiently strong to ground obligations and transfer rights (as the consent theorist must), where might we look to find widespread acts of express or tacit political consent in a free society? We are interested now in "the consent of the governed" only in the sense in which this refers to that consent that creates the political relationship, makes persons members (citizens) of the political society, and grounds their political obligations and the rights of their societies or governments. But can we find enough consent, even in a free society, to justify such a society's claim to govern by the consent of the governed? If we cannot, we face the dilemma outlined above in chapter 7: we must either abandon the thesis of natural human freedom (and so, a crucial aspect of Lockean political philosophy) or embrace the conclusion of philosophical anarchism (i.e., that there are no actual societies or governments that are morally "legitimate," which have the right to command and be obeyed). Locke, of course, found the consent in his free society primarily in the continued residence of the native born and in the conditions for landownership (a view to which I will return momentarily). But here I wish to widen our inquiry and ask whether *any* societies, in Locke's day or our own, really enjoy(ed) "the consent of the governed" (in the sense specified above).

Among contemporary societies, a seemingly uncontroversial starting point for the inquiry would limit our discussion to the case of liberal democracies (whose governments are the ones that most often *claim* to rule by consent). If such democracies turn out not to be governments by consent, it seems extremely unlikely that other kinds of political societies in the world will fare any better on this score. What, then, is so special about democracies in this regard? What is it about democratic political institutions that seems to us to display or draw forth the consent of the governed?

Presumably it is not that democracies are full of express consenters, persons who directly and explicitly authorize their societies or governments to make binding law or in other ways control them. Even in liberal democracies, this kind of consenter is rare (as they were also rare, if a bit less so, in Locke's England [as we saw in 4.1]). Perhaps the clearest candidates for the status of express consenter in today's societies are naturalized citizens, who typically must take an explicit oath of allegiance to the government (or constitution) of their new country. And even these oaths will seem to be fully voluntary acts of consent only where immigrants were free to seek refuge in other host countries, or to remain in their country of birth, so that their decision to take the oath looks like a free choice.[1] But for the majority of citizens in modern democracies (and, indeed, in the whole history of the modern nation-state), no such choice is ever faced. The occasions for giving one's express consent are few, and the circumstances surrounding most apparent "oaths of allegiance" are such as to render suspect any attempt to characterize them as acts of binding consent. The pledge of allegiance to the flag (and "to the Republic for which it stands"), taken by American schoolchildren (and some others), can hardly bind persons who have yet to reach the "age of consent"; and it is, in any event, so mechanical a performance for most that it could not be taken seriously as the extremely important act of making oneself a citizen. Similarly, the oaths taken in the past by American citizens on induction into the military were both taken under threat of punishment for refusal (as were most "loyalty oaths" in Locke's day) and regarded by those who did take it as a mere formality.[2] It may be true that democracies are likely to contain more express consenters (such as free immigrants) than other kinds of societies, but they seem unlikely to be present in numbers great enough to justify claims of government by express consent.

What seems more likely is that many (or even most) citizens in liberal democracies could be understood to have given their consent to the authority of their governments in subtler, less direct ways. Their consent might be tacit or indirect.[3] For instance, exercising

[1] See Sartorius, "Political Authority," 12–13; and my reply in "Voluntarism and Political Associations," 34–36. See also Woozley, *Law and Obedience*, 89–90.

[2] "Voluntarism and Political Associations," 33–34. Military induction oaths in the current (so-called) All Volunteer Force are taken by far fewer citizens and, even in those cases, are often tainted by problems with the economic necessity that motivates much enlistment.

[3] On tacit, implied, and indirect consent, in addition to the works cited above in 4.1, see Honore, "Must We Obey?" 56–59; Kraut, *Socrates and the State*, 152–54.

one's right to vote in a democratic election might seem to be a way of giving one's consent that is unique to democracies; political participation (of this or some other sort) might establish consent. Or one might suppose, with Locke, that by remaining in residence in a state that one is fully free to leave (as seems to be routinely the case in democracies), one can be understood to consent to the authority of its government. These seem to me to be the obvious reasons for supposing that democratic governments, before any others, enjoy the consent of the governed.

There is, of course, an immediate difficulty (which we noted above in 7.2) with those kinds of appeals to tacit, implied, implicit, or indirect consent. It will not be immediately evident what consent is being given *to*. If, for instance, consent is given by continued residence, there seems to be nothing in the nature of the "act" that specifies the extent of one's consent (as there is in cases of express consent: "I hereby consent to X"). Locke's solution to this problem, as we have seen, seems to have been to claim that binding consent can only be given to government of a certain type—government extensive enough to constitute an advance over the state of nature, but limited in its authority to use or endanger its subjects. Vague political consent is always to be understood as consent only to be governed within these limits, so even tacit consent must be understood to have this content. Others have suggested that tacit consent is given always to the constitution of the state. Since I believe that there can be no binding tacit or implicit consent except in clear choice situations that contextually determine what is being consented to, I propose to set this problem aside for now.

What, then, is to be made of the claims that voting or continued residence in a democratic state constitute ways of giving consent? Let me consider these suggestions in turn, beginning with the view that having or exercising the right to vote establishes that the governed have consented in an appropriate fashion to legitimate governmental control. This claim is a familiar feature of liberal democratic rhetoric; and it may be, as we saw in 4.2 above, an issue more directly relevant to Locke's thought than is commonly supposed. First, of course, it makes a difference whether it is claimed that consent is given by the mere possession of a right to vote, or only by actually *exercising* that right (i.e., voting).[4] The first, stronger version of the claim (that mere possession of a right to vote is sufficient)

---

[4] What one has a right to vote *for* obviously matters centrally as well. I will assume here that what is being voted for is an executive officer, a representative lawmaker, or a judge of limited term.

would justify asserting that *all* citizens in typical democracies are consenters.[5] It is hard to see, though, how consent could be given simply by having a right; this appears to conflate having the opportunity to consent with actually consenting. The weaker version of the claim (that actually voting is what gives consent) initially seems more reasonable.[6] It, however, faces difficulties of a different sort. In the first place, many citizens in existing democracies fail to vote in particular elections, many vote in none at all, and very few citizens vote in *all* democratic elections. Presumably, then, some citizens' consent is much more extensive than others', while nonvoters cannot be understood to have consented at all. And one would have to assume that since what is typically voted *for* is a candidate for a political office of limited term, consent is given only to the authority of that candidate for that term. This seems far short of the overarching consent to the authority of government that was supposed to be given in the act of voting.[7]

Perhaps this conclusion will incline us away from the weaker claim about voting back toward the stronger. Perhaps the stronger claim is really this: in possessing the right to vote in a democratic society, we possess the power to change laws, alter the constitution, remove public officials, and so on. Insofar as we do *not* do these things, we can be understood to consent to the authority of the law, constitutional provisions, and political officeholders. Again, this is all familiar enough from the rhetoric of democratic life, but it involves so many confusions that I despair of mentioning them all. It once again involves confusing "going along with" something, or acquiescing in it, with consenting to it (see 7.2 above). It involves supposing that consent can be given to arrangements (laws, officeholders) of which one may have no knowledge and without intending to consent to anything. *Failing* to do something can only be a

[5] For a defense of the strong version, see Gewirth, "Political Justice," 138; and Raphael, *Problems of Political Philosophy,* 112–13. For criticism of this view, see Smith, "Is There a Prima Facie Obligation?" section 2.

[6] Good examples of this weak version are those defended by Plamenatz (*Consent, Freedom,* 167–72, and *Man and Society,* 1:239–41), Lemos (*Hobbes and Locke,* 100), and Beran (*Consent Theory,* 76). I discuss Singer's version of this position below. See also Jenkins, "Political Consent," 60–61; and my comments on Plamenatz's views in *Moral Principles and Political Obligations,* 91–93. Plamenatz's stance(s) on this matter has not been entirely consistent, as far as I can see. He sometimes approaches the stronger version of the claim, as when he says that the English consent "because they can, if they so wish, change [their government] legally and peacefully" (*Man and Society,* 1:239). And his original view in *Consent, Freedom, and Political Obligation* (pp. 19–20) was that only those who voted *for* an elected candidate count as consenters.

[7] Beran, "Political Obligation and Democracy," 253–54, and *Consent Theory,* 74; Herzog, *Happy Slaves,* 183, 200.

way of consenting when that inactivity is in response to a clear choice situation, only when inactivity is significant as indicating that a choice has been made (and, as we will see, not always even then). Inactivity that results from ignorance, habit, inability, or fear will not be a way of consenting to anything. Citizens of modern democracies are not continuously, or even occasionally, presented with situations where their inactivity would represent a clear choice of the status quo.

But I have not yet mentioned the most obvious, and most damaging, shortcomings of the strong claim about voting. Individuals in democratic societies do not possess the right to change laws, constitutional provisions, or public officials. Only majorities possess this right. There is, then, no sense at all in which *my* failure to exercise *my* right to do these things constitutes *my* consent to the status quo. I have no such right. Nor is there any obvious sense in which I have granted the majority the right to act for me in these matters. For that one would need, in any event, a unanimous *prior* consent to majority rule that could not have been given by voting (as in Locke's account of the origin of a legitimate polity [4.2]). Majority rule in actual practice, however, is a product not of individual consent but of political convention. There is, of course, a clear sense in which "the people" as a whole or "the body politic" possess a right to alter their political institutions (and the like) in a democratic society. Is the failure of "the people" to accomplish such alterations a sign of the consent of the governed? Claiming that would involve the same confusions that I noted in the individual case. The maxim that "silence (or inactivity generally) gives consent" is a very misleading one. Silence virtually *never* gives consent. It does so only where that silence is a freely chosen response to a clear choice situation. And even if the silence of "the people" did give a kind of consent to democratic institutions, this "consent" in no way translates into the individual consent of particular citizens living in the state.[8]

One final but extremely important point: we would do well to

[8] Several further problems with the strong claim about voting are noted by MacIntyre. First, convicted felons are in some democratic states deprived of their right to vote. This would seem, according to the strong claim, (objectionably) to end their consent, and with it any further obligations to obey the law. Second, since the right to vote is typically granted to all permanent residents in democratic states, the "consent" this right gives is given no more or less voluntarily than the level of voluntariness of residence itself. Since there are serious problems about the voluntariness of continued residence (see 8.2–8.3 below), these problems infect the strong claim about voting as well. See MacIntyre, "Philosophy and Politics," 142–43.

remember that voting is often a way not of consenting to something, but only of *expressing a preference*.[9] If the state gives a group of condemned prisoners the choice of being executed by firing squad or by lethal injection, and all of them vote for the firing squad, we cannot conclude from this that the prisoners thereby *consent* to being executed by firing squad. They do, of course, choose this option; they approve of it, but only in the sense that they prefer it to their other option. They consent to neither option, despising both.[10] Voting for a candidate in a democratic election sometimes has a depressingly similar structure. The state offers you a choice among candidates (or perhaps it is "the people" who make the offer), and you choose one, hoping to make the best of a bad situation. You thereby express a preference, approve of that candidate (over the others), but consent to the authority of no one.

Those who wish to defend the weaker version of the voting-consent thesis in the face of such objections, insist that voting in a democratic election is necessarily a way of consenting because there are clear conventions governing such elections. It is made clear to voters that in casting their ballots they are participating in a political process designed to produce a result that all are morally obligated to accept. You cannot perform the acts that are clearly indications of consent (to the authority of the elected candidate) and then happily argue that you were only expressing a preference, not consenting, any more than a person can say (with a full knowledge of the implications), "I consent to X" and then claim not to have consented to X after all. Certain acts, when performed knowingly, intentionally, and voluntarily, just *are* acts of consent, like it or not.[11]

[9] Cohen, "Liberalism and Disobedience," 311–12. See also Kleinig, "Ethics of Consent," 107–9; Green, *Authority of the State*, 171–72; Siegler, "Plamenatz on Consent," 259; Herzog, *Happy Slaves*, 183. For a contrasting view, see Beran, *Consent Theory*, 76–77.

[10] Consent is absent because of the coercive background conditions in the example, which limit the range of available options to the uniformly unpalatable (as in the gunman case: "your money or your life"). I suggest below that the conditions of political life, even in liberal democracies, similarly involve background conditions that limit the available options in an objectionable way.

[11] This seems to be the view of Plamenatz, but the claim is too strong in at least one way. Those who genuinely do not understand the conventions that make certain behavior a sign of consent are not well described as nonetheless consenters (Jenkins, "Political Consent," 60–61). Most of us, of course, *do* understand what voting is about (although just *what* this involves understanding I address below). Singer (accordingly) presses the Plamenatz line in a rather different direction. Since "the normal case of voting must, because of what voting is, be a case in which there is consent," by voting we lead others reasonably to believe that in voting we give our consent. Even if we do not *actually* consent (lacking the necessary intentions), we have the same obli-

Is voting in a democratic election such an act? It seems obvious to me that it is not. In the first place, the conventions governing such elections are hardly crystal-clear; one could be forgiven for not understanding the (alleged) moral significance of casting one's ballot. I would guess that average voters have very little sense of what they have committed themselves to by voting. This conjecture, if true, is especially damaging to the argument under consideration; for the more centrally our important interests are involved (as they are in political cases), the clearer our signs of consent must be for them to bind us (as we saw in 7.2). But even if I am wrong in my guess, the government *itself* in effect routinely declares in modern democracies that voting is *not* a way of morally binding oneself to the state. For voting is typically portrayed not only as a right, but as a *duty* of citizens, suggesting that the status and duties of citizenship have some entirely different basis than the "consent" given in voting.[12] Nor is it ever suggested that by *not* voting one would be freed of obligations that voters voluntarily assume. In short, the government makes it clear that we should go to the polls and express our preferences, but that our political obligations (and its rights over us) in no way depend on this and will be in no way altered by failing to do it. Our conclusion must be that the conventions governing democratic elections, and the rhetoric surrounding them, do *not* establish that voting is a way of undertaking obligations and granting authority (i.e., a way of *consenting* in the sense that interests us here). And, of course, if the conventions in this area are not clear on that point, voting simply is not a way of giving consent, unless it is accompanied by some (nonmechanical) further act of consent.[13]

---

gations that we would have if we *had* consented. "After the event, one cannot say that one never consented—or to be strictly accurate, even if one says that one never consented, one is still obliged as if one had consented." Voting has the conventional significance of an act of consent; it is an act of "quasi-consent" (*Democracy and Disobedience*, 51–52). Weale, via a related argument, defends the view that voters tacitly consent to the results of the vote, because in voting they knowingly induce others to rely on the belief that, as voters, they will abide by the results ("Consent," 71–72). I outline a reply to Singer and Weale below in note 13.

[12] As Pateman notes, some democratic voting procedures actually involve legal compulsion to vote (i.e., penalties for failure to vote), which calls into serious question any "consent" alleged to flow from voting (*Political Obligation*, 86).

[13] This seems to me to be the proper response to Singer and Weale as well. If voting is not clearly a conventional way of undertaking political obligations, then it is not reasonable for others to take our voting as a consensual (obligation-generating) act, or to rely on it as an indication that we will feel obligated to abide by the results. If we subsequently act as if we have not consented, we frustrate no reasonable expectations about our behavior. Further, of course, Singer and Weale both seem, oddly, to make our political obligations (which stem from voting) depend on whether others

8.2. Consent and Residence

Let us turn, then, to the second (Locke's) proposal concerning the consensual basis of a free society: that by continuing to reside in a state that we are free to leave (whether by taking possession of land or not), we give our consent to the authority of its government, at least during our residence.[14] Some nondemocratic (and even quite oppressive) governments, of course, also give their citizens the right to free emigration. So if the consent theorist can defend this thesis, he will either have shown that government by consent is a reality (and hence that government is morally legitimate) in more states than we might initially have expected, or else he will be obliged to defend severe limits on what our consent can bind us to (as in Locke). But it is surely a standard feature (if not a defining characteristic) of democratic societies that they allow such free emigration. So in examining this line of argument we will also be saying something special about the respects in which democratic governments enjoy the consent of the governed.

The view that residence (at least in certain kinds of states) constitutes consent has enjoyed a long history. It was first suggested by Plato in the *Crito*, of course, long before Locke's *Treatises*. Others among the classical contract theorists (such as Hobbes and Rousseau) and many philosophers in this century have agreed with Locke.[15] In *Moral Principles and Political Obligations*, I argued against the view that continued residence, even in democratic states, could properly be taken as an act of consent to the authority of government.[16] While my views on the proper conclusion of the argument

---

do form beliefs or expectations (or rely upon their beliefs) about our future conduct; and our obligations would, in any event (and again quite oddly), seem to be owed (on Singer's and Weale's accounts of the matter) only to those of our fellow citizens who actually do form or rely upon such beliefs. For other responses to Singer, see Nelson, *On Justifying Democracy*, 43–44; and Green, *Authority of the State*, 170–72. Other arguments that voting should not be understood as a conventional way of giving consent can be found in ibid., 172; Kleinig, "Ethics of Consent," 107–9; and Siegler, "Plamenatz on Consent," 260.

[14] Locke, of course, argues that those who temporarily lodge or travel in the society give precisely the same consent to its authority as do tacit consenting, continuing residents. We have seen (in 4.1) how implausible this position is and what a Lockean should say on the subject. I concentrate here on continued residence as Locke's most plausible suggestion about a sign of tacit consent that might ground the full range of political obligations for the "right" group of persons.

[15] See the references in *Moral Principles and Political Obligations*, 95, and "Voluntarism and Political Associations," 20.

[16] *Moral Principles and Political Obligations*, 95–100.

have not changed significantly, I do believe that the case I presented there was too weak to establish that conclusion. I will try to remedy that defect here.

We must begin with the most general conditions for an act to be an act of binding consent (i.e., for consent to be a clear ground of obligation and right-transfer). Consent must, first, be given knowingly and intentionally. Second, binding consent must be given voluntarily. Consent can ground obligations only when it is freely given and adequately informed.[17] These requirements apply, I will suggest, even where the alleged consent is (as in the case of continued residence) tacit only. Let me take these requirements separately, beginning with the requirement that binding consent be given knowingly and intentionally.

Where an apparent consenter has tried to do something other than consent (or tried to do nothing at all), or where, as a result of incapacity, ignorance, confusion, or fraud, he does not fully comprehend what he is taken to have consented to, there is no (or only appropriately circumscribed) binding consent. When the (very) confused foreigner, speaking (very) little English, tries to order a pound of bologna with the words, "I consent to your authority over me," he has consented to nothing.[18] Only when the appropriate words, actions, or inaction are intentionally utilized with awareness of their significance can binding consent be given.

This seems to be taken for granted in the following passage from Hume's essay: "It is strange that an act of the mind, which every individual is supposed to have formed, and after he came to the use of reason, too, otherwise it could have no authority; that this act, I say, should be so much unknown to all of them, that over the face of the whole earth, there scarcely remain any traces or memory of it."[19]

Here Hume insists that consent is "an act of the mind," by which we may (charitably) understand him to mean that consent must be an intentional act, undertaken with reasonably full awareness of its significance and consequences. Where there is no awareness of having consented, no consent has been given. If Hume is right in this

<hr />

[17] Ibid., 77; Green, *Authority of the State*, 173; Kleinig, "Ethics of Consent," 99–107. *Failures* of consent, of course, correspond to these conditions—e.g., failures like defective belief, mental incapacity, coercion, etc. We have seen Locke's views on when consent is insufficient to bind (in 6.1 and 7.2 above). For the best recent discussion of the conditions for consensual failure, see Feinberg, *Harm to Self*, chapters 23–26.

[18] His act has "misfired," to use Austin's term (*How to Do Things with Words*, lecture 2).

[19] "Of the Original Contract," 259.

claim, then he is also right that the honest testimony of each of us will ultimately determine whether we have consented to our governments' authority (assuming only that our memories are accurate). And if we further accept, as I believe we should, that very few ordinary citizens are aware of ever having given consent to their governments' actions, this will count heavily against the "generality" of consent theory's account of political obligation and authority. Hume applies the point thus, in his challenge to the view that residence gives consent:

> Should it be said, that, by living under the dominion of a prince which one might leave, every individual has given a tacit consent to his authority, and promised his obedience; it may be answered, that such an implied consent can only have place where a man imagines that the matter depends on his choice. But where he thinks (as all mankind do who are born under established governments) that by his birth, he owes allegiance to a certain prince or a certain form of government; it would be absurd to infer a consent or choice, which he expressly, in this case, renounces and disclaims.[20]

Continued residence cannot be taken to ground political obligation unless residence is understood to be one possible choice in a mandatory decision process. Residence must be seen as the result of a morally significant choice. It is not enough that the choice is available; it must be understood by each person to be a required choice, with mere residence not constituting, for instance, a way of declining to choose.[21] And in Hume's view, of course, these conditions are not satisfied in our actual political lives. Residence requires no "act of the mind" as consent does.

To the consent theorist inclined to try to avoid this conclusion by *denying* that binding consent must be knowingly and intentionally given, it seems sufficient to point out that consent theory is in fact committed to *accepting* this requirement. As we have already seen in the case of Locke, the consent of which the consent theorist speaks must be consent knowingly and intentionally given, for several reasons. First, the consent theorist is attempting to utilize in his work a plausible theory of obligation; the consent with which he concerns himself must be a clear ground of obligation. But surely it is only consent that is intentionally given that satisfies this condi-

[20] Ibid., 263.
[21] Woozley, *Law and Obedience*, 82–84, 103; Beran, *Consent Theory*, 28.

tion. Consent in any looser, wider sense would be a considerably less convincing example of an obligation-generating act; where the "consent" is given unknowingly, its moral significance becomes extremely doubtful. Second, the most basic point of consent theory, we should remember, has historically been to advance an account of political obligation that is consistent with our intuitive conviction that political bonds cannot be forced on any individual, or fall upon him against his will. Political allegiance is to be a matter for each person's decision, for each is naturally free, with strong rights of self-government (the central thesis of any political voluntarism, like Locke's). Authority exercised over subjects without their permission is illegitimate. But if this ideal of a "free choice" is to be given more than mere lip service, the consent that legitimates political authority must be knowingly and intentionally given. Only the satisfaction of this condition will guarantee that a genuine decision has been made, and a consent theory that recognizes other sorts of consent as binding will undermine its own intuitive support.

We can understand Hume's argument, then, to have two points. It can be seen first as an attack specifically aimed at Locke. For when Locke claims that mere residence in a state constitutes consent to its authority, he seems to allow the possibility that we can give binding consent unknowingly, by merely going about our business. And Hume surely saw this as a case of Locke's sacrificing at once the plausibility and the integrity of his consent theory (and not, as I have urged, as a case of Locke's illegitimately extending the term "consent" to cover the grounds of nonconsensual special obligations). But the broader point of Hume's argument challenges any consent theory, not only Locke's. For if the consent theorist must insist on the intentionality of binding consent, as we have argued, then the consent of ordinary citizens cannot be a subtle process of which "people take no notice . . . thinking it not done at all" (II, 117). The act that binds us to our political community cannot be one whose true significance is unknown to the actor. Even the person of less than average intelligence must know that he consents when he does so. Hume's simple point, then, seems to strike home. If there is no widespread awareness of the process of political consent, consent theory's account of political obligation cannot have the wide application its proponents have supposed.

The argument cannot, however, be won so easily. Hume's attack on consent theory might be challenged at two points. First, it might be suggested that there are some cases in which unintentionally given consent can be taken to ground political obligations, without this suggestion conflicting either with good sense or with the spirit of consent theory. Second, one might claim that Hume is mistaken in his observation that most persons are unaware of ever having given their consent. Harry Beran, for instance, seems to argue in both of these ways in the course of defending the view that political consent is given by continuing to reside within the boundaries of the state after reaching the "age of consent."[22]

It is hard to deny that there might be some cases where it seems possible to give binding consent without intending to do so or being aware of the consequences of our act. We have already mentioned such cases—those where people perform an act that is clearly established by convention as an act of consent, but claim not to have intended to consent to anything in their performance. Where this claim is a result of understandable ignorance or confusion, we will not regard the performance as consensual (as in the case of the foreigner who uses words in ignorance of their meaning). But what about cases where the ignorance claimed is harder to understand? For instance, consider the case of a man who enters a restaurant, examines the menu, and asks for the filet mignon (clearly priced on the menu he has examined). After eating and being presented with the check, he claims not to have been aware that he would have to pay for the food. He takes himself to have consented to nothing.[23] Now assuming that the man in question is a normal, healthy, literate person, reared in a normal way, we can react to him in one of two ways. Most likely, we will take him to be a troublemaker who knew full well that his order amounted to an agreement to pay for the food. If he seems sincere and genuinely puzzled, however, we might check him out with our local polygraph examiner. When we find, to our surprise, that he has been speaking the truth, what should we conclude about his startling ignorance? Has he made a binding agreement (given binding consent) to pay for the meal, or not? One plausible answer is this: insofar as he has not been deprived in any way of the opportunity to learn about the conventions governing ordering in restaurants, and insofar as it would have seemed appropriate for him at least to have asked about the rules before eating, his ignorance is neither understandable nor excusable. It is genuine, but *negligent*, ignorance. And we will take him

---

[22] Beran, "In Defense of the Consent Theory." It is unclear whether Beran has abandoned these arguments, or only refrained from fully restating them, in his later *Consent Theory*.

[23] This example is a slightly altered version of one used by Kraut in *Socrates and the State*, 153. See Green's similar case in *Authority of the State*, 163–64.

to have made a binding agreement to pay for his food, despite the absence of any intention on his part to do so. Ordinary, excusable ignorance defeats the claim that consent was given. Negligent ignorance may not.

I emphasize this point only because it seems to be a key to Beran's response to the Humean argument we have been considering. Beran, in fact, admits that the Humean argument constitutes "a very persuasive objection," and he seems willing to grant as well its key premise: that "ordinary people are not aware that their remaining within a state when they cease to be political minors counts as their implicit agreement to obey."[24] How, then, can he avoid the conclusion that very few ordinary people have political obligations grounded in "consent through residence"? Beran's answer is that while people do not commonly see that continued residence counts as an agreement to obey, they *do* understand that by remaining in the state they "accept full membership" in it. And because the state is a rule-governed association like others with which they are familiar, they *should* be able to see that such "acceptance of membership" entails an obligation to follow the rules. If they do see this, then they properly understand the significance of continued residence, and can be taken to agree to obey. But if they do not make the necessary inference, their residence can *still* be taken as an agreement to obey. "For ignorance that doing W counts as agreeing to do X is only a conclusive defense against the claim that one has agreed to do X if such ignorance is not negligent."[25] And this failure to see that one's acceptance of membership involves obligations "may well be negligent, since people should consider what moral significance there is in their new status and their new rights."[26] So, Beran can conclude, in spite of the objection we have raised, that those who continue to reside in a state can be understood to have agreed to obey (at least, we might add, if they do not publicly reject the state's authority).

Beran's defense, in order to be convincing, must persuade us on two main points. First, we must be persuaded that ordinary people do in fact regard continued residence after their political minority as a way of "accepting full membership" in the state. And second, we must be convinced that they regard the "association" in which they "accept membership" as very much like other rule-governed associations with which they are familiar. For only if they "accept

[24] Beran, "In Defense of the Consent Theory," 270.
[25] Ibid.
[26] Ibid. This may also be what Machan has in mind in "Individualism," 511.

membership" with such an understanding could they possibly be considered *negligent* in failing to see that they have undertaken political obligations; it is only by virtue of their familiarity with ordinary, everyday rule-governed associations that they could be presumed to know that becoming a member necessarily involves assuming obligations (they are not, after all, moral philosophers).

Now both of these questions look like they would be best decided by a public opinion poll. Beran merely asserts that ordinary persons understand these matters, that clear conventions make continued residence a way of consenting. Hume (and I) would claim that they do not. Certainly there are many countries where the average citizen is not much better educated to political matters than he was in Hume's day; the claim that the ignorance of such persons is "negligent" seems ridiculous. And whatever accomplishments modern educational systems can claim, I doubt that a universally increased insight into problems of moral obligation is among them. But in order to try to add argument to opinion, let me suggest some reasons why it would seem peculiar (or even unreasonable) for ordinary persons to hold the views ascribed to them by Beran. First, if the transition to political majority is commonly regarded as involving a choice of no small significance, it should be viewed as a moment for careful thought and planning. One might also expect the transition to be accompanied by significant changes in behavior patterns, as is often the case when one becomes a new member of some association. None of this is in evidence in most political communities. Why is not this very important event in our lives the subject of elaborate rituals or formal pledges, as when other associations are joined? The most plausible answer is Hume's: residents of most countries believe themselves born to citizenship.[27] The transition to majority is no celebrated event for the simple reason that it is not regarded as a sharp break in one's political life. Rather it is regarded as a point at which certain important rights and duties are added to the list of those already possessed. Political minors are no strangers to the burdens of citizenship; they can have legal obligations, be tried and punished, be required to pay taxes on income. They are taught to think of themselves as citizens long before they cease to be minors. American children pledge their allegiance from their earliest school years and sit through units on "citizenship" regularly. At the "age of consent" they gain a legal freedom from the control

---

[27] "Of the Original Contract," 263. Locke, interestingly, agrees that this is what ordinary persons believe (II, 117). See also Woozley, *Law and Obedience*, 92–93.

of their parents, but this is by no means the time at which all their rights and duties begin. The rights to vote, to purchase alcoholic beverages, to hold political office, and to receive old-age benefits are among those that are not (or have not always been) received on reaching majority. Eligibility for military service may or may not begin at this time. The important point is that the course of one's political life does not appear as two distinct stages, with a moment of decision dividing them. Rather it appears as a smooth course involving the periodic gain or loss of rights and duties, and it would be extremely odd, given the state of political conventions, if ordinary persons regarded their political lives in any other way. It would be, then, more than surprising if they viewed continued residence at some point as a sign that one is accepting membership in the state, an agreement that would ground all future rights and duties. Beran's chief assumption, then, seems mistaken.

It follows from this, of course, that his second assumption is mistaken as well. For the points made above suggest that it would be equally surprising if persons regarded their "political associations" in the same light as the ordinary rule-governed associations with which they are familiar. Ordinary associations are joined in a way that political communities do not seem to be.[28] Homes, families, and friends are established in the state long before the age of consent; only the rare person thinks that there is anything to join at majority. Given these facts, the widespread "ignorance" of the moral consequences of continued residence can hardly be regarded as negligent. Indeed, it cannot even be regarded as "ignorance," for if residence is not understood to be a sign of consent, it cannot be one.

8.3. Duress, Hard Choices, and Free Choice

Our conclusion from the preceding section should be that continued residence, even within democratic communities, is not now a way of giving consent to the authority of government. But suppose, through reasonably painless alterations in political conventions, things were different. Suppose that the state really did present each person with a clear choice on reaching the age of consent: "either emigrate or continue to reside in our territories. If you choose the latter, we will take you to have consented to obey the law and sup-

---

[28] Honore, "Must We Obey?" 44–46. Compare the situation in contemporary democracies with that in ancient Athens, where becoming a citizen was very much like joining a "club." See Kraut, *Socrates and the State*, 154–55.

port the institutions of government in those ways necessary to its continued just functioning."[29] In the face of such a clear choice situation, there could be no confusion about how the government would regard the significance of continued residence. Would such a change be sufficient to establish residence as the giving of binding consent?

Here the second general condition on binding consent—that it must be given voluntarily—becomes a central concern. And, once again, one of Hume's arguments seems to strike to the heart of the matter:

> Can we seriously say that a poor peasant or artisan has a free choice to leave his country, when he knows no foreign language or manners, and lives, from day to day, by the small wages he acquires? We may as well assert that a man, by remaining in a vessel, freely consents to the dominion of the master; though he was carried on board while asleep and must leap into the ocean and perish, the moment he leaves her.[30]

Even when citizens understand the significance of the choice between residence and emigration, Hume is arguing, the latter option is not really one that is open to many citizens. Those who are poor or unskilled, for instance, could not emigrate without suffering disastrous consequences. And if a person is required to choose between two courses of action, of which only one is a real possibility, that person cannot really be understood to choose freely at all. In the absence of a genuine choice on his part, his exercising the only real option open to him will not have the sort of moral significance that a bona fide choice would have.

We can, of course, try to extend Hume's argument.[31] It is not only the poor and unskilled for whom emigration is an extremely unattractive option. For most of us the most important things in our lives—like home, family, friends, style of life—are firmly tied to our countries of residence. Similar problems surely faced those who considered emigration in Locke's day.[32] But it is a very hard thing

[29] Compare with the choice "the laws" are said to offer to all Athenians in Plato's *Crito*. On the significance of this offer, see Woozley, *Law and Obedience*, chapter 5; and Kraut, *Socrates and the State*, chapter 6.

[30] "Of the Original Contract," 263.

[31] As I do at greater length in *Moral Principles and Political Obligations*, 99–100. See also Herzog, *Happy Slaves*, 183; and Woozley, *Law and Obedience*, 104–9.

[32] Locke writes of the "frequent" examples in history "of men withdrawing themselves and their obedience from the jurisdiction they were born under, and the family or community they were bred up in, and setting up new governments in other

to ask anyone, and especially to ask one just arrived at the age of consent, to seriously consider leaving all this behind for the uncertainties and alienation of emigration. But if so much weight is placed on the side of continued residence, can we really be said to have a free choice to stay or go? Can the decision to stay have the moral significance that free choices have? If not, there would seem to be no conditions under which continued residence, even in a democracy, can be taken as a sign of tacit consent to the authority of government.

Now this conclusion may seem to involve a serious confusion between choices that are simply hard and those that are unfree.[33] We frequently have to make hard choices, where we feel constrained in one way or another; but we do not think that such choices are for that reason unfree and thus nonbinding. Hobbes famously pressed a similar confusion in a less liberal direction than the one suggested above. Hobbes argued that all political agreements are motivated by fear—those that are not the result of coercion as well as those that are. A consent given at the point of a sword is given through fear of what will happen if one chooses not to consent; but other consents are given just as much in fear of the consequences of not consenting. All political consent is equally free (or unfree). Hence, even coerced political consent must be morally binding, since the only alternative is to deny that *any* political consent is binding.[34]

Compare the following two acts of making a contract. The first contract is made at the point of a gun. Jones, owner of a small manufacturing firm, is forced by J. R., his ambitious competitor, to sign a contract selling J. R. his firm for a small fraction of its worth. Jones, afraid of being shot dead, complies with J. R.'s demands. The second contract is signed in a different possible world, one in which Jones' firm is slowly but surely failing. Jones calls his competitor J. R., they

---

places" (II, 115). But he cannot have thought such emigration an easy matter, even in his own day (when there were still wilderness areas to claim and settle). Not only was much given up by those who fled England in Locke's day, but considerable hardships awaited those who founded new communities; and similar or greater burdens (than those they left behind) were imposed by most existing societies on those who left England simply to enter another body politic.

[33] This appears to be what Tussman wants to claim in *Obligation and the Body Politic*, 37–38.

[34] *Leviathan*, chapter 20, paragraph 2: sovereignty acquired by force differs from sovereignty acquired from a "free" covenant "only in this, that men who choose their sovereign do it for fear of one another and not of him whom they institute, but in [the former case] they subject themselves to him they are afraid of. In both cases they do it for fear—which is to be noted by them that hold all such covenants as proceed from fear of death or violence void, which if it were true, no man, in any kind of commonwealth, could be obliged to obedience."

meet and negotiate, and finally Jones agrees to sell his firm for a small fraction of its worth. This time the contract is signed because of Jones' fear that if he does not sell for whatever he can get, he will lose everything.

Hobbes might say of these two contracts that both are made from fear of the consequences of not signing. Both are made equally freely (or unfreely), hence both are morally binding. The fact that one contract is signed under duress is irrelevant. But surely we will reply that the presence of duress makes all the difference in the world. The first contract is binding neither morally nor legally; duress is a condition that voids contracts.[35] Nor is it hard to say why. Where duress is used to extract an agreement, the party using coercion violates the rights of the one coerced. J. R., in our first scenario, wronged Jones, and must not be allowed to profit from his wrong-doing.[36] But this seems very different from the second scenario, where Jones faces not duress, but merely a difficult decision. And surely the difficulty of his decision does not affect the validity of the contract he signs. The second contract is both morally and legally binding.

So Hobbes is wrong. There is a significant moral difference between cases of coerced consent and cases where consent is the result of a difficult choice. But have I not followed Hume into the same kind of mistake that Hobbes made, supposing that because the choice of residence is motivated by fear of the alternative (emigration), this choice has no more moral significance than coerced choice? Where Hobbes assumes that *both* choices bind us, Hume assumes that *neither* binds us (as do I). Either way, it seems, the correct position, that difficult choices may bind while coerced choices cannot, is ignored.

Again, Beran has attacked precisely the position that I have followed Hume in defending. He considers the argument from Hume

[35] Scanlon has argued that coercion only obviously voids consent when that coercion is used to secure something to which the coercer is not entitled (thus explaining how defeated nations in war can still make binding treaties) ("Promises and Practices," 224n). While this condition is certainly satisfied in my example (J. R.'s coercion is used to secure from Jones something to which J. R. is not entitled), it is my view (and Locke's) that coerced consent never binds. For if I secure by coerced consent something to which I am independently entitled, it is not clear that the consent adds anything to the antecedent obligation the coerced party has to satisfy my entitlement. The (coerced) consenter already has the relevant obligations prior to consenting; and if further concessions are made by the consenter as a result of coercion, it is by no means obvious that he is obligated to act on them.

[36] Murphy, "Consent, Coercion," 81. The discussion below owes much to Murphy's interesting paper and follows his argument on a number of points.

(just quoted above) and suggests that the requirement of a genuine "free choice" for binding consent "can be regarded as a compendious way of claiming that a promissory obligation is created only if none of the defeating conditions hold." Examples of such conditions are "deception, mental incapacity, coercion or undue influence, and unfair bargaining position."[37] But clearly, Beran urges, none of these conditions is satisfied in the case Hume mentions. No one forces poor citizens to remain in the state, or tricks them into staying. It is their own poverty that prevents their emigration. "In general, it simply does not follow from one's being unable to leave a state that there is present one or more of the conditions which prevent one's promise to obey that state from creating an obligation."[38]

Against my attempt to extend the Humean argument, Beran proceeds similarly:

> People who do not wish to consent to the government under which they live but cannot bear the thought of losing homeland, family, and friends, could perhaps truly be said to be "forced by circumstances" to consent nevertheless. But common moral opinion does not endorse the claim that being "forced by circumstances" to consent to something necessarily prevents such consent from creating a right and an obligation. Therefore, Simmons has not *shown* that his objection to . . . consent theory from the high cost of emigration is a sound one.[39]

Is Beran right that agreements motivated by difficult circumstances are still binding, as long as no duress is involved? We have already seen one case that seems to support his claim: Jones' second contract with J. R. But there are other kinds of cases (as both Filmer and Locke saw[40]). Take the following:

Jones is wandering in the desert, dying of thirst, when he stumbles onto the front lawn of J. R.'s oasis estate. There on the porch swing sits J. R., in his hands a pitcher of cool lemonade. Jones begs him for a drink, and J. R. pours a glass of lemonade; but J. R. presents Jones first with a document for signature. Before he can have

[37] Beran, "In Defense of the Consent Theory," 267; see also *The Consent Theory,* 6–7.

[38] Ibid. See also Beran, *Consent Theory,* 105.

[39] Beran, "What Is the Basis of Political Authority?" 497–98.

[40] See Filmer's comments on the necessity of relief from unreasonable or unjust promises—i.e., those resulting not only from force, but from deceit, error, and fear, or those that it would be harmful to keep (*Patriarcha,* III, 7). On Locke's awareness that some contracts are unconscionable, see the discussion below.

a drink, Jones must sign a contract, selling his manufacturing firm to J. R. for a small fraction of its worth. Jones, in desperation, signs the contract and is rewarded with a life-saving glass of lemonade.[41]

Now that Jones has had his drink and recovered his strength, is the contract he signed binding? He was not, remember, forced to accept J. R.'s offer, nor was he tricked into accepting it or of unsound mind when he accepted. He just found himself "forced by circumstances" to accept. J. R. might claim that he violated none of Jones' rights (in any obvious fashion) along the way.[42] The lemonade, after all, was rightfully J. R.'s, and he was under no obligation to sell it at all. Beran seems committed to the position that this contract must be binding.

But surely it is *not* binding, legally or morally. In the law such a contract would be unenforceable because *unconscionable*.[43] Where one party to a contract has an unfair bargaining strength, created by another's special vulnerability, and he takes unfair advantage of that vulnerability in contract, the agreement is not enforceable. Again, the idea is that J. R. has acted wrongly, even granting his dubious contention that he has violated none of Jones' rights. He has unfairly required Jones to make an incredibly hard choice, where no such hard choice was necessary. J. R. has manipulated the situation to take unfair advantage of another's plight.[44] And he should not be allowed to profit from this wrongdoing. Thus, Jones has no obligation, moral or legal, to honor his contract with J. R. He is, perhaps, bound to give J. R. fair payment for the lemonade (which, in a desert, may be substantial). But no more than that is required.

I would not want to pretend that the idea of an unconscionable contract, in either law or morals, is an especially clear one. It is not immediately obvious what kind of principle distinguishes the un-

[41] Compare with Locke's example (of the robber who compels one to convey to him one's estate) in II, 176. The example used here is similar to those used in my "Voluntarism and Political Associations," 34–35; and in Murphy, "Consent, Coercion," 88–89.

[42] Whether J. R.'s claim is accepted, of course, will depend on one's views about positive rights. If Jones is taken to have a right to aid (as I argue in *Lockean Theory of Rights*, chapter 6), and J. R. a duty to give aid (without exploitive conditions attached to his aid), then J. R.'s actions will be wrong in an even more serious fashion. But even if Jones has no such right, J. R.'s actions fail to demonstrate that minimal decency that persons ought to practice toward one another. An act need not violate another's rights in order to be wrong.

[43] For brief philosophical treatments of unconscionability, see Murphy, "Consent, Coercion," 89–92; Fried, *Contract as Promise*, 103–11; Feinberg, *Harm to Self*, 249–53.

[44] On having and taking "unfair advantage," see Coleman, "Liberalism, Unfair Advantage."

conscionable contract signed by Jones in the example above from the hard bargain Jones felt he had to make in our second example (where he sold his failing firm for a fraction of its worth).[45] In both cases, for instance, J. R. "took advantage" of Jones' predicament to make a large profit. However, in one case I have claimed that J. R. "wronged" Jones, while in the other I have made no such claim. In what does the "wrong" consist in the case of the unconscionable contract?

I think that there are at least two elements of wrongdoing. First, it makes a difference that the unconscionable contract concerned harsh terms for the provision of an essential good (in our case, a good necessary to avoid the evil of death by dehydration). Minimally decent treatment of our fellows does not allow us to deny them essential goods or to provide them only on completely unreasonable terms. If J. R. had offered Jones some good that Jones merely *wanted* badly, instead of a good that he needed, our evaluation of a subsequent contract between them might be quite different—even if the profit J. R. obtained through the deal seemed to us ridiculously great.[46] Minimally decent treatment of others may not require that we make their lives easy. But it requires at least that we not withhold from them goods that they need, that we offer them reasonable terms for their procurement.[47]

At least as important is the second aspect of wrongdoing in the unconscionable contract we are considering: exploitation or manipulation.[48] While J. R. "took advantage" of Jones' plight in both of the contracts we have discussed, in only one of them was there any element of manipulation. The unconscionable contract was brought about by tailoring the terms in such a way as to guarantee that they

[45] The second example involves only what Murphy (quoting Justice Pitney) calls a "legitimate inequality of fortune" ("Consent, Coercion," 82). See Feinberg's discussion of Murphy's distinction, in *Harm to Self*, 196–97.

[46] As examples, we might use Fried's case of the stamp collector who must pay a steep price for the stamp he wants to complete his collection (*Contract as Promise*, 95), or Murphy's case of the boy who would love to have the ridiculously priced baseball autographed by Babe Ruth (in "Blackmail").

[47] That the terms are *harsh* is crucial here. Jones would have been equally unfree to refuse *reasonable* terms offered by J. R. (say, $5.00 for the lemonade), but our evaluation of the contract would then be completely different. See Feinberg, *Harm to Self*, 250–55.

[48] See Feinberg's extensive discussion of the concept of exploitation in *Harmless Wrongdoing*, chapters 31–32. Exploitation, according to Feinberg, is a wrongful or blameworthy way of using someone else for one's own purposes, which may or may not be coercive (p. 177). See also Raz's argument that while mere absence of choice may not void consent, "engineering" to secure consent from another does void it (*Morality of Freedom*, 88–89).

would be accepted. We can assume that J. R. would have been pre-pared to offer considerably more reasonable terms to one who was not so desperately needy as Jones. This makes his treatment of Jones exploitive, not merely opportunistic. And to exploit or manipulate others without good reason is wrong. In Kantian terms, exploitive conduct *uses* others objectionably, irrationally treating them as beings with less moral significance than oneself. Locke explicitly defends similar points in his essay "Venditio."[49]

When these two elements of wrongdoing are copresent in the background of a contract, we can confidently condemn it as un-conscionable.[50] People should not be allowed to profit from such wrongdoing. Where either element is missing, the status of the con-tract will seem less clear.[51] But however difficult it may be to draw neat, clean lines here, it seems undeniable that some contracts, even without the presence of duress, involve sufficient wrongdoing that they are not morally (and ought not to be legally) binding.[52]

Let us now return to Hume's argument. First, consider Hume's

[49] Locke argues there that it is *not* unjust to obtain high market prices for one's goods in a place where those goods are in short supply, provided the same high price is charged to all ("Venditio," 86)—as when J. R. charges the same high prices for everyone. But the seller, Locke argues, must accept a loss rather than charge another what will destroy him; we must sell to the distressed at the same (or *lower*) price as we sell to the undistressed (ibid., 86–87). We may not tailor our terms to take ad-vantage of distressed persons.

[50] On Feinberg's account, the terms of a contract are unconscionable if they are exploitive (i.e., if they are harsh in their costs or disproportionate in their benefits for one party) and if they are coercive in their intent and effect (*Harm to Self*, 249–52). Elsewhere Feinberg also explicitly mentions the importance of the fact that vital interests (needs) are involved in cases of the sort I have described (*Harmless Wrong-doing*, 232).

[51] As, for instance, if J. R. had only (1) exploited Jones' fervent desire to own a rare stamp, or (2) charged Jones for the lemonade the very steep price he charged even those much less desperate for a drink than Jones. Blackmail, another sort of exploitive contractual arrangement, typically does not involve threatening to deny others es-sential goods, unlike our example of an unconscionable contract. I make no effort here to deal with questions about the wrongness of blackmail. On this subject, see (again) Feinberg, *Harmless Wrongdoing*, 238–74.

[52] Murphy, "Consent, Coercion," 89–91. Whether the case described *does* involve duress or coercion (a so-called coercive offer) is not as clear as the preceding discus-sion suggests. Murphy believes that such agreements involve unfairness but no du-ress. Feinberg prefers to include unconscionable contracts in the category of those made under duress (*Harm to Self*, 250). My case here does not turn on the stance taken on this question. It is worth noting that Murphy elsewhere defines coercion in terms of "taking unfair advantage of his vulnerability by proposing, unless he accepts a certain offer, to treat him in a way that is unfair and in a way which he has no power to prevent" ("Total Institutions," 193–94). The terms of this account of coer-cion are so close to those used by Murphy in discussing unconscionability, that it seems fair to say there is no great philosophical distance between his position and Feinberg's.

shipbound man. He has two choices available to him: he can leap overboard and perish, or accept the arbitrary rule of the ship's master (remembering that he was not free to choose which master he sailed under). Is not his predicament similar to that of Jones above? If he is forced to make such a choice under these conditions, the choice is surely unfairly required of him, for it takes advantage of a difficult situation into which he entered through no fault of his own. Perhaps, then, Hume is right that remaining on board cannot be taken as a sign of binding consent, nor can it ground a moral obligation to obey the master's whims.

We arrive now at the case of Hume's peasant, and again the similarity with our case of Jones and J. R. is striking. The peasant lives in the land of his birth through no choice of his own. He has no choice of potential masters, like Jones and the shipbound man. He must either accept the dominion of a master who has allowed him to live a life of poverty, or embark on an almost certainly disastrous emigration (supposing this is even possible). Now even under these conditions Beran is certainly right that an unsolicited promise to obey would bind the peasant (within limits). But it is not at all clear that a required choice would also bind. Again I am inclined to think that it would not; for while the peasant is not prevented by coercion from choosing any particular option, he is after all forced by others (or perhaps by unjustifiable conventions) to make a choice, while in a very unfavorable position. Even if his choice is not coerced, it is still importantly *unfree*, by virtue of the severe limitation by others of his range of possible choices. It is precisely the poor and oppressed, of course, who would typically most desire but least be able to emigrate. The choice that they are forced to make results in "agreements" of very questionable force.[53]

The same reasoning applies, I believe, to the position of those who are not poor and oppressed, but remain in the state and accept the burdensome duties of citizenship because of the high cost of emigration. Such persons are not simply "forced by circumstances" to remain in the state, although they may not be coerced into staying either. They are unfairly required to choose between two hard options. They must either accept heavy taxation, unreasonably restrictive laws, terms of military service, official flouting of their basic principles, and the like (thereby sacrificing very important free-

[53] Needless to say, if Locke genuinely wanted to require express oaths of allegiance of all citizens in 1690 (as Farr and Roberts claim, in "John Locke on the Glorious Revolution," 390–91), this requirement would have resulted in similarly questionable agreements (as we saw in 4.1).

doms), or they must emigrate (they must "love it or leave it"). By requiring this choice, the state exploits the special vulnerability of its citizens. They are vulnerable through the fact of having been born, reared, and socialized within the territories of a demanding state, so that leaving it is a heavy burden; and they are vulnerable in their inability to resist the demands of the state by force. When the state takes advantage of this vulnerability by requiring a hard choice, it guarantees that continued residence is not an indication of binding consent.[54] Even if the choice situation it presents is clear and its expectations obvious, residence does not bind us in the way the state expects. Even within a democratic community, where every citizen is "free" to emigrate, this conclusion is sound. It is, of course (as we have seen), a conclusion that presupposes a particular view about how it is reasonable or decent of a state to treat those who reside within its territories. A state must not only respect the rights of residents, but it must also avoid manipulation designed to take advantage of special vulnerabilities suffered by those residents. And it must not deny essential goods (such as basic freedoms) to residents, or offer them only on unreasonably harsh terms. If it fails in this, any "agreements" exacted by such manipulation are non-binding on grounds of unconscionability.

States can, of course, offer their residents terms of membership that are not harsh, but reasonable and fair, so that the required choice between membership and emigration is not sufficiently "hard" to undermine its moral significance. States might tax only reasonably, protect the weak, restrict liberty only where necessary, refrain from requiring their citizens (or their poor, disadvantaged citizens) to risk their lives in foreign adventures (whether the "requirement" be one of law or one of economic necessity), use their powers to serve international justice, and so on. Under such conditions (and after suitable alterations in political conventions presented each resident with a clear choice situation), the state would not be extracting an unconscionable agreement from (at least the vast majority of) those who choose to consent by remaining resident. Residence might then constitute binding consent to the (appropriately limited) authority of government, might then ground

[54] The state does not, of course, tailor its demands to the vulnerability of particular citizens, as J. R. did to Jones. Its demands are rather tailored to a vulnerability shared by most of its residents. This does not, of course, make its exploitation more acceptable. In fact, because we can get no better terms from any other state (if we are lucky enough to be in that position), the "agreement" we are required to make in remaining in residence resembles unconscionable "contracts of adhesion" (where all the competitors for our business offer the same unfair terms).

clear political obligations. But no actual states, in our time or in Locke's, have offered such reasonable terms and clear choices to their residents.

And it is worth remembering here as well that what makes the terms offered by states unreasonably harsh (or not) may rest on very individual values or principles. Thus, for instance, for those who genuinely value independence highly enough, *any* terms of membership offered by a modern state may be unreasonably harsh (since membership itself has high disutility for such persons). To force such (admittedly unusual) persons to choose between membership and emigration will still seem wrong, and agreements made will still seem morally suspect, even if the terms of membership are quite reasonable for the majority of residents.

Such worries suggest a second way in which a state might offer residents a choice that is not unconscionable. A state might offer citizenship "grades" or "packages," where certain combinations of the possible benefits of citizenship could be purchased at the price of accepting some assortment of the possible associated burdens (with the lowest "grade" perhaps being the "noncitizen resident," who would bear none of the standard burdens and would be denied as many as possible of the benefits). Perhaps if a state were to offer residents a larger set of options (than simply full citizenship or emigration), its treatment of residents could more easily be regarded as reasonable and decent.[55] Even a required choice might then bind the resident, if there were less burdensome options lying between citizenship and emigration. But as things currently stand in (even democratic) political societies, such options are, of course, unavailable.[56] And most would, at any rate, regard the creation of interesting options (such as grades of citizenship and "internal emigration") as hopelessly impracticable within modern political

[55] Beran suggests that free consent will be maximized in societies that guarantee not only a right to emigrate, but also a right for groups to secede, and which preserve a "free territory" for dissenters who want neither citizenship nor emigration (*Consent Theory*, 125–27). But it is not clear how these additional options will solve consent theory's problem with voluntariness. Secession is only an option for groups of persons, not for individuals. And emigration to a free territory has many (or more) of the same kinds of associated high costs as does emigration to another country. Only options such as internal (individual) emigration (i.e., resident nonmembership) or grades of citizenship will attack the voluntariness problem, since they eliminate the high costs of leaving home, family, etc.

[56] See Kraut's argument to a related conclusion in *Socrates and the State*, 192–93; and Klosko's rejection of "consent or leave" mechanisms in "Reformist Consent," 678–82.

communities.[57] Even, then, if modern states presented their residents with clear choice situations, the agreements secured by this process would be mostly nonbinding because unconscionable (at least without very dramatic further changes in modern states).

There is more, it seems, to Hume's attack on Locke than Beran has noticed. We have seen already that Locke is explicitly committed to accepting the force of at least some arguments from unconscionability (although he seems not to see very clearly how this commitment might affect his position on political consent). Locke's commitments in this area are probably nowhere made more clear than in the *First Treatise*, where he writes: "A man can no more justly make use of another's necessity, to force him to become his vassal, by withholding that relief God requires him to afford to the wants of his brother, than he that has more strength can seize upon a

---

[57] The immediate practical difficulties involved in implementing such schemes are not quite as severe as is commonly supposed, as the successful evolution of (e.g.) "subscription" fire departments and medical rescue services (where service is denied to those who are not paid up) seem to show. Differential police protection, highway tolls, and so on, could be accomplished with no (or easily imagined) technical innovations. More severe, I believe, would be the likely "morale" and "character" problems such schemes would introduce (such as unwelcome class distinctions, likely hardheartedness toward those who suddenly need services for which they have not paid, endless worries about cheating and free riding, etc.). But none of these problems seems to me to make all kinds of "graded citizenship" schemes either practically impossible or morally indefensible.

Klosko has argued that "benefit deprivation schemes" (which he regards as "the most defensible" mechanisms for facilitating free consent) cannot ground political obligations ("Reformist Consent," 690)—i.e. (for our purposes here), that a "graded citizenship" scheme would not really result in free, binding consent by residents. His argument seems to be that even if a government allowed residents to forego certain benefits (such as police protection), so that the lower "grade" of those residents could be regarded as freely chosen, government would still have to coercively prevent those residents from providing such benefits for themselves (e.g., by banding together for self-defense)—since the state must have a monopoly on force. And this necessary state coercion would, of course, undermine the voluntariness of the scheme (pp. 689–90).

Klosko's argument seems weak in at least two crucial regards. First, the use of force for protection is only one of many public benefits that might be differentially distributed within a society; the argument from the necessity of a monopoly on force does not extend to schemes that withhold from some citizens various of the other commonplace benefits of citizenship. Second, however familiar such claims may have become, it is not at all obvious that states either must have a complete monopoly on the use of force within their territories (rather than having, say, sufficient assets and power to monitor private use of force by some and to prevent or punish it where morally permissible), or that they are entitled to insist on such a monopoly. Societies are obliged to offer those affected by their operation legitimate options and reasonable terms. Individuals are not required to freely give up just anything that makes it awkward or inconvenient for societies to function in their preferred or traditional ways. To deny these assertions is simply to deny out of hand those reasons one might have for finding consent theory attractive in the first place.

weaker, master him to his obedience, and with a dagger at his throat offer him death or slavery" (I, 42).[58] But if "a man" cannot justly use another's vulnerability to extract from him favorable terms, neither can a government or political society. And if the options a government offers individuals reared in its territories are limited to a range that is unreasonably harsh, it is *not* true that the existence of that society and its government "injures not the freedom of the rest [i.e., those still in the state of nature]" (II, 95). Their freedom may be significantly enough reduced to deprive their "agreements" of all moral force. The problem is not just that there are compelling reasons for joining any (legitimate) civil society, or that there are compelling reasons not to leave the land of one's birth.[59] The problem is rather that the choices left open to individuals by the state are unfairly restricted so as to exploit these compelling reasons. Unless the alternatives offered by the state are clearly presented and significantly restructured, continued residence cannot be taken as a free choice that could ground political obligations and the rights of governments.[60]

Perhaps it will seem that, however fair this argument might be as an attack on some general claim that residence gives consent, it cannot be fair as a criticism of Locke or of Lockean consent theory. For Locke is a proponent of severely limited government, and the political obligations he thinks will issue from the tacit consent given by continued residence are also, as a result, suitably limited and reasonable. Requiring a choice by residents between such limited obligations and emigration will not force agreements that are unconscionable. Indeed, the content of political obligation in Locke's philosophy might seem to amount to no more than: (a) obeying valid civil law, which law in a just (i.e., authoritative) society will simply reinforce and further specify our natural law duties (and so add no new duties we did not have already, independent of civil society); (b) refraining from enforcing natural law ourselves, allowing instead the free operation of the state's legal apparatus (which is surely no

---

[58] Cohen seems also to see some of the extensive consequences of this passage for Locke's political philosophy ("Structure, Choice, and Legitimacy," 308–9).

[59] Dunn rightly notes that powerful motivations do not, for Locke, render acts nonvoluntary. But he seems wrongly to suppose that this is all that is at issue in the consent given by remaining in the land of one's birth ("Consent," 51).

[60] This is one of the central themes of an unpublished paper by Farrell entitled "Tacit Consent and the Justification of Political Power." While Farrell arrives at his conclusion in a very different way than I do here, many of his remarks helped me to clarify my thoughts expressed above.

great burden); and (c) assisting the state financially (and perhaps physically) in protecting the rights of society's members.[61]

But how fair I have been to Locke depends, first, on how far Locke wished to claim that citizens in *actual* states give their consent by continued residence (etc.). We know that Locke at least wished to claim this about his own postrevolutionary England. And it can certainly not be plausibly maintained that England in 1689 either presented all of its residents with a clear choice situation or offered reasonable and fair terms of membership to all (or even the great majority) of its residents. In any event, to whatever extent Locke was willing to accept the anarchist implications of his consent theory (and I believe that extent was quite small), to that extent my argument is not an argument against Locke. It is not the Lockean ideal of government by consent that is here under attack.

Second, however, I think the content of political obligation that is consistent even with Locke's ideal could be in most respects as burdensome as that imposed in most modern democracies. For, as we saw in 3.1: (a) Valid civil laws for Locke are not simply those that reinforce or specify natural law; rather, they are all laws "preserving or regulating property" and promoting the "public good" (II, 3) that are *"conformable to* the law of nature" (II, 135; my emphasis)—that is, all such laws that are *consistent with* the requirements of natural law. And this leaves open the possibility that there will be many civil laws that require or forbid actions beyond those required or forbidden by natural law. Civil law may legitimately extend into the (previously optional) realm of morally indifferent (i.e., merely permissible) conduct, since in doing so it will not contradict any natural law requirement or proscription. (b) Citizens are required not only to themselves refrain from enforcing law, but also to "assist the executive power of the society, as the law thereof shall require" (II, 130) and to be part of "the force of society" (II, 148) in repairing injuries done "to a member of their body" by "those that are out of it" (II, 145). Both assisting in domestic law enforcement and participating in military actions against other nations are, at least potentially, extremely heavy burdens. (c) Whether tax burdens in a society will be excessive depends heavily on both the efficiency of its government and the wealth and needs of its people and territories. Even a legitimate society cannot guarantee the absence of problems in either area. Again, of course, to the extent that Locke can be taken to intend that residence gives consent only when the options and

---

[61] This line of objection was suggested to me by Jeremy Waldron.

need for choice are clear and when the terms of membership for all are reasonably unburdensome (and, again, I think that extent is probably small), then my arguments are not with Locke's positions on that subject. They are rather only with Locke's refusal to clearly acknowledge that his consent theory requires us to draw anarchist conclusions with regard to actual, existing polities.

Let us stop now and take stock. What exactly has thus far been shown by the arguments of this chapter? Perhaps, it will seem, only this: that those who remain in a free society and take on the burdens of citizenship *unwillingly* cannot be understood to consent to the authority of their governments by doing so. And this may seem a conclusion of only limited interest. For surely, in "states whose governments are, and are believed by most of their citizens to be, reasonably efficient and reasonably just," many citizens will choose residence quite willingly, not out of fear of the consequences of emigration.[62] Where a choice is made willingly, it is surely binding, even if the available alternatives are bleak. So my conclusion may appear to "apply only to a small proportion of the adults of the kind of state which consent theory would claim to be authoritative."[63]

I think, in fact, that this severely understates the force of my arguments. I agree, of course, that wherever citizens make entirely unsolicited express agreements to support their governments, these agreements bind them, regardless of the costs of emigration. For where no choice between residence and emigration has been required, the choice to reside and assume the duties of citizenship is quite free (assuming, of course, that no other defeating conditions are present). But this in no way bears on the question of when mere continued residence, without any express agreement, counts as a way of giving consent. I have argued that under current political conditions, residence is not a way of giving consent. And this argument applies just as forcefully even to those who might accept the duties of citizenship quite willingly. Our concern is not with their attitude toward the state, but with whether they have performed binding acts of consent.[64] Regardless of their willingness to undertake political duties, their mere residence does not count as such an undertaking. For, as I argued earlier, present political conventions do not make continued residence a way of binding oneself

<hr />

[62] Beran, "What Is the Basis of Political Authority?" 495, and *Consent Theory,* 101, 106.

[63] Ibid., 494–95; also *Consent Theory,* 98–107. Inability to emigrate is, Beran claims, only a problem for consent theory when combined with the *desire* to emigrate.

[64] *Moral Principles and Political Obligations,* 93.

to the state, any more than they make voting the source of these bonds. Given that fact, the willingness of persons to undertake the duties of citizenship is irrelevant to any determination of their consensual obligations. There is simply no good reason to understand their continued residence as a sign of binding consent, in the absence of appropriate conventions.[65]

Changes in political conventions of the sort described at the beginning of this section (such that a clear choice situation *is* offered by our governments) will, of course, alter our conclusion. As a result of such changes, those who willingly continued to reside, uninfluenced by the costs of emigration, could be taken to consent to the authority of their governments. Even then, however, those who regarded the choice between residence and emigration as a choice between two very unpleasant options could not be understood to consent by continued residence.

Our conclusion is not, then, that government by consent is impossible. It remains, in one sense, the ideal toward which all governments should strive, and an ideal not perhaps hopelessly impracticable. But it is necessary to admit that this ideal is not approximated by any governments currently exercising authority, nor was it approximated in any societies with which Locke was familiar. It is here—in Locke's apparent empirical assumptions about the status of existing governments, in his application of his account of the political relationship—that we seem to find the most serious weaknesses in his commitments. Locke believed that some actual governments govern with the consent of their subjects, in a sense of "consent" sufficiently strong to ground political obligations and legitimate authority, and thus in a sense of "consent" consistent with his basic doctrine of natural human freedom. But even modern liberal democratic governments do not enjoy the consent of the governed (in this strong sense of "consent"). Perhaps consent theory tells the whole of the story about political obligations and authority. If so, however, it is a very short story, with philosophical anarchism as its (for some, unhappy) ending.

Where, then, does this conclusion leave the conception of the political relationship examined and developed in parts 1–3 of this work—the conception that I claimed was the best, strongest version available to Lockean political philosophy? Nothing in my arguments thus far has attacked that (revised) Lockean conception of the political relationship. All that has been attacked is the effort to portray

[65] As Murphy sees, in "Consent, Coercion," 93.

existing societies as embodying the Lockean ideal. Thus, for instance, the Lockean account of justified resistance in a legitimate,
consensual community (i.e., in one that has "gone bad" in certain
respects) is in no way undermined by the fact that no legitimate,
consensual political communities actually exist. It can still be regarded as a (or the) valid theory of political resistance. But most of
us do not stand in (Lockean) political relationships with respect to
others, however accustomed we may have become to thinking of
ourselves in that way. The best Lockean political philosophy insists
rather that we are in, admittedly complex and highly structured,
nonpolitical states of nature with regard to most of our peers. It is
not Locke's theory of political resistance that applies to us here and
now, but his account of rights and justifications in our natural condition. Thus, our practical "political" lives are described more in
chapters 1 and 2 of this book than they are in chapter 6.

If we wish our lives to have the moral sanction of the Lockean
term "political," we must cease our contentment with lives built
upon layers of force (threatened or real) and passive acquiescence,
and restructure our laws and conventions to permit the freedom on
which any political legitimacy is premised. Lockean consent theory
and resistance theory are more defensible than political theorists
usually suppose, although their defensibility turns less than we
might have thought on their applicability to our actual lives. What
is indefensible is not Lockean political philosophy—which is, after
all, supposed to be describing not *our* "political" lives, but morally
acceptable ones. What is indefensible is rather our ordinary ways of
thinking about the legitimacy (rights, authority) of existing governments and societies and about the political obligations of real people, ourselves importantly included. The final section of this chapter
(and this book) attempts to defend these claims against two prominent and initially persuasive objections.

8.4. Lockean Anarchism

Locke's most basic commitments, I have argued, are, first, to the
natural freedom (from political subjection) to which each person is
born; and second, to the voluntarist conception of the political relationship that is necessitated by that first commitment (to natural
freedom). When Locke writes of the basis of the political relationship, as a result, he most often mentions agreements, contracts, and
other straightforwardly consensual acts. But we have seen (in 7.2),
as well, that Locke may have been willing to extend the meaning of

political "consent" in his philosophy to cover other voluntary, but not literally consensual, possible grounds of special obligation— such as willing benefaction (the "enjoyment" of the "dominions of any government"). The most natural way to characterize a theory of political obligation that relies on such grounds, however, is not as a "consent theory" of political obligation, but rather as a "reciprocation theory" of political obligation—that is, as a theory that holds that obedience to law (with the other components of political obligation) is morally required reciprocation for benefits received or accepted by citizens from the workings of their political communities, legal and political institutions, or officials.

The most popular recent version of such a reciprocation theory, of course, utilizes the so-called principle of fairness (to use John Rawls' name for it), according to which "when a number of persons engage in a mutually advantageous cooperative venture . . . , and thus restrict their liberty in ways necessary to yield advantages for all, those who have submitted to these restrictions have a right to similar acquiescence on the part of those who have benefited from their submission."[66] Political obligation, according to the account using this principle, is the obligation (of fairness) of each benefiting participant in a cooperative political scheme to do his or her fair share in bearing the burdens necessary to the production of the benefits shared by all. Citizens who obey the laws and pay their taxes (etc.) within just civil societies have a right that other citizens do the same, since all benefit from their society's cooperative structure.

Now one might reasonably believe that Locke had such ideas in mind when he stretched the term "consent" to cover all instances in which people willingly "enjoy" the benefits political societies provide.[67] The obligations of such "enjoyers" may not be strictly consensual in nature (so that it is certainly misleading for Locke to insist on that characterization of them); but they are *like* consensual obligations in being created, special obligations (i.e., not natural ones), in being voluntarily assumed (by willing benefaction), and in grounding particularized obligations of obedience and support to the one society that provides the benefits.[68] Perhaps it is because of

---

[66] Rawls, *Theory of Justice*, 112. For fuller statements of this principle (and its early formulations), its possible forms, and the problems it faces, see my *Moral Principles and Political Obligations*, chapter 5; and Klosko, *Principle of Fairness*.

[67] See *Moral Principles and Political Obligations*, 89–95.

[68] Indeed, the legal doctrine of "quasi-contracts" importantly relies on these similarities between contractual relations and the relations of those who voluntarily interact within a climate of mutual expectation. See Lessnoff, *Social Contract*, 121.

these similarities that Locke calls the acts of both proper (express or tacit) consenters and willing beneficiaries acts of "consent."

This reading of Locke seems even more persuasive when we note his account of the transfer of rights from member to society:

> For being now in a new state, wherein he is to enjoy many conveniences from the labour, assistance and society of others in the same community, as well as protection from its whole strength; he is to part also with as much of his natural liberty in providing for himself as the good, prosperity and safety of the society shall require: which is not only necessary, but just, since the other members of the society do the like. (II, 130)[69]

Since Locke is here describing the act, elsewhere called contract or consent, by which each member gives up certain rights to the political society (in the transaction that creates it), it seems fair to conclude that Locke is prepared to draw no very sharp lines between obligations of consent and what we would now call obligations of fairness. For he here describes the "act" of political consent in terms not at all unlike those used by contemporary authors to describe the basis for obligations generated under the principle of fairness.

Now the first three sections of the present chapter were concerned to argue that political consent (properly or strictly understood) is not sufficiently in evidence in actual political communities (no matter how democratic) to ground political obligations for even a substantial minority of their residents. Our conclusion was that a commitment to true consent theory is in fact a commitment to a moderate philosophical anarchism. A voluntarist in political philosophy might now respond, however, that there is no reason why voluntarism must allow only consent (strictly construed) as the ground of political obligation. The voluntarist may, perhaps following Locke's own example, embrace other voluntary grounds of moral obligation as possible sources of political obligation—grounds such as the willing benefaction within cooperative schemes that generates obligations of fairness. Each person's own voluntary act would still be necessary for that person's political obligations. But the act in question might not be strictly consensual.[70] The essential Lockean commitment to voluntarism, one might argue, thus need not be a commitment to (pure) consent theory, or to the philosophical anarchism it requires.

[69] See Den Hartogh's discussion of this passage in "Express Consent," 108.
[70] See Den Hartogh, "Made by Contrivance," 215.

The failure of pure consent theory, then, leaves two possible avenues for Lockean political philosophy to take. Either (1) it must successfully defend an extension of the voluntarist account of political obligation and authority (with the move to utilization of the principle of fairness being the only very plausible candidate); or (2) it must accept the conclusion that most actual citizens have no political obligations and that no actual governments or societies have de jure political authority over most of those residing in the territories they control—that is, it must accept (empirical) philosophical anarchism. I consider these two possibilities in turn in the remainder of this chapter.

Will the supplementation of pure consent theory with a fairness account of political obligation in fact substantially assist the political voluntarist in producing a suitably general account of the obligations of actual citizens in actual states? Recent philosophical debate about obligations of fairness strongly suggests a negative answer. H.L.A. Hart's 1955 formulation of the principle of fairness (the principle he called "mutuality of restrictions"), of course, was presented more as an attractive alternative to consent (or contract) theory's account of political obligation than as a supplement to it.[71] But even in its more limited role as a voluntarist supplement to consent theory, most have been skeptical about the principle's ability to account for the political obligations of many actual citizens. Rawls, after initially accepting Hart's arguments, later concluded that the nonvoluntariness of actual political schemes makes inappropriate the suggestion that many people really freely accept the benefits those schemes provide (or at least, accept them in ways that would ground clear obligations to make substantial contributions to the schemes).[72] And Nozick employs related concerns (about our inability to refuse many cooperatively produced goods) to reject not only fairness accounts of political obligation, but the principle of fairness itself. Our only obligations to contribute to or comply with cooperative schemes are those we assume by acts of strict consent.[73] My own arguments against fairness accounts of political obligation, while concerned to argue (against Nozick) that the principle of fairness is a valid moral principle and (against Rawls) that it is meaningful to talk about

[71] "Are There Any Natural Rights?" 185.

[72] *Theory of Justice*, 112–14.

[73] *Anarchy, State, and Utopia*, 90–95. I will not attempt here to comment on the apparent status in Nozick's theory of a class of nonconsenters (independents) that he seems to think may be legitimately incorporated into the minimal state (i.e., those who are forbidden to exercise their rights to enforce natural law and are then compensated with state protection).

freely accepting pure public goods, still aim to reinforce those same doubts about the principle's ability to account for the political obligations of many actual persons.[74] Indeed, even the most recent defense of a fairness account of political obligation in effect expresses these concerns; for it rejects altogether the original voluntaristic point of the principle of fairness, instead basing obligations of fair reciprocation not in the voluntary acceptance of benefits (or in willing benefaction), but in the mere (possibly unwilling) receipt of substantial goods that flow from the (possibly unwilling) sacrifices of others.[75]

Because of Locke's apparent interest in willing benefaction within political society as a ground of political obligation (as a sign of "tacit consent"), however, we should try to be very clear about just why a fairness account of political obligation seems so unlikely to be congenial to his theoretical goals. To begin, the kinds of benefits ("enjoyments") in which Locke was likely to have been interested (as a possible source of obligation) are almost certainly those we might call "public goods," "open benefits," or "nonexcludable goods."[76] These are the kinds of goods that are typically provided by governments or communities to the people in an area, rather than to particular individuals. All who are in that area receive the good, regardless of their willingness to pay for or to receive it. Standard examples of such goods in political societies are national defense, the rule of law, pollution control, a stable economy, and the availability of (i.e., the opportunity to use) public highways, recreational facilities, hospitals, and the like. A government will usually try to extend such goods "to all parts whereof the force of its laws extends" (II, 122). These goods can be contrasted with others, which can (without extraordinary expense) be supplied to or withheld

---

[74] *Moral Principles and Political Obligations,* chapter 5. The text below in part restates several of the prominent points from my earlier treatment.

[75] Klosko, *Principle of Fairness.* See especially 148: "Because the principle of fairness grounds obligations on the receipt of benefits rather than voluntary actions by recipients, it is not forced to construe political relationships as voluntarily assumed." On Klosko's account, even unwilling recipients of "presumptive public goods" will often have obligations of fairness to duplicate the sacrifices made by (indeed, will have obligations owed to) possibly unwilling "cooperative" producers of those goods (such as citizens who unwillingly pay taxes or obey restrictive, but "fairly enacted" laws). No possible rendering of these views about "fairness" or "cooperation" could make them look even remotely voluntaristic. Klosko thus willingly strips the principle of fairness of what was originally taken to be one of its chief virtues—its continuation of consent theory's concern for voluntary action as the source of special obligation.

[76] For defense of this claim, see *Moral Principles and Political Obligations,* 90. For a quick and concise analysis of collective and public goods, see Arneson, "Principle of Fairness," 618–19.

from specific individuals without the necessity of affecting similarly all others in the area. Any good that can feasibly be supplied in a "pay-for-use" scheme belongs in this latter group (including the benefits received from the *actual use of* hospitals, harbors, highways, fire departments, museums, schools, and so on).[77]

In the case of goods of this latter sort, of course, it is generally clear when a person willingly (freely, voluntarily) benefits from receipt. Since such goods do not fall on persons automatically, simply by virtue of their being in a certain area, individuals must go out of their way to secure the goods. Provided their actions are free and adequately informed, their thus going out of their way to secure a good can be taken to indicate the kind of free acceptance (willing benefaction) in which a voluntarist ought to be interested. But the case is more difficult with goods of our first sort (public goods or open benefits), for these goods fall unavoidably on all persons within an area. This unavoidability may seem to make nonsense of the idea that such goods even *could* be voluntarily accepted.[78] And since it is precisely the *public* goods—important goods received by all residents—which seem the most interesting in developing a reciprocation theory of political obligation (and precisely these in which Locke is most interested), their unavoidability seems to pose an unpleasant dilemma for the Lockean voluntarist who wishes to follow Locke's suggestion (about the moral importance of the citizen's "enjoyment" of the benefits of political society). Either the Lockean must reject on voluntarist grounds the relevance of such "enjoyments" to our political obligations (since the benefits in question cannot be voluntarily accepted); or the Lockean must pursue a nonvoluntarist account of the importance of such enjoyments to political obligation, thus sacrificing the central Lockean commitment to political voluntarism.[79]

---

[77] Few large-scale schemes provide only one of these kinds of benefits. And few benefits fall cleanly into one group or another. National defense and the rule of law, for instance, are standard examples of public goods and are normally provided to all of the area within a nation's recognized boundaries. But it is certainly feasible to exclude certain groups or areas, and even to exclude particular individuals in some circumstances (e.g., the United States could exclude Alaska or Florida or an island with one or two inhabitants). What is usually difficult or impossible in the case of public goods, of course, is excluding particular individuals, while still supplying the good to others in surrounding areas.

[78] "Notice that once a pure public good is supplied to a group of persons, there cannot really be any voluntary acceptance or enjoyment of the benefit by individual consumers. One cannot voluntarily accept a good one cannot voluntarily reject" (Arneson, "Principle of Fairness," 619).

[79] To select the first horn is essentially to follow Rawls (in his account of the obli-

I believe the dilemma, as stated, is a false one; for it makes perfectly good sense, in my view, to speak of voluntarily accepting goods that one unavoidably receives. Just as we may freely take those *avoidable* benefits we go out of our way to get, we may freely take *unavoidable* benefits that we knowingly and willingly accept (when they fall upon us). Provided I am adequately informed about the benefits and their costs (so that I can accurately be said to want the benefits *as they are provided*) and want them independent of the presence of factors that would make suspect my desire (such as duress, addiction, brainwashing, etc.), benefits I unavoidably receive can surely be viewed as voluntarily accepted by me. The relevant contrast here is not that between voluntary acceptance of a good and nonreceipt of it. Nonreceipt is not a possibility in the case of public goods. The relevant contrast is rather between voluntary acceptance and nonvoluntary receipt, where nonvoluntary receipt may be a matter of receiving goods one does not want, goods one does not want at the price demanded or in the manner provided, or goods of whose cost one is non-negligently ignorant (as when one reasonably, but falsely, believes the goods to be given freely as a gift, say, or to be already paid for by some previous contribution).[80]

---

gations of "ordinary" citizens). To select the second is to follow Klosko (see below) or Arneson (whose version of the principle of fairness allows that persons who "simply receive" a benefit from a scheme, where "voluntary acceptance of it is impossible," may still be obligated "to contribute to the support of the scheme" ["Principle of Fairness," 623]). Den Hartogh suggests that tacit consent in Locke's own writings should similarly be understood as the not-necessarily-voluntary receipt of the benefits of a government's labors (at least within communities with clear "exit options") ("Made by Contrivance," 215–16). This reading seems to me to (in effect) accuse Locke not just of a wishful and implausible attempt to portray his (internally consistent) voluntarist ideal as embodied in his own society (as I have done), but rather of a fundamental contradiction in his political philosophy (i.e., that between his political voluntarism and a nonvoluntarist theory of political obligation).

[80] Notice that these claims do not rely on the idea that emigration (or, more generally, leaving the area to which public goods are supplied) is the available option that makes it possible for "unavoidable" goods to be voluntarily accepted. I of course agree with Arneson ("Principle of Fairness," 619) that this option is inadequate to render receipt of goods voluntary (as the arguments earlier in this chapter should have made clear). Arneson objects more generally to the appeal to "subjective requirements" (of the sort I defend here), such as recipient knowledge or desire, as necessary for the generation of obligations of fairness. While he actually says only that the requirements I defend "are too stringent" (p. 632), his own account seems to ignore the subjective elements altogether (in the case of obligations to reciprocate for the receipt of pure public goods). But his only real objection to relying on subjective requirements seems to be that persons might have "bizarre beliefs" about the source of goods, the level of required payments relative to others, etc. (p. 632). These objections can be answered by the simple insertion of a requirement of non-negligence in one's beliefs (as stated above in the text, and as implied in the text criticized by Arneson). Arneson thinks that the requirement that "the benefit is un-

Making sense of the idea of voluntary acceptance of unavoidable benefits thus relies centrally on taking account of psychological facts about the recipient (that the recipient wants the benefit, wants it at the price, etc.). While appeals to such facts are obviously a difficult basis for public policy decisions about, say, whom should be taxed for what (given each individual's relatively privileged access to the relevant facts and given natural variations in desires across communities), the moral relevance of such appeals seems clear. And it is only by means of such appeals that we can explain how the principle of fairness, understood in voluntaristic terms, could be taken to ground obligations to reciprocate for the receipt of public goods. We are obligated to do our part in cooperative schemes supplying public goods, on my account, only if (and only to the extent that) we have voluntarily accepted the public goods those schemes provide.

Unfortunately, this rendering of the principle of fairness still severely limits the principle's ability to ground political obligations for many actual citizens in actual states. Chief among the reasons for this is the fact that most citizens, even in those states that are sufficiently just and nonauthoritarian to in any way resemble cooperative schemes, not unreasonably take the public goods they receive to be fully "bought and paid for" (indeed, overpaid for) from governments with tax payments. Mandatory purchase of overpriced public goods with compulsory tax payments does not leave much to account for the alleged additional aspects of political obligation (e.g., general obedience to law, military service, etc.) that the principle of fairness is supposed to explain. That people do in fact not only pay their taxes but obey the law (etc.) seems more a function of habit, fear of punishment, and belief in the independent moral wrongness of most legally criminal conduct than it does a function of a general belief that the receipt of public goods comes with this additional price (beyond payment of taxes). It will be hard, then, to portray the receipt of public goods by the average citizen as the kind of informed, voluntary acceptance of benefits that could ground political obligations of fairness or reciprocation.[81]

Recent defenders of a more wide-ranging principle of fairness re-

---

controversially a benefit for all" is a stringent enough condition without the addition of subjective requirements (p. 633). But, as we will see below, Arneson's requirement will either justify extensive and untoward limitations of individual liberty or must be read in a way that itself incorporates subjective requirements (i.e., in order to explicate what it is for something to be "uncontroversially a benefit for all").

[81] For additional arguments to the same conclusion, see my *Moral Principles and Political Obligations*, section 5.5.

ject my attempt to use psychological facts to explicate the idea of voluntary acceptance of public goods (and to explain in terms of voluntary acceptance the obligations that might arise from receiving unavoidable goods). They argue that mere receipt (however unwilling) of goods that flow from the sacrifices or labors of others, at least if these goods are substantial enough, can obligate one to contribute one's fair share.[82] But this view not only plainly constitutes an abandonment of political voluntarism, it constitutes in my view an abandonment of all the bases of intuitive support for the principle of fairness. That intuitive support revolves around the idea that it is unfair to take advantage of, to "ride free on" the good-faith efforts of others, taking desired benefits that others provide while refraining from contributing oneself. The classic free rider, whose behavior the principle of fairness is concerned to condemn, wants the goods a cooperative scheme produces, and wants them at the price demanded and in the manner they are provided (i.e., he prefers taking the goods with their associated costs to not taking them). But he wants still more to get the goods free; so he takes the goods, parasitically taking advantage of the efforts of others to support the scheme, all the while refusing to do his fair share within it.

Both my (voluntaristic) version of the principle of fairness and recent nonvoluntaristic versions (such as those of Richard Arneson and George Klosko) condemn the classic free rider's behavior. For the classic free rider not only receives, but freely accepts (on my account of that notion) the goods he gets from the cooperative scheme. In trying to capture the wrongness of such free riding, however, the nonvoluntarist accounts of the principle of fairness cast far too large a net. They catch not only the classic free rider, but also the person who genuinely does not want the goods some cooperative scheme is providing or who would genuinely prefer to do without those goods rather than pay the price demanded for them.[83] And that is not to worry about *fairness* at all. It is rather to justify a quite different sort of unfairness than the one they are interested in condemning. It is to justify a kind of tyranny by ourselves or our neighbors over those whose tastes, needs, or values are different, over those for whom allegedly "uncontroversial benefits" are in fact controversial. But surely the right to have tastes and values different

[82] See Arneson, "Principle of Fairness," 623, 628, 633; Klosko, *Principle of Fairness*, 39, 148.

[83] Klosko allows that the noncontributor who is really willing to "let others do the same" has not violated the principle of fairness (*Principle of Fairness*, 45, 102). But he seems unwilling to pursue the consequences of this claim, as I do here.

from those of one's neighbors, and not to suffer for this, is at least as basic as the right of our neighbors to a return for benefits we incidentally receive as a side effect of their freely chosen cooperative activities. We may not reasonably demand from others just whatever is necessary to supply what we (but not they) want to have reliably supplied at that price. Nor is a group entitled to demand repayment for whatever benefits happen to spill over on nonparticipants, as undesired but unavoidable side effects of the group's activities.[84] It is to demonstrate the illegitimacy of such tyranny that my appeal to psychological conditions (and to the distinction between voluntary acceptance and nonvoluntary receipt of public goods) is essential.

Klosko tries to avoid these objectionable consequences of embracing a nonvoluntaristic principle of fairness by appealing to the idea of goods that are "presumptively beneficial." Because some goods are indispensable (needed) for (almost) any decent life, every person can be presumed to want them. And only the receipt of those public goods that are thus presumptively beneficial will obligate one to reciprocate for unavoidable benefits.[85] Klosko allows that if one can show one genuinely does not need the presumptive good in question, one can escape obligations to reciprocate (the good is, after all, only *presumptively* beneficial).[86] Otherwise, mere nonvoluntary receipt of the good (and the satisfaction of several other conditions[87]) will ground obligations of fairness to contribute to the cooperative scheme that produces the presumptive good.

This addition to the principle of fairness is designed to counter voluntarist objections (like my own) that we must not be made liable to obligations for the unavoidable receipt of goods we do not want (and indicates that Klosko is in fact more concerned with psychological facts about recipients than he professes to be[88]). But Klosko's

---

[84] Americans could not demand payment from Canadians who benefited as a result of American national defense policy or American law and order. Nor does "invisible hand" production of some collective good (where all are simply pursuing their own business, with no thought of cooperation) justify collecting payment from all who happen to benefit. Nor can I demand payment for the undesired but inevitable benefits others may receive from activities I pursue for purely private reasons. Nobody is unfairly taken advantage of by being denied payment for goods he is not even trying to provide for others (and without any beliefs about common purpose).

[85] *Principle of Fairness*, 39–44. I believe that in the final analysis the guiding moral idea in Klosko's account is not really *fairness*, but *need*: we may require others to take and to pay for what they need. Klosko's concerns are thus less about fair distribution of benefits and burdens than they are about insuring the supply of needed goods (see my "Anarchist Position," 271–72).

[86] *Principle of Fairness*, 49.

[87] Ibid., 39.

[88] Klosko claims that his appeal to presumptive goods greatly reduces the need for

nonvoluntarist revision of the principle of fairness fails for several reasons, of which I will mention only two here. First, there are no public goods produced by cooperative schemes that are needed or indispensable *simpliciter*, and so there is no product of a cooperative scheme that can be said to be on balance a benefit (presumptively beneficial) for anyone without further qualification. Goods are only benefits to persons on balance if their costs and the manner in which they are provided are not sufficiently disvalued by those persons. Even a good like physical security (Klosko's primary example of a presumptive good) may be reasonably regarded by an individual as on balance a burden if it is provided at a prohibitive cost—such as one's independence, say, or the violation of one's pacifist convictions—or in a manner that is unnecessary and objectionable (e.g., many public goods supplied by the state can be provided by alternative, private means, often at lower cost and without the imposition of oppressive or restrictive conditions). One who genuinely prefers doing without even a "presumptively beneficial" public good, given its cost, or who prefers to try to provide the good privately, can hardly be accused of unfairly taking advantage of a group that unilaterally foists that good upon her on their own terms. If anything, it is surely the group that tries to take unfair advantage in such a case. That the public goods a cooperative scheme produces are central or important will thus not adequately answer concerns about licensing tyranny under the nonvoluntarist principle of fairness.

Second, however, Klosko's only response to such objections threatens to justify even more massive infringements of individual rights. Despite his occasional nods to the importance of individual liberty,[89] Klosko's arguments commit him to the conclusion that even very substantial numbers of, say, serious pacifists (who wish to do without armed defense) or rugged individualists (who wish to defend themselves) can legitimately be forced to accept a community's provision of physical security (national defense, law and order). For he seems to allow that states may prohibit individualists

---

"making inquiries about [the beneficiary's] values or beliefs" (ibid., 48). It might be fairer to say that his appeal to presumptive goods at most just hides the central relevance to his account of beneficiaries' values and beliefs (subjective requirements). For calling a benefit "presumptive" seems to mean precisely that we can safely assume that almost everyone will *want* the benefit and will *believe* it to be worth any reasonable price (see my "Anarchist Position," 272–73).

[89] *Principle of Fairness*, 36, 114. Klosko allows interference for communitarian and paternalistic reasons that few of the classical liberals (to whose views he often appeals) would accept (see, e.g., ibid., 60; note 36).

from providing needed services for themselves, then provide for them those same services through state mechanisms and demand whatever payment is acceptable to the majority of state citizens (and all in the name of fairness!).[90] And pacifists seem unable to show that they do not need security in a fashion acceptable to Klosko;[91] so they too may apparently be coercively absorbed. Indeed, given Klosko's conception of a community, it seems clear that groups may on his account coercively extend themselves to absorb unwilling independents almost indefinitely and without interesting geographical limitation.[92] Surely this, however, is to advance (too) far beyond

[90] Klosko's arguments on this important subject are for some reason buried in a footnote (ibid., 108; note 8). Indeed, Klosko there seems uncomfortable with his own conclusions. But it is clear that if he were to allow to individuals the right to choose for themselves how they will secure needed goods (as I have urged), he would scuttle his efforts to ground political obligation in the mere (possibly unwilling) receipt of state-supplied presumptive goods.

[91] The only way Klosko allows that one could escape obligation to a scheme for the receipt of physical security benefits is by showing "one's ability to live off the land in a remote wilderness area," where security is not required (ibid., 115–16, 49). This is not the sort of thing a pacifist would always be able to show (or would think it necessary to show). Klosko's requirement really seems to amount to a virtual demand for emigration (to the wilderness) as the sole means of avoiding obligation for receipt of presumptive goods from (otherwise) reasonably just states.

[92] Klosko defines a community as "the collection of individuals who receive indispensable benefits from the cooperative scheme in question" (ibid., 62; note 55). The absence of any criterion of community membership other than benefaction (and of any geographical constraint on the conception of community) implies that groups providing physical security for their members may legitimately extend this service to any number of independent nonmembers, in any location whatsoever, and demand that these independents (who by merely benefiting, even if not on balance, are made community "members") carry their "fair share" of the group's burdens. For instance, nation A may unilaterally extend its security services to adjacent territory B, in effect annexing it, regardless of the wishes of those residing in B; for even "excludable" presumptive goods may be forcibly imposed on those who "need" them (ibid., 60; note 36). Or territory B may be annexable because it receives security as an utterly unintended consequence of its proximity to A (whose bristling defensive posture intimidates all would-be aggressors in the area). A may prohibit those residents of B (if any) who were providing security for themselves from continuing to do so (since A must monopolize force in its "community"), thereby creating the "need" that A's security benefits satisfies (in whatever way the majority of A's residents deem best). This is roughly like my stealing your motorcycle safety helmet, then forcing you to pay a tax to provide helmets for a large group in which you are forcibly included, and justifying my acts by appealing to your need for a helmet (and to the unfairness of allowing others to pay the tax without forcing you to do so as well)! Klosko may have intended his arguments to justify only the coercive assimilation of those within a territory who wish to remain independent while nearly all of their surrounding colleagues wish to form a cooperative group. But since he has no territorial criterion for community membership, all independents everywhere end up being similarly vulnerable to coercive assimilation. In any event, there is in my view certainly no better reason for forcing genuine dissenters (i.e., those who are *not* classic free riders) to participate in the cooperative schemes of others, than there is

any reasonable concern for fairness to cooperators or for the prohibition of selfish free riding.

These brief remarks, while obviously inadequate as a careful discussion of the principle of fairness, seem sufficient to support the first conclusions I wish to draw in this section. Nonvoluntarist versions of the principle of fairness are not only in one important sense non-Lockean. They are also sufficiently ill motivated and implausible in their own rights to discourage any reasonable Lockean from abandoning the commitment to a voluntarist account of political obligation (and of the political relationship generally). We have seen as well, however, that the most convincing voluntarist rendering of the principle of fairness is unlikely to entail political obligations for many citizens in existing states. It follows from this, of course, that the reasonable Lockean, pursuing the defensible, voluntarist version of the principle of fairness as a supplement to Lockean consent theory, will not be much aided by this pursuit in producing a suitably general account of political obligation. Most actual citizens in actual states have neither consensual obligations nor obligations of fairness to support and comply with their governments or communities.

Serious political voluntarism commits us to the acceptance of philosophical anarchism. Since Lockean political philosophy is *essentially* voluntarist, in my view, this means that Lockeans must also accept philosophical anarchism. And because I believe political voluntarism to be the correct view to take on its subject (a claim supported in part by the rejection of nonvoluntarist fairness theory outlined above),[93] I believe as well that Lockean political philosophy is on secure ground in its commitment to this form of anarchism. Lest this seem a depressing conclusion, however, I will suggest below that Lockean anarchism in fact entails a view of our actual political lives that is free of many dramatically counterintuitive im-

---

for forcing cooperators to limit their activities so as to leave genuine dissenters free of new obligations.

[93] More precisely (and as I have suggested earlier in this study), I think Locke is correct in claiming that each person is born to natural freedom (i.e., to *moral* freedom from political obligation and the de jure authority of others). And I think that only political voluntarism is consistent with acceptance of the natural freedom of persons. The only political obligations we have are those we have voluntarily assumed, at least for the cases of polities even remotely like our own. I take my arguments in *Moral Principles and Political Obligations* to be support for these claims, and to establish that *nonvoluntarist* accounts of political obligation (such as those utilizing a principle of utility, a principle of gratitude, or natural duties of justice or allegiance) are uniformly unsuccessful when applied to modern political communities.

plications, implications that might force us to reassess the arguments that lead us to that view.[94]

It might seem, of course, that Lockean philosophical anarchism could hardly be a more counterintuitive position. For Lockean anarchism might seem to imply both that (a) all existing governments are morally equal (since all are equally illegitimate or nonauthoritative, equally lacking "political power" over their subjects), and (b) residents of existing "communities" may do as they please, lacking any political obligations to obey valid law in their societies or support the other institutions of government that preserve public order and supply vital goods. A position that had those consequences would, indeed, be sufficiently odd to make reasonable persons question the arguments that led to it. But Lockean anarchism in fact implies neither of these counterintuitive claims.[95]

First, of course, from the mere fact that all existing governments or societies are illegitimate (in the sense in which a Lockean must use that term), it in no way follows that they are all morally equal. Governments may do more or less good, for their "subjects" and for others, and they may do more or less harm. They may violate the rights of persons more or less regularly, systematically, and seriously. They may be more or less merciful, responsive, beneficent, efficient, and wise. In short, governments may still, within the Lockean anarchist model, be properly said to exemplify to varying degrees all of the virtues and vices that we normally associate with governments.

Nothing in Lockean anarchism prevents us from ranking governments morally, as better or worse, in just the ways that we are normally inclined to do. We may even say that good governments are those that most deserve our free consent, those that it would be most reasonable for people to *make* legitimate (in existing or modified form) by the free contract (consent) and trust that establish the political relationship. The one thing we must *not* say, according to Lockean anarchism, is that good governments are, by virtue of those qualities that make them good, therefore legitimate, or that they therefore wield genuinely political power. Good governments, however extensive their virtues, cannot obtain over free people (without their consent) "the right to command and be obeyed." And to the

---

[94] As examples of those who disagree with me here, arguing that the consequences of philosophical anarchism *are* damningly counterintuitive, see Lessnoff, *Social Contract*, 89; and Senor, "What If There Are No Political Obligations?"

[95] For a fuller defense of several of the claims argued immediately below, see my *Moral Principles and Political Obligations*, chapter 8.

extent that good (but still illegitimate) governments, albeit with the best of intentions, utilize ("nonpolitical") force in violation of the rights of free persons, they act (prima facie) wrongly.

Second, the fact that most residents of existing societies must be understood not to have political obligations, on the Lockean anarchist view, in no way implies that these persons may act however they please. All persons have basic, natural moral duties to one another (as we saw in 1.2 and 5.2–5.3)—duties not to harm others in their lives, liberty, health, limb, or goods (II, 6). Even with no general obligation to obey the law, then, individuals in existing societies still have duties to refrain from those actions that in all legal systems constitute the most serious crimes (e.g., murder, assault, rape, theft, fraud). Similarly, I have argued that Lockeans (and others) ought to accept some positive duties and rights—that is, duties to aid those in need and to extend their surplus wealth to the poor.[96] This implies, of course, that even if legal duties in this realm (where they exist) have no moral force, persons are still morally bound to care for one another in certain ways. They may even choose to (or, in hard cases, need to) discharge such duties by supporting salient cooperative efforts to help those in need, possibly including efforts by (their own or other) governments. And where others are abiding by innocent laws or conventions, and my violation of those rules would endanger them, I am bound not to violate those rules—even though the rules have *in themselves* no force with respect to me, and even though the behavior to which I am bound is not *naturally* obligatory. Thus, if others follow the convention of driving their vehicles on the right (and in so doing violate no right of mine), I must not knowingly endanger them by driving on the left, for I am morally forbidden to deliberately harm the innocent. This is true even if I am not a party to their practices and even though driving on the left is not naturally (i.e., in all times and places) immoral. The natural law prohibition on harming others extends itself to cases where their choices (e.g., innocent convention-following) or other (e.g., medical) developments make other persons vulnerable to harm in ways that are not natural or typical.

Lockean anarchism, then, insists that persons in existing societies are by no means free to do as they please, but rather that they have a wide range of moral duties that will overlap considerably (i.e., require the same conduct as) their nonbinding legal duties. And in most societies these moral duties overlap the most central and im-

[96] See *Lockean Theory of Rights*, chapter 6.

portant legal duties, prohibiting physical harming and most serious disruption of others' lives. Further, however, even where persons owe no natural moral duties to others, there can still be additional moral reasons not to interfere with or upset the innocent plans or arrangements of others.[97] Even if I do not count as harming you by upsetting your plans (and so am entitled to upset them), it would plainly be malicious to do so gratuitously. We are not morally obligated to act, nor ought we to act, just whenever we have a right to do so.[98] Indeed, simple decency demands that we not press others to secure our unimportant rights, where doing so will result in no substantial gain for us and serious cost for others. We have, in short, good moral reason, even if no moral duty, to practice the virtues of patience, courtesy, consideration, and so on, toward others. Again, Lockean anarchism does not advocate insensitive or destructive conduct.

It is easy to see, then, that Lockean philosophical anarchism does not have the direct and profoundly counterintuitive consequences that we considered initially. But we can see already as well several ways in which Lockean anarchism pushes us to substantially revise our thinking about ordinary "political" life. While we live in structured societies with laws and governments, we are not "subject" to those laws or governments, bound to obey them. We cannot act on the general presumption that obedience is obligatory, advisable, or even morally permissible. We must, rather, view legal requirements and the governments that make them with a certain skepticism,[99] with a (in my view healthy) focus on their actual moral standing. Our obligations to comply with laws (i.e., to act in the ways they require) have nothing to do with any special bond to the community whose laws they are, but only with the specific content of the laws. The same laws, imposed in some other similar country, would call for compliance by us in the same ways and for the same reasons.[100] We are bound to act toward our colleagues, our governors, and members of other societies all as fellow residents in a highly socialized state of nature, one in which we all are surrounded by many

[97] See *Moral Principles and Political Obligations*, 193–94, and "Anarchist Position," 278.

[98] See *Lockean Theory of Rights*, 119–20.

[99] Green, *Authority of the State*, 254–55.

[100] That is, those laws whose point is territorially limited (e.g., specific traffic laws) will call for compliance when we are in the relevant territory, while those whose point is universal (e.g., laws forbidding murder) will call for compliance regardless of which country enacts them.

people with false beliefs about their rights and duties with respect to us.

The extent to which existing governments should be complied with, disobeyed, or resisted (and the respects in which such conduct is optional) is, of course, in part just a function of the specific character of the government in question. But the content of each person's natural rights provides a set of basic guidelines, as a common background for all such considerations. According to Lockean moral and political philosophy (and as we saw in 3.1 and 3.3), each person is born to a broad right of self-government, which includes the right to be free of coercive interference by others (except to prevent or in response to wrongdoing), the right to act in pursuit of "innocent delights" and to advance one's own and others' well-being (within the limits set by others' equal rights), and the powers to make property, to alienate or acquire rights by contract or promise, and so on. Each person also has the right to punish others who act immorally (up to the limits set by natural law) and to secure just reparation for injuries done them.[101] Free residents of existing societies may, of course, have alienated or forfeited some (or all) of these rights or acquired others in private activities, transactions, or interactions. But we must otherwise think of ourselves and others as (at least for the most part) possessors of this basic set of natural moral rights.

Viewed in this light, it is easy to see in what areas typical existing governments most often wrong (i.e., violate the rights of) those who reside within their territories. For (to simplify substantially) the most familiar types of (restrictive) laws imposed and enforced by governments can be divided into five categories: (1) those that prohibit acts that wrongly harm (including those that wrongly fail to benefit) others—that is, acts that are naturally immoral or *mala in se*; (2) those that impose systems of coordination on morally permissible activities, in order to prevent unintended harm (as in traffic laws); (3) those that prohibit private conduct that is harmless (and thus not forbidden by natural morality), but which is for other reasons deemed wrong or unnatural; (4) those that require or forbid acts in order to protect the government or the state (as in laws prohibiting treason or requiring military service); (5) those that require payments (or which permit seizures of property) to finance or facilitate government operations, provision of public benefits, and the like.

---

[101] For a fuller account of these basic rights, see *Lockean Theory of Rights*, especially chapter 2.

Of these five categories, it seems clear that governments will most often be justified in enforcing laws in the first two. For while it is true that the residents of existing states still possess their natural rights to punish moral wrongdoers, those who govern and administer the law are also persons possessing this right. When states punish those who harm others, officials of the state may in fact be justifiably exercising their natural rights to do so.[102] States may not demand that we *obey* their laws; but they may legitimately punish us for doing what is in fact contrary to law, when our so acting also breaches a moral duty.

In categories (3)–(5), however, governments routinely wrong those against whom their laws are enforced. No one may interfere with harmless, morally innocent activities (as the law does in category [3]). Nor does an illegitimate government have the right to force free people to protect it or the territories it claims (by enforcing laws in category [4]). If persons cannot be brought to voluntarily uphold a government or defend a territory (or to freely consent to do so in the future), the state is not entitled to insist that it continue to exist.[103] Good governments may merit our support, but they are not entitled to require it (without our free consent). And even the best governments wrong us in many ways (as the present argument is in part designed to show). Finally, governments may not demand or seize payment to support their operations or programs (by using laws in category [5]) from those who never authorized such activities. Even the state's enforcement of laws in categories (1) and (2), although possibly a permissible activity, is not an activity for which the state may demand payment. For governments were never authorized to be the sole enforcers of natural morality, nor did typical residents ever consent to pay for this. Payment from another may only be required in order to enforce a right (e.g., to repair a wrong or secure what has been promised). Only in the very rare instance when a government program provides the *only* way for an individual to do his or her moral duty can the government legitimately require participation and payment.[104]

---

[102] Provided, of course, that their punishments are just in kind and amount. States invariably act wrongly in prohibiting private citizens (or outsiders) from exercising *their* equal rights to punish (i.e., in seizing a monopoly on force); but this wrong is usually not a very serious one. For reasonable persons will not wish to compete for the right to punish (possibly dangerous) wrongdoers, at least if the state is punishing immorality efficiently and fairly.

[103] Wolff, *In Defense of Anarchism*, 80.

[104] This claim, with others in this paragraph, is in fact slightly too strong. Governments may sometimes act justifiably even when they violate individual rights. For

Lockean anarchism maintains that existing governments regularly and systematically wrong their "citizens," no matter how many good qualities (some of) these governments may otherwise display. Good governments limit this wrongdoing by, for instance, minimizing the number of laws in category (3), making military service voluntary, taxing citizens as little as possible, and so on. And good governments often act in ignorance of any wrongdoing and with the intention (and sometimes the effect) of benefiting persons within and without their societies. But even good governments still wrong us, still violate our rights.

How shall we view this wrongdoing in assessing our moral positions? Those of us who live under good governments (to whose authority we never consented) are not, of course, in precisely the situation of any of the persons discussed in chapter 6—that is, we are not members of an originally legitimate community who are now being wronged by the society's breach of its legitimating contract or by the government's breach of its trust. We never contracted with those around us or entrusted any government with our rights. Neither, however, are we in precisely the situation of the persons described in chapter 2—that is, we are not in a state of war with our governments. For while our governments have used against us "force without right," we have seen (in 2.1 and 6.2) that such a wrong is not in fact sufficient to originate a state of war (Locke's own claims to the contrary notwithstanding). Most of our governments (or at least most of those whose legitimacy might seriously have been maintained) have not conspired or acted to deprive us of our lives or freedom, and so have not made war upon us (in the reasonable Lockean sense detailed in 2.1). Rather, most of us in the "free world" are in Lockean terms just persons in the state of nature (simpliciter), subjected by our governments to a variety of (usually) relatively minor, but frighteningly regular, wrongful acts and policies. Illegitimate governments need not be warmakers. They can be quite benign, even progressive or responsive. They can govern the sorts of societies to which residence *would* give consent, if only residents were offered a clear choice situation. They can also, of course, be the sorts of governments we are entitled (or even obligated) to

---

rights may conflict and other morally relevant factors (such as dramatic utilities) may need to be considered. Moral justification is not a simple matter of respecting rights. Governments may, then, sometimes be justified in coercing individuals, even where they lack the right to do so (and even where they violate the rights of others in the process). But coercion on the massive scale necessary to the enforcement of laws in categories (3)–(5) is unlikely to be defensible except in circumstances of serious crisis.

oppose with all means at our disposal. Most often in the "free world," however, they are merely bumbling and inefficient, sometimes well-intentioned, sometimes moved by personal or partisan concerns, occasionally oppressive or tyrannical, and still somehow able to do a reasonable amount of good.

Should those of us living under such governments, then, just obey our moderately good laws and support our moderately good polities? Or should we pursue some alternative course? Here we do well to attend to the Lockean position on justified *individual* resistance, even though that position was framed primarily for those who began in a consensual political relationship (as we did not). For while "the majority" has no moral standing in the state of nature (there being no "people" there on whose behalf they may decide), individuals (such as ourselves) whose rights are violated by de facto governments or societies are in much the same moral situation as individuals who are *returned* to the state of nature by a previously legitimate government's or society's violation of their rights (with this exception: that a contract is breached in the latter case, but not in the former). And in 6.3–6.4 we saw what Lockean political philosophy must say about such individuals. Individuals have the right to resist and repair violations of their rights and to recruit others who are entitled to assist them in this, regardless of whether the individuals live within or without political society. And in the state of nature (but not in political society) they may resist, repair, and punish even nonsystematic, nondeliberate violations. In thus enforcing our rights, we are limited only by the requirements that we avoid infringing the more pressing rights of others and avoid causing dramatic social harm (or preventing the accomplishment of dramatic social good).

When we confront a moderately good (but still illegitimate) legal system and government, then, we must weigh the importance of the rights it violates against the consequences of our various possible strategies. If the government is a good one, its violations of our rights would need to be very serious indeed (which will be unusual under a good government) for us to be justified in doing anything that will cause it to be unable to function effectively. For it will likely be doing significant good and preventing significant harm. And while we have no contractual duty to resist wrongs done to others (as we would toward fellow members of a legitimate polity [6.4]), we have a natural moral duty to aid those in need, as far at least as we comfortably can (and perhaps farther). This duty may require us to in certain ways support the efforts of governments (if only by

267

refraining from disabling them) when they assist those in need. Finally, of course, unless a government's violation of our rights is very serious, the acts we will be morally entitled to perform (in order to justly resist, punish, and repair those wrongs) will be anyway unlikely to be violent or destructive enough to cause serious disruption of a government's functions. For we are not at war with such governments as I am considering here. These moral facts, plus considerations of simple prudence (i.e., our interest in avoiding legal punishment), seem to dictate that moderately good governments, which violate our rights only in the ways such governments typically do, ought not to be resisted in ways that threaten to destroy them or to replace them with distinctly inferior alternatives. Lockean anarchism acknowledges that there can be strong moral reasons for supporting, or at least not actively resisting, even (certain) illegitimate governments. In this regard again, Lockean anarchism is not dramatically counterintuitive in its implications. It is only philosophically, not practically anarchic.

In the face of the wrongs done us by moderately good existing governments, of course, it will still usually be morally permissible to simply disobey those laws that are wrongly enforced against us, and it will be reasonable to do so as far as it remains possible to avoid detection or serious legal consequences. For simple individual disobedience almost never has dramatic social consequences. And it remains permissible, even if almost never prudent, to attempt to forcibly secure just compensation for the wrongs done us. It will usually be best to press for public recognition of these wrongs, sometimes even by conspicuous disobedience, within the legal frameworks offered in our society. To disobey conspicuously and pursue legal remedies is not to acknowledge the legitimacy of those frameworks (as the proponent of civil disobedience insists we must do); it is rather only to take action that is well within morally permissible limits in the context of illegitimate, but virtually unavoidable, legal mechanisms.

What we certainly have good reason to do is to press by legal means for those changes in our political arrangements that will permit the establishment of genuinely voluntary political societies. Thus, changes that would clarify the resident's choice situation, expand membership options, reduce the cost of membership, facilitate internal or external emigration, and so on, would all go far toward making the choice between membership and its alternatives adequately informed and fully voluntary. Such changes would help to secure the natural right of self-government to which each of us is born, a right that includes the privilege of genuine freedom in the choice of political (or nonpolitical) forms of life. Although Locke (as we saw in 2.2) may have been wrong in claiming that life in the state of nature is always precarious and unstable (our lives in *this* state of nature are not, for instance, as he described them), he was surely right at least in maintaining that life in a free, consensual polity is *morally* preferable to life in even a stable, structured society built on force and acquiescence.

It would be foolish to pretend that many actual societies are likely to change or emerge in the ways Lockean political philosophy prescribes. In the world of illegitimate states that will continue, moral persons must cast off their childhood lessons in good citizenship, and proceed by selectively supporting or opposing their governments' actions and policies solely according to the particular moral standing of each governmental move. Even if we find that we can seldom justify or bear the consequences of active disobedience or substantial opposition, we can at least lobby for the elimination of those laws that interfere with harmless choices, impose needless regimentation of behavior and lifestyle, limit personal liberty without securing important social benefits. For any movement in such directions, as we have seen, will at least help to reduce the violation of basic personal rights.

Even when Lockean political philosophy directs us to obey the laws and support the government (of, say, a moderately good but still illegitimate state), and so tells us to do what common intuition prescribes, however, it still forces us to view our conduct in a new light. Lockean philosophical anarchism demands of us that we be more thoughtful about and more sensitive to the particular moral issues in our lives. For we can no longer just appeal to a general presumption of governmental legitimacy or political obligation, viewing it as overriding or outweighing more specific questions about the moral merits or defects of the individual laws, actions, or policies of our governments. We must confront directly and balance carefully the effects of such laws or policies on the performance of our natural duties and the exercise of our natural rights. Perhaps many of us have preferred to avoid the burden of these concerns. Perhaps in our complacency we have assisted the progress of political unfreedom and helped to further popularize the comfortable myth of easy legitimacy. If so, we have, in Locke's words, "done the truth and the public wrong." We owe both, as well as ourselves, a better effort.

WORKS CITED

Aaron, Richard. *John Locke*. Oxford: Oxford University Press, 1971.

Aarsleff, Hans. "The State of Nature and the Nature of Man in Locke." In *John Locke: Problems and Perspectives*, ed. J. W. Yolton. Cambridge: Cambridge University Press, 1969.

Altham, J. E. J. "Reflections on the State of Nature." In *Rational Action*, ed. R. Harrison. Cambridge: Cambridge University Press, 1979.

Andrew, Edward. "Inalienable Right, Alienable Property and Freedom of Choice: Locke, Nozick and Marx on the Alienability of Labour." *Canadian Journal of Political Science* (September 1985).

————. *Shylock's Rights: A Grammar of Lockian Claims*. Toronto: University of Toronto Press, 1988.

Anglim, John. "On Locke's State of Nature." *Political Studies* (March 1978).

Aquinas, Thomas. *Summa Theologica*. New York: Benzinger Bros., 1947.

Arneson, Richard. "The Principle of Fairness and Free-Rider Problems." *Ethics* (July 1982).

Arnhart, Larry. *Political Questions*. New York: Macmillan, 1987.

Ashcraft, Richard. "Locke's State of Nature: Historical Fact or Moral Fiction?" *American Political Science Review* (September 1968).

————. "The *Two Treatises* and the Exclusion Crisis: The Problem of Lockean Political Theory as Bourgeois Ideology." In *John Locke*, ed R. A. Ashcraft and J. G. A. Pocock. Los Angeles: Clark Memorial Library, 1980.

————. *Revolutionary Politics & Locke's Two Treatises of Government*. Princeton: Princeton University Press, 1986.

————. *Locke's Two Treatises of Government*. London: Allen & Unwin, 1987.

Austin, J. L. *How to Do Things with Words*. Oxford: Oxford University Press, 1970.

Baldwin, Thomas. "Toleration and the Right to Freedom." In *Aspects of Toleration*, ed. J. Horton and S. Mendus. London: Methuen, 1985.

Barker, Ernest. "Introduction" to *Social Contract*. New York: Oxford University Press, 1962.

Bayles, Michael. "Limits to a Right to Procreate." In *Ethics and Population*, ed. M. Bayles. Cambridge, Mass.: Schenkman, 1976.

Beitz, Charles R. "Tacit Consent and Property Rights." *Political Theory* (November 1980).

Benn, S. I., and R. S. Peters. *Social Principles and the Democratic State*. London: Allen & Unwin, 1959.

Bennett, John G. "A Note on Locke's Theory of Tacit Consent." *Philosophical Review* (April 1979).

Bentham, Jeremy. *Anarchical Fallacies*. In *Human Rights*, ed. A. Melden. Belmont: Wadsworth, 1970.

Beran, Harry. "Political Obligation and Democracy." *Australasian Journal of Philosophy* (December 1976).

———. "In Defense of the Consent Theory of Political Obligation and Authority." *Ethics* (April 1977).

———. "What Is the Basis of Political Authority?" *Monist* (October 1983).

———. *The Consent Theory of Political Obligation*. London: Croom Helm, 1987.

Best, Judith A. "The Innocent, the Ignorant, and the Rational: The Content of Lockian Consent." In *The Crisis of Liberal Democracy*. ed. K. L. Deutsch and W. Soffer. Albany: State University of New York Press, 1987.

Brandt, Richard. *Ethical Theory*. Englewood Cliffs: Prentice-Hall, 1959.

Brown, Alan. *Modern Political Philosophy*. Harmondsworth: Penguin, 1986.

Brown, Stuart M., Jr. "Inalienable Rights." *Philosophical Review* (April 1955).

Cohen, Joshua. "Structure, Choice, and Legitimacy: Locke's Theory of the State." *Philosophy & Public Affairs* (Fall 1986).

Cohen, Marshall. "Liberalism and Disobedience." *Philosophy & Public Affairs* (Spring 1972).

Coleman, Jules L. "Liberalism, Unfair Advantage, and the Volunteer Armed Forces." In *Conscripts and Volunteers*, ed. R. Fullinwider. Totowa: Rowman & Allanheld, 1983.

Colman, John. *John Locke's Moral Philosophy*. Edinburgh: Edinburgh University Press, 1983.

Cook, Thomas. "Introduction" to Locke, *Two Treatises of Government*. New York: Hafner, 1947.

Cox, Richard. *Locke on War and Peace*. Washington, D.C.: University Press of America, 1982.

———. "Introduction" to Locke, *Second Treatise of Government*. Arlington Heights: Harlan Davidson, 1982.

Cranston, Maurice. "John Locke and Government by Consent." In *Political Ideas*, ed. D. Thomson. New York: Basic Books, 1966.

———. *John Locke: A Biography*. Oxford: Oxford University Press, 1985.

———. "John Locke and the Case for Toleration." In *On Toleration*, ed. S. Mendus and D. Edwards. Oxford: Oxford University Press, 1987.

De Beer, Esmond S. "Locke and English Liberalism: *The Second Treatise of Government* in Its Contemporary Setting." In *John Locke: Problems and Perspectives*, ed. J. W. Yolton. Cambridge: Cambridge University Press, 1969.

Den Hartogh, G. A. "Express Consent and Full Membership in Locke." *Political Studies* (March 1990).

———. "Made by Contrivance and the Consent of Man: Abstract Principle and Historical Fact in Locke's Political Philosophy." *Interpretation* (Winter 1989–1990).

Drury, S. B. "Locke and Nozick on Property." *Political Studies* (March 1982).

Dunn, John. *The Political Thought of John Locke*. Cambridge: Cambridge University Press, 1969.

———. "Consent in the Political Theory of John Locke." In *Political Obligation in Its Historical Context*. Cambridge: Cambridge University Press, 1980.

———. "The Politics of Locke in England and America in the Eighteenth Century." In *Political Obligation in Its Historical Context*.

———. *Locke*. Oxford: Oxford University Press, 1984.

———. "The Concept of 'Trust' in the Politics of John Locke." In *Philosophy in History*, ed. R. Rorty, J. B. Schneewind, and Q. Skinner. Cambridge: Cambridge University Press, 1984.

———. "What Is Living and What Is Dead in the Political Theory of John Locke?" In *Interpreting Political Responsibility*. Princeton: Princeton University Press, 1990.

Dworetz, Steven M. *The Unvarnished Doctrine*. Durham: Duke University Press, 1990.

Ellerman, David P. "On the Labor Theory of Property." *Philosophical Forum* (Summer 1985).

Farr, James. "'So Vile and Miserable an Estate': The Problem of Slavery in Locke's Political Thought." *Political Theory* (May 1986).

——— (with Clayton Roberts). "John Locke on the Glorious Revolution: A Rediscovered Document." *Historical Journal* (June 1985).

273

Farrell, Daniel. "Coercion, Consent, and the Justification of Political Power: A New Look at Locke's Consent Claim." *Archiv für Rechts- und Sozialphilosophie* 65/4 (1979).

———. "Tacit Consent and the Justification of Political Power" (unpublished).

Feinberg, Joel. *Social Philosophy.* Englewood Cliffs: Prentice-Hall, 1973.

———. "Voluntary Euthanasia and the Inalienable Right to Life." *Philosophy & Public Affairs* (Winter 1978).

———. *Harm to Self.* New York: Oxford University Press, 1986.

———. *Harmless Wrongdoing.* New York: Oxford University Press, 1988.

Filmer, Robert. *Patriarcha.* In Locke, *Two Treatises of Government,* ed. T. Cook. New York: Hafner, 1947.

Fox Bourne, H. R. *The Life of John Locke.* London: Henry S. King, 1876.

Frankena, William K. "Natural and Inalienable Rights." *Philosophical Review* (April 1955).

Franklin, Julian H. *John Locke and the Theory of Sovereignty.* Cambridge: Cambridge University Press, 1978.

———. "Bodin and Locke on Consent to Taxation: A Brief Note and Observation." *History of Political Thought* (Spring 1986).

Fried, Charles. *Contract as Promise.* Cambridge, Mass.: Harvard University Press, 1981.

Friedman, W. *Legal Theory.* New York: Columbia University Press, 1967.

Gale, George. "John Locke on Territoriality." *Political Theory* (November 1973).

Gewirth, Alan. "Political Justice." In *Social Justice,* ed. R. B. Brandt. Englewood Cliffs: Prentice-Hall, 1972.

Glenn, Gary D. "Inalienable Rights and Locke's Argument for Limited Government: Political Implications of a Right of Suicide." *Journal of Politics* (February 1984).

Goldwin, Robert. "Locke's State of Nature in Political Society." *Western Political Quarterly* (March 1976).

———. "John Locke." In *History of Political Philosophy,* ed. L. Strauss and J. Cropsey. 3d ed. Chicago: University of Chicago Press, 1987.

Gough, J. W. *John Locke's Political Philosophy.* Oxford: Oxford University Press, 1950.

Grady, Robert C., II. "Obligation, Consent, and Locke's Right of Revolution: 'Who Is to Judge?'" *Canadian Journal of Political Science* (June 1976).

Grant, Ruth. *John Locke's Liberalism.* Chicago: University of Chicago Press, 1987.

Green, Leslie. *The Authority of the State.* Oxford: Oxford University Press, 1988.

Green, T. H. *Lectures on the Principles of Political Obligation.* Ann Arbor: University of Michigan Press, 1967.

Grotius, Hugo. *De Jure Praedae Commentarius,* tr. G. Williams and W. Zeydel. Oxford: Oxford University Press, 1950.

———. *Inleidinghe tot de Hollansche Rechts-gheleerheydt,* tr. R. Lee. Oxford: Oxford University Press, 1926.

Hacker, Andrew. *Political Theory.* New York: Macmillan, 1961.

Hampsher-Monk, Iain W. "Resistance and Economy in Dr. Anglim's Locke." *Political Studies* (March 1978).

———. "Tacit Concept of Consent in Locke's Two Treatises of Government: A Note on Citizens, Travellers, and Patriarchalism." *Journal of the History of Ideas* (January–March 1979).

Hampton, Jean. *Hobbes and the Social Contract Tradition.* Cambridge: Cambridge University Press, 1986.

Hardin, Russell. "The Utilitarian Logic of Liberalism." *Ethics* (October 1986).

Hart, H. L. A. "Are There Any Natural Rights?" *Philosophical Review* (April 1955).

Herzog, Don. *Without Foundations.* Ithaca: Cornell University Press, 1985.

———. *Happy Slaves: A Critique of Consent Theory.* Chicago: University of Chicago Press, 1989.

Hobbes, Thomas. *Leviathan,* ed. C. Macpherson. Harmondsworth: Penguin, 1975.

Honore, A. M. "Must We Obey? Necessity as a Ground of Obligation." *Virginia Law Review* (February 1981).

Hughes, Martin. "Locke on Taxation and Suffrage." *History of Political Thought* (Autumn 1990).

Hume, David. "Of the Original Contract." In *Hume's Ethical Writings,* ed. A. MacIntyre. London: Collier, 1970.

———. *A Treatise of Human Nature.* Oxford: Oxford University Press, 1968.

Jefferson, Thomas. *Notes on the State of Virginia.* New York: Harper & Row, 1964.

Jenkins, John J. "Locke and Natural Rights." *Philosophy* (April 1967).
———. "Political Consent." *Philosophical Quarterly* (January 1970).

Kavka, Gregory. *Hobbesian Moral and Political Theory.* Princeton: Princeton University Press, 1986.

Kendall, Willmoore. *John Locke and the Doctrine of Majority-Rule*. Urbana: University of Illinois Press, 1959.

———. "John Locke Revisited." *Intercollegiate Review* (January–February 1966).

Kilcullen, John. "Locke on Political Obligation." *Review of Politics* (July 1983).

King, Peter, Lord. *The Life of John Locke*. 2 vols. London: Henry Colburn & Richard Bentley, 1830.

Kleinig, John. "The Ethics of Consent." *Canadian Journal of Philosophy*, Supp. Vol. 8 (1982).

Klosko, George. "Reformist Consent and Political Obligation." *Political Studies* (December 1991).

———. *The Principle of Fairness and Political Obligation*. Lanham, Md.: Rowman & Littlefield, 1992.

Kraut, Richard. *Socrates and the State*. Princeton: Princeton University Press, 1984.

Kraynak, Robert P. "John Locke: From Absolutism to Toleration." *American Political Science Review* (March 1980).

Kuflik, Arthur. "The Utilitarian Logic of Inalienable Rights." *Ethics* (October 1986).

Laslett, Peter. "Introduction" to Locke, *Two Treatises of Government*. Cambridge: Cambridge University Press, 1963.

Lemos, Ramon. *Hobbes and Locke*. Athens: University of Georgia Press, 1978.

Lessnoff, Michael. *Social Contract*. Atlantic Highlands: Humanities Press, 1986.

Locke, John. *Two Treatises of Government*, ed. P. Laslett. Cambridge: Cambridge University Press, 1963.

———. *An Essay Concerning Human Understanding*, ed. P. Nidditch. Oxford: Oxford University Press, 1975.

———. *Essays on the Law of Nature*, ed. W. Von Leyden. Oxford: Oxford University Press, 1965.

———. *A Letter Concerning Toleration*. In *The Second Treatise of Civil Government* and *A Letter Concerning Toleration*, ed. J. Gough. Oxford: Basil Blackwell, 1947.

———. *Two Tracts on Government*, ed. P. Abrams. Cambridge: Cambridge University Press, 1967.

———. *An Essay Concerning Toleration*. In H. R. Fox Bourne, *The Life of John Locke*. London: Henry S. King, 1876.

———. *The Fundamental Constitutions of the Government of Carolina*. In *The Works of John Locke*, vol. 10. London: Thomas Davison, 1823.

———. "On the Difference between Civil and Ecclesiastical Power, Indorsed Excommunication." In King, *The Life of John Locke*.

———. "Venditio." In Dunn, "Justice and the Interpretation of Locke's Political Theory."

———. "A Call to the Nation for Unity." In Farr and Roberts, "John Locke on the Glorious Revolution."

———. "Some Thoughts Concerning Reading and Study for a Gentleman." In *The Educational Writings of John Locke*, ed. J. Axtell. Cambridge: Cambridge University Press, 1968.

Loewenberg, Robert. "John Locke and the Antebellum Defense of Slavery." *Political Theory* (May 1985).

Mabbott, J. D. *John Locke*. London: Macmillan, 1973.

McClure, Kirstie M. "Difference, Diversity, and the Limits of Toleration." *Political Theory* (August 1990).

McConnell, Terrance. "The Nature and Basis of Inalienable Rights." *Law and Philosophy* (1984).

MacCormick, Neil. "Law, Obligation and Consent: Reflections on Stair and Locke." *Archiv für Rechts- und Sozialphilosophie* (1979).

Mace, George. *Locke, Hobbes, and the Federalist Papers*. Carbondale: Southern Illinois University Press, 1979.

Machan, Tibor. "A Reconsideration of Natural Rights Theory." *American Philosophical Quarterly* (January 1982).

———. "Individualism and the Problem of Political Authority." *Monist* (October 1983).

———. *Individuals and Their Rights*. La Salle: Open Court, 1989.

MacIntyre, Alasdair. "Philosophy and Politics." In *Philosophy and Human Enterprise* (USMA Class of 1951 Lecture Series, 1982–1983).

McNally, David. "Locke, Levellers and Liberty: Property and Democracy in the Thought of the First Whigs." *History of Political Thought* (Spring 1989).

Macpherson, C. B. *The Political Theory of Possessive Individualism*. Oxford: Oxford University Press, 1962.

———. "Natural Rights in Hobbes and Locke." In *Democratic Theory*. Oxford: Oxford University Press, 1973.

———. "Introduction" to Locke, *Second Treatise of Government*. Indianapolis: Hackett, 1980.

Madison, James. *Memorial and Remonstrance Against Religious Assessments*. In *The Complete Madison*, ed. S. Padover. New York: Harper, 1953.

Malone, Dumas. *The Story of the Declaration of Independence*. Oxford: Oxford University Press, 1975.

Mansfield, Harvey C., Jr. "The Right of Revolution." *Daedalus* (Fall 1976).

Mayo, Bernard. "What Are Human Rights?" In *Political Theory and the Rights of Man,* ed. D. D. Raphael. London: Macmillan, 1967.

Medina, Vincente. *Social Contract Theories.* Savage: Rowman & Littlefield, 1990.

Melden, A. I. "Introduction" to *Human Rights.* Belmont: Wadsworth, 1970.

Mendus, Susan. *Toleration and the Limits of Liberalism.* Atlantic Highlands: Humanities Press, 1989.

Meyers, Diana T. "The Rationale for Inalienable Rights in Moral Systems." *Social Theory and Practice* (Summer 1981).

———. *Inalienable Rights: A Defense.* New York: Columbia University Press, 1985.

Monson, Charles H., Jr. "Locke's Political Theory and Its Interpreters." In *Locke and Berkeley,* ed. C. Martin and D. Armstrong. Notre Dame: University of Notre Dame Press, 1968.

Murphy, Jeffrie G. "Total Institutions and the Possibility of Consent to Organic Therapies." In *Retribution, Justice, and Therapy.* Dordrecht: D. Reidel, 1979.

———. "Blackmail: A Preliminary Inquiry." *Monist* (April 1980).

———. "Consent, Coercion, and Hard Choices." *Virginia Law Review* (February 1981).

Nelson, William. *On Justifying Democracy.* London: Routledge & Kegan Paul, 1980.

Nickel, James. *Making Sense of Human Rights.* Berkeley: University of California Press, 1987.

Nino, C. S. "A Consensual Theory of Punishment." *Philosophy & Public Affairs* (Fall 1983).

Nozick, Robert. *Anarchy, State, and Utopia.* New York: Basic Books, 1974.

Ozar, David T. "Rights: What They Are and Where They Come From." In *Philosophical Issues in Human Rights,* ed. P. H. Werhane, A. R. Gini, and D. T. Ozar. New York: Random House, 1986.

Paine, Thomas. *Rights of Man,* ed. H. Collins. Harmondsworth: Penguin, 1969.

Pangle, Thomas L. *The Spirit of Modern Republicanism.* Chicago: University of Chicago Press, 1988.

Parry, Geraint. *John Locke.* London: Allen & Unwin, 1978.

Passmore, J. A. "Locke and the Ethics of Belief." *Proceedings of the British Academy* 64 (1978).

Pateman, Carole. *The Problem of Political Obligation*. Berkeley and Los Angeles: University of California Press, 1979.

———. "Women and Consent." *Political Theory* (May 1980).

Pitkin, Hanna. "Obligation and Consent." *American Political Science Review* (December 1965; March 1966).

Plamenatz, John. *Man and Society*. 2 vols. London: Longmans, Green, 1963.

———. *Consent, Freedom and Political Obligation*. 2d ed. Oxford: Oxford University Press, 1968.

Plato. *Crito*. In *Plato: The Collected Dialogues*, ed. E. Hamilton and H. Cairns. Princeton: Princeton University Press, 1961.

Pocock, J. G. A. "The Myth of John Locke and the Obsession with Liberalism." In *John Locke*, ed. J. G. A. Pocock and R. Ashcraft. Los Angeles: Clark Memorial Library, 1980.

Polin, Raymond. *La Politique Morale de John Locke*. Paris: Presses Universitaires de France, 1960.

———. "Justice in Locke's Philosophy." In *Nomos VI: Justice*, ed. C. Friedrich and J. Chapman. New York: New York University Press, 1963.

———. "The Rights of Man in Hobbes and Locke." In *Political Theory and the Rights of Man*, ed. D. D. Raphael. London: Macmillan, 1967.

———. "John Locke's Conception of Freedom." In *John Locke: Problems and Perspectives*, ed. J. W. Yolton. Cambridge: Cambridge University Press, 1969.

Rapaczynski, Andrzej. "Locke's Conception of Property and the Principle of Sufficient Reason." *Journal of the History of Ideas* (April–June 1981).

Raphael, D. D. *Problems of Political Philosophy*. London: Macmillan, 1976.

Rawls, John. *A Theory of Justice*. Cambridge, Mass.: Harvard University Press, 1971.

Raz, Joseph. "The Obligation to Obey the Law." In *The Authority of Law*. Oxford: Oxford University Press, 1979.

———. *The Morality of Freedom*. Oxford: Oxford University Press, 1986.

Reeve, Andrew. *Property*. Houndmills: Macmillan, 1986.

Replogle, Ron. *Recovering the Social Contract*. Totowa: Rowman & Littlefield, 1989.

Richards, B. A. "Inalienable Rights: Recent Criticism and Old Doctrine." *Philosophy and Phenomenological Research* (March 1969).

Richards, David A. J. *Toleration and the Constitution.* New York: Oxford University Press, 1986.

Richards, Judith, Lotte Mulligan, and John K. Graham. "'Property' and 'People': Political Usages of Locke and Some Contemporaries." *Journal of the History of Ideas* (January–March 1981).

Riley, Patrick. *Will and Political Legitimacy.* Cambridge, Mass.: Harvard University Press, 1982.

Robins, Michael. "The Primacy of Promising." *Mind* (July 1976).

Rothbard, Murray. *The Ethics of Liberty.* Atlantic Highlands: Humanities Press, 1982.

Rousseau, J. J. *Social Contract,* tr. G. Cole. New York: Dutton, 1950.

Russell, Paul. "Locke on Express and Tacit Consent." *Political Theory* (May 1986).

Ryan, Alan. "Locke and the Dictatorship of the Bourgeoisie." In *Locke and Berkeley,* ed. C. Martin and D. Armstrong. Notre Dame: University of Notre Dame Press, 1968.

Sabine, George H. *A History of Political Theory.* New York: Henry Holt, 1937.

Sartorius, Rolf. "Political Authority and Political Obligation." *Virginia Law Review* (February 1981).

Scanlon, Thomas. "Liberty, Contract, and Contribution." In *Readings in Social and Political Philosophy,* ed. R. M. Stewart. New York: Oxford University Press, 1986.

———. "Promises and Practices." *Philosophy & Public Affairs* (Summer 1990).

Schiller, Marvin. "Are There Any Inalienable Rights?" *Ethics* (July 1969).

Schochet, Gordon. "The Family and the Origins of the State in Locke's Political Philosophy." In *John Locke: Problems and Perspectives,* ed. J. W. Yolton. Cambridge: Cambridge University Press, 1969.

———. *Patriarchalism in Political Thought.* Oxford: Basil Blackwell, 1975.

Seliger, M. *The Liberal Politics of John Locke.* London: Allen & Unwin, 1968.

———. "Locke, Liberalism, and Nationalism." In *John Locke: Problems and Perspectives,* ed. J. W. Yolton. Cambridge: Cambridge University Press, 1969.

Senor, Thomas. "What if There Are No Political Obligations? A Reply to A. J. Simmons." *Philosophy & Public Affairs* (Summer 1987).

Shapiro, Ian. *The Evolution of Rights in Liberal Theory.* Cambridge: Cambridge University Press, 1986.

Siegler, Frederick. "Plamenatz on Consent and Obligation." *Philosophical Quarterly* (July 1968).

Sigmund, Paul E. *Natural Law in Political Thought*. Cambridge, Mass.: Winthrop Publishers, 1971.

Simmons, A. John. *Moral Principles and Political Obligations*. Princeton: Princeton University Press, 1979.

———. "Voluntarism and Political Associations." *Virginia Law Review* (February 1981).

———. "Reasonable Expectations and Obligations: A Reply to Postow." *Southern Journal of Philosophy* (Spring 1981).

———. "Inalienable Rights and Locke's *Treatises*." *Philosophy & Public Affairs* (Summer 1983).

———. "Consent, Free Choice, and Democratic Government." *Georgia Law Review* (Summer 1984).

———. "The Anarchist Position: A Reply to Klosko and Senor." *Philosophy & Public Affairs* (Summer 1987).

———. "Locke's State of Nature." *Political Theory* (August 1989).

———. *The Lockean Theory of Rights*. Princeton: Princeton University Press, 1992.

Singer, Peter. *Democracy and Disobedience*. Oxford: Oxford University Press, 1973.

Skinner, Quentin. *The Foundations of Modern Political Thought*. 2 vols. Cambridge: Cambridge University Press, 1978.

———. "The Origins of the Calvinist Theory of Revolution." In *After the Reformation*, ed. B. Malament. Philadelphia: University of Pennsylvania Press, 1980.

Smith, M. B. E. "Is There a Prima Facie Obligation to Obey the Law?" *Yale Law Journal* (1973).

Snare, Frank. "Consent and Conventional Acts in John Locke." *Journal of the History of Philosophy* (January 1975).

Snyder, David. "Locke on Natural Law and Property Rights." *Canadian Journal of Philosophy* (December 1986).

Steiner, Hillel. "The Natural Right to the Means of Production." *Philosophical Quarterly* (January 1977).

Stell, Lance K. "Dueling and the Right to Life." *Ethics* (October 1979).

Strauss, Leo. *Natural Right and History*. Chicago: University of Chicago Press, 1953.

Stumpf, Samuel E. *Socrates to Sartre*, 4th ed. New York: McGraw-Hill, 1988.

Tarcov, Nathan. "Locke's *Second Treatise* and 'The Best Fence Against Rebellion.'" *Review of Politics* (April 1981).

————. *Locke's Education for Liberty.* Chicago: University of Chicago Press, 1984.

Tassi, Aldo. "Two Notions of Consent in Locke's *Second Treatise.*" *Locke Newsletter* (Autumn 1970).

————. "Locke on Majority-Rule and the Legislative." *Locke Newsletter* (Summer 1973).

Thomas, Craig. *There to Here.* New York: HarperCollins, 1991.

Trevelyan, G. M. *The English Revolution, 1688–1689.* Oxford: Oxford University Press, 1938.

Tuck, Richard. *Natural Rights Theories.* Cambridge: Cambridge University Press, 1979.

Tully, James. *A Discourse on Property.* Cambridge: Cambridge University Press, 1980.

————. "Political Freedom." *Journal of Philosophy* (October 1990).

Tussman, Joseph. *Obligation and the Body Politic.* Oxford: Oxford University Press, 1960.

VanDeVeer, Donald. "Are Human Rights Alienable?" *Philosophical Studies* (February 1980).

Vaughn, Karen I. *John Locke: Economist and Social Scientist.* Chicago: University of Chicago Press, 1980.

Vlastos, Gregory. "Justice and Equality." In *Social Justice*, ed. R. B. Brandt. Englewood Cliffs: Prentice-Hall, 1962.

Von Leyden, Wolfgang. *Hobbes and Locke.* New York: St. Martin's, 1982.

Waldman, Theodore. "A Note on John Locke's Concept of Consent." *Ethics* (October 1957).

Waldron, Jeremy. "Enough and as Good Left for Others." *Philosophical Quarterly* (October 1979).

————. *Nonsense upon Stilts.* London: Methuen, 1987.

————. "Locke: Toleration and the Rationality of Persecution." In *Justifying Toleration*, ed. S. Mendus. Cambridge: Cambridge University Press, 1988.

————. *The Right to Private Property.* Oxford: Oxford University Press, 1988.

————. "Rights in Conflict." *Ethics* (April 1989).

Walzer, Michael. *Just and Unjust Wars.* New York: Basic Books, 1977.

Weale, Albert. "Consent." *Political Studies* (March 1978).

White, Morton. *The Philosophy of the American Revolution.* Oxford: Oxford University Press, 1978.

————. *Philosophy, The Federalist, and the Constitution.* Oxford: Oxford University Press, 1987.

Wills, Garry. *Inventing America: Jefferson's Declaration of Independence.* New York: Doubleday, 1978.

Windstrup, George. "Freedom and Authority: The Ancient Faith of Locke's Letter on Toleration." *Review of Politics* (April 1982).

Winfrey, John C. "Charity versus Justice in Locke's Theory of Property." *Journal of the History of Ideas* (July–September 1981).

Wolff, Robert Paul. *In Defense of Anarchism.* New York: Harper & Row, 1970.

Wood, Neal. *The Politics of Locke's Philosophy.* Berkeley: University of California Press, 1983.

———. *John Locke and Agrarian Capitalism.* Berkeley: University of California Press, 1984.

Woozley, A. D. *Law and Obedience.* London: Duckworth, 1979.

Yolton, John W. *Locke: An Introduction.* Oxford: Basil Blackwell, 1985.

Zvesper, John. "The Utility of Consent in John Locke's Political Philosophy." *Political Studies* (March 1984).

INDEX

Aaron, Richard, 13n, 159n
Aarsleff, Hans, 28n
absolute power (government), 6, 20n, 33, 41–42, 41n, 48–55, 52n, 99–100, 107, 113, 115–17, 121–22, 126n, 137–39, 144–45, 157, 157n, 208–9; defined, 54–55. *See also* despotical power
absolute rights. *See* rights
acceptance (of benefits), 253–58, 253–54n, 254–55n. *See also* receipt; subjective requirements; voluntariness
acquiescence, 210–16, 211n, 211–12n, 212n, 216n, 221, 248. *See also* consent
alienation (of right), 46–48, 46n, 47n, 50, 51n, 69, 71–72, 103–4, 106–7, 109–12, 121, 153–54, 215n, 264; defined, 46. *See also* transfer of rights
aliens, 16, 17, 21, 21n, 22, 29–30, 81–82, 82n, 85–87, 171, 199, 203
American Declaration of Independence, 103n, 106–7n, 181n
American Revolution, 101, 103, 105, 106–8
anarchism, philosophical. *See* philosophical anarchism
anarchism, political, 210, 268
anarchy, 33, 53, 162n, 165n, 168–69, 179, 188–89, 201, 210
Andrew, Edward, 95n, 113n, 114n, 116n, 132n, 136n, 159–60n, 173n, 174n, 179n
Anglim, John, 173n
animals, 43, 43–44n, 45, 51n, 112n
annullment, 48, 109
appeal to heaven, 149, 149n, 173, 174–75, 179, 189. *See also* revolution
Aquinas, Thomas, 44n, 205n
arbitrary power, 16, 33, 44n, 97, 116–18, 116n, 138, 154, 174–75, 209n; defined, 54–55. *See also* absolute power; despotical power
Aristotle, 36
Arneson, Richard, 252n, 253n, 253–54n, 254–55n, 256
Arnhart, Larry, 45n

artificiality: of governments, 37, 59, 203–4; of obligations, 200n
Ashcraft, Richard, 8n, 13n, 18n, 22n, 27n, 28n, 29n, 30n, 51n, 86n, 89n, 90n, 91n, 95n, 115n, 127n, 128n, 129n, 130n, 148n, 149n, 158n, 162n, 167n, 168n, 172n, 174n, 176n, 184n, 212n, 213n
Athens, 232n, 233n
atheists, 73n, 126–27, 127n
attitudes (and consent). *See* consent
Austin, J. L., 226n
authority, 11, 13, 27, 29, 74–75, 94, 162–63, 182–83, 197–269. *See also* legitimacy; political power
authorization, 38–39, 39n

Bagshaw, Edward, 124
Barker, Ernest, 71n, 159n
Beitz, Charles, 206n, 207n
belief (religious), 125, 130n, 131–34. *See also* religion; toleration
benefit/reciprocation theories, 76, 203–4, 249–60
benefits of government, 73, 76, 187, 187n, 203, 211, 216, 242, 243n, 249–60. *See also* acceptance; receipt; voluntariness
Bennett, John, 199n, 203n
Bentham, Jeremy, 101n, 104n
Beran, Harry, 74n, 198n, 201n, 221n, 223n, 227n, 229–32, 235–36, 240, 242n, 243, 246n
Best, Judith, 28n, 209n
blackmail, 239n
Bodin, Jean, 96
body politic, 4, 5n, 61n, 172, 222. *See also* civil society
breach of trust. *See* trust
Brown, Alan, 35n
Brown, Stuart, 205n

Calvinist political theory, 149n, 182
capital punishment. *See* punishment
Catholics, 73n, 40, 126–27, 126n, 127n, 130

285

charity, 67n, 242, 262, 267–68. *See also* need; positive rights

Charles II, 155

choice, 211–17, 211n, 211–12n, 212n, 213n, 214n, 221–24, 227–28, 233–44, 233n; hard vs. free, 234–44. *See also* consent; voluntariness

church, 11, 131n, 213n. *See also* religion

civil, 5–6, 15n

civil disobedience, 268

civil law. *See* law

civil rights, 4, 85–86, 94n, 97, 108–9. *See also* rights

civil society, 14, 15n, 19, 27, 29n, 39, 43–44, 53n, 59–60, 61n, 99, 164, 175–76; defined, 4, 5n; end of, 124–35, 138, 204–5, 204n, 205n, 209–10. *See also* body politic; commomwealth; political society; society

claim rights, 38, 39n, 119–22, 150, 152; optional, 119–20; mandatory, 119–20, 121–22, 130, 140–41, 151n, 182

claims, 142–43, 151–52. *See also* rights

clear choice situation, 80–81n, 83, 83n, 87, 213, 213n, 220, 221–22, 232–33, 241, 245–46, 247, 266, 268. *See also* tacit consent

coercion. *See* consent; voluntariness

Cohen, Joshua, 26n, 90n, 244n

Cohen, Marshall, 223n

Coleman, Jules, 237n

Colman, John, 15n, 26n, 28n, 29n, 150n

common good, 204, 245

common judge, 17–21, 27, 29–30, 44, 62, 161, 168–70, 172–73

commonwealth, 4–5, 5n. *See also* civil society

communitarian fallacy, 37–38

community, 4–5, 5n, 68n, 159n, 167–68, 259n,; natural, 4. *See also* civil society

compensation, principle of, 38n, 251n

conflict of rights, 108n, 190–91

conquest, 6, 16, 50, 73, 154, 160–62, 163–65, 168–69, 171, 177, 200, 211, 214–15. *See also* violence

consent, 6–7, 68–70, 70n, 84–85n, 193–94, 197–251, 260; actual vs. hypothetical, 76–79, 205–8, 209n; attitudinal sense of, 214, 214n, 246; coerced, 38n, 57, 74, 85n, 137, 154–55, 209, 211–13, 215–16, 223n, 226n, 233–41, 235n, 239n; defined, 69–70, 70n; duration of, 81, 87–88; insincere, 69; limits on, 153–55; natural, 213, 213n; obligation to give, 75, 75n; personal, 59, 68–69, 90–92, 94, 97–98, 99, 205–8, 216; positive, 212–13; and sufficiency for obligation, 54n, 69, 69n, 73, 91n, 198, 203, 206, 208–9, 209n; unanimity of, 92–93, 222. *See also* consent theory; express consent; inexplicit contract; intentionality; limited government; majority consent; political consent; reliance; tacit consent; taxes; voiding conditions; voluntariness

consent theory (Lockean), 72–79, 194–95, 197–251, 260; appeal of, 72–75, 99, 216–17, 228; conservative evaluation of, 198n; critical evaluation of, 198n, ; defined, 197–98; revisionist, 76–77, 198n; standard critique of, 199–201, 202–3, 204, 206, 210, 216

consequentialism. *See* rule-consequentialism; utilitarianism

consideration (in contract), 71

constructive intention, 41n

contract, 68–72, 70n, 71n, 78, 117–18, 130–31, 164, 171, 176–77, 180–81, 183–85, 188, 194, 197, 213, 234–39, 248, 249n, 250, 261, 267; of adhesion, 241n; irrational, 137–39, 143–44; private, 18–19, 25, 44n, 51n, 264; stages of, 68, 68n. *See also* historical contract; inexplicit contract; quasi-contract; unconscionable agreements

contractarianism. *See* hypothetical contractarianism

conventions, 200n, 222, 223–24, 223–24n, 224–25n, 229, 231–33, 241, 246–47, 262

Cook, Thomas, 31n

cooperation, schemes of, 249–60, 262

coordination, 262, 264

correlation: of political power and political obligation, 59–60, 60–61n, 207–8, 207n; of rights and duties, 119–20, 140, 152

Cox, Richard, 14n, 18n, 28n, 102n, 109n, 167n

Cranston, Maurice, 125n, 129n, 148n, 180n

Cumberland, Richard, 153

defeating conditions (for consent). *See* voiding conditions

democracy, 68n, 77, 90–98, 91n, 149, 167–68, 218–44; perfect, 91, 167–68, 172

Den Hartogh, G. A., 28n, 35n, 64n, 65n, 69n, 84n, 88n, 89n, 131n, 187n, 206n, 213n, 250n, 254n despotical power, 11, 46, 49–53, 49n, 50n, 59n; defined, 49–50; and natural executive right, 51n. *See also* absolute power; arbitrary power; slavery

disability, 103

discretion, 71, 116–17, 181

dissolution: of government, 6, 22n, 114, 161–73, 163n, 178, 182–87; moral vs. physical, 163–64, 182–84; of society, 22, 22n, 161–72, 186–87; with respect to individuals, 187

dramatic social utilities, 190–91, 265–66n, 267–68

drudgery, 50n, 116–17, 131n, 138–39. *See also* slavery

Drury, S. B., 184n

Dunn, John, 8n, 13n, 23n, 30n, 43n, 45n, 49n, 60n, 71n, 73n, 74n, 82n, 83n, 88n, 90n, 92n, 97n, 147n, 148n, 150n, 151n, 171n, 173n, 174n, 180n, 181n, 189–90n, 190n, 205n, 207n, 210–16, 214n, 215n, 216n, 244n

duress. *See* consent; voluntariness

duty, moral. *See* law of nature; imperfect duty

duty to resist, 149, 149n, 151, 179–82, 180n, 181n, 187–89, 192

Dworetz, Steven, 180n

economical power, 50, 50n

elections, 94–96, 162. *See also* voting, right of

emigration, 225–27, 232–37, 233–34n, 240–41, 242n, 246–47, 246n, 254n, 259n, 268. *See also* residence

enjoyment (of benefits), 80–81, 80–81n, 83–86, 202–4, 203n, 204n, 249–50, 252–55. *See also* benefits of government

equality, 5, 5n, 11–12

estoppel, 70n

Exclusion Crisis, 115n, 126n, 148n

executive power, 155, 162, 162n, 169–70, 170n, 244–45. *See also* natural executive right

explanation, 34–35

exploitation, 237n, 238–39, 238n, 239n, 240–41, 241n

express consent, 69n, 80–90, 93, 99, 168, 197, 209, 211, 213n, 214n, 219, 246, 249–50; defined, 83–86, 84–85n; dispositional account of, 88n, 206. *See also* consent

expropriation (of right), 48, 109, 154

fairness, principle of, 35n, 76, 249–60; basic formulation of, 249–50

Farr, James, 84–85n, 240n

Farrell, Daniel, 244n

federative power, 60n, 62

Feinberg, Joel, 46, 103n, 104n, 106n, 216n, 226n, 237n, 238n, 239n

fiduciary relationships. *See* trust

filial relationships, 11–12, 37–38, 110, 212n

Filmer, Robert, 11, 31, 31n, 32, 36, 46–47, 48–49, 49n, 52, 93, 111, 111n, 159n, 160n, 165–66, 165n, 172, 175, 186n, 204, 210, 236, 236n

first try, right of, 67–68

forgiveness, 186

forfeiture of rights, 43–44, 45n, 46–48, 46n, 51n, 57, 59n, 72, 74n, 104, 104n, 106, 108, 111, 112n, 114, 114n, 153–54, 155–59, 164, 183, 186n, 264; defined, 46. *See also* nonforfeitable right

franchise. *See* voting, right of

Frankena, William, 105n

Franklin, Julian, 65n, 97n, 149n, 158n, 159n, 162n, 174n, 189n

free choice. *See* choice; voluntariness

freedom and blameworthiness, 45–46, 45n. *See also* choice; liberty, right to; natural freedom, voluntariness

free rider, 256–57. *See also* fairness, principle of

French Declaration of Rights, 103n, 104n, 106n, 113

Fried, Charles, 201n, 237n, 238n

full transfer theories, 155. *See also* transfer of rights

fundamental law of nature. *See* law of nature

generality (of political obligation), 227

general rights. *See* rights

Gewirth, Alan, 221n

Glenn, Gary, 109n, 114n

Goldwin, Robert, 14n

Gough, J. W., 14n, 60n, 64n, 70n, 71n, 92n, 113n, 125n, 127n, 159n, 173n, 185n, 205n, 212n, 213n

government, 57–59, 68, 69n, 70–72, 97–98, 99, 114, 158–59, 162–63, 167–68, 172–73, 203–4, 208–10; defined, 68n; good, 261–69. *See also* civil society; dissolution; political power; trust

grades of citizenship, 242, 242n, 243n

Grady, Robert, 65n, 173n

Grant, Ruth, 20n, 22n, 55n, 64–65n, 68n, 69n, 92n, 93n, 94n, 113n, 114n,

Grant, Ruth (*cont.*)
  131n, 136n, 148n, 159n, 165n, 166n,
  167n, 169n, 174n, 179n, 180n, 203n,
  208n, 210n
gratitude, 76, 163, 260n
Green, Leslie, 37n, 69n, 70n, 76n,
  198n, 201n, 207n, 215n, 216n, 223n,
  225n, 226n, 229n, 263n
Green, T. H., 200n
Grotius, Hugo, 44n, 46, 49, 108n, 135–
  36, 151, 153

Hacker, Andrew, 64n, 106n, 211n
Hamilton, Alexander, 101n
Hampsher-Monk, Iain, 83n, 88n, 89n,
  214n
Hampton, Jean, 53n, 70n
hard choice. *See* choice; voluntariness
Hardin, Russell, 122n
Hart, H.L.A., 251
Hegel, G.W.F., 36
Herzog, Don, 77–78, 77n, 85n, 127n,
  133n, 198n, 203n, 207n, 212n, 221n,
  223n, 233n
historical argument, 30–33, 92–93
historical contract, 30–32, 73, 153
Hobbes, Thomas, 14–17, 22–23, 26–28,
  29–31, 29n, 33–34, 34–35n, 36, 38–39,
  38n, 39n, 42n, 48, 49n, 137, 137n,
  151–52, 152n, 164, 166, 205, 225, 234–
  35
Hohfeld, W. N., 38, 103, 119
Honore, A. M., 219n, 232n
honour, right of, 110–11
Hooker, Richard, 153
Hughes, Martin, 95n, 96n
human rights, 101, 103, 106–7, 112. *See
  also* natural rights; rights
Hume, David, 32, 76n, 197–98, 200–
  202, 200–201n, 226–31, 233–34, 235–
  36, 239–40, 243
Hutcheson, Francis, 135n
hypothetical contractarianism, 33n,
  54n, 76–77, 77n, 78–79, 79n, 205–8,
  216; and ideal contract theory, 76n.
  See also quality of government
  theories

immunity, 103
imperfect duty, 71
imprescriptible right, 47–48, 101n, 103,
  109n, 154; defined, 104. *See also*
  prescription
inalienable things, 135–36

inalienable rights, 7, 25, 47, 47n, 99,
  101–46, 153, 154, 158, 193; defined,
  103–5
incompetence (of governors), 157, 157n,
  165
incompetents, 16, 21–22, 24–25, 45,
  51n, 171, 226, 226n, 236
incorporation, 61n, 82n, 175, 175n, 191
indefeasible rights, 103–5, 104n; defined, 104–5
indifferent acts, 63–64, 63n, 64n, 66,
  124–28, 124n, 129–30, 130n, 133, 245
individualism, 36–37, 36n, 61n, 66, 75–
  76, 150–51, 151n, 197
individual resistance. *See* resistance,
  right of
inexplicit contracts, 93–94, 131n, 138–
  39, 153–54, 153n, 209–10, 220
inheritance, 88–90, 89n, 110–11, 110–
  11n, 213
innocent delights, right of, 62–63, 67,
  118, 264–65
insanity, 137, 137n, 143–44, 145
intentionality (of consent), 199, 202,
  211–16, 223, 226–32
interpretation of law, 19, 62, 114, 114n.
  See also "Who shall judge?"
interpretive charity, principle of, 108n,
  138, 153. *See also* inexplicit contracts

James II, 40, 51, 155
Jefferson, Thomas, 101, 103n, 106,
  106n, 127n, 135n
Jenkins, John, 28n, 223n
Jephtha, 149n, 175
judge. *See* common judge; "Who shall
  judge?"
jurisdiction, 19n, 33, 67n, 86n
jus ad bellum, 44n
jus in bello, 44n
justice, 15, 76, 151, 166, 169, 183, 192,
  204–6
justification, 34–35n, 35, 265–66n, 267–
  68
just war theory, 44n, 49n, 50–51, 157–
  58, 158n. *See also* war

Kant, Immanuel, 41n, 71, 136, 142–43,
  142n, 239
Kavka, Gregory, 17n, 33n, 53, 79n
Kendall, Willmoore, 13n, 31n, 93n,
  102n, 104n, 109n, 120n, 173n, 185n
Kilcullen, John, 60–61n, 64n, 91n,
  206n, 207n
Kleinig, John, 223n, 225n, 226n

Klosko, George, 198n, 242n, 243n, 249n, 252n, 254n, 256, 256n, 257–60, 257n, 257–58n, 259n
Kraut, Richard, 219n, 229n, 232n, 233n, 242n
Kraynak, Robert, 67n, 124n, 126n
Kuflik, Arthur, 122n

Laslett, Peter, 84n, 148n, 173n
law, civil, 60, 63–64, 160n, 245; categories of, 264–65
law enforcement, domestic, 60, 85, 244–45
law of nature, 23–25, 26n, 41, 44–45, 45n, 51n, 60, 62n, 63–64, 66–68, 108, 112, 112n, 120–23, 127n, 140–41, 156, 179, 188, 208, 244–45, 262–64, 269; content of, 23–25, 115–19; fundamental, 44–45, 115, 122
Lawson, George, 159n
legal rights, 102, 103n. See also rights
legislative power, 19, 62, 62n, 68–72, 90, 94–97, 118–19, 137–39, 155, 159n, 160–62, 162n, 165, 169–70, 170n, 191, 208
legitimacy, 15n, 16, 19, 22, 29–30, 31n, 33, 34, 34–35n, 37–38, 52–54, 54n, 57–58, 69, 72–73, 79, 91n, 164, 183, 186–87, 198–99, 201–2, 205–9, 207n, 218, 248, 261–62, 265–69; presumption of, 269. See also authority; political power
Lemos, Ramon, 16n, 43n, 74n, 91n, 221n
Lessnoff, Michael, 36n, 65n, 71n, 75n, 76n, 86n, 149n, 159n, 182n, 198n, 201n, 249n, 261n
Levellers, 66, 95, 95n, 137n
libertarians, 210
liberty rights, 15n, 38–39, 39n, 119, 121, 150, 150n, 152, 154–55; protected, 39n, 152. See also rights
liberty, right to, 107, 111n, 115n, 116n
life, right to. See rights
limited government, 33, 40, 62, 62n, 91n, 99–100, 108–9, 118–19, 137–39, 144–45, 204, 210, 220, 244
loss of right. See alienation; forfeiture; prescription; rights; transfer of rights

Mabbott, J. D., 28n, 89n, 128n
McConnell, Terrance, 46n, 103n, 105n, 113n, 115n
Mace, George, 104n, 149n
Machan, Tibor, 230n
MacIntyre, Alasdair, 222n

Macpherson, C. B., 14n, 27n, 28n, 47n, 59n, 66n, 88n, 88–90, 90n, 92n, 95n, 98n, 102n, 109n, 184n
Madison, James, 113, 132n
majority consent, 91–94, 97, 194, 206
majority rule, 68–69, 91–94, 97, 99, 101–2, 149, 159, 172–91, 193, 210, 222, 267
majority tyranny, 91n, 94n, 173, 175
man, 3n, 137–38, 141–43. See also person
mandatory decision process, 227, 232–33, 240–43, 240n, 246
manhood suffrage, 94–96. See also voting, right of
mankind, 4
Malone, Dumas, 103n
manipulation, 237–41
Medina, Vincente, 209n, 211n
members (of society), 82–90, 82n, 88n, 89n, 90n
membership, 230–32, 259–60n
Mendus, Susan, 129n
Meyers, Diana, 139n, 141–42n, 142n
minorities: intense, 93; rights of, 101–2, 172–91. See also majority rule
minors, 16, 21, 24–25, 29, 45, 51n, 171, 231–32
Molina, Luis de, 96
monarchy, 27, 31, 31n, 53–54, 91, 131n, 168
money, 27, 27n, 28, 211, 211–12n. See also property
monopoly on force, 64n, 243n, 259n, 265n
moral philosophy, 3
moral rights. See natural rights; rights
Murphy, Jeffrie, 235n, 237n, 238n, 239n, 247n

national defense, 60, 82, 83n, 85, 87, 183, 232, 241, 245, 252, 253n, 255, 258–59, 264, 266
natural disasters, 165, 170, 177
natural executive right, 19–22, 20n, 24–25, 51n, 62–64, 64n, 68n, 114, 114n, 159, 176–77, 186, 264–65, 265n. See also executive power
natural freedom, 5n, 31–32, 36–37, 50, 74–75, 110, 112, 115, 118, 150, 159, 162, 200, 204, 216, 218, 228, 244, 247–48, 260n. See also self-government, right of
naturalism (political), 36–38, 36n, 75, 204
naturalized citizens, 219

natural law. *See* law of nature
natural rights, 59, 61–68, 94n, 101–3,
    103n, 104–5, 108–9, 112, 119–23,
    128–29, 149–55, 162, 193, 204, 249,
    263–65, 269; enumeration of, 23–25,
    115–19; types of, 119–20. *See also*
    rights
need, 243–44, 257–58, 257n, 259n, 262,
    267–68. *See also* charity
negligence, 229–32, 254, 254–55n
Nelson, William, 225n
neutral acts. *See* indifferent acts
Nickel, James, 107n, 150n
Nino, C. S., 46n
Ninth Amendment (to U. S. Constitu-
    tion), 62n
nonconsensual obligations, 203–4
nonconsensual relations, 11–12, 39, 57,
    100, 193–94. *See also* state of nature;
    war
nonforfeitable right, 104
nonreductionism (social), 61n, 175–76n
nonviolent political action, 188–89
Nozick, Robert, 20n, 34–35, 34–35n, 38,
    101n, 251

oaths of allegiance, 84–85, 84–85n, 87,
    90, 219, 219n, 240n
obedience to law, 60–61n, 87, 244–45,
    249–50, 255, 261–69. *See also* political
    obligation
objectivism (moral), 9
obligation. *See* law of nature; noncon-
    sensual obligations; particularized
    obligations; political obligation

pacifism, 258–59, 259n
pagans, 127n
Paine, Thomas, 153n
Pangle, Thomas, 17n, 101n
Parry, Geraint, 26n, 65n, 83n, 162n,
    166n, 173n, 185n, 208n, 210n
participation, political, 82, 89–92, 94–
    98, 197–98, 219–20
participation theory, 77–78
particularized obligations, 203–4
Passmore, J. A., 131n
Pateman, Carole, 69n, 74n, 77, 77n,
    212n, 224n
paternalism, 101n, 109–10, 129, 204–5,
    258n
paternal power, 11, 49n, 50, 59n, 80,
    80–81n, 108n, 110–12, 119, 212n
people, 61n, 159n, 172–73, 174–77, 175–
    76n, 179–82, 184–86, 184n, 191–92,
    222; defined, 4,

performative judgment, 185–87, 185–
    86n
person, 3n, 43–44, 123, 142–43. *See also*
    man
personal consent. *See* consent
philosophical anarchism, 7, 195, 201–2,
    201n, 216, 218, 245–46, 247, 250–51,
    260–69, 261n
Pitkin, Hanna, 54n, 64n, 206, 210n, 216
Plamenatz, John, 8, 73–74n, 75n, 94n,
    97n, 192n, 202n, 206n, 213n, 221n,
    223n
Plato, 225, 233n
Polin, Raymond, 45n, 109n, 113n
political, 5–6, 11–12, 13, 37–38, 247–48,
    261–62
political consent, 59–70, 61n, 115–17,
    176, 208–10. *See also* consent; transfer
    of rights
political obligation, 5–6, 13, 25–26, 26n,
    59–64, 60n, 72–79, 85–86, 164, 179–
    80, 197–269, 200–201n, 260n
political participation. *See* participation,
    political
political philosophy, 3–4, 193–94, 247–
    48
political power, 4, 4n, 5–6, 11, 37, 46,
    49n, 50, 57–65, 59n, 60–61n, 64n, 64–
    65n, 68, 68n, 72–73, 91, 107–8, 124–
    35, 158–59, 164–65, 182–83, 203–4,
    207–8, 207n, 212n, 216, 218, 250,
    261–62; domestic component of, 64.
    See also authority; legitimacy
political relationship, 1–7, 11–13, 57–58,
    61, 80–81, 86, 99, 146, 147, 174, 192,
    193–94, 218, 247–48, 260, 261. *See also*
    civil society
political society, 4, 5–6, 5n, 68n, 218.
    See also civil society
politic society. *See* civil society
polity. *See* civil society
positive rights, 237n, 262. *See also*
    charity; need
power (Hohfeldian), 106–7n, 119, 264
prerogative, 55, 71–72, 160n, 162n
prescription, 46–48, 47n, 57, 59n, 104,
    104n, 106, 108–9, 154, 215n; defined,
    46–47; legal doctrine of, 47n; positive
    and negative, 47n. *See also* impres-
    criptible right
presumptive goods. *See* public goods
principle of compensation. *See* compen-
    sation, principle of
principle of fairness. *See* fairness, prin-
    ciple of
private contracts. *See* contracts

promising, 69–70, 69n, 71n, 73n, 77–78, 82–83n, 107, 120, 127n, 154, 171, 180–81, 197, 200–201n. *See also* consent; contract
property, 6, 19n, 27, 40, 47, 62n, 67, 67n, 74, 106–7n, 108, 109n, 111, 113, 117–18, 117–18n,, 118n, 139, 176–77, 180–81, 190, 204, 215n, 218, 264; defined, 4n; and membership, 85–86, 86n, 88–90, 89n, 90n, 95–98, 95n, 184–85, 184n; regulation of, 96–97. *See also* money; natural rights
proportionality, 42n, 157, 158n
protected liberty. *See* liberty right
public goods, 252–58, 252n, 253n, 254–55n; presumptive, 252n, 257–58, 257–58n, 259n
Pufendorf, Samuel, 49, 152
punishment, 44, 45n, 108n, 151, 156–58, 158n, 159, 171–72, 176–77, 186, 186n, 189–90n, 231, 264–65, 265n, 268; capital, 64n, 158. *See also* natural executive right
Puritan theory, 75n, 205n
Putney debates, 95, 95n

quality of government theories, 76, 78–79, 204–10, 208n, 216, 261–62
quasi-contract, 249n

radical views, 109n, 137n, 148–49, 151n, 158n, 159n, 162n, 174–75, 176n, 181
Raphael, D. D., 221n
Rawls, John, 54n, 76–77, 77n, 249, 251, 253–54n
Raz, Joseph, 69n, 70n, 164n, 202n, 207n, 238n
realism (and consent), 198–99, 216–17
realism, moral, 9
rebellion, 114, 149n, 163, 165–66. *See also* resistance, right of; revolution
receipt of benefits, 253–59, 253–54n, 254–55n. *See also* acceptance; voluntariness
reciprocation. *See* benefit/reciprocation theories
redistribution (of rights), 48
Reeve, Andrew, 47n
regulatory statutes, 63
reliance (and consent), 70n
religion, 66–67n, 124–36, 124n, 129n, 905, 205n. *See also* belief; church; indifferent acts; toleration
renouncement, 47–48, 111, 121, 140

reparation, 44, 62n, 151, 158n, 175–77, 178–79, 186–87, 189–90n, 191, 264, 267–68
representatives, 91–92, 94–98, 94n, 174, 174n, 220n
required choice. *See* choice; mandatory decision process
residence (and consent), 199–200, 216, 218, 220, 222n, 225–44, 244n
resistance, right of, 66, 70–72, 70n, 73, 73–74n, 99–100, 107–8, 124–25, 126–28, 147–92, 193–94, 248; defined, 149–50, 149n; for individuals, 17n, 149, 159, 159n, 172–92, 267–68
responsiveness (of state), 77–79
retained rights. *See* rights
revolution, 107–8, 113–14, 113n, 145–46, 147–55, 158, 182, 188, 188n. *See also* resistance, right of
Richards, B. A., 105n
Richards, David, 74n, 126n, 132n, 136n, 190n, 205n
Richards, Judith, 95n, 184n
Riley, Patrick, 59n, 84n, 92n, 200n, 208n, 211n
rights: absolute, 104–5, 105n, 108n, 126, 190; general, 111n; to life, 101n, 106–7, 111n, 113n, 115, 115n; loss of, 46–48, 106–7; of nature, 38–39; retained, 61–68, 62n, 65n, 90, 102, 108–9, 114, 114n, 117–18, 128–34, 176–77; special, 11n, 249–50; waiver of, 47, 105, 105n. *See also* civil rights; claim right; conflict of rights; disability; immunity; honour, right of; human rights; imprescriptible rights; inalienable rights; indefeasible rights; legal rights; liberty, right to; liberty rights; natural executive right; natural rights; power; resistance, right of; self-defense, right of; self-government, right of; transfer of rights; tuition, right of
Robins, Michael, 201n
Rothbard, Murray, 136n
Rousseau, J. J., 51n, 65, 94, 94n, 137, 137n, 198, 199n, 225
rule-consequentialism, 41n, 45, 122–23, 141, 141n, 182, 190–91
rule of law, 252, 253n
Russell, Paul, 84n, 88n, 89n, 214n
Ryan, Alan, 158n, 184n
Rye House Plot, 51n

Sabine, George, 8, 68n, 102n
Sartorius, Rolf, 207n, 219n

Scanlon, Thomas, 200–201n, 235n
Schochet, Gordon, 70n, 201n
secession, 242n
Selden, John, 151
self-defense, right of, 42n, 45n, 47n, 149–50, 152n, 158, 162, 176–77
self-government, right of, 61–64, 67, 74–75, 78–79, 106, 115, 158–59, 176, 228, 264, 268–69
Seliger, M., 49n, 83n, 89n, 149n, 162n, 167n, 172n, 214n
Senor, Thomas, 261n
Shaftesbury, first Earl of, 49, 125, 125n, 150n
Shapiro, Ian, 73n, 94n
Sherman, William T., 44n
Siegler, Frederick, 214n, 223n, 225n
Singer, Peter, 221n, 223–24n, 224–25n
Skinner, Quentin, 26n, 109n, 149n, 182, 182n, 205n
slavery, 6, 41–42, 43–44, 48–52, 90, 99, 113, 114–17, 134, 142–45, 154, 155–57, 209, 243–44; and drudgery, 50n; factual and moral, 49–50. See also absolute power; arbitrary power; despotical power
Smith, M.B.E., 202n, 221n
Snare, Frank, 60n, 70n, 204n, 213n, 214n
Snyder, David, 28n
society, 4, 5n, 68n, 177; natural, 4, 11. See also civil society
sovereign, 16n, 17n, 39, 39n, 152n
sovereignty, 64, 64–65n, 152, 159n
special bond to state, 203–4, 263–64
special rights. See rights
state of nature, 11–12, 13–39, 48, 53–54, 57, 59–60, 63, 80–81, 82n, 84–86, 93, 115, 158, 161–62, 161n, 167–72, 171n, 177, 187–88, 193, 204, 210, 248, 263–64, 267, 269; defined, 14–23; historical instantiations of, 14–15, 22, 30–33; individualistic character of, 16–17, 21; moral characterization of, 14–15, 22–26, 34; ordinary, 20n; original, 23n, 24, 24n; perfect, 20n; relational character of, 16–17, 17n, 20–22, 22n, 171–72; simpliciter, 21–22; social characterization of, 14–15, 22–23, 26–30, 34; stages of, 26–27, 26–27n; and state of war, 42–43
state of war. See war
Steiner, Hillel, 104n
Stell, Lance, 101n, 117n, 142n
Strauss, Leo, 18n, 27n, 102n, 109n, 167, 173n

Suarez, Francisco, 49, 96, 151
subjective requirements, 254–58, 254–55n, 257–58n
subjects, 81–82, 82n, 88–89
suffrage. See elections; manhood suffrage; voting, right of
suicide, 50n, 67n, 115–17, 176n

tacit consent, 7, 17n, 38n, 61n, 69n, 80–90, 99, 107–8, 139, 193, 198–201, 209–10, 211n, 211–12n, 213, 213n, 214n, 216, 218, 219–44, 219–44n, 252, 266; defined, 83–84, 83n. See also consent
Tarcov, Nathan, 68n, 149n, 165n, 167n, 169n, 172n, 205n
Tassi, Aldo, 93n, 96n
taxes, 60, 60n, 63, 85, 87, 89, 91, 94n, 95–98, 231, 240–41, 245, 249, 252n, 255, 264–65; consent to, 91, 96–98
territory (of society), 86n, 259–60n
Thomas, Craig, 31n
toleration, 66, 66–67n, 73n, 113–14, 117–18, 117–18n, 123–36, 150n, 176, 190n, 213n. See also belief; religion
Tories, 162n
torture, 107, 143–44
transfer of rights, 152–55; in political consent, 18–20, 21–22, 24–26, 37, 38–39, 46, 57, 59–68, 60n, 62n, 96–97, 102n, 117–19, 124–25, 176–77. See also alienation; full transfer theories; rights
Trevelyan, G. M., 151n
trial by combat, 149n
trust, 68, 70–72, 70n, 71n, 72n, 114, 114n, 115n, 116–17, 116n, 117n, 128–29, 136, 147–48, 156–60, 160n, 162–63, 180–81, 185–86n, 194, 261; breach of, 42, 72, 72n, 74n, 114, 114n, 156–60, 162–63, 163n, 164, 169, 171–73, 171n, 177, 180–86. See also government
Tuck, Richard, 108n, 136n, 137n, 151n
tuition, right of, 110–11
Tully, James, 8n, 27n, 90n, 95n, 120n
tyrannicide, 158, 158n, 177
tyranny, 160–61n, 163, 166–67, 169n, 175, 177
tyranny of the majority. See majority tyranny
Tyrrell, James, 127n

unanimity. See consent
unconscionable agreements, 143–44, 236n, 237–43

unfair bargaining position, 137, 236, 237, 239n
usurpation, 160–61n, 169n
utilitarianism, 76, 103n, 200, 200–201n, 260n

VanDeVeer, Donald, 101n, 143n
"Venditio," 239, 239n
Vindiciae Contra Tyrannos, 182
violence, legitimate uses of, 158n, 160–61, 160–61n, 190–91. *See also* war
Virginia Declaration of Rights, 103n, 113, 153n
virtue, 75–76, 151n, 261
Vlastos, Gregory, 46n
voiding conditions (for consent), 110, 137–39, 143–45, 226–44, 226n. *See also* consent
voluntariness: in taking benefits, 252–55; of consent, 154n, 199–200, 211–17, 219, 219n, 222n, 224n, 226, 232–44. *See also* choice; consent
voluntarism, 8, 36–39, 57, 59–61, 59n, 75, 193–95, 197, 201–4, 216, 228, 248–51, 253–60, 253–54n; defined, 36
Von Leyden, Wolfgang, 71n, 155n, 157n, 166n, 173n, 208n, 209n, 212n
voting, right of, 94–96, 97, 219–24, 222n, 223–24n, 232. *See also* elections; manhood suffrage

Waldman, Theodore, 82n, 84n

Waldron, Jeremy, 65n, 67n, 129n, 130n, 132n, 132–33n, 199n, 245n
Walzer, Michael, 44n, 211n
war, 6, 11–12, 15n, 27, 28n, 29, 40–46, 48, 50–51, 57, 108, 116n, 155–58, 160–61, 161n, 164, 168, 170, 171, 171n, 193, 266, 268; defined, 40–42; Hobbes on, 42n; moral consequences of, 43–46; relational character of, 42–43, 155n; and state of nature, 42–43. *See also* just war theory; violence, legitimate uses of
warmaker, 43–44n, 44n, 127n, 155–56; defined, 42; moral standing of, 45–46. *See also* war
Weale, Albert, 69n, 70n, 223–24n, 224–25n
Whigs, 51n, 95n, 109n, 149, 150n, 162n, 176n
White, Morton, 101n, 106–7n, 120n, 135n
"Who shall judge?," 72n, 114, 114n, 180, 184–86, 185–86n, 186n, 187
William III, 148, 148n, 199n
Wills, Garry, 106n
Windstrup, George, 129n, 206n
Winfrey, John, 22n
Wolff, Robert, 201, 201n, 265n
Wood, Neal, 49n
Woozley, A. D., 202n, 219n, 227n, 231n, 233n

Yolton, John, 15n, 124n

Zvesper, John, 209n

The Princeton University Press series "Studies in Moral, Political, and Legal Philosophy" is under the general editorship of Marshall Cohen, Professor of Philosophy and Law and Dean of Humanities at the University of Southern California. The series includes the following titles, in chronological order of publication:

Understanding Rawls: A Reconstruction and Critique of A Theory of Justice by R. P. Wolff (1977). Out of print

Immorality by R. D. Milo (1984)

Politics & Remembrance: Republican Themes in Machiavelli, Burke, and Tocqueville by B. J. Smith (1985)

Understanding Marx: A Reconstruction and Critique of Capital by R. P. Wolff (1985)

Hobbesian Moral and Political Theory by G. S. Kavka (1986)

The General Will before Rousseau: The Transformation of the Divine into the Civic by P. Riley (1986)

Respect for Nature: A Theory of Environmental Ethics by P. W. Taylor (1986). Available in paperback

Paternalist Intervention: The Moral Bounds on Benevolence by D. VanDeVeer (1986)

The Longing for Total Revolution: Philosophic Sources of Social Discontent from Rousseau to Marx and Nietzche by B. Yack (1986)

Meeting Needs by D. Braybrooke (1987)

Reasons for Welfare: The Political Theory of the Welfare State by R. E. Goodin (1988)

Why Preserve Natural Variety? by B. G. Norton (1988). Available in paperback

Coercion by A. Wertheimer (1988). Available in paperback

Merleau-Ponty and the Foundation of an Existential Politics by K. H. Whiteside (1988)

On War and Morality by R. L. Holmes (1989). Available in paperback

The Rhetoric of Leviathan: Thomas Hobbes and the Politics of Cultural Transformation by D. Johnston (1989). Available in paperback

Desert by G. Sher (1989). Available in paperback

Critical Legal Studies: A Liberal Critique by A. Altman (1989)

Finding the Mean: Theory and Practice in Aristotelian Political Philosophy by S. G. Salkever (1990)

Marxism, Morality, and Social Justice by R. G. Peffer (1990)

Speaking of Equality: An Analysis of the Rhetorical Force of "Equality" in Moral and Legal Discourse by P. Weston (1990)

Friedrich Nietzsche and the Politics of the Soul: A Study of Heroic Individualism by L. P. Thiele (1990). Available in paperback

Valuing Life by J. Kleinig (1991)

The Lockean Theory of Rights by A. J. Simmons (1992). Available in paperback

Liberal Nationalism by Y. Tamir (1993). Available in paperback

On the Edge of Anarchy by A. J. Simmons (1993). Available in paperback

Authority and Democracy: A General Theory of Government and Management by C. McMahon (1994)